SOUTH KOREAN POLITICS

The Search for
Political Consensus
and Stability

Koon Woo Nam

UNIVERSITY
PRESS OF
AMERICA

Lanham • New York • London

Copyright © 1989 by

University Press of America,® Inc.

4720 Boston Way
Lanham, MD 20706

3 Henrietta Street
London WC2E 8LU England

British Cataloging in Publication Information Available

Library of Congress Cataloging-in-Publication Data

Nam, Koon Woo.
South Korean politics : the search for political consensus and
stability / by Koon Woo Nam.
p.   cm.
Bibliography: p.
Includes index.
1. Korea (South)—Politics and government.   I. Title.
DS917.8.N36   1989   951.9504'3—dc20   89–33844 CIP

ISBN 0–8191–7507–2 (alk. paper)

This book is dedicated

TO MY PARENTS

CONTENTS

ABBREVIATIONS

AMG	American Military Government
ANSP	Agency For National Security Planning
CRP	Civil Rights Party or Civil Rule Party
DJP	Democratic Justice Party
DKP	Democratic Korea Party
DMZ	Demilitarized Zone
DNP	Democratic Nationalist Party
DP	Democratic Party
DRP	Democratic Republican Party
DSP	Democratic Socialist Party
DUP	Democratic Unification Party
FKTU	Federation of Korean Trade Unions
KCIA	Korean Central Intelligence Agency
KDI	Korea Development Institute
KDP	Korean Democratic Party
KMA	Korean Military Academy
KNCC	Korean National Council of Churches
KNP	Korea National Party
LCNS	Legislative Council For National Security
LP	Liberal Party
NCFU	National Council For Unification
NCFRD	National Council For the Restoration of Democracy
NDP	New Democratic Party
NDRP	New Democratic Republican Party
NFDYS	National Federation of Democratic Youth-Students
NKDP	New Korea Democratic Party
NSCC	North-South Coordinating Committee
PPD	Party for Peace and Democracy
PRP	People's Revolutionary Party
PP	Progressive Party
RDP	Reunification Democratic Party
RMC	Revolutionary Military Committee
ROK	Republic of Korea
SCNSM	Special Committee For National Security Measures
SCNR	Supreme Council For National Reconstruction
UP	Unification Party

PREFACE

The Korean peninsula, about half the size of the state of California and adjacent to Sino-Soviet borders and Japan, has historically been perceived as a buffer against invasion or as a spring board either from the Asian continent to Japan or from Japan to the continent. And today, the peninsula has become the geopolitical-strategic fulcrum of East Asia, where the interests of the world's four major powers (United States, Soviet Union, People's Republic of China, and Japan) converge. It is not surprising, therefore, that in the last 100 years or so three major international wars have been waged over the control of Korea: the Sino-Japanese War of 1894-1895, the Russo-Japanese War of 1904-1905, and the Korean War of 1950-1953, in which the United States and China fought against each other.

During the last and the latest international bloodshed, the opposing forces clashed to the point of world war, raising the spectre of nuclear destruction in the eyes of the Korean people, while reducing the entire country to a smoldering ruin. Still the war that ended in 1953 had merely restored the status quo and solved nothing concerning the underlying issues which had led to that conflagaration. Three and a half decades later the problems remain unresolved. On the contrary, Korea--once known as "the Land of the Morning Calm"--has in the 1980's been transformed into two opposing armed camps, each supported by its allies of major power standing, becoming one of the most tense areas in the world.

The division of Korea in 1945 was the first of its kind for an extended period since 668 A.D., and it was the product of a U.S.-Soviet wartime contingency plan to accept the surrender of Japanese troops in Korea toward the end of the Pacific War. This division subsequently became frozen as a result of the U.S.-Soviet rivalry in the Cold War. However, before that occurred, the Koreans--homogenous racially and culturally and speaking one language--had sought to solve the problems brought about by the tragedy of the division.

xi

They had done so in the presence of the two new great powers that dominated the post-World War II era, the United States and the Soviet Union, and amidst the transmutation of the neighboring two ancient nations, China which was involved in its own civil war, and Japan whose empire crumbled to the ground. Faced with the great power rivalry as well as the reality of inter-Korea competition, the Koreans' efforts had ended in failure. This led to the emergence of two separate states on the peninsula in 1948. Thus Korea, which had been subjected to the domination of the Japanese empire, escaped that grip only to be split in two in the aftermath of the Pacific War.

The Korean War did not alter the divided state of Korea; if any, the bloodletting hardened the division. Yet the concept of territorial unity of their country has remained dear to all Koreans--whether in the South, the North, or overseas. The tragic consequences of the division, along with the burdensome arms expenditures that continue to consume major shares of both national budgets, have been so obvious that no Korean leader in either half of the peninsula can afford to be reticent about the need for reunification. Since 1972, North and South Korea have indeed been in agreement that their unification must be achieved peacefully and through their own efforts by transcending their ideological differences, without relying upon foreign powers.

The only important change that has occurred is that since 1973 South Korea has been willing to relegate the question of unification to that of an aspiration, to be fulfilled in the distant future. She has worked for the stabilization and legitimization of the existing status quo through the simultaneous admission to the United Nations of herself and the North as two separate entities. This policy of Seoul has been backed by the United States and Japan, both of which see South Korea as a bulwark against communism. Moreover, they have indicated their support for the idea of cross recognition of both Korean states by all four major powers closely involved in Korean affairs, and of mutual recognition of each other by the two Koreas.

As South Korea tried to have the division of the peninsula accepted by all the parties concerned, such a stance found itself at variance with the nationalistic aspiration of Koreans to acquire a single personality in the international community. The process of South Korea's endeavours at nation-state building, carried out within such a context, has been uneven and stormy. Indeed, since its inception as a liberal democracy in 1948, the political scene in the Republic of Korea has been punctuated by a series of turbulences including violent endings of regimes.

The First Republic under President Syngman Rhee was toppled by the students' upheaval of April 19, 1960. The Second Republic, governed by Premier Chang Myon, was overthrown by the military coup of May 16, 1961. President Park Chung Hee's prolonged and repressive rule ended abruptly on October 26, 1979, when he was murdered by the director of the Korean Central Intelligence Agency. And the Fifth Republic, launched in the spring of 1981 led by President Chun Doo Hwan, was racked by endless and stormy confrontations between the government and its opponents. Mr. Chun's grip on power, never firm from the beginning because of the way he had seized it, was further weakened by a series of sensational financial scandals involving his relatives and public figures. Under the circumstances, Chun continued to be frustrated in his efforts to legitimize his power, thus leaving the political situation of the country unstable and volatile.

Through this period, the South Korean society has undergone tremendous changes. Its once predominantly agricultural economy has been transformed into a mainly manufacturing and industrial one. The overwhelmingly rural population of the past, who generally had little or no formal education, has become primarily urban in the process, becoming one of the world's best educated peoples. Furthermore, the traditional class structure has been altered: the old upper class the Yangban has been destroyed; in its place, the military and a new business elite have emerged as powerful interest groups side by side with the traditionally influential intellectuals.

The cumulative effects of these changes accelerated transformation of Korean society, which had been under the influence of Confucianism, and has resulted in the development of new patterns and trends in social relationships. The relatively closed, occupation-related social class structure has given way to increasing occupational mobility, leveling social distinctions to some extent. The once male-dominated hierarchical family system has greatly weakened its grip on society, and authoritarian parental influences have declined in the face of individuals' increasing social role. Furthermore, when combined with the recent improvements in mass media and transportation, the growing socio-economic mobility has eroded traditional barriers of isolation among the people, who in the past clustered around their villages. This has helped to bring them together as national citizens.

Underlying the political disorders and cleavages, taking place amidst the socio-economic transformation, were the unresolved issues concerning the basic direction of the country. In addition to the ever-present question of unification of the divided peninsula, there was the problem of the democratic aspirations of a growing number of South Koreans versus authoritarian penchant of those who were in power. Still more, there was doubt among many intellectuals about the policy of economic development in the country carried out since the mid-1960's, which was heavily dependent upon trade, exposing the economy to the vagaries of foreign markets. Because the social and political fissures on these issues ran deep, South Korea's efforts at a new nation-building was made without a basic national consensus on the fundamental course of the country and thus without a clear notion of the political community it was attempting to create.

Concerning the controversy over the problem of authoritarian vs. democracy, which had been perennial since the imposition of the Yushin rule in 1972, both Park Chung Hee and Chun Doo Hwan defended their authoritarian military-dominated regimes which were decked out in some of the trappings of democracy, by citing the threat from the North. On the other hand, the proponents of democracy, whose psyche was deeply scarred by nearly 30 years of military rule, demanded that the government open up the political process so that the people could meaningfully participate in the governing process. Because only when the government was based upon an open democracy, it could acquire popular legitimacy and thus ensure enduring political stability. This state of affairs in turn would automatically provide the most reliable guarantee for national security, so they argued. For the advocates of democracy, political participation by the general population was especially desirable in view of the growing sophistication of the people, which was accelerated by the rapid socio-economic changes occurring in the country.

In addition, as they had done during the regime of the late Park, the advocates of democracy rebuked the labor

policy of the Chun regime. The Chun government--in order
to keep Korean products competitive in the international
market--met the "revolution of rising expectations" among
the people with draconian restrictions on workers' attempts to organize and improve their position. And
Chun's critics never ceased to accuse his regime of being
inherently repressive, corrupt, and illegitimate.

As Chun's foes remained irreconcilable with his political leadership, anti-American sentiments rose among
the South Koreans, who until Chun's ascendancy had been
friendly to the United States. The ill-feelings toward
the U.S. were fed by the belief that the U.S. was tolerating or even embracing the Chun government. Notable in
this connection was an increasing role of the "radical"
students in the dissident movement, who had expanded the
sphere of student political activities through coalition
with labor and rural communities. This trend toward
"leftist extremism" was so worrisome and intolerable to
the Chun government that it did not hesitate to brand the
radical students as "pro-Communist radicals and destruc-
tionists."

Throughout this period, the Chun regime, beleaguered
as it was with unceasing student opposition and increasingly virulent labor disputes, proved to be a government
of "crisis management" rather than one that truly governed. On the other hand, the traditional opposition
political leaders--who like Kim Dae Jung and Kim Yong Sam
had been relatively cautious--were finding themselves
losing ground to the anti-American radicals in the whole
opposition movement to the Chun regime. Under the circumstances, even after the rise and fall of the series
of regimes in succession since 1948, South Korea had to
continue to search for the principles of socio-economic
order that could be acceptable to broad strata of the
population, thus providing the ideological foundation of
a viable political system.

An ideology provides a set of aims and values for a
given socio-political structure, so that various groups
in the society can develop a sense of collective identity
with these aims and values; similarly it infuses common
goals and symbols into the institutional structure, and
transforms it according to them. By addressing itself
to the problems and goals of the society, the ideology
draws wide groups into the central institutions, while
legitimizing these institutions in general and the ruling
groups in particular. In South Korea none of the suc-

cessive political leaderships was able to forge an ideology that was coherent and relevant to the major issues faced by the country. Thus the political controls exercised by them did not penetrate the society, and the political systems devised by these leaders sat only precariously upon the population whose attitude to their political leaders had oscillated between apathy and "eruption."

As was generally the case with political leaders of newly independent nations in the immediate post-World War II period, the first president of South Korea, Syngman Rhee (1875-1965), had distinguished himself in anti-colonial struggle. It was Rhee's anti-Japanese activities aimed at Korea's independence that had initially accorded legitimacy to the First Republic which was headed by him. The act of national liberation, however, tied legitimacy only to the ascension to power; and the political leaders of former colonies could not rely exclusively on their revolutionary political activity as the enduring source of their legitimacy. Once in power, they held it in the name of national aspirations, which involved the establishment of a national identity and sovereignty along with socio-economic modernization; and they had to accomplish the task quickly. It was here that President Rhee failed and squandered his early popularity.

Rhee's First Republic espoused democracy, an anti-Japanese stance, and anti-communism. However, because of Rhee's growing authoritarianism and the harboring of Korean collaborators of Japanese colonialism in his government for political expediency, the former two principles became devoid of substance and incongruent with reality. This engendered cynicism among the public. As Rhee was engrossed in unceasing schemes to stay in power in the face of mounting opposition, his government failed to attend to socio-economic problems plaguing the country, especially in the aftermath of the Korean War, leading to the alienation of the people from the government.

The background of the new leadership which ultimately emerged after the overthrow of Rhee's government nullified the links between the anti-Japanese independence movement and legitimacy. The new ruling group, headed by Park Chung Hee and composed of former army officers, had ties with the Japanese military in Manchuria before Korea's independence. Unable to claim any association with national liberation activities, Park's regime upheld "economic development" as the national ideology. This reversed the feelings of alienation and cynicism prevalent among South Koreans, as the country achieved its economic goals and took pride in the accomplishment. However, as the economy ran into snags with the resersal of previously favorable market conditions, such an ideology proved effective only temporarily.

Ultimately, it turned out empty because growth as an end in itself--the assumption implicit in the ideology of "economic development"--was devoid of the notion of growth as an end to achieve overall nationalistic purposes, a notion crucial for the country like South Korea which had only recently been freed from colonial status. Furthermore, as recognized by a growing number of observers, the political underpinnings of "economic progress" were endangered when its benefits were not widely and "fairly" shared and wealth was concentrated in the hands of a small group of "haves." As proved in South Korea and other newly developing countries, economic growth at the expense of "distributive justice" often was a time bomb.

Growth unaccompanied by "social equity" was even more detrimental to the creation of a stable polity, if the process of growth was punctuated by corruption on the part of political leaders, which again had been the case in South Korea and elsewhere. Corruption signified a diversion of the political system to private and self-aggrandizement, while generating disaffection among the general public with the system and undermining it. It indicated the failure of the political elite in a crucial test of their legitimacy---the projection of their image as men of self-sacrificing dedication to a national cause.

Finding it difficult to rule through persuasion and loyalty, the Seoul government increasingly resorted to coercion and force. In addition, it exploited certain negative cultural and behavioral carry-overs from the Yi dynasty (1392-1910)--such as "family-centrism," "factionalism," and "regionalism." Because the ideology of the Yi dynasty was Confucianism, the family was accorded extreme sanctity and the family-centrism exerted a powerful influence--often to the detriment of the general well-being of the society.

The factionalism under the Yi dynasty was a form of power struggle among Confucian scholar-officials, and

xvii

factional affiliations were centered around leading personalities rather than ideological differences. The actions of one's opponents were seldom judged on their merits, and any political authority was relentlessly resisted as illegitimate, when not derived from one's own political faction. Such factional clashes had a debilitating impact on the Yi dynasty rule. The regionalism was a corollary of the family-centrism and factionalism, and was a bane of the Korean society. These behavioral remnants were obstacles to modernization and thus dysfunctional for the creation of a modern state; and they were so acknowledged and denounced by contemporary Korean leaders of every political persuasion.

As the Seoul government continued to remain in power through force and other negative means in the supportive environs provided by the United States and Japan, some of the various democratic opposition movements were turning to radical nationalism. The radical nationalism, when combined with democratic activism, seemed determined to burst the extreme anti-communism which the government placed upon the country severely restricting political and intellectual freedom.

This book intends to describe the process of South Korea's search for a stable political system and to analyze the various factors that contributed to the failure of the successive Seoul regimes to legitimize themselves and institutionalize the structures they had erected. In doing so, this study examines the value orientations and power positions of the major sociopolitical sectors of South Korean society such as party politicians, the bureaucratic elite, the military, business leaders, student activists, Christian intellectuals, and workers. Concentration on the analysis of the relationship of these groups was justified, because there tended to be relatively little differentiation in political attitude within each of these groups and because it was the conflicts of the value orientations among these groups which were responsible for the perennial political disturbances in South Korea.

The period covered is mainly from 1972 to 1981, because by the early 1970's the political cleavages in the country's direction had become markedly pronounced, revealing the lack of consensus on it. And by 1981 the opportunity provided by the assassination of Park for restructuring the political system, based upon a broad popular consensus, had been lost and the country had settled back into the old mould of repression and aimlessness. Finally, because some of the political problems faced by South Korea were not unique to her but common among other newly developing societies which have difficulties creating durable polities, this study may help us understand some of the problems of these societies.

As a general rule, Korean words and names appearing in this book follow the McCune-Reischauer system of transliteration. Exceptions were made for the individual names which are widely recognized and accepted in their idiosyncratic renderings such as Syngman Rhee, Kim Il Sung, Park Chun Hee, and Chun Doo Hwan. Otherwise, family names preceded given names and given names were not hyphenated, except individual authors in the reference materials who preferred hyphenation of their given names. For the romanization of Japanese, the Hepburn system of transliteration was used.

In closing, I wish to express my thanks to those who helped make this publication possible. I am deeply indebted to the late Professor Eugene Kim of Western Michigan University, who read an early draft of the work and offered constructive comments. I am also grateful to Professor Young Whan Kihl of the Iowa State University for his critical suggestions on the manuscript. My thanks are extended to Georgia Thorstenson, who typed the final version of the manuscript with professionalism, and to Stewart Hobson, Debra Campbell, Thomas Pirog, Douglas George, and Marjorie Nichols for their untiring editorial support.

Mr. Key P. Yang at the Library of Congress helped me in locating a number of books and other materials used in writing this book. Many other materials were found at the Harvard-Yenching Library, where I was a frequent visitor while preparing this book.

Finally, the presentation of all facts and their interpretations, with their possible errors and shortcomings, are my own responsibility.

Monterey, California   Koon Woo Nam
Spring 1989

CHAPTER 1

THE CRIPPLING OF DEMOCRACY

The First Republic: Autocratic Precedents

Upon liberation in 1945 from Japanese colonial rule, which had begun in 1910, Korea was divided into two zones along the 38th Parallel.   They were placed under separate military controls exercised by the Soviet Union and the United States, that had accepted the Japanese surrender in the northern half and southern part respectively.   The foreign military rules had lasted for three years until 1948, when they were replaced by indigenous but mutually hostile regimes.

For South Korea, the immediate post-liberation period was a difficult one, profoundly affecting the course of its subsequent development as an independent political entity.   First of all, during that period there was a hardening of the two divided zones--supposedly the result of a temporary wartime military measure by the United States and the Soviet Union--into two antagonistic political units because of the failure of the occupying powers to agree on a program of unification as well as the inability of the Koreans themselves to find a consensus on the course of their country.   For the Koreans, whose country had developed as a homogeneous society for nearly one and one-third millennia since it was unified in 668 A.D., the division of the country was a grave event.   Since the two areas had been economically interdependent, the division deprived South Korea of access to mining and power resources and heavy industry-- all concentrated in the north--thus curtailing industrial production.

The division also brought in a heavy influx of refugees from the north and abroad, who far outnumbered the Japanese in Korea who were then repatriating.[1]   A galloping inflation rate sprang up in the wake of reduced production and the sudden increase in population growth.

The difficulties were compounded by the repatriation of Japanese managers and technicians, who had run the economy using Koreans almost exclusively as laborers and who were now leaving Korea with no trained personnel in management and technology. All of this led South Korea to immediate dependence on the United States, foreshadowing the future of South Korea's economic development. As the division was detrimental to the economy, its political consequences also were grave.

While the collapse of the Japanese colonial administration revealed a severe shortage of experienced Koreans to replace the departed Japanese, the American occupation authorities had no knowledge of Korea and thus were ill-prepared to administer it. Compounding the immediate problem of maintaining law and order, the domestic political forces in South Korea split into leftists and rightists--a legacy of the pre-liberation Korean independence movement which also was now aggravated by the division of the country.

The rivalry and hostility between them, especially between Communists and Anti-Communists, became increasingly bitter and violent. It reflected the ideological competition of the two superpowers and increased the prospect (in view of the deadlock between the U.S. and U.S.S.R. over the Korean unification) that either the leftists or Nationalists, but not a coalition group, would assume power in an independent Korea. During this time, the Nationalists, in their battle against the leftists, were aided by the American Occupation authorities, who, fearful of Communist takeover, pursued the policies which weakened the leftists as well as the moderates.

It was in this setting that Syngman Rhee (1875-1965), an American-educated conservative whose political credentials dated back to the late 19th century, came successfully to power.[2] In addition to his strong Anti-Communist stance, Rhee, unlike most of his political rivals, sided with the Americans when they granted the formation of an independent South Korean government in 1948.[3] Ultimately, Rhee's stance on this crucial issue made him the acceptable candidate as the future leader of South Korea in the eyes of the American authorities.

Rhee was supported in his bid for power by former Korean members of the Japanese bureaucracy and police, most of whom were rehired by the American Military

2

Government (AMG) and who feared a leftist take-over. There were strong feelings against these former intermediaries of Japanese rule among the population, but they were kept by the AMG for their administrative efficiency and other conveniences.[4] Rhee also received support from the Christians as well as the Korean Democratic Party (KDP), which was formed in September 1945 by landlords, businessmen, and former anti-Japanese Nationalists, who were held together by anti-communism.

With the United States ready to grant independence to South Korea and all the supporters of Rhee in favor of the American move because "half a loaf is better than none,"[5] elections were held on May 10, 1948, in the South under the auspices of the United Nations to form a constitutional assembly and to establish a government. The elections, the first opportunity for Koreans to elect their legislators, were violently opposed and boycotted by the Communists and Centrists as well as by some rightists. This meant that the legitimacy of the yet-to-be-formed government would be narrowly circumscribed.[6] Nevertheless, on August 15, 1948, the third anniversary of the country's liberation, South Korea gained independence under "a democratic system of government," patterned largely after that of the U.S. and with Syngman Rhee as the president.

Immediately, the fledgling republic was faced with a series of crises. Despite increasing U.S. aid, the economy had been "one of endless despair."[7] The outcome of the Land Reform Act of 1949--carried out despite the conservative bias of the government--proved dubious. to be sure, the reform eliminated tenancy as a major political issue, the tenancy which the leftists could have taken advantage of to cultivate rural support. Yet its "overall effect was to create a basic rural structure of small--very small--owner-operated farms"[8] to the detriment of production efficiency. And the traditionally agrarian South, which had been the breadbasket of Korea, could not even produce enough food for its own inhabitants, even though nearly three-fourths of its population engaged in farming.[9]

In addition, the infant republic was faced with a series of rebellions. The gravest insurrection was the Yosu-Sunch'on Incident of October 1948, in which an army regiment, inspired by leftists, mutinied in the southwestern towns of Yosu and Sunch'on. The regiment rebelled on the eve of its departure to Cheju Island to subjugate Communist-led guerrillas, and the rebel soldiers kept the two towns under their control for about two weeks until retaken by troops loyal to the government.[10]

The outbreak of the Korean War (1950-1953) taxed the viability of South Korea as a democratic state virtually to the breaking point. It did so not only because of the death and destruction spawned by the fighting but also because of corruption and misrule under the growing "personalism" of President Rhee, for which the war provided impetus. The most glaring examples during the first year of the war were the National Defense Corps scandal and the Koch'ang massacre.[11]

The Defense Corps was hastily organized in December 1950 to deprive the Communist army of a chance to enlist South Korean youths in its ranks in case the battle line pushed south again. As the corps members numbering some 200,000 marched south during the second evacuation of Seoul in January 1951, some 90,000 of them died from cold, starvation, and illness. The tragedy resulted from embezzlement by the corps commander and a few other top officers of the funds allocated to support the corps. The scandal was exposed at the National Assembly in the wartime capital of Pusan in March 1951, leading to the execution of five officers of the corps including the commander himself.

The Koch'ang massacre involved the slaying of some 200 villagers at Koch'ang, a mountainous village in South Kyongsang Province, by South Korean troops assigned to the area late in 1950 to mop up Communist guerrillas planted in the fall by the retreating North Korean army.

The South Korean troops found themselves frustrated in getting information from the villagers and called them in February 1950 "to hear an order" and killed them. In April the National Assembly committee sent to the spot to investigate the killings was ambushed by South Korean soldiers disguised as Communist partisans, and the investigation was abandoned. The army colonel who staged the fake ambush was later appointed the director of the national police by President Rhee. During this time, the National Assembly, which in July 1948 had overwhelmingly elected Syngman Rhee as the president, was rapidly losing confidence in his administration, and there developed a growing split between Rhee and his original conservative backers in the Assembly.[12]

4

Following the May 1950 National Assembly elections in which the administration had emerged with far fewer seats than it had wished for, the opponents in the newly elected Assembly began to accuse the administration of having committed a series of malfeasances and other irregularities. This presented a serious problem for Syngman Rhee, because under the Constitution the president was elected by the National Assembly and Rhee's first presidential term was to expire in 1952. Rhee's weak position in the National Assembly became evident in January 1952, when his proposal for constitutional amendment, providing for popular elections of president and vice-president, was decisively defeated.[13] It was masterminded by the conservative Democratic Nationalist Party (DNP)(Minju Kungmindang), which advocated a parliamentary cabinet system and was determined to oust Rhee in the forthcoming 1952 presidential elections.[14] However, since Rhee was resolved to obtain a constitutional amendment, a fight was inevitable.

During his struggle, Rhee was assisted by the Liberal Party (LP)(Chayu-dang), established in November 1951 following the defeats of many of Rhee's supporters in the May National Assembly elections of the previous year. Built and developed as a political instrument for Rhee's hold on power, it was headed by Rhee himself, who had previously rejected the idea of leading a political party in order to conduct "suprapartisan" politics. The new party was to play a key role in Rhee's battle against the National Assembly.

In May 1952, only a few months after the humiliating defeat in the January elections, the 77-year-old Rhee imposed martial law in the vicinity of Pusan, still the wartime capital, ostensibly to check guerrillas, who "certainly did not exist in the area at the time."[15] Then, aided by the LP, police, and hired thugs, Rhee proceeded to intimidate the legislators with mass demonstrations for violating "the will of the people," which was presumably also the will of Rhee himself. Subsequently through the roundups of those Assemblymen in hiding and physical threats to them and their colleagues, in July Rhee forced the Assembly to adopt the constitutional amendment providing for popular presidential and vice-presidential elections.[16] Capitulation of the legislature was complete. The following month Rhee was elected to his second four-year presidential term. The whole affair dealt a crippling blow to the fledgling Korean democracy, while setting the stage for steadily

5

increasing corruption and the discarding of a host of democratic freedoms.

In protest against Rhee's brazen "abuse of power" unimaginable in a "democratic state," in June Vice-President Kim Song Su (1891-1955, a pre-liberation businessman and Nationalist leader) resigned. Kim had been chosen by the National Assembly only in May of the previous year to succeed the country's first Vice-President Yi Shi Yong (1868-1953, an anti-Japanese revolutionary), who quit his post angry with the growing autocratic tendencies of President Rhee.[17]

Meanwhile, in the National Assembly elections of May 1954, the LP, aided by the police as well as the army, gained a majority, making it the first majority party in the Assembly of the Republic of Korea. Then in the fall of 1956, looking ahead to the end of President Rhee's second term, the administration again introduced constitutional amendments which included a provision to remove the two-term restrictions on presidential tenure. As it turned out, however, the Rhee Administration suffered an "agonizing defeat," because it received 135 of the 203 votes when the exact two-thirds majority required 135.3 votes. The presiding officer momentarily announced that the amendments had been rejected. At the next session, however, he retracted his earlier decision declaring that by rounding off to the nearest whole number, only 135 votes were required for the passage and therefore the bill passed.[18]

By now, the humiliation and submission of the National Assembly was complete, largely thanks to Rhee's control of the police and the army through manipulation. Indeed, the arbitrariness of the Rhee government had become such that there had remained no social organizations which could effectively function without giving unconditional support to the LP. Under the circumstances, Rhee's position had become almost absolute.

Because of Rhee's tactics to hold onto power along with the growing oppressiveness of his regime, the populace were fast losing faith in the government, particularly in conjunction with the discomforts of the postwar period. The discontents were centered in the then growing urban areas, where the inhabitants were becoming increasingly literate and articulate.[19] The public sentiments manifested themselves in the presidential and vice-presidential elections of May 1956, in which presidential and vice-presidential candidates from the same party had to run on separate tickets as stipulated in the 1952 constitutional amendment.

With only 55 percent of the popular vote compared with 72 percent in the wartime elections of 1952, Rhee, then 81 years old, was nevertheless elected for a third presidential term. However, Rhee's "anointed" would-be successor and the LP vice-presidential candidate Yi Ki Bung was defeated by Chang Myon of the opposition Democratic Party (DP)(Minjudang).[20] The election result was "allowed to stand" and Chang Myon won the vice-presidency.

The outcome of the elections was indicative of the loss of public faith in the LP rule under Syngman Rhee, which was dependent upon the police for maintaining political power instead of working for genuine popular support. In fact, the pre-election campaign rallies held in major cities for Democratic candidates were much larger than those for their Liberal counterparts. Moreover, alarmingly for the LP as well as the DP, Cho Bong Am, an ex-Communist and the presidential candidate of the Progressive Party (PP)(a socialist group, 1956-1958), ran a strong second with 24 percent of the popular vote. This was more than 2.5 times the percentage Cho had garnered in the 1952 presidential campaign (9 percent).[21] It was an extraordinary phenomenon because South Korean politics had been predominantly conservative and extremely inhospitable to leftists.[22]

Shaken by the election results, the Rhee government was seriously worried about the next presidential elections to be held in 1960. The 1956 elections, which revealed the fast ebbing popularity of the ruling LP, suggested that another defeat in Yi Ki Bung's bid for vice-president could be reversed only by drastic measures. Furthermore, the LP was nervous because the Vice-President-elect Chang Myon of the opposition DP could constitutionally drive the LP out of power, should President Rhee die prior to the 1960 elections when he would be 85 years old. As such, the Korean political scene, though relatively calm following the 1956 elections, was expected to become turbulent once again.

In April 1958 the government, which had begun to suppress the activities of the PP, arrested Cho Bong Am for allegedly engaging in espionage activities for North Korea. He was sentenced to death and executed in July

7

1959.[23] With Cho gone, his followers dispersed and the socialist movement, which already had lost its momentum, disintegrated, ending the leftist challenge to the existing socio-economic system.

Besides eliminating the leftist threat, the LP set out to capture two-thirds of the National Assembly seats in May 1958 elections to ensure that Yi Ki Bung would succeed Syngman Rhee. That would enable the LP to pass another constitutional amendment introducing a joint election ticket of president and vice-president. But they failed. On the other hand, the opposition DP increased its seats substantially--to slightly more than one-third of the Assembly seats.[24] Now the Liberals set about exploring other means to help them carry the 1960 elections. In November 1958 they attempted to force through the National Assembly a series of bills which could be used to foster their power vis-a-vis the DP. These ranged from a bill revising the existing National Security Law to a bill abolishing elections to local offices.

In particular, the provisions for the National Security Law were so sweepingly prohibitive of criticism of government that practically no critical comments could be made without violating the law.[25] For example, it was stipulated that those who had gathered "information on government or public offices, political parties, organizations or individuals for the purpose of benefiting the enemy" should be punished by death or life imprisonment. Furthermore, it was declared that anyone who had "benefited by disturbing the people's minds by openly pointing out or spreading false facts" would be punished by penal servitude for not more than five years. Virtually every word in these provisions could be applied and interpreted to suit the government. Indeed, these provisions would "in effect" give the police "almost unlimited authority to arrest and imprison anyone for vaguely defined anti-state activities." Rhee and Yi, the latter now being the Speaker of the House, would be "legally placed above any meaningful political criticism."[26]

The Democrats attacked the bill for the National Security Law as a legal device to lump all criticism of the Rhee regime with Communist propaganda. Such a law, they claimed, would be used to ensure the success of the LP in the upcoming elections, in which Rhee would try to put his trusted follower Yi into the position of Vice-

President and thereby ensure that Yi would become his successor. The opponents of the bill conducted a sit-down strike on the Assembly floor but were forcibly carried away by guards. The bill was passed in December with only the LP assemblymen present. With the "passage" of the National Security Law, most of the democratic civil rights guaranteed in the 1948 Constitution could now be "formally and legally crushed."[27]

Meanwhile, the government bureaucracy had remained completely obsequious to the demands of the LP, engrossed in their grab for power. It had "retreated into stric-test kind of ritualism and routine" with no innovations ever suggested, let alone attempted, even though it should have been urgently and innovatively tackling the socio-economic problems rising fast in the aftermath of the war.[28] Under the circumstances, the socio-political atmosphere in early 1960 was "suffocating," in which a growing number of people--particularly, intellectuals--had been profoundly alienated from the government.

The political repression itself moved to a climax in connection with that year's March presidential and vice-presidential elections, in which Yi Ki Bung and the then incumbent Vice-President Chang Myon once again faced each other. No clearer indication of the self-centered disregard of political reality and of blatant violations of the rule of law was given than in the official election results. The official tallies of the ballots cast showed Yi defeating Chang by a more than 4-to-1 margin, although there were very few people who would have found Yi's victory--even a narrow one--credible.[29]

As early as on the election day, in the southern port city of Masan there was a demonstration spontaneously staged by students, who were convinced that there were irregularities in the election. As evidence became widespread that the ruling LP had resorted to fraud, intimidation of opposition politicians and voters, and other means of securing a victory in the elections, the demonstration spread to other areas including Seoul, culminating in bloody confrontations between police and demonstrators in April. However, in the face of angry crowds, the police finally disintegrated; martial law was declared on April 19 in five major cities including Seoul, and army units were called in.

However, unlike the police, the soldiers enforcing martial law took little action against the demonstrators,

9

indicating that Rhee's ability to manipulate the military on behalf of his political fortune had ceased. Under the circumstances, after 12 years in power, the Rhee regime collapsed. On April 26 Rhee himself resigned the presidency, and shortly afterwards he left the country in disgrace to seek refuge, once again the United States whence he had come as a national hero in 1945.[30] Rhee's downfall marked the end of the First Republic and paved the way for the rise of the Second Republic.

Notably, Rhee's exit from the political scene signified a change in the backgrounds of South Korean political leadership. The political activities in the immediate post-liberation South Korea had been dominated by the Koreans with anti-Japanese revolutionary records. However, for various reasons including assassinations, all of the renowned leaders except Syngman Rhee had faded away from the political scene by late in the 1950's. Thus the departure of Rhee, a life-time anti-Japanese activist, marked the end of the political legitimacy that was based upon the anti-Japanese independence movement.[31]

The Second Republic: A Democratic Interval

Following the fall of the Rhee regime, an interim government, headed by an American-educated conservative politician Ho Chong, was installed.[32] Ho, a former acting premier and mayor of Seoul, was appointed by the outgoing President Rhee to the post of Foreign Minister. This entitled him to become the Acting President on April 28, 1960, with the endorsement of the National Assembly. As head of the caretaker government, Mr. Ho stated that he would carry out" revolutionary reforms" aimed at eliminating "the remnants of dictatorship" in an "unrevolutionary fashion." Under this slogan, the interim government during its 100-day existence exerted itself in maintaining a "delicate balance"[33] between the policies inherited from the previous administration, on the one hand, and the high expectations of the students and intellectuals who had engineered the April uprising, on the other. At the same time, it arranged for a new constitution and elections for the new National Assembly.

The new constitution, adopted by the National Assembly on June 15, aimed at ensuring the maximum guarantee of the rights of citizen, which had been provided for but trampled on under the Liberal regime. Also the new basic law replaced the presidential system exploited by Syngman

Rhee as a tool of autocracy with a parliamentary-cabinet system; and provided for a bi-cameral National Assembly composed of the House of Councilors (upper house) and the House of Representatives (lower house). During this time, the populace generally took a "wait and see" attitude.[34]

The general elections for the National Assembly were held on July 29. Despite the recasting of ballots in 13 electoral districts due to irregularities, the elections were "the most honest and democratic ones" that South Koreans had experienced.[35] As expected, the former opposition DP emerged victorious, capturing 31 of the 58 seats in the House of Councilors and 175 of the 233 seats in the House of Representatives. On the other hand, the LP, which had begun to disintegrate with Rhee's fall in April, won only four seats in the upper house and two seats in the lower house. This put an end to the LP as a significant political group, indicating the super-ficiality of its former strength and unity, which emanated not from an ideological bond but rather from the lure of power and the assistance of the police.[36]

The triumphant Democratic Party recommended its two leading members to the two top governmental posts: Yun Po Son to the now ceremonial presidency and Chang Myon to the premiership, which was vested with administrative power and was the most important governmental position. The two party nominees were duly approved by the National Assembly, and the Second Republic was launched in August 1960.

The new government under Premier Chang continued the policies initiated by the Interim Government, while instituting new policies of its own. While permitting a greater degree of freedom than South Koreans had known before or have known since, it continued the purges (already started under the Interim Government) of those who were closely associated with corrupt and illegal practices of the toppled Liberal regime. The new government also made efforts to promote the economy, and the urgency of their endeavors was succinctly expressed in the slogan of "Economic Development First." In addition, it started to reform the bureaucracy, manned largely by men schooled during the Japanese colonial period and which had been elitist and aloof from general social currents as well as "legalistic." And for the first time the bureaucracy was widely opened to the post-

11

liberation college graduates who had broad backgrounds in liberal arts.[37]

The Democratic Party regime, however, was not the millennium which many had hoped for. From the very beginning, it was beset by serious internal and external problems. Though the DP had become the symbol of the opposition to Rhee's autocracy during the latter part of the 1950's, it did not plot--let alone organize--the April Revolution. Rather the uprising was a spontaneous reaction of angry students against the rigged elections of the previous month as well as against other accumulated misdeeds of the Rhee regime. And when students had participated in the upheaval of the spring, they had "not done so with the thought either of supporting Chang or of overthrowing Rhee"[38]--even though the political storm that destroyed the Rhee regime was set off by Chang's failure to win the vice-presidency in the March elections.

As such, the decisive election victory of the DP in July could be attributed mainly to the fact that it was the only nationally organized political force with any degree of effectiveness as well as to the desires on the part of many voters to reward the party for its resistance against the Rhee regime.[39] Thus the party's right to rule was a "gift" from the "April Revolutionists."

Moreover, the DP's stance was not representative of the restive social forces of growing importance in the rapidly urbanizing South Korean society: the urban masses led by disgruntled intellectuals and students of generally youthful post-liberation schooling who had brought about the April Revolution. Instead, the social backgrounds of the Democratic elite were similar to those of the now ousted Liberal elite. Like their Liberal counterparts, the Democratic leaders were mostly in their early fifties, were predominantly the sons of landlords, had their last schooling during the Japanese colonial period, and started their careers in the colonial civil service.[40] Indeed, the DP was a coalition of those who, intent upon seizing power, opposed Rhee's "dictatorship" without challenging his conservatism and pro-U.S. foreign policy.

An examination of the two highest political leaders of the Second Republic would further elucidate the characteristics of the Democratic governing elite. The President-elect Yun Po Son was born in 1897 to a rich land-owning family, and studied in Japan as well as at the University of Edinburgh in Scotland. Though he refused to cooperate with the Japanese authorities throughout their rule, Yun remained passive without participating in any activities which could endanger his personal safety and wealth. After 1945 it was mainly through his wealth that Yun made his presence felt on the political scene. He served as the appointed mayor of Seoul during 1948-1949 and as Rhee's Minister of Commerce and Industry during 1949-1950 without showing initiative or risking controversy. Yun's passivity and unwillingness to involve himself in controversy helped him advance in the DP.[41]

Like President Yun, Premier Chang Myon too was a gentle and cautious personality. Born in a fairly well-to-do Catholic family in 1899 and educated in Korea and the United States, Chang had devoted himself since 1925 to educational projects of the Catholic Church. For 17 years until the end of World War II, Chang served as the principal of a Catholic commercial middle school in Seoul, thus not having to involve himself in political activities. Following the completion of his mission as the first ambassador of South Korea to the United States, Chang served as President Rhee's Prime Minister (November 1950-April 1951). Then he became an "opposition" politician.[42]

However, during the 1952 "political turmoil"--when the anti-Rhee Assemblymen were arrested and intimidated by the pro-Rhee forces--Chang showed timidity and indecision by withdrawing from the scene of political battle, as if to presage his several-day disappearance following the military coup of May 1961. Although he stood against Rhee during the rest of the 1950's and defeated Rhee's vice-presidential choice in 1956, Chang's opposition continued to be tinged with moderation and gingerliness. Though always well-meaning and sincere, he was more like "a dean of a divinity school" than a political leader who could steer his country through a stormy path.[43]

The Democrats' claim to rule was made more dubious due to the eruption of intraparty factional fighting between the Old Faction led by Yun and the New Faction headed by Chang. The two factions had originated from two major anti-Rhee conservative parliamentary groups that had coalesced in September 1955 to form the Democratic Party, while aiming at introducing a parliamentary cabinet system in place of the presidential system headed by

Rhee.[44] From the very beginning, the union of these two major anti-Rhee groups, however, was an uneasy one. During the days of their common struggle against Rhee in favor of a parliamentary form of government, factionalism remained dormant.

However, with Rhee gone, the parliamentary system introduced, and the party winning the coveted position of power, there was little to contain factionalism. Because the two factions were practically indistinguishable ideologically and the factional divisions stemmed from personal links and consideration of private interests, the antagonism and hostility were expressed in the form of personal attacks on the integrity of the opposition faction members.[45]

The Democratic Party's nomination of Chang Myon for the office of Prime Minister, which was the most important political post in the Second Republic, was accompanied by acrimonious factional disputes. The subsequent election of Chang as the Premier by the National Assembly led to the split of the DP. Having come into close proximity with power but unable to grasp it because of the New Faction's "takeover" of the government, the Old Faction, whose parliamentary strength had virtually matched that of the New Faction, formed in November a new political party called the New Democratic Party (NDP).

The NDP, now standing in opposition to the DP, deprived Premier Chang of his parliamentary majority. The situation for Chang became more difficult when the "young group" in his DP, realizing that they would not be awarded a large share of power by the DP leadership dominated by the "old group," joined the newly formed NDP as a gesture of retaliation against the Chang Administration.[46] Thereafter, the main concern of the new government was not how to run the country but rather how to survive by securing enough support among the assemblymen.

From the initial formation of his administration in August and until the next May when it was overthrown, Premier Chang carried out a series of cabinet shuffles including three "major ones," which meant on the average a two-month tenure for each of the cabinets. Yet Chang was still unable to placate dissidents and the situation remained as fluid as ever.[47] Due to its preoccupation with political survival and the perpetual factional paralysis in the National Assembly, the new government was unable to undertake socio-economic policies effectively, discrediting itself in the eyes of the public and arousing their fury. Thus the internal split and dissension within the ruling elite of the Second Republic were their fatal weakness.

While it was rapidly disintegrating as an organization, the DP, other than its vague conservatism, was unable to provide an ideological focus. Without a clear-cut guiding doctrine and weakened by internal splits, the party sought to remain in power by reacting to the demands of the various social forces unleashed by the April upheaval rather than initiating its own independent policies. The result was a mob rule. Not only did mobs rule on the streets but they even invaded the National Assembly, which dismayed South Korea's ruling elements.

It was estimated that 2,000 separate demonstrations occurred with about one million participants during the nine months of the DP Administration.[48] The most alarming to South Korea's entire Establishment was the resurgence of the reformist parties (leftist parties) along with the emergence of leftist elements among school teachers and students in the milieu of the "new freedom," granted in the aftermath of the downfall of the repressive Rhee regime.

Though the numerical strength of the reformist parties in the National Assembly was negligible[49] and the extent of the leftist activities was not wide, the "radical" nature of their movement was disturbing to the country's governing class and the well-to-do. It became especially disquieting in early 1961, when students at several universities started a movement for direct debates with their North Korean counterparts for peaceful reunification of the country. The initiative of the students, which was endorsed by the reformist parties and other leftist organizations, received "enthusiastic support" from North Korean students.[50]

The leftist agitations provoked rightist forces, usually right-wing youth organizations and veterans' groups, to hold their own rallies and demonstrations denouncing the "pro-Communist" activities of the reformists and the "radical" students. There was a growing fear of social chaos, leading to an increasing doubt about the efficacy of the new political system to deal with the situation.[51] It was in this uneasy and confrontational atmosphere that the Chang government was brought

15

down by a military <u>coup</u> on May 16, 1961--barely nine months after its inception. This brought about an end to the attempt for liberal democracy based upon a parliamentary-cabinet system of government.

Notes

1. Kim Joungwon Alexander, Divided Korea: The Politics of Development 1945-1972, (Cambridge: Mass.: Harvard University Press, 1975), p. 47; and Gregory Henderson, Korea: The Politics of Vortext, (Cambridge, Mass.: Harvard University Press, 1968), p. 137.

2. Robert T. Oliver, Syngman Rhee, the Man Behind the Myth, (New York: Dodd Mead Company, 1955), pp. 237-259.

3. Ibid., pp. 259-263.

4. Han Sangjoo, The Failure of Democracy in South Korea, (Berkeley: University of California Press, 1974), p. 11; and Bruce Cummings, The Origins of the Korean War: Liberation and the Emergence of Separate Regimes, 1945-1947, (Princeton, N.J.: Princeton University Press, 1981), pp. 151-178.

5. John K. C. Oh, Korea: Democracy on Trial, (Ithaca: Cornell University Press, 1968), p. 7.

6. Ibid., p. 9.

7. Ibid., p. 34.

8. After the reform, those having less than one Chongbo (one Chonbo is about one hectare) rose to 45 percent of the total farm families from 41 percent in 1947. Virtually, no families had the legal limit of three Chongbos of paddy-fields. Tenancy itself later reemerged when some farmers sold their lands for debts and other reasons. David Cole and Princeton N. Lyman, Korean Development: The Interplay of Politics and Economics, (Cambridge, Mass.: Harvard University Press, 1971), p. 21.

9. Oh, Korea, p. 35.

10. Hong Sung Myon, et. al., eds., Haebang Isipnyon(The Twenty Years of Liberation)(Seoul: Semunsa, 1965), pp. 322-325.

11. Ibid., pp. 384-391.

12. The Constituent Assembly in 1948 would have adopted a parliamentary-cabinet system of government had it not been for the opposition of Rhee who was then a national

hero. Subsequently, many Assembly members were further disappointed when they were refused a share of power in the Rhee Administration.

13. It was defeated by a vote of 143 to 19. Pak Chi-Young, Political Opposition in Korea, 1945-1960, (Seoul: Seoul National University Press, 1985), p. 96.

14. The DNP was formed in February 1949 by a merger of the KDP and other conservative elements.

15. Oh, Korea, p. 42.

16. Pak, Political Opposition in Korea, 1945-1960, pp. 96-111.

17. Ham T'ae Yong (1873-1964), a pastor with a record of anti-Japanese activities, became the third Vice-President. Hong et. al., eds., Haebang Isipnyon, pp. 390-391, 398-399.

18. Pak, Political Opposition in Korea, 1945-1960, pp. 111-119.

19. For explanation, see the next chapter.

20. The DP was formed in September 1955 by coalition of the main opposition DNP, on one hand, and Liberals and Independents who had been disappointed because of Rhee's failure to appoint them and their followers to coveted bureaucratic positions, on the other. The DP presidential candidate Sin Ik Hi died of a heart attack on the eve of the elections. Kim, Divided Korea, pp. 205-206; and Oh, Korea, pp. 52-53.

21. Pak, Political Opposition in Korea, 1945-1960, pp. 192-195.

22. The political dissent of the main opposition parties of the time, the DNP and the DP, had been largely non-ideological. They differed from the Rhee regime primarily in how a democratic yet socio-economically conservative system should be run within a strong anti-Communist framework buttressed by close ties with the United States. Among the factors inhibiting leftist movement were the popular resentment against Communists along with suspicion about leftists in general because of the unfortunate experiences during the Korean War, and the loss and liquidation of the Centrists and leftists during the war.

23. Hong, et. al., eds., Haebang Isipnyon, pp. 491-493.

24. Ibid., pp. 80, 494. The DP increased its seats to 69 from 45, and the LP retained the 126 seats held by the party on the eve of the elections despite the increase in the Assembly seats. The Independents captured 27 seats, and the Unification Party (UP) won only one seat.

25. Pak, Political Opposition in Korea, 1945-1960, pp. 125-129.

26. Military Revolution in Korea, (Seoul: The Secretariat, Supreme Council for National Reconstruction, 1961), p. 5; and Oh, Korea, pp. 56-57.

27. Pak, Political Opposition in Korea, 1945-1960, pp. 129-131.

28. Cole and Lyman, Korean Development, p. 30. The GNP growth averaged less than 3.7 percent per annum during 1958-1960. Since the population increased about 2.9 percent annually, per capita income barely improved. Charles R. Frank, et. al., Foreign Trade Regimes and Economic Development: South Korea, (New York: National Bureau of Economic Research, 1975), pp. 11-12.

29. Pak, Political Opposition in Korea, 1945-1960, pp. 195-198. Rhee was unopposed because his opponent, Cho Pyong Ok of DP, had died shortly before the elections.

30. Hong, et. al., eds., Haebang Isipnyon, pp. 543-558.

31. This claim of political leadership stemming from anti-Japanese revolutionary activities was also true with the post-liberation North Korean leadership.

32. Korea Annual 1964, p. 91. Chang Myon had already resigned the vice-presidency in protest over the election irregularities.

33. Hahn-Been Lee, Korea: Time, Change, and Administration(Honolulu: East-West Center, 1968), p. 114.

34. Kim Divided Korea, p. 203.

35. Lee, Korea, p. 117; and Hapton Yongam 1980(Haptong Yearbook 1980)(Seoul: Haptong T'ongshinsa, 1980), p. 58.

36. Korea Annual 1964, pp. 91-92.

37. Lee, Korea, pp. 101-108, 130-132.

38. Kim, Divided Korea, p. 207.

39. Han, The Failure of Democracy in South Korea, p. 103.

40. This characterization was drawn from a study of cabinet ministers, national assemblymen, and other "high officials" of the Democratic regime. Lee, Korea, p. 134.

41. Han, The Failure of Democracy in South Korea, pp. 109-111, 114.

42. Hanguk Inmyong Sajon, (A Korean Biographical Dictionary)(Seoul: Haptong T'ongshinsa, 1980), p. 361; and Han, The Failure of Democracy in South Korea, pp. 115-117.

43. Kim Chae Chun, Pomyong'gi(Diary of An Ordinary Man), II,(Toronto, Canada: Chilsong Kwang'gosa, 1982), p. 248.

44. The Old Faction had been the DNP prior to September 1955; and the New Faction had been Independents or LP members who had supported Rhee but then turned against him and joined the DP when it was formed.

45. Han, The Failure of Democracy in South Korea, pp. 104-105; and Lee, Korea, p. 128.

46. Korea Annual 1964, pp. 111-112.

47. Kim, Divided Korea, pp. 208-209.

48. Lee Yong-Ho, "The Politics of Democratic Experiment: 1948-1974," in Edward R. Wright, ed., Korean Politics in Transition, (Seattle: University of Washington Press, 1975), p. 26.

49. The reformist parties held five seats in the lower house and two seats in the upper house. Han, The Failure of Democracy in South Korea, pp. 96-97, 179-187.

50. Korea Annual 1964, p. 118; and Hong, et. al., eds., Haebang Isipnyon, pp. 609-610.

51. Han, The Failure of Democracy in South Korea, pp. 203-204.

CHAPTER 2

THE RISE OF THE MILITARY TO POWER

Korean Military and the May 16, 1961 <u>Coup</u>

The erosion of the civil authority and the rise of the military in South Korea presented a pattern similar to the politics of developing nations in recent decades. Indeed, the Korean military <u>coup d'etat</u> on May 16, 1961 was closely preceded by those in Egypt (1952) and Pakistan (1958) and was immediately followed by those in Burma (1962) and Indonesia (1965).

The South Korean armed forces began to form under the American aegis and essentially as a "police reserve" with personnel of heterogeneous backgrounds. Instead of being trained as a force capable of defending South Korea's borders, the new force was primarily inculcated in the techniques of riot suppression to be used against internal disorder, which was feared by the Occupation authorities. Among the initial recruits of this force were "social marginals," and among its officers were many opportunists who had served in the Japanese or Japanese-Manchurian armies as officers.[1] Indeed, with the encouragement of the Occupation authorities, who were alarmed by the "civil disorders and guerrilla-like activities by Communist elements" that "dotted South Korea from 1946 to 1950," the new embryonic military force became the preserve of "those officers with a Japanese military background." Officers with different backgrounds resented this, but they were a "minority."[2] As such, the new military force lacked the <u>esprit de corps</u>.

The armed forces were further demoralized by defections of troops to North Korea as well as mutinies, the bloodiest being the Yosu-Sunch'on Rebellion in October 1948 by the 14th Regiment. Refusing to embark for the Cheju Island to fight guerrillas there, the regiment occupied the two towns of Yosu and Sunch'on and massacred

21

local leaders. As late as the eve of the Korean War, this group of motley backgrounds and low morale had remained a poorly trained constabulary force of some 100,000 men, many of whom being engaged in counter-guerrilla activities. Then, they were practically decimated within a matter of weeks from the time that North Korean troops moved south of the 38th Parallel beginning June 25, 1950.[3]

The present-day South Korean military is primarily a product of the Korean War. With American help and guidance, the strength of the Army had been rebuilt up to 82,000 men by August 1950, and then to 100,000 men by February 1951, which was some three months after the Chinese entry into the conflict. The expansion continued. When the war ended in July 1953, the army's size rose to more than 525,000 troops, "one of the largest in the world in absolute number." By 1956 the armed forces had expanded to more than 600,000 men, making it the world's fourth largest military establishment and "one of the very best equipped and trained organizations" among the developing countries.[4]

Now the military became relatively more important to the society than it had been previously. Not only did the war enhance its prestige but the possibility of another war with North Korea along with a greater fiscal commitment by the government to military purposes strengthened the voice of military leaders in the council of government. Moreover, a growing number of Koreans in civil life, through their service in the armed forces, had exposed and accustomed themselves to military ideas and ways of life in a society where traditionally the military and its values had been held in low esteem. In addition, the military, unlike the police, had maintained reasonably good relations with the populace--thanks largely to its stand during the April Revolution.

All this time, the armed forces had been undergoing their own internal transformation. First of all, the officers' mental attitudes had been profoundly influenced by the Korean War. Through the crucible of the war, the survivors as a whole had been transformed from a pre-war ragtag group into a hardened group with firm convictions about their role in the country. The military continued to be a career opportunity for lesser-privileged members of society because of lingering cultural bias against the military profession. However, through intense exposure to the United States from its very inception, the military became "one of the most intensively Westernized sectors of the society."[5]

Significantly, following the paralysis of the police force in the aftermath of the April uprising, the armed forces emerged as the only organization with sufficient coercive power, capable of preventing a rise of leftist groups and of assisting the conservative politicians in power to maintain the status quo. Thus substantial political resources were at the disposal of the military. Yet the Chang Myon Administration, unlike the Liberal and Interim counterparts, hardly accorded due recognition to the military, as evidenced by the fact that there was not a single cabinet minister with military backgrounds.

Meanwhile, the military became increasingly restive with the general drift of the Democratic regime. When the Democratic Administration confirmed its election campaign pledge to reduce the size of the Korean Army by some 100,000 men, army officers, who saw reduced promotional and professional opportunities, strongly opposed the plan. The army officers' position was supported by the United States. Faced with the opposition from the Army, the Chang Government scaled down the proposal twice and then altogether abandoned it. This exposed the inability of the government to carry out its own reform program in the face of pressures from the military, while arousing their enmity.[6]

Another serious misstep of the DP regime was its promise to purge the armed forces of undesirable elements but failing to follow through on the promise. Incidentally, the military as a whole had preserved a relatively favorable image among the populace for its role in the Korean War and for its stand in the turbulent spring of 1960. Many senior officers, however, had been deeply involved in the scandalously corrupt practices of the Liberal regime, which included blatant employment of military units against opposition politicians as well as election riggings.[7]

Many of these senior officers had served in the Japanese or Japanese-Manchurian armed forces, and after 1945 they received limited training of short duration--no more than six months. Yet they were catapulted during the wartime growth of the military into senior positions within a very short time; and most of them were still very young--young enough to be many years away from retirement.[8] The promotional patterns of much larger

23

numbers of officers, who closely followed these senior officers and were trained longer and somewhat better, were considerably slower and limited.

A case in point is the Eighth Graduation Class of the Korean Military Academy (KMA), who were to become the initiators of the plot for the coup of May 1961. This class, trained for one year (1948-1949), bore much of the brunt of the combat during the war as platoon or company leaders. After the war, they took advantage of newly available training opportunities and served in command and staff posts under the very top-ranking officers who were not much older.

By the end of the 1950's, opportunities for quick promotions within the Army had been virtually exhausted, and junior officers with field grade ranks of colonel or lieutenant colonel felt frustration.[9] Their senior officers, seemingly with many years of service ahead, were blocking their rise to the top leadership positions. Yet these senior officers were identified with the toppled Liberal regime not only in the eyes of the general public but also the soldiers under their commands, thus substantially compromising their authorities.

Demands for a cleanup of the military had become popular in and out of the armed forces following the April uprising, and the new Democratic Government promised a thorough "purification" of the services. The governmental plan, however, was caught up in cross currents. Lower-ranking military officers, encouraged by the appearance of support in the government, demanded an all-out purge of dishonest elements in the officer corps, especially at the highest levels; and they sought to bring to light evidence of misconduct among the senior officers. On the other hand, the high-ranking officer most of whom were denounced by the reform-minded young officers, exerted pressures on the Administration to retain their jobs. They were supported by American officials, who warned that toleration of the efforts of junior officers to have their seniors removed was a kind of insubordination which would undermine the discipline of the entire South Korean military.[10]

Warned by the representatives of the American Government and alarmed by the number of incidents in which subordinate officers defied the authorities of their superiors, the Chang Government abandoned its plan for the "purification of military." Thereafter, the government shifted its concern from corruption among the top officers to the problem of insubordination and rebelliousness within the Army, and took a hardened position against revolting junior officers.[11] The abandonment of the purge program left in power the very senior officers who were blocking the promotion of junior officers. Mistrust and resentment of such power among many junior officers led to bitterness toward the Government.

Furthermore, the officer corps as a whole—juniors and seniors alike—were aggrieved at the Government's inability to curb the "radical" students who, to the consternation of the whole South Korean Establishment, in early May 1961 proposed an immediate North-South student conference to seek unification of the divided peninsula.[12] This provided an additional impetus for executing a military coup, which, inspired by the Eighth Class of the KMA, had been quietly mapped out.

It was in the early hours of May 16, 1961 that approximately 5,000 troops (less than one percent of the armed forces) were committed in the execution of the planned coup d'etat. Upon being informed of the approaches of the rebel soldiers, instead of taking steps to counter the rebellion, Premier Chang hurriedly went into hiding, and the rebels met little or no resistance from domestic quarters. The public, meanwhile, generally took the attitude of indifference. The challenge to the coup came from American officials in Korea, including General Carter B. Magruder, Commander of the United Nations Forces.

The Americans, however, were unable to enlist the support of President Yun Po Son, a bitter political enemy of Premier Chang, who thought the coup was inevitable in view of the ineptitude of the Chang Administration. The Americans also failed in their attempts to mobilize Korean military units against the rebellious troops. Under the circumstances, the American challenge fizzled.[13] By May 18, it had become apparent that the coup had been successfully carried out virtually with no bloodshed, putting an end to the nine-month-old civilian government as well as the Second Republic.

The Military Junta (May 1961-December 1963) and the Emergence of the Third Republic

On May 16, 1961, a military junta referred to as a Revolutionary Military Committee (RMC) was formed. On May 20, when the success of the coup was assured, the RMC was renamed the Supreme Council For National Reconstruction (SCNR), with all the powers of government concentrated in it. The SCNR ruled the country by fiat, and its rule lasted until December 1963. During its existence the composition of the SCNR shifted several times. Yet, its members were always military officers on active duty, and they hardly exceeded 30 men at any given time, of whom a dozen or so were the core members.[14]

The success of the coup brought into the arena of national politics military men who traditionally had not had access to the elite social stratum in Korea. Indeed, very few of the participants in the coup and in the junta represented the prestigious ranks of Korean society, such as the families of large landowners or high governmental officials, from whom the power-elites of the First and Second Republics had sprung up. Rather most of the coup leaders came from social classes traditionally held in low esteem, such as the families of merchants and farmers, who in many cases had known poverty at close range.[15]

Despite their humble origins, the coup leaders seemed to show few basic ideological differences from the DP regime they had replaced. According to the six "Revolutionary Pledges" issued by the RMC on May 16, the new military government, like the previous two regimes, was strongly anti-Communist and pro-U.S.[16] And its position on socio-economic issues was murky. In justifying their seizure of power, the coup leaders seemed to assert that they would pursue basically the same socio-economic policies as the DP but they were more capable of implementing these policies than the DP, which was little more than the "twin" of the discredited LP leadership.[17]

The SCNR contended that the Chang Myon regime failed in nation-building because of its "corruption" and "incompetence" and "factional feuds." They asserted that the domestic unrest which had prevailed under the Democratic government stimulated Communist subversion which could invite a Communist takeover. The SCNR continued claiming that only the Korean armed forces were capable of preventing Communists from taking root among the people, and that only through their timely action was the country saved from a North Korean Communist takeover.[18] As a matter of fact, the leftist agitation during the Democratic rule provided a useful justification for the military to intervene in the political process; and it led many people in and out of the government to support the military coup.

As if to justify the ruling style of the SCNR, its leaders argued that Korea was not yet fully ready for a full-fledged democracy and that a period of guided "Administrative Democracy" was necessary to have the South Koreans develop the ability for self-government and prepare for the eventual establishment of "genuine democracy." Finally, the SCNR leaders insisted that the coup was not a counterrevolution to the student revolution of April 1960. Rather they saw the coup as an extension of the April revolution and themselves as heirs of that revolutionary spirit, which they claimed was "betrayed" by the DP leaders.[19]

In its efforts to consolidate its newly acquired position, the all-powerful SCNR moved rapidly both in domestic and diplomatic fronts. Following the proclamation of martial law on May 16, the SCNR banned all political activities, while disbanding the National Assembly as well as all political parties and pressure groups with the exception of those engaged in charitable, relief, academic, and religious activities. Also the SCNR outlawed many newspapers, news agencies and magazines (more than 900 altogether) that had mushroomed during the Second Republic, and placed the remainder (only 82) under strict censorship.

Furthermore, the SCNR arrested hoodlums, who had terrorized urban areas during the First and Second Republics; imprisoned or forced underground suspected Communist sympathizers, who had advocated peaceful unification with North Korea; and screened government officials, both civil and military, for corruption firing some 19,000 who were found guilty of misdeeds.[20] The attention of the coup leaders was also drawn to the country's economy, which had not recovered from the ravages of the war and had remained stagnant. In order to remedy the ailing economy and further develop it, the SCNR inaugurated a Five-Year Economic Plan in 1962, the first of its kind in South Korea.[21]

In external affairs, the junta took steps to ease tense relations with Washington which stemmed from the outright hostility to the coup of the American military officers and diplomatic personnel in Seoul. First, the SCNR

27

persuaded President Yun Po Son, who had no real power, to remain in office. This enabled the junta to avoid the problem of seeking diplomatic recognition from the United States and other countries. Second, the junta made efforts to explain to the U.S. government that the coup was needed to keep South Korea strong against the threat from P'yongyang, while promising to return the control of government to civilians in due time.[22]

Washington, on the other hand, pressed the SCNR to return power to the civilian administration if the latter wanted continued American economic aid, which along with U.S. military assistance was a fact of life in South Korea. Under the U.S. pressures the SCNR pledged on August 12, 1961 that it would permit a resumption of political activities early in 1963 and it would relinquish power to a civilian government in the summer of that year following general elections.[23]

With the timetable for return to civil rule set, the SCNR decreed a Politics Purification Act in March 1962. The Act prohibited 4,368 "old" politicians, who had already been under ban, from any future political activity until August 15, 1968. The blacklist included not only almost all prominent politicians since the country's independence but also the former junta members who had been ousted from the SCNR. The list also included student activists who had been involved in the movement for peaceful unification with the North, and the journalists who had been critical of the junta.[24] By blacklisting these people, the SCNR did narrow--in sharp contrast to the practices under the Democratic regime--the scope of permissible political activities. It was a continuation of the earlier policy under the Rhee government, and it remained under the subsequent civil government which would succeed the SCNR.

However, many of those purged were "cleared" or "pardoned" over the next 12 months so that by February 1963 only 268 persons still remained on the blacklist. Nevertheless, among these 268 were some of the most prominent political figures including Chang Myon and some "reformist" politicians.[25]

In anticipation of the return to "civilian rule," a new constitution establishing a strong presidential system was adopted by a national referendum in December 1962. In the same month, the SCNR promulgated a stringent political party law.[26] On New Year's Day of 1963, the

28

junta lifted the ban on political activities. Incidentally, the clearance of the banned politicians was timed by the coup makers to establish their own political party, which would serve as a dressing room where the junta leaders could change their uniforms for muftis to participate in the anticipated civilian government. The new party, named the Democratic Republican Party (DRP), began to be organized secretly in the summer of 1963 (when it was still illegal to engage in political activities) by Kim Jong P'il, one of the colonels who had instigated the coup, and his associates in the Korean Central Intelligence Agency (KCIA).[27]

The KCIA itself was the creature of the junta leaders. It was established under the direction of Kim Jong P'il, who became the agency's first head. The new agency, unlike its American counterpart, was designed to "supervise and coordinate both international and criminal investigations by all government agencies, including the military."[28] With such a sweeping mandate and given its origins, the agency exercised ubiquitous and almost absolute power during the junta rule. It implemented the anti-corruption crusade waged by the SCNR, while seeking out potential counter-coup elements. Over the years, the agency was to develop into an all-powerful and multipurpose organization--loyal only to the President and representing a pervasive force of state control.

The KCIA-created DRP organizers claimed it to be the heir of the ideals of the "military revolution" executed in order to carry out the "modernization of the fatherland." The party was to provide for the emergence of a "new leadership" into the national political arena, and would spearhead a drive to enlist popular support at the polls for those sympathetic to the goals of the junta leaders. The DRP structure and its political role were said to have been patterned after those of Communist parties: the party was highly centralized with a single command and a disciplined party membership, and the party would control the government, not vice versa.[29]

When the DRP emerged officially in January 1963, the new party turned out to be primarily the preserve of the "new generation" of young colonels, largely those in the KCIA under Kim Jong P'il. Senior members of the junta, who joined the DRP only in January 1963, were dismayed to find out that the party structure was already built with its power base strongly supportive of junior officers; and they demanded the dissolution of the party

in favor of a broadly based "pan-national" party.[30] As
factional disputes erupted within the junta, the anti-
Kim Jong P'il faction brought into the open the existence
of a series of massive swindlings--known as the "Four
Scandals"--whereby Kim had not only extracted funds to
finance the DRP but also lined his own pocket.[31]

Throughout the political feuds within the junta, one
officer, named Park Chung Hee, remained the unchallenged
arbitrator. As a major general, Park had been the active
leader of the coup.[32] Born into a southern farming
family in 1917, Park attended a cadet officers' school
in Manchuria run by the Japanese from 1940 to 1942. He
received an additional military training for two more
years in Japan, and in 1944 he joined the Japanese army
in Manchuria as an officer. In 1946 Park joined the
newly created South Korean army, and received a three-
month officers' training course at the newly established
South Korean military academy.[33]

In 1948 Park, then a major, was arrested and sentenced
to death for his involvement in the army mutiny in Yosu-
Sunch'on area.[34] However, Park turned up a prosecution
witness and his sentence was commuted to life imprisonment. He was then reinstated in the army after the
outbreak of the Korean War. Park's rise through the
ranks was slower than most of his comrades, perhaps
because the Rhee regime had been unwilling to place full
confidence in him. If that was the case, such a lack of
trust gave Park the chance to emerge as one of the few
high-ranking officers untainted by the corruption in the
army, which was rampant during the First Republic.

Although the colonels were the instigators and organizers of the 1961 coup, the cooperation of higher ranking
officers was needed for the success of the coup in a
country that was still imbued with Confucian tradition.
Furthermore, the cooperation of senior officers would
broaden support of the coup within the military. Major
General Park, willing to join forces with the younger
coup-makers, became the link between the young "revolu-
tionaries" and the more senior officer group. Thus,
although his life history revealed him to be a "switcher
or opportunist" or even "the very incarnation of betrayal,"[35] Park became the leader of the junta.

Meanwhile, the schism within the DRP became so serious
and so threatening to the junta's chances in the forthcoming elections that Park intervened in February 1963.

He arranged a compromise among the feuding factions that involved modifying the highly centralized DRP's structure and broadening the sources of its leadership. In the process many politicians of "the old generation"--largely those who had been closely associated with the Liberal regime--had been recruited into the DRP in order to utilize their "experience" and to maintain "political stability."[36]

The February compromise, however, did not end the party's internal dissension. Nor was the compromise a clear victory for senior officers because many of them were subsequently arrested on charges of conspiracy against the government or other irregular activities. Park's intervention, however, reversed the original plan for the relationship between the Administration and the DRP by establishing the former's leadership in the affairs of the latter, a precedent that was observed thereafter.[37]

Early in January 1963 when political activities were permitted, pre-coup conservative politicians scurried to restructure parties in order to take part in the forthcoming general elections in opposition to the DRP. Not surprisingly, the Old Faction and New Faction members of the former DP retained the bitter enmity that had divided them during the Second Republic. And they formed two separate parties in January, which were the two major opposition parties of the time: the Civil Rule Party (CRP) under Yun Po Son and the Democratic Party (DP) whose leader Chang Myon still remained blacklisted. In addition, by June two more parties had been formed by other conservative politicians of pre-coup days.[38]

The primary campaign issues of the 1963 general elections were what type of government would replace the junta and how to bring a stable democracy to South Korea. As the junta-sponsored DRP faced the electorate, it had mixed record on which to run. Under the SCNR rule, social order had been restored but living conditions for the ordinary people had worsened.[39] And the financial scandals and factional strife erupting inside the junta indicated that the "new" leadership was no better than its civilian predecessors. Yet the DRP maintained that unless they were elected to national political leadership, the country would again plunge into the old vicious circle of corruption, instability, and poverty.[40]

The opponents of the junta, on the other hand, argued that a genuine and stable democracy could be brought about by the restoration of civilian leadership, and urged the voters to reject another form of military rule by repudiating DRP candidates. They made a restoration of civil rule their cause celebre under the common slogan of "Let's put an end to the military rule."[41] Despite the common banner and strong public pressures calling for integration of opposition parties, the foes of the junta--not unlike the parties and factions of the pre-coup days--were unable to unite because of disagreement over who should be their presidential candidate.

In the presidential election held in October 1963, four opposition candidates ran against the DRP's candidate Park Chung Hee, who had retired from the service in August. Among the four, Park's chief opponent was CRP's Yun Po Son, who was the president of the Second Republic and, for a short time, of the military government.[42] The race became largely a contest between Yun and Park, the latter winning the presidency with a plurality of 46.65 percent of the vote over the former who received 45.10 percent. Indeed, Park won the election by a hair's breadth margin of 156,000 votes over Yun, while the other three opposition candidates polled over 700,000 votes altogether.[43]

In the National Assembly elections held in November, the DRP garnered only 33.5 percent of the votes cast, while the opposition parties drew 66.5 percent altogether. Yet the competition among the opposition candidates was so widespread and intense (in all 11 opposition parties ran) that the DRP won 110 seats in the 175-member Assembly or 62.8 percent of the Assembly seats--in contrast to 65 seats or 37.2 percent of the total Assembly seats gained by the opposition parties.[44]

Thus, though Park won the presidency and his DRP swamped the opposition in the National Assembly, the elections were inconclusive for the DRP to claim a clear mandate to rule. Another aspect to be noted was that 79 of the newly elected Assemblymen, accounting for 44.6 percent of the total members, were "old" politicians.[45] This made many observers highly doubtful--doubt already aroused when the DRP admitted "old" politicians into its ranks--whether the Park regime would be able to break completely with the past which it had so roundly denounced. Be that as it may, in December 1963 the SCNR was dissolved and a new civilian government emerged,

inaugurating the Third Republic with Park Chung Hee as
its first president.

The Korea-Japan Normalization Treaty and Its Aftermath

No sooner had Park's military-turned-civilian government been established than its legitimacy was severely
challenged because of its decision to resolve the
unfinished business for normalization of diplomatic
relations with Japan. The dispute over the restoration
of Seoul's relations with Tokyo involved virtually all
the political, social, and economic issues which South
Korea faced. It polarized South Korean society with
bitter antagonism in 1964-1965. On the one hand,
students, intellectuals, the press, opposition parties,
and religious organizations were mobilized against the
normalization of relations between Seoul and Tokyo. One
writer estimated that 3.5 million persons took part in
the protest against the normalization treaty, one of the
most active political mobilizations modern Korea had
experienced. On the other side stood the government,
government-sponsored organizations, and business groups--
all with the firm support of the United States.[46]

The preliminary talks for negotiations between Seoul
and Tokyo had commenced in October 1951, in the midst of
the Korean War and only one month after the signing of
the San Francisco Peace Treaty between the Allied Powers
and Japan which took effect in April 1952. The talks
were the first official contact between the two countries
after the surrender of Japan in 1945.[47] Over the next
eight years, the Rhee government and the newly independent Japan, both prodded by the United States, had made
intermittent attempts at restoring diplomatic relations
but the contacts had remained unproductive.

Among the stumbling blocks were Seoul's insistence that
normalization be preceded by a Japanese apology for their
colonial exploitation of Korea and demand for a payment
of approximately $2 billion in reparations. Japan, on
the other hand, claimed that the 1910 annexation treaty
was a valid instrument of international agreement, and
refused to consider any obligations at all. Rather, some
Japanese officials occasionally mentioned the "benefits"
of Japanese colonial rule to the Koreans.[48] As the
Japanese were unyielding with regard to their position,
President Rhee too remained adamant in his stance.
Indeed, Rhee seemed to be in no hurry to reach a solution

with Japan--apparently because his anti-Japanese posture had enjoyed a strong public support and had been a rallying point for his government. A turning point in the Seoul-Tokyo relations came with the emergence of the Chang Myon government. The new Seoul government approached the problems with a conciliatory attitude and resumed the talks on a somewhat more promising note; but they were cut short by the coup.[49]

Meanwhile, the issues between South Korea and Japan had grown complex. This was reflected in the fact that seven formal conferences had taken place--not to mention numerous other contacts--in the 14 years since the 1951 preliminary talks; all this before the two sides reached a final agreement or the treaty was signed.[50] The points in dispute between the two sides could be grouped under four major categories. The first was the "basic relations" that should be maintained between the two countries. Here, Seoul demanded Japan's apology as well as Japan's recognition of the Seoul government as the only legitimate and sovereign government of all Korea (to the exclusion of the P'yongyang regime).

The second category dealt with property claims, which primarily concerned compensation to South Korea for losses of property incurred by the Japanese colonial exploitation.[51] The third category dealt with fishery and the Peace Line. The Peace Line was proclaimed unilaterally by President Syngman Rhee in 1952 as South Korean fishery and defense zone from 50 to 60 miles seaward around Korea; but its main goal was to protect the fishery resources from Japanese fishermen, whose equipment and techniques were superior to those of their Korean counterparts. However, to the chagrin of the Koreans, Japanese fishing vessels routinely crossed the Peace Line and Seoul could not defend it. The matter became one of the key stumbling blocks in the Seoul-Tokyo negotiations.[52]

The fourth category concerned the legal status and treatment of some 600,000 Koreans who had chosen to remain in Japan after the Pacific War. Their legal status was uncertain, varying from that of Japanese national to special status nationals and to aliens. Many of them were unskilled laborers who accepted jobs which Japanese normally would not take and were wretchedly poor, victims of Japanese prejudice and discrimination. The objective of the Seoul government was to win for them the privilege of permanent residence, to have Japan discontinue discriminatory policies in education and employment, to facilitate business and property transactions between them and Korea, and to have Japan to treat all of them as nationals of South Korea. Seoul's claim for a single nationality was made, even though the Koreans in Japan were divided between those who were loyal to P'yongyang and those who supported Seoul.[53]

Each of the categories described was fraught with potentially strong emotional reactions in Korea. Indeed, when the Park government in June 1965 finally signed the treaty with Japan compromising on every category, it came under attack. First, although the South Korean government was recognized as "the only lawful government in the Korean peninsula," the treaty neither specified the extent of the territorial jurisdiction (obviously because of Japan's cognizance of the existence of the North Korean government) nor was it accompanied by Japanese apology.[54] Second, the Japanese payment in the property claims settlement was made in the name of "economic cooperation" rather than compensation or reparations as originally demanded by Seoul. In the fishery agreement, the Peace Line was abandoned in return for a 12-mile exclusive fishery zone for South Korea.[55]

Concerning the Korean minority, Japan agreed to recognize their "special status" as distinct from other foreign nationals in Japan, while specifying that the benefits of such an agreement would be made available only to those Koreans who were loyal to the Seoul government. Tokyo, however, refused to assign a single nationality to all Korean residents in Japan.[56] As such, the agreements on the various categories represented "one-sided" concessions for many South Koreans, and they severely criticized the accords. But these agreements were the maximum the Park government could extract from Tokyo government.

The leaders of the junta and later President Park looked upon a Japanese settlement as urgent business, because it promised to be a major aid for Korea's faltering economy and would also broaden its international ties. The execution of the First Five-Year Economic Plan (1962-1966) of South Korea required a huge amount of foreign capital[57] as well as extensive technical aid; yet at the time, the American economic aid to Seoul was decreasing rapidly. Indeed, the active interest of the United States in the Korea-Japan talks had been accompanied by a steady contraction of its grant-aids to South Korea,[58] which had been gradually replaced by development loans. In this gloomy and desperate situation, the Seoul government was forced to look for other countries for economic assistance; and Japan was a major source, the most accessible source for such help, provided that the outstanding issues between the two countries could be resolved.

In addition to the economic need, the Seoul government also was interested in expanding its diplomatic contacts. This interest was stimulated by the growing influence of Communist China in the Third World since the mid-1950's and its subsequent emergence in October 1964 as a world power with the detonation of its first nuclear device-- to the advantage of P'yongyang vis-a-vis Seoul.[59] This being the case, a logical step for the Seoul government would be to gain diplomatic recognition and support from Japan, Seoul's close neighbor geographically and ideologically.

After the coup, the junta moved quickly to resume the talks with Japan. In November 1961 the SCNR Chairman Park Chung Hee conferred in Tokyo with Japanese Premier Ikeda Hayato, which resulted in a general understanding between the two leaders. Park assured Ikeda that the Peace Line would be modified if Japan showed sincerity in settling Korea's property claims. Park also went along with the long-standing Japanese position that its monetary payments would not be construed as reparations or compensations and that the amounts would hardly reach the ones demanded by the previous Seoul governments.[60]

Then in November 1962 the KCIA Director Kim Jong P'il met in Tokyo with Japanese Foreign Minister Ohira Masayoshi. The two men reached a basic agreement on the sum for the property claims settlement. In the agreement, which was kept from the Korean people but subsequently became known as the Kim-Ohira Memorandum, Japan agreed to pay $300 million in grants, $200 million in government-to-government loans, and $100 million or more in commercial credits.[61]

After the formation of the civilian government under President Park, steps were taken to resolve the other issues. By March 1964 it had appeared that an overall agreement would shortly be reached between Seoul and Tokyo. However, the protracted negotiations, all conducted behind closed doors, had aroused considerable concern among the public in South Korea. In particular, the secret Kim-Ohira Memorandum, whose existence had since been exposed and finally made public, served to stimulate the suspicions which the opposition parties and their allies had already entertained about the new Korean leaders, especially Park.[62]

The opponents of the treaty in Seoul were apprehensive that the Japanese money, once introduced into Korea in the wake of the Seoul-Tokyo accord, would be used by the Park government to consolidate its political control initially snatched by coup, leading to their government's dependence on Japanese economic power to stay in power. In conjunction with such a feeling of uneasiness, the critics suspected that the Japanese money, once infused into the Korean economy as stipulated in the Seoul-Tokyo settlement, would create a situation in which Korean businessmen would become mere "compradors" working for the Japanese, as Korean politicians, unable to resist Japanese financial allurement, would bend their will. Thus the foes of the treaty feared all along that Japanese money would open Korea to Japanese economic penetration as well as political manipulation, while aggravating the level of already existing internal corruption in Seoul.[63]

This kind of nationalistic apprehensiveness was deepened by concerns over the basic direction of the country. Many felt that the Japan-Korea treaty would make the prospect for reunification of their divided peninsula even more distant, because the settlement would facilitate the absorption of the South Korean economy into the Japanese and would place Korean hopes for reunification at the mercy of Japanese international politics. Thus the opponents, among whom were many renowned conservative politicians, questioned their government's judgement in giving priority to the Japanese problems over the reunification issue.[64]

In the spring of 1964 it was widely speculated that a successful conclusion of Korea-Japan talks was imminent. This galvanized treaty opponents, sparking widespread protests. The protest against the ongoing negotiations commenced early in March with opposition party speaking tours around the country. Late in the month, students in all major cities--aroused by the turn of events and supported by the press--took to the streets and vented their anger against the government despite the government's use of military forces to disperse them. This marked the beginning of a 18-month-long violent anti-

37

treaty struggle, in which the demonstrators denounced the government leaders for their "low-posture diplomacy" in dealing with Japanese negotiators and even impugned them as traitors.[65] By May the situation had become critical.

In Seoul the May demonstrations climaxed on June 3 with bloody battles between beleaguered policemen and 15,000 students who, demanding the resignation of President Park, attempted to storm government buildings including the Presidential residence. The attackers were driven back by combat troops who had been called in. On the very same day, martial law was proclaimed in the vicinity of Seoul. With Seoul under martial law (until July 29), the press was placed under strict censorship, assembly was forbidden, and schools were closed down until the fall semester. In addition, 168 student leaders, seven reporters, and 173 other people were arrested and prosecuted.[66] By then, the fierceness of the anti-treaty activities of the year lessened.

The anti-treaty campaign of 1965 commenced in February, when the Japanese Foreign Minister Shinna Etusaburo visited Seoul. By summer the campuses and streets in every major city in South Korea had been filled daily with protesting students. In April--the most violent month in the year's anti-treaty turbulence--some 45,000 protestors in Seoul clashed with thousands of riot policemen, resulting in injuries to hundreds of demonstrators (including four opposition national assemblymen) and many policemen.[67] Notably, the American support of the Seoul government on the Japanese issue engendered an anti-American feeling among the demonstrators, who regarded the U.S. stance as selfish and shortsighted in pushing Korea into the arms of Japan.[68]

On June 21 the hard-pressed Park government closed down 13 universities and 58 high schools, which had been the centers of the student protest movement, for an early vacation. The next day the treaty was signed, while the opposition politicians, restrained by police from carrying out a street protest, staged a sit-in demonstration in the National Assembly. Pending ratification, the protests continued, though their ferocity abated somewhat due to the systematic and relentless crackdowns by the determined government.[69]

On July 14, amid a scene of violence in the National Assembly between the members of the ruling DRP and the outnumbered opposition, the treaty was placed on the agenda. On the night of August 11, the Democratic Republicans forcibly concluded the debate and voted the consent bill out of committee, while physically barring opposition members from the rostrum. Three days later, the National Assembly, with the presence of only 110 Democratic Republicans and one Independent, approved the ratification bill by 110 votes with one abstention.[70] The protests against the Japan-Korea treaty were finally brought to an end with the squashing by combat troops of demonstrations in Seoul on August 26. The troops were called into the city under the decree of "garrison state," a state of affairs similar to martial law but without press censorship or other administrative control by the military.[71]

On August 18--while the public attention was still riveted on the Japan-Korea accord--the still one-party National Assembly pushed through a bill authorizing the government to send 20,000 combat troops to Vietnam by a vote of 101 for, one against, and two abstentions. This increased the level of South Korea's involvement in the Vietnam conflict--the involvement already begun with the dispatch of a 133-man army medical unit the September before along with the expedition of a 2,000-man "logistical support unit" the following spring. In March 1966 the National Assembly authorized the government by a vote of 95-27 to send an additional 20,000 combat troops to Vietnam. As the Seoul government broadened its Vietnam commitment, there were more than 50,000 Korean troops in the war-torn country as of 1969. In addition, more than 15,000 Korean civilians were engaged in various work to assist the war efforts; this number subsequently peaked to some 23,000.[72]

With the Japan-Korea treaty turmoil and the Vietnam decision now behind, a sense of quietude and stability settled over the country. The tranquility was facilitated by the new money flowing in from the two settlements, which provided the Seoul government with funds for its economic development plan as well as its political machines.[73] In the economic field, the First Five-Year Economic Plan was completed successfully in 1966, exceeding by 1.2 percent the annual GNP growth rate of 7.1 percent expected under the plan. And there had been marked improvements in the country's overall economic situation, which was reflected among others in the growth of the per capita income from $83.60 in 1962 to $123.50 in 1967.[74] Buoyed by the improving economy, the national mood was changing from the earlier uncertain, even le-

thargic, desperation to one of hopeful expectation. The
political structure, established late in 1963 and
preserved shakily in 1964-1965, appeared to be stabil-
ized. Thus when the government faced general elections
in 1967, its position seemed unbeatable, particularly in
view of the lack of sustained solidarity and purposeful-
ness in the opposition camp.

On June 14, 1965--amidst the upheaval over the
Japan-Korea treaty--the two major opposition parties, the
CRP and DP, merged into a single party called the
People's Party (PP).[75] The PP as a unified party lasted
only a few months because of an intraparty factional
disagreement over how to block passage of the Korea-Japan
treaty by the DRP-dominated National Assembly. The
"extreme" faction led by Yun Po Son was willing to resign
en masse from the National Assembly as a protest against
the treaty; but the "moderate" faction insisted upon a
"parliamentary" opposition. Infuriated at the position
taken by the moderates, the extremists withdrew from the
PP, and early in 1966 they formed the New Korea Party
(NKP). However, in February 1967--only a few months away
from the general elections--the NKP merged with the PP
to form the New Democratic Party (NDP). Yun was selected
as the new party's presidential candidate.[76]

The presidential election in May 1967 once again became
primarily a two-man race between Park Chung Hee of the
DRP and Yun Po Son. However, unlike in 1963, Park
defeated Yun rather convincingly--by winning 51 percent
of the total valid ballots (5,688,000 votes), as opposed
to 41 percent (4,526,000) for Yun and eight percent
(1,000,000) for five minor candidates. In the National
Assembly elections held in June, 11 parties put up
candidates. The DRP won 129 of the 175 seats (more than
two thirds) at stake, the NDP captured 45, and a third
party took one.[77] The election outcomes seemed to
suggest that by 1967 the Park regime--thanks largely to
the success of its economic development plan and abundant
political funds--had not only established a fair degree
of control over the society, but was well on its way to
acquiring an aura of political legitimacy.

Notes

1. Kim Se-Jin, The Politics of Military Revolution in Korea, (Chapel Hill: University of North Carolina Press, 1971), pp. 37-55; and Cumings, The Origins of the Korean War, pp. 169-178.

2. John P. Lovell, "The Military and Politics in Postwar Korea," in Wright, ed., Korean Politics in Transition, pp. 159-164.

3. Sasaki Harutaka, Hangukchon Pisa, (Hidden History of the Korean War, trans. from Japanese by Kang Ch'ang Koo), Vol. I, (Seoul: Pyonghaksa, 1977), pp. 205-224.

4. Lovell, "The Military in Postwar Korea," in Wright, ed., Korean Politics in Transition, p. 165.

5. Kim, The Politics of Military Revolution in Korea, pp. 64-69; and Lee, Korea, p. 159.

6. Korea Annual 1964, pp. 110-114; and Hong, et. al., eds., Haebang Isipnyon, pp. 609-612.

7. Henderson, Korea, pp. 345-350, 359; and Han, The Failure of Democracy in South Korea, pp. 53, 172.

8. Sasaki, Hangukchon Pisa, Vol. I, pp. 501-577, Vol. III, pp. 105-655.

9. Kim, The Politics of Military Revolution in Korea, pp. 69-76.

10. Ibid., pp. 77-86.

11. Han, The Failure of Democracy in South Korea, pp. 171-176; and Korea Annual 1964, pp. 115-117.

12. Korea Annual 1964, p. 106; and Han, The Failure of Democracy in South Korea, pp. 199-204.

13. Kim, The Politics of Military Revolution in Korea, pp. 93-102.

14. Lovell, "The Military and Politics in Postwar Korea," in Wright, ed., Korean Politics in Transition, pp. 183-184.

15. Hahn Bae-ho, "The Authority Structure of Korean Politics," Wright, ed., Korean Politics in Transition, p. 316.

16. The six "Revolutionary" Pledges contained the following goals: (1) anti-Communism, (2) pro-United Nations, pro-Western and pro-United States foreign policy, (3) elimination of governmental corruption, (4) economic betterment, (5) national unification through strength, and (6) eventual restoration of civilian government. Hong, et. al., eds., Haebang Isipnyon, p. 619.

17. Park Chung Hee, Our Nation's Path: Ideology of Social Reconstruction, (Seoul: Tong-A Publishing Company, LTD, 1964), pp. 171-195.

18. Ibid., pp. 189-198.

19. Ibid., pp. 171-177, 207-215.

20 Korea Annual 1964, pp. 126-127.

21. Kim Sung hee, "Economic Development of South Korea," in Kim Se-Jin and Cho Chang H., eds., Government and Politics of Korea, (Silver Spring, Maryland: Research Institute on Korean Affairs, 1972), p. 150.

22. Kang Song Chae, "Park Chung Hee e 'Poni'wa Kwollyok Naebu e Amt'u" (Park Chung Hee's Reversal of Will and the Secret Feud Within the Ruling Group), Shin-Tong-A, No. 327 (December 1986), pp. 288-291.

23. Kim, The Politics of Military Revolution in Korea, pp. 125-126; and William J. Bards, "The United States and the Korean Peninsula," in William J. Bards, ed., The Two Koreas in East Asian Affairs, (New York: New York University Press, 1976), p. 173.

24. Kim, Divided Korea, pp. 237-238.

25. Lee Hahn-Been, Korea, pp. 156, 163. By the end of the military junta in December 1963, only 74 persons were on the blacklist.

26. Kim, Divided Korea, p. 244. The law prohibited almost all voluntary political activities of the type which make political parties effective channels for public participation in political process. Under the law, only registered members of a party could campaign for the party. It outlawed door-to-door canvassing for votes, prohibited soliciting or accepting donation except from one's own registered party members, and strictly restricted the use of the news media to solicit votes.

27. Kang Song Chae, "Park Chung Hee ege Onsong nop'in Mitaesa 'Berger'" (American Ambassador Samuel Berger Who Raised Voice to Park Chung Hee), Shin-Tong-A, No. 328, (January 1987), p. 340.

28. New York Times, October 28, 1979.

29. Kim Kwan Bong, The Korea-Japan Treaty Crisis and the Instability of the Korean Political System, (Hereafter cited as Korea-Japan Treaty Crisis), (New York: Praeger Publishers, 1971), pp. 180-186.

30. Kang, "Park Chung Hee ege Onsong nop'in Mitaesa 'Berger'," p. 340.

31. All the scandals occurred during the SCNR rule. They were: the importation by the KCIA of Japanese cars duty-free and their resale; the importation of pinball machines by the KCIA from Japan duty-free and their resale; the covert manipulation of the Korean stock market, whereby the KCIA raked in money at the expense of many investors; and the construction of the Walker Hill Resort near Seoul to attract money from American GIs, and diversion by the KCIA of money from the construction fund. Lee Sang Woo, "Park Chongkwon ha Kwollyokhyong Pup'ae e Chongch'e," (The True Character of Power-Associated Corruption Under the Park Regime), Shin-Tong-A, No. 328 (January 1987), p. 290.

32. At first Park had remained as the Deputy Chairman of the SCNR behind a frontman. In July 1960, he replaced the frontman as Chairman and remained in that capacity until December 1963, when the SCNR was dissolved.

33. Park's life history up to the 1961 coup was based upon various scattered materials. They included: New York Times, October 27, 1979; Far Eastern Economic Review, November 9, 1979, pp. 12-13; and Yang Sung Chul, Korea and Two Regimes: A Study of Kim Il Sung and Park Chung Hee, (Cambridge, Mass.: Schenkman Publishing Company, Inc., 1981), pp. 47-57.

34. One of the reasons for the instant American hostility to the coup was supposedly Americans' suspicion of the ideological backgrounds of Park and some other coup leaders. Lee Sang Woo, "Hanguk Kwa Miguk: ku Kaltung e Choryu," (Korea and the United States: The Undercurrent of Conflict), Shin-Tong-A, No. 322, (July 1986), pp. 456-457.

35. Kim, Pomyong qi, II, p. 258.

36. Han Y. C., "Political Parties and Elections in South Korea," in Kim and Cho, eds., Government and Politics of Korea, pp. 130-132.

37. Korea Annual 1964, pp. 141-143; and Hong, et. al., eds., Haebang Isipnyon, pp. 660-663, 736. In a sense, that the compromise was reached by Park's intervention was suggestive that Korean political parties could be made and unmade overnight by the decisions of personal leaders. Indeed, the DRP, like the previous ruling parties, was primarily a personal instrument for a few leading members of the party, and it derived its strength from its connections with the administration rather than from mass support.

38. Hong, et. al., eds., Haebang Isipnyon, pp. 670-671, 733.

39. Lee, Korea, p. 156; and Kim, Divided Korea, p. 249; and Kim, Korea-Japan Treaty Crisis, p. 86. During the 31 months of junta rule, the average price of consumer goods increased by 32 percent and the price of rice by 64 percent, while the average wage of industrial workers rose by only 19 percent. Unemployment, which was officially 8.4 percent in 1962, rose to 8.6 percent in 1963.

40. Kim, Korea-Japan Treaty Crisis, pp. 143-146.

41. Ibid., p. 148.

42. Yun resigned the presidency in protest against the March 1962 Politics Purification Act, which exempted him but prohibited many of his colleagues from participating in politics.

43. Kim C. I. Eugene, "Significance of the 1963 Korean Elections," Asian Survey, IV, No. 3, (March 1964), p. 770.

44. Kim, The Politics of Military Revolution in Korea, pp. 135-136.

45. Kim, "Significance of the 1963 Korean Elections," pp. 765-773.

46. Kim, Korea-Japan Treaty Crisis, p. 116; Lee Changsoo and George De Vos, Koreans in Japan, (Berkeley: University of California Press, 1981), pp. 102-104, 108; and Bards, "The United States and the Korean Peninsula," in Bards, ed., The Two Koreas in East Asian Affairs, p. 173.

47. Nakagawa Nobuyuki, Chosen Mondai eno Kihonteki Shikaku, (Hereafter cited as Chosen Mondai...) (Korean Problems Viewed from Fundamental Angle) (Tokyo: Tobata Shotten, 1976), pp. 74-75, 135.

48. Gavan McCormack, "Japan and South Korea, 1965-1975: Ten Years of 'Normalization'," in Gavan McGormack and Marck Selden, eds., Korea, North and South: The Deepening Crisis, (New York: Monthly Review Press, 1978), p. 173.

49. Jo Yung-Hwan, "Japanese-Korean Relations and Asian Diplomacy," Orbis, XI, No. 2, (Summer 1967), pp. 583-584.

50. Nakagawa, Chosen Mondai..., pp. 84-86, 134-136.

51. Jo, "Japanese-Korean Relations and Asian Diplomacy," pp. 587-588.

52. Ibid., p. 3. Premier Chang Myon called the Peace Line "a kind of cancer" in Korea-Japan relations and promised a modification of the line in case Japan showed sincerity in settling Korea's property claims. Kim, Korea-Japan Treaty Crisis, pp. 58-64.

53. Nakagawa, Chosen Mondai..., p. 89; and Lee and De Vos, Koreans in Japan, pp. 133-158.

54. Jo, "Japanese-Korean Relations and Asian Diplomacy," pp. 586-587.

55. Nakagawa, Chosen Mondai..., pp. 84-88; and Kim, Korea-Japan Treaty Crisis, pp. 52-54, 57-58.

56. Korea Annual 1964, p. 192; and Kim, Korea-Japan Treaty Crisis, p. 64.

57. The First Five-Year Economic Plan required a total foreign capital of between $630.3 million and $684 million, and Japanese contribution constituted 29 percent of the total. Hahn Bae-ho, "Korea-Japan Relations in the 1970's," Asian Survey, XX, No. 11, (November 1980), p. 1088.

58. Jo, "Japanese-Korean Relations and Asian Diplomacy," p. 586. The U.S. grant-aid to South Korea in 1960 amounted to $225 million; and declined to $165 million in 1962, to $119 million in 1963, to $88 million in 1964, and to $71 million in 1965. Kim, Divided Korea, p. 258f.

59. Jo, "Japanese-Korean Relations and Asian Diplomacy," pp. 585-586. After French President Charles de Gaulle recognized the Peking regime in January 1964 and Peking detonated its first atomic bomb in the fall, the Seoul government felt that the tension in Asia, then centered on the escalating Vietnam conflict, had heightened.

60. Already the Chang Myon government reduced the amount of the property claim to $800 million from Rhee's claim of $2 billion. McCormack, "Japan and South Korea, 1965-75," in McCormack and Selden, eds., Korea, North and South, p. 174.

61. Nakagawa, Chosen Mondai..., pp. 87-88; and Jo, "Japanese-Korean Relations and Asian Diplomacy," p. 584.

62. Like the Four Scandals, the existence of the Kim-Ohira Memorandum was brought into the open in January 1963 by Kim John P'il's opponents in the SCNR. A former South Korean diplomat in exile in the United States told an American news agency that large "pay-offs" were made by Seoul to Japanese politicians to make the agreement. Economist, February 12, 1977, p. 69.

63. McCormack, "Japan and South Korea, 1965-1975," in McCormack and Selden, eds., Korea, North and South, p. 176; and Kim, Korea-Japan Treaty Crisis, pp. 101-105.

64. Nakagawa, Chosen Mondai..., p. 87.

65. Oh Byung-Hun, "Students and Politics," in Wright, ed., Korean Politics in Transition, pp. 109-110; and Hong, et. al., eds., Haebang Isipnyon, pp. 682-687.

66. Walter Easey and Gavan McCormack, "South Korean Society: The Deepening Nightmare," in McCormack and Selden, eds., Korea, North and South, pp. 81-82.

67. Oh, "Students and Politics," in Wright, ed., Korean Politics in Transition, p. 127; and Kim, Korea-Japan Treaty Crisis, pp. 111-112.

68. Kim, Divided Korea, pp. 146, 261.

69. Kim, Korea-Japan Treaty Crisis, pp. 111-113; and Oh, "Students and Politics in Wright, ed., Korean Politics in Transition, p. 127. By the time the treaty was ratified by the one-party Assembly, no less than 52 students and 18 "political" professors had been expelled from universities by the order of the government. Demands for their reinstatement were made in September, when campuses opened. However, demonstrations on their behalf were crushed by troops, who pursued students into at least two of the campuses which had hitherto been sanctuaries for students.

70. Kim, Korea-Japan Treaty Crisis, pp. 114-116.

71. Nakagawa, Chosen Mondai..., p. 136.

72. Selig S. Harrison, The Widening Gulf: Asian Nationalism and American Policy, (New York: The Free Press, 1978), pp. 186-189; and Koo Youngnok, "The Conduct of Foreign Affairs," in Wright, ed., Korean Politics in Transition, pp. 222-223.

73. In 1966 and 1967 South Korea received $49.08 million from Japan in grants, $80.03 million in public loans, and $103.4 million in commercial loans. The Vietnam commitment provided Seoul with additional revenues, which were approximately $118 million in the fiscal year 1965, $135 million in FY 1967, and over $165 million in FY 1968. Kim, "Economic Development of South Korea," in Kim and Cho, eds., Government and Politics of Korea, p. 159; Kim, Divided Korea, pp. 156, 264; and Lovell, "The Military and Politics in Postwar Korea," in Wright ed., Korean Politics in Transition, p. 191.

74. Kim, Divided Korea, pp. 165, 268; and Kim, "Economic Development of South Korea," in Kim and Cho, eds., Government and Politics of Korea, p. 156.

75. Hong, et. al., eds., Haebang Isipnyon, p. 733.

76. Han, "Political Parties and Elections in South Korea," in Kim and Cho, eds., Government and Politics in Korea, p. 136.

77. Kim, The Politics of Military Revolution in Korea, pp. 148, 150-152. The DRP won 102 district seats and 27 of the 44 proportionally distributed seats, and the NDP captured 28 district seats and 17 proportional ones.

CHAPTER 3

The 1969 Constitutional Amendment

Following the 1967 elections, the South Korean political scene was overshadowed by a power play within the
ruling Democratic Republican Party over an amendment of
the country's constitution. Because the basic law
carried a two-term limitation on an individual as
president, Park Chung Hee was required to step down in
1971 when his second four-year presidential term would
expire. This kindled contention for succession within
the DRP between the mainstream faction centered around
Kim Jong P'il and its opposition from the very early days
of the party, the non-mainstream faction. The overriding
issues dividing the two factions had little to do with
policy differences but revolved around the question of
power. Thus, the battle for succession too was acted out
with no discernible divergences in policy.

While the mainstream faction was hoping that Kim Jong
P'il would become the party's presidential standard
bearer in 1971, the non-mainstream faction moved to block
any activities to recruit support for Kim as Park's
successor and made plans to remove constitutional
obstacles in the way for a third consecutive presidential
term.[1] They did so presumably with a tacit approval of
Park, while contending that Park was indispensable for
the country, because only he could provide a "strong"
leadership--the prerequisite for political stability
which, in turn, was essential for economic development
and national security.[2]

As the intra-party maneuverings came out into the open
in January 1969, pressures were applied on the dissenters
of the constitutional amendment for Park, who "always had
a 'darkest Africa' or 'midnight sun' embassy ready for
anyone who stepped over the bounds." By late July all
DRP assemblymen had been "persuaded" enough to be brought

into line, enabling the party to avoid a split which would have been disastrous for the party in the 1971 elections. And the DRP drafted a bill permitting Park to seek a third term and submitted it to the National Assembly early in August.[3]

The upshot of the DRP intraparty strife over the amendment was that the party had become incapable of selecting a presidential candidate to run on the party's programs independent of the personality of Park. The DRP, instead of functioning as the vehicle through which broad consensuses were achieved and translated into political actions, was relegated to the shadowy status of being a personal appendage of Park, as the defunct Liberal Party was that of Syngman Rhee's. During this time, the opposition New Democratic Party repeatedly remonstrated against the pending constitutional amendment,[4] while students staged violent street demonstrations against it throughout the summer of 1969.

The outcome of the confrontation between the DRP and its opponents turned out to be similar to the final passage by the National Assembly of the Japan-Korea Treaty some four years before, because at the dawn of September 14, the DRP-drafted amendment bill passed the Assembly with only the supporters of the bill present. At the time, the Assembly rostrum was forcibly occupied by the opposition assemblymen who were determined to prevent any voting on the bill. Those assemblymen in favor of the bill gathered surreptitiously in another Assembly room and passed it by a vote of 122-0. On October 17 the amendment was approved by national referendum and duly became law.[5]

A contributing factor for the endorsement of the amendment by the plebiscite could have been the tension which had heightened suddenly between Seoul and P'yongyang, which in South Korea could not have failed in engendering public support for the incumbent President. Both the attempted North Korean commando raid on the Blue House (the presidential palace) and the seizure of the U.S.S. Pueblo occurred in January 1968, and the U.S. reconnaissance plane EC 121 was shot down off the North Korean coast in April of the following year.

In addition, 1969 was a good year for the South Korean economy. The GNP grew by more than 15 percent in contrast to 13.3 percent in 1968 and an average of 7.8

percent between 1962 and 1966. It was the highest growth rate thus far. The wages and per capita income, both of which had steadily risen for at least a few years, continued to rise. The inflation of consumer prices was 10.1 percent, which was one of the lowest since 1961, and farmers had bumper crops.[6]

Fragility of the Economic Development

The economic development program of the Park government was centered on an "export-oriented growth model." It was carried out under the slogans such as "Work and Seat" and "Productive Politics," meaning that material productions were the very essence of politics itself. Indeed, the economic program was "one of the central elements" of the Park government's entire socio-economic policies as well as of "its claim to public support."[7] Judging from the performance during the latter half of the 1970's, the economic program appeared to be working and the Park regime seemed entitled to public support. However, the development strategy based on the growth of exports was to enjoy ephemeral popularity.

Between 1959 and 1969 exports expanded at a much greater rate than imports (the former 23-fold in value and the latter only five to six times), but the total value of imports far exceeded that of exports. Despite the rapid growth of exports, the exports in 1970 were still only 46 percent of the imports of the year in value. In order to finance the deficits in the expanding foreign trade, the government borrowed money abroad. The foreign debt in 1969 reached a peak of $556 million. By 1970 the total outstanding foreign debt had reached $1.931 billion, some 24 percent of that year's GNP. In 1971 it was $2.396 billion, in 1972 it went up to $2.978 billion, and in 1973 it climbed to $3.575 billion.[8]

To execute its economic plans in the face of growing foreign debts, the government was forced to increase the domestic taxation. The taxes collected rose from 111.4 billion won in 1966 to 313.7 billion won in 1969, to 398 billion won in 1970, and to 492.9 billion won in 1971. This meant that taxation rose from 10.8 percent of South Korea's GNP in 1966 to 15.1 percent in 1969, to 15.4 percent in 1970, and to 15.6 percent in 1971.[9] All this while, the fruits of the economic development were not shared equitably, which created serious social problems. The problems were compounded by the conspicuous consumption of the country's new elites, the millionaire industrialists and high government officials; and apparently it had a debilitating effect on social cohesion. A widely shared feeling that the government was less than sensitive to the matters of distribution of wealth and socio-economic justice was dramatized in Kim Chi Ha's satirical poem entitled, "The Five Thieves." In the poem, published in the May 1970 issue of the monthly Sasangge (The World of Thought), the poet denounced the world of privilege, corruption, and ruthless authority.[10]

South Korea's export-oriented economy was predicated on "harnessing cheap labor to an international viewpoint," that is, on low wages paid to Korea's skilled and industrious work force. During the First and Second Economic Plans (1962-1971) factory workers received extremely low wages, which averaged only 15 to 19 percent of the comparable Japanese levels.[11] There were no fringe benefits.

Labor unions were controlled by management and the government, and protests against unsatisfactory working conditions were not tolerated.[12] As such, there were "many cases of employer abuse of unskilled workers, reminiscent of nineteenth century sweat shops in Western nations." The exploitation of workers was dramatically attested to at the P'yonghwa Market in Seoul by the tragedy of a garment maker Chon T'ae Il, who in November 1970 immolated himself in protest against deplorable working conditions. The incident brought to "public attention the human cost" which economic development, "based on exports made cheap by low wages, was placing on the workers."[13]

Meanwhile, the international scene in Asia changed unhappily for the Seoul government. In pursuance of the Nixon Doctrine enunciated in July 1969, the United States informed Seoul in July of the following year that it would withdraw by June of 1971 the 7th Division, a third of its 63,000 troops then stationed in South Korea. The withdrawal notification--coming at a time when Seoul's position in the United Nations had been weakening--[14] made the Seoul government nervous, since it construed the American plan as a step toward America's eventual complete military disengagement from Korea. Also because the stationing of American troops in Korea had been an important source of revenue for South Korea, the pullout would reduce earning from that quarter.

Furthermore, the American economic assistance, given almost entirely in the form of grants, began to be replaced by loans after 1965, and it was virtually terminated after 1971. In addition, the U.S. food assistance program under Public Law 480, under which Korea from 1955 on had received U.S. agricultural commodities virtually free, started to be supplanted as early as 1966 by commercial imports. The U.S. food aid program was to be terminated in 1975.[15]

The conclusion of the Vietnam conflict adversely affected the Korean economy further. The war in Vietnam, which provided the first overseas venture of South Korean military and business firms, proved an important source of foreign exchange earnings, which totalled more than $1 billion through military remittances and Vietnam-related businesses. The war provided a boost to Korean economy, perhaps comparable to the effect the Korean War had on Japanese economy. However, as the war began to wind up after President Richard Nixon's program of its "Vietnamization" went into effect in 1969, the numbers of South Korea's civilian and military personnel in Vietnam declined with concomitant reductions in the economic benefits. The earnings from Vietnam ceased with the complete withdrawal of all Koreans after the cease-fire agreement in January 1973.[16] On top of all this, in October 1971 the United States, a major buyer of Korean goods, imposed a quota on Korean textiles and apparel, South Korea's most important export items.[17]

1971 Presidential and National Assembly Elections

Amidst the growing restiveness with the unfolding political and economic difficulties, presidential and national assembly elections were held in April and May 1971, respectively. The campaign themes of the two major parties, the ruling DRP and the opposition NDP, echoed the partisan debates then going on among the South Koreans who were concerned about the state of the nation.

The DRP, whose presidential candidate was again Park Chung Hee, asserted that South Korea, facing danger and insecurity as it was, needed a president who had military experience. This was an allusion that the presidential candidate of the opposition NDP Kim Dae Jung lacked military background.[18] Another theme of the ruling DRP was that of the 1967 presidential election: namely, an uninterrupted modernization and economic development under Park. As he hit the campaign trail, Park himself stated that "We have just begun to write a historic sentence. Who will put a period to this unfinished sentence if we ourselves do not complete it?"[19]

The NDP presidential candidate Kim Dae Jung (45 years old in 1971), selected after a series of intraparty factional maneuverings, proved himself a formidable challenger to Park. Addressing himself to the future of the divided country, Kim advocated its neutralization through cooperation with the United States, Japan, China, and the Soviet Union--the four major powers directly involved in the affairs of Korea. Regarding the reopening of Japan-Korea relations, which since its inception in 1965 had created externally-supported privileges in Korea while bringing about growing financial debt to and economic dependence on Japan, Kim declared that it did not reflect the genuine wishes of the people.[20] Indignant at the corruption, which was believed to be endemic in high places in South Korea and was causing resentment among the populace, Kim told his audiences: "Let's put an end to the corrupt 10-year rule" of the Park regime.

Furthermore, pointing to the glaring gap between urban and rural incomes, with the latter being only half of the former on a per capita basis, Kim promised a redistribution of wealth should he become president.[21] Finally, Kim warned that Park, if elected, would probably perpetuate his rule for life under a "dictatorial generalissimo system." As Kim proved an attractive campaigner and his campaign crescendoed, Park, on the eve of the election day, pledged that this would be his "last bid" for the presidency.[22]

When ballots were cast and counted in late April, Park received 53.2 percent of the almost 12 million votes as compared to 45.3 percent for Kim Dae Jung (the remainder going to three other runners). Thus Park won again but his margin of 940,000 votes against Kim was smaller than the 1.2 million margin he had received in 1967 against the aging Yun Po Son.[23] The electoral showing of young Kim, until then a relatively obscure leader of a minor faction in the NDP, was considered very "strong" and surprised many people.

In the National Assembly elections in May, the opposition NDP once again garnered more votes than anticipated, especially in view of the bitter factional wranglings over the selection of the party's nominees before the elections. It captured 89 seats (65 by districts and 24 by proportional representation)--more than one-third of the 205 Assembly seats and a considerable gain over the 45 seats won out of the total 175 in the 1967 elections. The NDP's improved position was sufficient to thwart any move on the part of the ruling DRP to initiate another constitutional amendment. The ruling DRP, on the other hand, captured 113 seats (86 district seats and 27 proportional ones)--a decline from 129 seats won in the previous elections.[24]

The election returns of 1971 gave little comfort to Park and his DRP, since they showed a considerable advance of the opposition NDP despite the mobilization of abundant funds and bureaucracy and the police in support of the DRP candidates.[25] It was especially so in the view of the growing demographic decline of the rural population in whom the electoral strength of the DRP lay.[26]

The North-South Dialogue, the Yushin Constitution, and the Inauguration of the Fourth Republic

As the DRP suffered an election setback and problems were looming in the country's economy, Park government's sense of insecurity further sharpened because of a series of events unfolding abroad. In April 1971 the Sino-American "Ping-Pong Diplomacy" started, leading to President Richard Nixon's visit to Peking in February of the following year. In October 1971 the United Nations General Assembly voted in favor of seating the Peking government in that world organization at the expense of the Taiwan government, Seoul's ally. In September 1972 Tokyo and Peking agreed to establish diplomatic relations. The rapprochement among the powers and Peking's enhanced international status caused uneasiness for the Seoul government,[27] because its tight reign over its population was facilitated by the cold war-like atmosphere that had been prevailing in South Korea.

At home, the Park regime was faced with increasingly restive population. On August 10, 1971 some 30,000 low-income dwellers in Seoul rioted at a public housing development, demanding that sale prices of building lots be lowered and burning police stations. The same month also witnessed violent demonstrations of industrial workers for higher wages.[28] Two months later several thousand university students in Seoul took to the streets in protest against political corruption, compulsory military training at schools, and the surveillance of campuses by the ubiquitous KCIA. The government had to call out troops and police to quell the campus disturbances.

The extent of students' distrust of their government could be adduced from an anti-Japanese manifesto clandestinely circulated in September at Korea University. The manifesto charged that Korea:

> has reentered the Japanese sphere through plots between Korean commercial-political gangsters and government-backed Korean chaebol (financial conglomerates). Japan wants us to be dependent and seeks to divide and rule the two Koreas.

> Let us not repeat the history of 1910-1945. If we think only of comfort, we will produce another ruler who calls himself Korean but is actually like Yi Wan Yong in 1910.[29]

Besieged by the converging economic and political crises, President Park on December 6, 1971 proclaimed a state of "national emergency," declaring that rapid external changes posed an unprecedented peril for South Korea's "national security." He stated that as a trend emerged toward detente between great powers, tensions on the Korean peninsula were constantly rising primarily because of P'yongyang's "preparations for an invasion" and the stepped-up infiltration of Communist agents and terrorists. Park proclaimed that his government would henceforth give top priority to "national security" and that, for the sake of national security, "all social unrest" and "irresponsible" arguments would not be tolerated and that every citizen had to sacrifice part of the freedom he was enjoying.[30]

Park's assessment was, however, disputed not only by Park's domestic critics but also by foreign observers. They noted that the state of national emergency was proclaimed not for the sake of the nation's safety but rather for the sake of "the security of the Park regime" and that "the external threat Mr. Park evidently fears is not military attacks but the opposite--detente."[31] Be that as it may, the proclamation of a state of "national emergency" was followed on December 27 by the enactment of a Special Measures Law For National Security and

Defense, which was railroaded by a predawn National Assembly session with no opposition assemblymen present.

Under the Special Measures Law, President Park was empowered to proclaim national mobilization, to control the press and other publications, to restrict labor disputes, to control wages and prices, and to regulate or forbid outdoor gatherings and demonstrations--all without consulting the National Assembly.[32] Thus the law granted sweeping emergency powers to the President, who on January 11, 1972 once again justified them by citing "the basic strategy of the northern puppet regime to unify the country by force and through communization."[33]

While U.S.-China relations improved in 1971-1972 with potentially far-reaching consequences for the entire Korean peninsula, the relationship between North and South Korea, that had been characterized by continued tension and confrontation, entered a new phase. It did so in August 1971 when Seoul and P'yongyang agreed to open bilateral talks through "liaison personnel" of their respective Red Cross Societies at the truce village of P'anmunjom for the reunion of family members separated between the North and South. It was followed in September by the first preliminary meeting of the two Red Cross societies. Subsequently 19 more preliminary conferences had been held at P'anmunjom before August 30 of the following year, when the first full-dress meeting was held.[34]

The Red Cross negotiations were paralleled by behind-the-scenes contacts at the highest political level in the capitals of the two sides.[35] Out of these meetings came a dramatic joint communique issued by both South and North Korean governments on July 4, 1972. In the communique, the two Koreas pledged to seek the reunification of the divided country through independent solution without relying upon any outside force, by peaceful means, and in the spirit of national harmony transcending differences in ideology or political system.[36]

The joint communique also contained an agreement to expedite the ongoing Red Cross talks held since the summer of the previous year at P'anmunjom and to establish a North-South Coordinating Committee (NSCC) to implement the agreed points in the communique. The NSCC was to be co-chaired by KCIA Director Lee Hu Rak and Kim Yong Chu, Director of the Organization and Guidance

Department of the Korean Workers' Party and also the younger brother of Kim Il Sung.[37]

Spurred on by the accord, the North and South Korean Red Cross Societies held their first full-dress conference in P'yongyang on August 20, 1972. It was followed by a second session in Seoul on September 13-14, thus alternating the conference site between the two capitals. A third session was held on October 24 and a fourth one on November 22.[38]

Meanwhile, a conference of co-chairmen of the NSCC (not to be confused with a conference of the NSCC itself which was yet to be formed) was held at P'anmunjom on October 12. From the North, Second Deputy Premier Park Song Ch'ol represented Kim Yong Chu. Park was to continue to represent Kim, who did not participate in the subsequent conferences of the co-chairmen of the NSCC nor the meetings of the NSCC. The meeting on October 12 was followed by a second one in P'yongyang on November 2-4. At a third conference, held in Seoul on November 30-December 1, the two sides inaugurated the NSCC with five regular members from each side, making the meeting also the first regular NSCC session.[39] Thus nearly five months after the announcement of the historic July 4th communique, two key avenues of communication were established between the two Koreas: the meetings of the Red Cross Societies and the NSCC.

For the Park government, entering into talks with P'yongyang for "peaceful unification" of the divided country, however, was an about-face. Because South Korea had maintained its independent status in the Cold War atmosphere with the support of the United States, and it had been taboo to advocate "peaceful unification" with the North. The notion of "peaceful unification" with the North was advanced by Cho Bong Am, the Progressive presidential candidate executed in 1959 on treason charges. It was also advocated by students and reformist parties on the eve of the May 1961 coup. The movement for "peaceful unification," however, made the South Korean Establishment jittery and was suppressed by the military junta.

Despite the official suppression, the territorial division had remained repugnant to the peoples in the North as well as the South. In Seoul, as in P'yongyang, national unification had continued to be the supreme national goal and had been officially proclaimed as such time after time. Thus the Park government had been ambivalent on the unification issue, while realizing that it could not continuously ignore tackling the problem with impunity.

When the Park government opened dialogue with the northern counterpart following the issuance of the July 4th joint communique, it was greeted in Seoul with great surprise, "considerable misgivings among some quarters," and much euphoria among the general public.[40] Also it helped divert the attention of the public away from their country's growing politico-economic difficulties, provided the government with an escape from its defensive position on the reunification issue, and made President Park popular among many South Koreans. Riding on the wave of his sudden popularity engendered by the euphoria over the North-South dialogue, President Park railroaded a series of measures, which would have been impossible under normal circumstances. Indeed, the "boldness" of these measures and the "stakes" at which these actions were aimed made Park's "earlier exercise in risk over rapprochement with Japan look like a parlor game."[41]

As the attention of South Koreans was riveted on the North-South talks, on October 17, 1972 Park suddenly clamped down martial law throughout the country. This was the third martial law since Park's seizure of power in 1961. Under the latest martial law, the National Assembly was dissolved, political parties were banned, tight press censorship was imposed, and all colleges and universities were closed down "for an early winter vacation."[42]

Park declared that these steps were necessary to create a new political system that was essential for his efforts to eliminate the causes and symptoms of "disorder and inefficiency" at home and to "foster and develop the free democratic institutions most suitable for Korea." Furthermore Park stated that the soon-to-be-built political structure would be able to cope more effectively with the fluid domestic and external situations arising from the opening of the talks with P'yongyang. Also Park promised a comprehensive constitutional revision and to hold a national referendum on it.[43]

The newly drafted constitution of South Korea,[44] endorsed by an Emergency Cabinet Conference on October 27, made it possible for Park to prolong his presidency indefinitely through an indirect presidential selection process. Freed from the previous constitutional provision that required him to relinquish his position in 1975 when his third consecutive four-year presidential term would expire, Park could now be reelected to an unlimited number of six-year terms by an electoral body, known as the National Conference For Unification (NCFU) which would consist of 2,359 popularly elected "non-partisan" deputies.

The President under the draft charter was empowered to nominate one-third of the National Assemblymen for "election" by the deputies of the NCFU, and to dissolve the Assembly whenever he deemed it necessary. In addition, the constitution stipulated that a constitutional revision proposed by the National Assembly had to be ratified by the NCFU, of which the President would be Chairman, and that the government could restrict civil liberties and rights of citizens at its own discretion. Significantly, in conjunction with the ongoing North-South dialogue, the new draft constitution made the NCFU the sole constitutional organ responsible for determining unification policies.[45]

The draft constitution was approved by an overwhelming majority (91.5 percent) of the votes cast (91.9 percent of the eligible voters) in a national referendum on November 21, while the nation was still under martial law (until December 13). It duly became the fundamental law of the nation on November 24, referred to as the Yushin (Revitalizing Reform) Constitution.[46] In accordance with its stipulation, on December 15 South Koreans elected 2,359 deputies to the NCFU. Most of the new deputies were local dignitaries such as landowners, "nonpolitical" lawyers, or other men of "conservative" inclination. On December 23 the NCFU deputies gathered in Seoul and without debate elected to the country's presidency Park Chung Hee, who acted as the presiding officer of the gathering and was the only presidential candidate. On December 27 Park was sworn in as the eighth president of South Korea, inaugurating the Fourth Republic.[47]

On February 27, 1973 elections were held to pick 146 lawmakers, two-thirds of the 219 National Assemblymen, in the nation's 73 two-member electoral districts. The pro-government DRP won 73 seats, half the seats at stake, with only 38.7 percent of the total popular votes cast. The opposition NDP captured 52 seats with 32.5 percent of the votes, and another opposition Democratic Unifica-

58

tion Party (DUP) took two seats with 10.2 percent of the ballots cast. The Independents garnered 19 seats with 18.6 percent of the votes.[48]

Though the ruling DRP captured only half of the elective assembly seats, pro-government legislators subsequently constituted two-thirds of the total national assemblymen. Seventy-three legislators, one-third of the assemblymen yet to be chosen, were nominated on March 7 by President Park, and they formed a pro-government Yujonghoe (Political Fraternity for Yushin) in the National Assembly.[49] Under the circumstances and in view of the fact that the two opposition parties together outpolled the DRP, the general elections as the genuine reflection of popular political mandate in the National Assembly became meaningless.

With the Yushin Constitution in force, which was ironically claimed by its supporters as the legal embodiment of the "Korean-style democracy," South Korea's faltering experiment with democracy since 1948 had come to an end. The basic charter provided Park with a legal framework for perpetuation of his dictatorial presidency, while wiping out virtually any vestiges of democracy that had survived until then. Notably, the new constitution did not help the on-going North-South dialogue realize its declared goal of reunification of the divided peninsula. The new basic law entrusted the task exclusively with the government, specifically with the NCFU of which Park was the chairman by virtue of his being the president, and the government proved to have no positive programs for the accomplishment of the task.

Although it endorsed the July 4th communique, the Park government approached the talks with its northern counterpart with "a high degree of sensitivity to the pitfalls" the situation provided. And the Seoul regime looked "less confident of its supporters" than the P'yongyang regime and appeared apprehensive of being "outsmarted and possibly outfought" by the North, which assumed "a more sanguine, positive, and demanding posture."[50]

The contrasting postures had become abundantly clear by March 15, 1973, when a second plenary meeting of the NSCC got under way in P'yongyang. At the conference the North proposed a peace treaty, which would end the Korean War halted by the 1953 Armistice and "lift the confrontational atmosphere hindering peaceful and independent

59

unification." The proposed treaty was to be implemented, inter alia, by mutual reduction of troops to the level of 100,000 on each side, withdrawal of foreign troops from Korea, and the convocation of an all-nation congress to solve the question of reunification. The all-nation congress was to be attended by the representatives of the people from all walks of life from both sides.[51]

The South, which had maintained a "gradualist" approach, rejected the proposal on the ground that it was "premature" to tackle political issues. Instead, it offered cultural and economic exchanges in order to first build a "mutual trust" before any political negotiations could take place. The North refused the Seoul's proposal, denouncing it as an "obstructionist and delaying tactics." The mutually unacceptable proposals continued to be the very bases of the positions of the two sides. The third session of the NSCC--which convened on June 12-13 and which turned out to be the last conference of its kind--confirmed that the differences were fundamental and could not be resolved.[52]

The confidence of one side and the apprehensiveness of the other were also reflected in the Red Cross talks. At their third plenary meeting held in P'yongyang on October 24, 1972, the northern delegation proposed that the two Red Cross Societies each dispatch its own personnel to the territory of the other side and verify the fates of dispersed family members as a step toward their eventual reunion. The Seoul representatives, however, counterproposed that the verification be done through written applications. At the subsequent Red Cross talks neither side budged from its positions advanced on October 24.[53]

The Seoul government's position on the reunification was finally spelled out in Presidents Park's speech on June 23, 1973. Stating that North and South Koreas must not interfere in each other's "domestic affairs" and that unification "appears difficult to be achieved in a short period," Park declared that his government would drop all its previous oppositions to P'yongyang's entering into the specialized organs of the United Nations and would welcome the two Koreas' becoming U.N. members as separate entities.[54] Park's statement clearly indicated that for the South, reunification--no matter how desirable--was a distant goal.

Park's proposal was rejected the very same day by President Kim Il Sung, lest simultaneous admission of two Koreas as two separate political bodies could imply P'yongyang's formal acceptance of the divided status leading to perpetuation of the division. Instead, Kim called for convening of an All-Nation Congress to be comprised of the representatives of the people from all strata of society in the North and South. Kim proposed that the Congress establish a North-South confederation under the name of the Confederal Republic of Koryo and that the two Koreas join the United Nations under that name as a single body, while leaving intact the two political systems existing in the two halves until unification.[55]

The North-South dialogue, as hopelessly stalemated as it had been, came to a halt. The halt occurred shortly after the kidnapping of Kim Dae Jung, an incident not directly related to the talks themselves. Mr. Kim was in Japan at the time of the political denouement of October 1972. Instead of returning home, he traveled between Japan and the United States campaigning against what he called the "military dictatorship and tyranny" in South Korea. But on August 8, 1973 he was kidnapped from a Tokyo hotel in broad daylight by five Korean CIA agents and five days later he was released in front of his house in Seoul, blindfolded and bruised.[56]

The abduction instantly brought out angry reactions from P'yongyang, which, despite Seoul's firm denials, denounced the kidnapping as work of the KCIA. And on August 28 North Korea's co-chairman of the NSCC Kim Yong Chu launched a personal attack on South's counterpart Lee Hu Rak. Kim specifically charged that the crime was committed by KCIA agents under the direction of their "chieftain" Lee, because the victim had struggled for "democracy" and peaceful unification of the country. Kim demanded that the men from the KCIA on the NSCC be replaced by persons who "have national conscience, oppose the freezing of the national split, and aspire after reunification of the country."[57] Finally, Kim declared that under the prevailing circumstances the North would no longer engage in the Seoul-P'yongyang talks.

The North-South dialogue had achieved very little or nothing in redeeming the pledges contained in the July 4th joint communique. Rather the dialogue was used by Park Chung Hee as a rationale for cracking down on dissidents and tightening up political control, claiming that such measures were needed to conduct the dialogue from a position of strength and internal cohesion. It was through such justification, extracted from the extraordinary circumstances created by the opening of the North-South talks, that Mr. Park circumvented the existing constitution and carried out the "Revitalizing Reforms."

Notes

1. For details of the controversy over the 1969 constitutional amendment, see the lengthy account entitled, "The Third Republic" which appeared serially in Tong-A Ilbo between January 2 and March 1, 1982.

2. New York Times, February 2, May 9, July 13, 26, 31, 1969; and Tong-A Ilbo, May 10, 21, August 12, 1969.

3. Michael Keon, Korean Phoenix: A Nation From the Ashes, (Englewood Cliffs, N.J.: Prentice-Hall, 1977), pp. 117-118; and New York Times, July 26, 31, August 8, 1969.

4. Tong-A Ilbo, February 16 and 22, 1982.

5. New York Times, October 20, 1969; and Han, "Political Parties and Elections in South Korea," in Kim and Cho, eds., Government and Politics of Korea, pp. 140-141. In the national referendum 65.1 percent of voters cast their approval.

6. Parvez Hasan, Korea: Problems and Issues in a Rapidly Growing Economy, (Baltimore: John Hopkins University Press, 1976), pp. 50, 52, 239; Kim, "Economic Development in South Korea," in Kim and Cho., eds., Government and Politics of Korea, p. 162; and Cole and Lyman, Korean Development, p. 127.

7. From President Parks' speeches of January 16 and May 27, 1965, in Park Chung Hee, Major Speeches by Korea's Park Chung Hee, (Seoul: Hollym Corporation Publishers, 1970), pp. 299, 315; and Bards, "The United States and the Korean Peninsula," in Bards, ed., The Two Koreas in East Asian Affairs, p. 173.

8. Hasan, Korea, pp. 43, 66; and Patricia M. Bartz, South Korea, (London: Oxford University Press, 1972), p. 96. South Korea's balance of payments worsened in part by a rash of failures among the firms dependent upon these foreign loans, mostly Japanese commercial loans; and the failures were the result of the lack of careful feasibility studies of new enterprises. By 1969 the situation had become serious enough to alarm the government, which under prior agreements was obliged to assume

responsibility on defaulting foreign loans. By 1971 no less than 85 percent of the enterprises which had borrowed private loans from Japan had become insolvent and unable to repay their loans, forcing government-owned banks to assume the repayment burdens. Nakagawa, Chosen Mondai, pp. 96-98; and Kim, "Economic Development of South Korea," in Kim and Cho., eds., Government and Politics of Korea, p. 159.

9. Haptong Yongam 1977, p. 528.

10. Kim Chi Ha had been known for his biting poems attacking the "modern" Korea Park's regime was building. Park Sil, "Hanguk Ollon Sunansa" (A History of the Sufferings of Freedom of Speech and Writing in South Korea), Shin-Tong-A, No. 295 (April 1984), pp. 281-282.

11. Park Eul Yong, "An Analysis of the Trade Behavior of American and Japanese Manufacturing Firms in Korea," in Karl Moskowitz, ed., From Patron to Partner: The Development of U.S.-Korean Business and Trade Relations, (Lexington, Mass.: D.C. Heath and Company, 1984), p. 24. In 1968 average daily wages in manufacturing industries in Asian countries were: $1.15 in South Korea, $1.61 in Taiwan, $2.50-3.00 in Singapore, and $6.00 in Japan. The wage differential between Korea and the United States early in the 1970's ranged as high as one to ten. Bartz, South Korea, p. 49; and Harrison, The Widening Gulf, p.227.

12. For labor laws under Park regime, see Edward J. Baker, "'Within the Scope Defined by Law': The Rights of Labor Under the Yushin System," Monthly Review of Korean Affairs, II, No. 3 (July 1979), pp. 2-3.

13. Frank, et. al., Foreign Trade Regimes and Economic Development, p. 243; and Monthly Review of Korean Affairs, I, No. 5 (September 1979), pp. 2-3. According to the New York Times of March 1, 1981, most of the workers at the garment factories in the P'yonghwa Market were teen-age girls. They worked up to 12 hours a day, six days a week for wages starting at less than $50 a month.

14. South Korea--not a U.N. member--has been represented in the U.N. since 1951 by a permanent observer mission. During the 1950's the U.N. served as a major forum where the Seoul government sought to advance its claim as the only lawful government of the entire Korean peninsula and to isolate North Korea as an international outlaw. However, Seoul's reliance on the U.N. became increasingly tenuous during the 60's and early 70's, because the newly independent and nonaligned nations of the Third World took more often than not an anti-colonial and anti-Western stance in their voting

behavior in that world organization. Nena Vreeland, et. al., Area Handbook for South Korea, (Washington, D.C.: American University Press, 1975), p. 202; and Park Chung Hee, To Build A Nation, (Washington, D.C.: Acropolis Books, 1971), pp. 157-160.

15. The Economic and Social Modernization of the Republic of Korea, (Cambridge, Mass.: Harvard University Press, 1980), pp. 2, 199, 455; and Karl Maskowitz, "Limited Partners: Transnational Alliances Between Private Sector Organizations in the U.S.-Korea Trade Relationship," in Moskowitz, ed., From Patron To Partner, pp. 154-161.

16. The withdrawal of South Korean troops from South Vietnam started in December 1971 and was completed in March 1973. Korea Annual 1981, (Seoul: Yonhap News Agency, 1981), pp. 317, 319.

17. New York Times, December 28, 1971; John S. Odell, "Growing Trade and Growing Conflict Between the Republic of Korea and the United States," in Moskowitz, ed., From Patron To Partner, pp. 123-131; and Lee Seung-Yun, "Major Achievements and Problems of the South Korean Economy: 1962-74," in Kim Young C. and Abraham M. Halpern, eds., The Future of the Korean Peninsula, (New York: Praeger Publishers, 1977), p. 19. Exports of textiles constituted 39 percent of South Korea's total export value in 1971, bringing in $1.068 billion and accounting for 12.2 percent of that year's GNP. In addition, in 1971 the textile industry accounted for over 32 percent of the employment in the manufacturing industry.

18. New York Times, March 29, 1971. Park had four opponents, but Kim Dae Jung was the only serious challenger.

19. Boston Globe, October 27, 1979; and New York Times, March 29, April 11, 15, 1971.

20. New York Times, March 29 and April 25, 1971. Out of the total foreign capital of $7.6543 billion (both loans and direct investments by foreign companies) introduced to South Korea between 1959 and 1974, the Japanese capital accounted for 25.2 percent--second only to the United States (36.5 percent). Seoul's dependence on Tokyo was especially pronounced in the lopsided pattern of two-way trade that reached a two-way volume of $4.33 billion by the end of 1974 from mere $210 million in 1965, with the trade imbalances in Japan's favor jumping from $123 million in 1965 to $1.28 billion in 1974. Nakagawa, Chosen Mondai, p. 129; and Vreeland, et. al., Area Handbook for South Korea, pp. 305, 309.

21. The per capita income of a rural household in 1967 was 49.8 percent of its urban counterpart, 50.7 percent

in 1969, and 63.6 percent in 1971. Tong-A Ilbo, April 7, 1980; Monthly Review of Korean Affairs, V, No. 2 (March/April 1983), p. 2; and Franklin B. Weinstein and Kamiya Fuji, eds., The Security of Korea: U.S.-Japanese Perspective on the 1980's, (Boulder, Colorado: Westview Press, 1980), p. 4.

22. New York Times, April 1, 25, 28, 1971; and Tong-A Ilbo, April 7, 1980.

23. New York Times, April 29, 1971.

24. New York Times, May 27, 1971. Two seats went to two splinter parties.

25. In addition to routine contributions from Korean big business, which was dependent on the government for bank loans and government contracts, the DRP in 1971 received at least $8.5 million from American companies doing business in South Korea; and the bulk of the American money was paid by two firms: Gulf Oil ($3 million) and Cartex Petroleum ($4 million) through its Korea partner, Honam Oil. Asian Wall Street Journal, March 10, 1977; and Newsweek, May 26, 1975, p. 39. In the absence of local autonomy, all local officials were appointees of the central government; as such, local officials campaigned for the candidates of the ruling party.

26. Following the 1953 cease-fire, urbanization was rapid both in absolute and relative terms. In 1955 there were about 5.3 million people in administratively defined urban areas, and they accounted for roughly 24 percent of the total population. In 1971 some 42 percent of the 15 million eligible voters lived in urban areas. In 1975 there were 16.8 million urbanites, representing more than a three-fold increase since 1955 and accounting for 42 percent of the total population. New York Times, April 25, 1971; and Kim Son-ung and Peter J. Donaldson, "Dealing with Seoul's Population Growth: Government Plans and Their Implementation," Asian Survey, XIX, No. 7 (July 1979), pp. 660-661, 663.

27. New York Times, October 13, 23, 1971; and Tong-A Ilbo, July 16, 17, October 27, 28, 1971.

28. Tong-A Yongam 1975 (Tong-A Yearbook 1975), (Seoul: Tong-A Ilbosa, 1975), P. 110; and Kamada Mitsunori, "Boku Taitoryo Ansatsu no Hamon" (The Impact of the Assassination of President Park), Supplement to Special New Year Edition of Chuo Koron, (Tokyo) 1982, p. 125.

29. Harrison, The Widening Gulf, p. 227. Yi Wan Yong was the Korean Prime Minister who on August 22, 1910 signed the Treaty of Annexation that turned Korea into a Japanese colony. Since then Yi has become the symbol of treason to the Korean people.

30. <u>Tong-A Ilbo</u>, December 6, 1971.
31. <u>New York Times</u>, December 28, 1971.
32. <u>Tong-A Ilbo</u>, December 27, 1971; and <u>New York Times</u>, December 27, 1971.
33. <u>Tong-A Ilbo</u>, January 11, 1972.
34. <u>Kim Kyung-Won</u>, "South Korea: The Politics of Detente," in Kim and Halpern, eds., <u>The Future of the Korean Peninsula</u>, p. 56.
35. Between May 2 and 5, 1972 KCIA Director Lee Hu Rak was in P'yongyang secretly in order to confer with North Korean leaders including Kim Il Sung. From May 29 to June 1 North Korean Deputy Premier Park Song Ch'ol visited Seoul on a similar mission.
36. <u>Tong-A Ilbo</u>, July 4, 1972.
37. <u>Ibid.</u>
38. <u>Nam</u> Koon Woo, "North-South Korean Relations: From Dialogue To Confrontation," <u>Pacific Affairs</u>, Winter 1975-1976, pp. 478-479.
39. <u>Ibid.</u>
40. <u>Kim</u>, "South Korea," in Kim and Halpern, eds., <u>The Future of the Korean Peninsula</u>, p. 57; and Yang, <u>Korea and Two Regimes</u>, p. 263.
41. Keon, <u>Korean Phoenix</u>, p. 120.
42. <u>Tong-A Ilbo</u>, October 18, 1972.
43. <u>Ibid.</u>
44. <u>Tong-A Ilbo</u>, November 25, 1972.
45. <u>Ibid.</u>
46. <u>Tong-A Ilbo</u>, November 21, 23, 24, 25, 1972.
47. <u>Tong-A Ilbo</u>, December 15, 16, 27, 1972. There was a story revealing Park's determination to hold onto power for lifetime. after the ratification of the Japan-Korea Treaty, Park reportedly spoke to his aides:

> Now that I have the U.S. in my grasp by dispatching (South Korean) troops to Vietnam and have Japan behind me through the Japan-Korea Treaty, who would dare to touch me? Do you thing I would ever leave the Blue House before I enter a coffin?

Kim, <u>Pomyong'gi</u>, II, p. 297.
48. <u>New York Times</u>, March 2, 1973. the DUP was formed only one month before the elections by a splinter group from the NDP.
49. <u>New York Times</u>, March 6, 1973.
50. Abraham M. Halpern, "Introduction," in Kim and Halpern, ed., <u>the Future of the Korean Peninsula</u>, p. 7.
51. <u>Tong-A Ilbo</u>, March 15, 16, 17, 20, 1973.

52. Tong-A Ilbo, March 15, 16, 17, 20, June 13, 14, 1973.

53. Before the two-pronged North-South talks came to a halt in August 1973, four more Red Cross plenary sessions were held; and the last, the seventh such meeting, was held on July 11-12. Tong-A Ilbo, October 24, November 23, 1972; March 21, 22, May 10, 11, July 12, 1973.

54. Tong-A Ilbo, June 23, 1973. It should be noted that already on May 17, 1973 North Korea was admitted into the World Health Organization (WHO), a specialized organ of the U.N. Through its admission to the WHO, P'yongyang was entitled to observer status in the U.N., and it established a permanent mission in New York in the fall of 1973.

55. Nam, North-South Korean Relations, p. 480.

56. Vreeland, et. al., Area Handbook for South Korea, p. 176; and Kim, "South Korea," in Kim and Halpern, eds., The Future of the Korean Peninsula, p. 60.

57. Nam, "North-South Korean Relations," p. 481.

CHAPTER 4

THE DEMOCRATIC OPPOSITION

As President Park was instituting the Yushin system, many people were suspicious of his ulterior motives and opposed to the measures he was implementing; but they were kept quiet by the effects of the martial law and the ongoing North-South dialogue. The hostility toward the Yushin structure became vocal and gained momentum following the kidnapping of Kim Dae Jung and the breakup of the dialogue with P'yongyang. Indeed, the conjunction of these two seemingly only superficially related incidents galvanized the forces of opposition to the Yushin system and helped them initiate an active movement for a "revival of democracy."[1]

Democratic Movement

From early October 1973 and throughout the middle of the month, students at the Seoul National University and a few other major universities in Seoul staged demonstrations, demanding the "truth" about the Kim Dae Jung affair and an establishment of a "liberal democratic system" of government and guarantee of "basic civil rights." The students also asked for an immediate end to "subjugation of [South Korea] to Japan" and an "assurance of people's rights to livelihood by establishing a self-supporting economic system."[2] In addition, the protestors called for an immediate dissolution of the KCIA, the withdrawal of police agents from campuses, and the restoration of the freedom of the press.

The demonstrating students further demanded that the politicians and journalists repent their sins of aligning themselves with the government rather than criticizing it, and that the press and the opposition NDP perform their "original mission." Apparently, the students' involvement in political issues was reinforced by their dissatisfaction with the opposition NDP and the press, both of which had been too intimidated to perform their "original mission," as castigated by the students. Under the circumstances, the students through demonstrations expressed their view of the government in the ways the cowed opposition party and press could not do.[3] By the end of November, the initial protests had spread to other campuses in Seoul as well as in provincial capitals, whereupon the authorities closed all major universities and colleges for premature winter recess.[4]

The modern political activism of Korean students harks back to the Japanese colonial period, when the students including high-school ones had been an important locus of nationalist fervor and activity. All major anti-Japanese movements within Korea during the period--such as the March First Movement in 1919, the June 10th Incident in 1926, and the Kwangju Students' Incident in 1929--were spearheaded by the students. Since the liberation in 1945, Korean college and university students--not unlike their counterparts in other developing countries--have continued their historical role as a powerful political force. They have been at the center of many currents of public opinion and social conflicts in the country, and their reactions of sociopolitical issues have often reflected the prevailing mood of the nation.[5]

Under the American Military Government (1945-1948), the students were divided between the leftists and the rightists and they battled against their ideological opponents, often bloodily. The underlying issues were for or against the presence of the American military government, for a liberal democracy vs. Marxism, and other ideological and nationalistic concerns regarding the best course for Korea's independence and unification. The agitations of the leftist students were focussed on protesting the dismissals of leftist professors and on boycotting "reactionary" professors. The leftists also demanded "democratic" education, which, among other things, would grant them a voice in the management of campuses.[6]

The campus agitations of the leftist students slowed down somewhat after the open suppression of leftist movements in general from 1946 on by the American occupation authorities. By the time when the Korean War broke out in 1950, the leftist students had been either converted or had gone underground. Shortly afterwards many of them fled to North Korea, bringing their sporadic agitations to an end. On the other hand, the rightist students, being content with the existing sociopolitical order, saw no reasons to continue political activities.[7] Throughout the war years, the students had remained politically nonactive even though the Rhee regime's authoritarian character had begun to show its signs. Because most of them were in the military services and/or were simply resigned to the oppressive situation as an unavoidable evil for the country in peril.[8]

It was only after students had returned to regular academic life following the 1953 armistice that they began to be stirred by the plight of the nation under Rhee's autocratic rule. By then, the Korean schools--like other sectors of the society--had been under the crosscurrents of American, Korean, and Japanese influences that had operated in South Korea since 1945. And the students had been exposed to new ideals of democracy--such as the concept of a free individual, respect for basic human rights, and popular participation in political process.[9] Another reason for the resurging campus political activism was the sharp rise in the school population, especially in higher education.

In the traditional Korea under the Yi Dynasty (1392-1910), it was normally through excellence in the Confucian scholarship that persons obtained governmental appointments, which meant not only power and honor but also wealth. Thus, scholarly accomplishments were cherished and educational aspiration was widespread. Under the Japanese rule, most of the Korean youth were excluded from educational opportunities other than for elementary schooling; because the colonial authorities were bent upon making docile and barely literate subjects out of Koreans. After the liberation in 1945, the pent-up traditional aspiration for learning was suddenly unleashed and the student population of secondary schools and higher educational institutions increased dramatically, a trend influenced and accelerated by the American idea of mass education.[10]

In 1945 there was a total of 7,819 college students attending 19 colleges. By 1965 the combined college enrollment increased to nearly 142,000, a 18-fold rise in two decades. In 1973 the number was about 223,600, representing about eight percent of the college-age population; in 1975 it reached almost 297,000, a 38-fold increase since 1945; and in 1977 some 306,000 students were attending the country's 95 (possible 98) junior or four-year colleges.[11]

The potential of university students for becoming a formidable political force inherent in their numerical strength was enhanced by the heavy concentration of colleges and universities in large cities, especially in densely populated Seoul, where direct actions of students in the explosively crowded streets tended to maximize potential nationwide impact.[12] The effectiveness of the students as a political force was further enhanced by the traditional veneration the common people in Korea had held for the intellectuals, because the former had regarded the latter as being sincere and motivated by lofty ideals. The prestige and honor held by the intellectuals permitted the students, widely regarded to be untainted by dubious compromises of the pragmatic world, to exercise substantial influence on the general public.[13]

Once their political consciousness was awakened, the students, through collective endeavours, displayed their political strength in the April 1960 uprising by overthrowing the unpopular Rhee regime. And in that revolution they acquired the prestige and power that have led them to be looked upon as a major political force in the post-Korean War era. since that revolution, students' demonstrations have become indications of popular unrest and bellwethers of political instability.[14] Viewed in this context, the campus disturbances in the fall of 1973 could have meant that the students were not the only group who were discontented with the existing state of affairs.

Indeed, already during the latter part of the 1950's when the Rhee regime was descending into autocracy, country's college professors and other intellectuals considered their government less than trustworthy and sporadically voiced criticisms of its oppressive measures. The college professors' suspicion of the government, nourished toward the end of Rhee regime, grew conspicuously during their helpless experiences with the military government which, while seeking advice from intellectuals, left them without real influence in the government.[15] Emergence among the college professors of spokesmen for democracy was not only an indication of their distrust of repressive regimes; it was also manifestations of their concerns about the country's enduring political instability as well as the relative decline of their social status.[16]

Since the liberation in 1945, the academic intelligentsia in South Korea had been in a state of difficult transition. They had been moving away from the traditionally prestigious position to one of uncertain social influence and of relatively lower pay. The college professors' social status declined in the face of increasing competition for prestige and influence with new contenders, the military and businessmen, the groups which the academics had traditionally looked down upon and which were now standing on the side of government on various key political issues. In this unsettling and merciless world, the defense of democracy had become important as a means for the defense of the freedom of the universities, of the status of academic intelligentsia, and of their right to criticize the government from which they had been estranged.[17]

Also by actively involving themselves in the anti-government movement, the academics voiced their conviction that the endemic political disturbances were generally caused by a lack of genuine freedom and not by its abundance, the very opposite of government's insistence. And many of them, like in other groups, paid heavily for voicing their convictions. Among the early victims under the Yushin rule was Professor Ch'oe Chong Kil of the Law School of Seoul National University, who in October 1973 was found dead mysteriously following his arrest by the KCIA.[18]

In addition to professors and students, Christian churches too stood up against the governmental repression. Before the introduction of the Yushin system that extinguished the flickering flame of democracy, the South Korean Christian community had hardly been active as an anti-government force. It was only after the grave events of 1972-1973 that some of the politically more conscious clergymen and theologians took upon themselves the role of public advocates for human rights and democracy.[19] As churchmen were arrested and incarcerated for their opposition to the government, angry protest movements spread through the then rapidly growing Christian community, arousing it to what the persecuted church leaders considered the plight of the country.[20] The resistance of the Christian churches to oppressive authorities and their association with reformist activities in the 1970's were not a new phenomenon.

73

Christianity was introduced into Korea surreptitiously in the 18th century. Since then, young Korean churches, unlike the old and tradition-bound churches in the West, had worked for sociopolitical changes, despite persecution by the Yi Dynasty and then repression by the Japanese authorities. Especially during the Japanese colonial rule, Christianity was associated with Korea's independence movement; and it was also a channel, though very limited due to the small number of its adherents, through which Western ideals of democracy were filtered into the country.[21] As such, the Christians played an important role--well beyond their numerical strength--in the post-liberation South Korea.

In 1945 there were some 300,000 Christians in the entire Korean peninsula, approximately one percent of the population. Many of those in the North, however, fled to the South because of the persecution of churches by the Communist authorities. In South Korea the number of Christians grew slowly but steadily thanks to conversion. The real surge in conversion came in the 60's and 70's and overwhelmingly among young urbanites. The urban converts found moorings in this Western faith amidst a growing sense of uncertainty and uprootedness, which were brought about by the long period of political instability and the unsettling social changes accelerated by the rapid industrialization the country had been undergoing.[22] Furthermore, due to its association with the West, conversion to Christianity was seen by many young people as part of their country's "modernization."[23]

The numbers of Christians in South Korea in the recent decades have varied considerably depending upon sources, and the numbers given here should be treated with caution and reservation. In 1974 there were about 4.3 million Christians (3.5 million Protestants and 800,000 Catholics), roughly 13 percent of the total South Korean population, and Christianity ranked third after Buddhism and Confucianism in popularity. In 1979-1980 the number increased to about five to seven million, approximately 12.8 percent to 17.9 percent of South Korea's 39 million people, making Christianity the second most popular religion after Buddhism.[24] Such an explosive growth was unparalleled in Asian history since the conversion of the Philippines by Roman Catholic Spain during her colonial rule of the islands.

Following the massive involvement of Christians in the anti-Yushin activities, the dissident movement broadened.

What held together the diverse elements of the Park regime's foes--students, intellectuals, and Christians--was their common desire for wholesale alteration of the Yushin system, as expressed in their catchword the "Restoration of Democracy." And until the assassination of President Park in October 1979, their movement, frequently forced to go underground, was led by some 2,000 core activists.[25]

As if to signal the birth of a common front among various anti-government forces, 15 prominent intellectuals, scholars, and Christians issued early in November 1973 a "declaration of the state of affairs," echoing the anti-government sentiments of the rebellious students. The statement claimed that South Korea was "now faced with the worst conditions" internally as well as externally because of "the present regime's dictatorship and rule by terror"; and it called upon the people to "rise up and struggle" for revival of democracy.[26]

At this juncture, the authorities closed all universities and high schools for the winter recess earlier than usual, while releasing some of the arrested students. In order to further mollify its critics, the government early in December announced changes in the Cabinet, which included the ouster of the KCIA chief Lee Hu Rak under whose direction KCIA agents had kidnapped Kim Dae Jung and who since then had been identified in the mind of the public with the ill-fated North-South dialogue.[27] The government, however, declared that any move challenging the substance of the constitutional structure itself would not be tolerated.

Given the lack of intention for genuine reforms on the part of the government, however, its critics called the cabinet reshuffle a "trickery." And late in December some 30 civic and religious leaders launched a grassroots campaign to collect one million signatures to petition for the replacement of the Yushin Constitution with a democratic charter. Among the originators of the campaign were a renowned Quaker Ham Sok Hon and a Christian intellectual Chang Chun Ha.[28] Mr. Chang was the editor of the monthly Sasangge whose May 1970 issue printed the poet Kim Chi Ha's "Five Thieves," a satire about the corruption of South Korea's high society; the magazine was closed down on the government's order in September of the very same year.[29]

Repression vs. Resistance

Faced with mushrooming opposition to his assumption of almost unlimited power under the Yushin Constitution, President Park Chung Hee took a series of new repressive measures. On January 8, 1974, the government proclaimed presidential "emergency measures" Number 1 and Number 2 in order to cope with a "potentially serious threat to the security of the state and the public safety." The former made it a crime punishable by imprisonment of up to 15 years for anyone to criticize the Constitution or to advocate its revision. Violators could be arrested without warrants and tried at courts-martial to be established under the latter decree.[30] The proclamation of the two decrees was shortly followed by arrests of the leaders of the grassroots campaign for constitutional revision, including Chang Chun Ha and Ham Sok Hon.[31]

The two harsh decrees notwithstanding, students at Seoul National University and several other colleges in Seoul staged protest marches on April 3. In the name of the National Federation of Democratic Youth-Students (NFDYS), the marchers shouted demands for ending of "president's dictatorship" and termination of the curbs on political activities.[32] On the very same day, the government clamped down on the disturbances with a fourth presidential "emergence measure."

Decree Number 4 outlawed the NFDYS labelling it as a subversive group controlled by a clandestine organization called the People's Revolutionary Party (PRP). And it forbade anyone to join the NFDYS or carry out any activities associated with it, including publishing news about it; violators could be arrested without warrants and be punished by the "death penalty, life or more than five years of imprisonment."[33]

All those involved in the NFDYS-sponsored marches were brought to trial; and eight members of the PRP, that had been allegedly behind the NFDYS's anti-government activities, were given death sentences. In terms of the number of the arrested as well as the harshness of penalties, this was said to be the largest and the most severe since the 1960 April Revolution.[34] In all during 1974 more than 1,000 dissenters were arrested, and no less than 180 were sentenced to various terms ranging from short imprisonments to deaths.

Notably, most of the convicted were known anti-Communists including former President Yun Po Son, Bishop Chi Hak Sun of the Roman Catholic Church, Professor Kim Tong Kil of Yonsei University, and Rev. Park Hyon Kyu. The four were charged with having aided and/or abetted the students in conjunction with the NFDYS marches.[35] Concerning the government's persecution of these known anti-Communists who were also anti-Park, an analyst commented that "a vacuum is being created that could be filled by skilled Communist agitators."[36]

The persecution of the vocal critics of the government failed in subduing the opposition, while giving a rise to international disapproval of the Seoul regime. Subsequently, Park repealed the first and fourth emergency decrees on August 23, 1974, amidst widespread expressions of grief and sympathy that followed his wife's death from an assassin's bullets (presumably aimed at Park himself) during the Independence Day ceremony at the National Theatre in Seoul. Park, however, retained the courts-martial and also kept in prison those who had been already incarcerated.[37] If the repeal of the two decrees was intended as a gesture of reconciliation with its opponents, the government woefully miscalculated.

At its convention on August 23, 1974, the opposition New Democratic Party elected Kim Yong Sam as the new party head. Unlike his predecessor Yu Chin San who had been opportunistic and had tended to toe the ruling DRP lines, Kim had not hesitated confronting the government by making critical remarks. Thus Kim's election had the effect of "radicalizing" the NDP. On August 30 at his first news conference as head of the NDP, Kim called on President Park to end "the dictatorial political method" under which he sought "political stability through political oppression and a controlled press." Then early in September in the National Assembly, Kim urged the government to "open the way for a peaceful change of government through constitutional change." Kim made these remarks, even though either of them could well be construed by the authorities as "subversive."[38]

Meanwhile, the South Korean Christian community became concerned about the fate of their leaders who had been incarcerated, especially so because of the abundant allegations of tortures. Thus the imprisonments of priests and ministers became a catalyst for political awakening of the Christian community as a whole. After the arrests of those implicated in the NFDYS affairs in

1974, a growing number of Christians participated in anti-government agitations including "prayer meetings."[39] The students, too, who had been relatively quiet for several months following the issuance of Decree Number 4, renewed once again their anti-government demonstrations in the fall.[40]

Still more, the press--censored and restricted in its news coverage since the declaration of national emergency in December 1971--showed a sign of restiveness while upholding the principle of free press. On October 24, 1974 some 200 editors and journalists of the Tong-A Ilbo adopted a "declaration of free speech," demanding an end to the governmental interference in news reporting, and had their reluctant publisher agree to print the resolution in the paper. Within a week or so, the Choson Ilbo and 34 other news medias followed suit.[41] At the time the Tong-A Ilbo and the Choson Ilbo carried the two largest circulations among South Korea's 34 dailies then being published.[42] The two were also the oldest papers in Korea and the only ones with a history reaching back to the Japanese colonial period.

Oriented nationalistically and avowing the principle of free press, the Tong-A Ilbo and the Choson Ilbo were established in 1920; since then not infrequently they challenged the Japanese colonial authorities. Early in the 1940's both were closed down by the Japanese who would not tolerate political dissent.[43] During the Rhee regime and virtually throughout the 1960's, the two papers, along with other newly established ones and several intellectual magazines, continued the tradition of dissent while upholding the principle of press freedom. Thereby they provided a forum for the expressions of internal criticisms of the government and of South Korea's democratic and progressive political thoughts.[44] Thus, the press exerted a strong influence on the public, thanks largely to high literacy of the Koreans and their wide readership. Consequently, the press was in constant danger of suppression, and it had to walk a narrow line to avoid outright closure or indirect control through threats of violence and/or economic pressures.

Despite its oppositional character, the press in South Korea had maintained too cautious and conservative posture to be branded as dangerously radical. With rare exceptions, the press had been unrelentingly anti-communist and only gingerly had questioned the official policy on the reunification of the country, which, in many ways, had been the touchstone of the orthodoxy in South Korean politics. The tendency of the press to be accommodating to the authorities during the Rhee and Park regimes was accelerated by the "intimidatingly vague and all-inclusive" Anti-Communist Law, of which Article 4 in part read:

1. Those who have praised, encouraged, or sympathized with the activities of anti-state organizations, members thereof, and foreign communist organizations...shall be punished by not less than seven years' imprisonment.

2. The same punishment shall be meted out to those who have produced, obtained, reprinted, kept,...distributed, sold and imported books, drawings, and other materials with a view to doing the same.[45]

On the other hand, the press usually had been sharp in criticizing governmental corruptions including irregularities in elections and parliamentary procedures; and it was almost vitriolic on the issues of nationalistic concern such as the relationship with Japan, as manifested during the 1964-1965 treaty crisis. Furthermore, the press as a whole had been generally quick to react to gross violations or flagrant disregards of human rights or civil liberties. It had been within these bounds that the press until December 1971 had attempted to carve out its free domain of expression.

Well aware of the power of the press, the Park regime from its very inception had attempted to strengthen its control over news reportings; it did so, however, without resorting to direct censorship.[46] On the other hand, editors and journalists, accommodating governmental wishes, followed moderate editorial policies under the concept of self-restraint. However, not all news stories and comments were welcome to the authorities. Thus with the declaration of national emergency in December 1971, KCIA men were assigned to the press rooms to serve as censors, who banned discussions of the issues which the government felt would be socially disruptive. Under the circumstances, the declarations for free press by editors and journalists in the fall of 1974 were manifestations of their resolve to break away from the governmental constraints.[47]

79

By the autumn of 1974 various segments of South Korean society--the press, the opposition NDP, the Christians, and the students--had become conspicuously defiant of the government. For these diverse elements of the opposition, the Yushin Constitution was the symbol of all the political ills of South Korea. As the fall wore on, they increasingly clamored for constitutional revision and President Park's resignation for the sake of a "restoration of democracy."

Representing these diverse dissident groups, 71 prominent individuals in November formed a broad anti-government coalition, called the National Council for the Restoration of Democracy (NCFRD) (Minju Hoebok Kungmin Hoe'i) in order to restore the country to "democratic rule by peaceful non-partisan means." By January 1975 the National Council had established some 50 local branches.[48] Among the Council's 71 charter members were Yun Po Son, the most famous KCIA kidnap victim Kim Dae Jung, the new NDP head Kim Yong Sam, Cardinal Kim Su Hwan of Seoul Diocese, and Chong Il Hyong who was foreign minister in Chang Myon cabinet and who was now an opposition NDP national assemblyman.

The February 1975 Referendum

Faced with the gathering storm of protests, President Park on January 22, 1975, told the nation that he would hold a national referendum on the Yushin Constitution to determine if it should be retained or abolished. The voting date, announced by the government on February 5, was set for February 12. The voters were to decide whether they supported or opposed the unspecified "major policies of the President," which, however, were understood to mean the current constitution and Park's system of the "revitalizing reforms."[49]

The results of the plebiscite were both comforting and disturbing for the President. He won a substantial margin of victory. Out of the total electorate of 16.8 million, 79.8 percent cast their ballots, and 73.1 percent of them supported and 25 percent (other votes invalid) opposed the "major policies." Thus, 58.3 percent of the total eligible voters approved Park's policies.[50] This was a sizable drop compared with the results of the 1972 constitutional referendum, in which some 84 percent of all eligible voters approved the basic law.

Nevertheless, the plebiscite officially proved what Park always claimed--that a solid, though not overwhelming, majority of the voters favored his rule. And Park lost no time in asserting that the voting proved that there was a national consensus behind him, and that he would dedicate himself to strengthening national security as well as riding out economic difficulties brought about by the "oil crisis." The President suggested that he would seek reconciliation with his critics and even might form a new cabinet to bring in some of them, by pledging that he would institute a "pan-national political structure based on total harmony."[51]

To make his interest in "harmony" seem even more sincere, Park on February 15 ordered an immediate release of all political prisoners incarcerated under his emergency decrees No. 1 and No. 4, except "Communists," to allow them to join in the work of "national revival." And 148 of the 183 dissidents were freed, who had been imprisoned since the summer or the spring of the previous year for advocating constitutional revision.[52] Among the released were Rev. Park Hyon Kyu, Professor Kim Tong Kil, the poet Kim Chi Ha, and 100 students. Of the 35 alleged Communists still in prison, 22 were the PRP members, of whom eight had been on death row. The remaining 13 were "fellow travellers."[53]

President Park's offer of reconciliation, however, was rejected, proving that his post-referendum scheme for harmony was as ephemeral as the consensus he claimed was achieved. Members of the chief opposition NDP charged that the figures in the final votes in the plebiscite had been fabricated. They vowed that they would not participate in the President's pan-national cabinet and would continue their anti-Park offensive until they had received a promise of constitutional revision.[54]

The released dissidents too felt as aggrieved as ever because, though freed, they still remained guilty as charged and could be rearrested at any time. In case of freed campus protestors, they were barred from reenrolling at their former schools. Already, the outspoken Professor Kim Tong Kil just outside the gate of the prison, where he could have spent 15 years had it not been for the February 15 amnesty, stated that he would be "ready to return to this prison for continuing my struggle for democracy." The poet Kim Chi Ha too, whose works had rankled the authorities and whose original death sentence (because of his alleged involvement in the

81

NFDYS incident) had been commuted to a life, said that Park regime was "as rotten as the most rotten fish" and called on Park to step down.[55]

Students, too, remained restive, and some were even incensed by stories of the tortures of the released former classmates. Early in April they staged demonstrations, the biggest and the most violent in many months, clamoring for constitutional revision and resignation of the entire cabinet. The renewed campus turbulence was climaxed by the tragic death on April 12 of a Seoul National University student Kim Sang Jin, who the previous day had stabbed himself in protest against Park's repressive government.[56]

It was clear that neither the referendum nor Park's appeal for unity had silenced the demands for the amendment of the constitution; and it appeared that the unrest would develop into yet another serious challenge to the President. The government returned to a hard-line policy. Vexed by persistent reports abroad on the anti-government activities, pro-government legislators on the night of March 19, 1975, forced through a controversial press bill in the National Assembly lounge, while the opposition legislators were staging a sit-down strike on the Assembly rostrum to prevent the passage of the bill. The new law forbade foreigners to criticize the Seoul government; and authorized imprisonment up to seven years for anyone who would make "slanderous or libelous remarks against the state" while abroad or in conversation with foreigners at home.[57]

The passage of the "gag law" had been preceded by government's financial offensive against the Tong-A Ilbo, which in the previous fall had launched the free press movement with the Choson Ilbo. since then, the paper had reported on the activities of the dissidents, while editorially making critical comments about the government. By doing so, the paper provided South Koreans with their "most intense taste of media freedom for several years." To steer the Tong-A Ilbo away from such a course, the government in December 1974 clamped an almost total advertising boycott against the paper through pressure on corporations using the paper's advertising columns. And the daily's revenues from advertising instantly fell by about half. A similar advertising boycott was applied in January of the next year to the paper's affiliate the Tong-A Broadcasting System.[58]

At this critical juncture in the struggle for free press, the managements of the Tong-A Ilbo as well as of the Choson Ilbo succumbed under government pressures; and in March 1975 they carried out massive dismissals of those editors and reporters who had been active in the free press movement.[59] This brought about the reassertion of official control over the news medias, which was followed by lifting of the advertisement ban imposed against the Tong-A's advertisement columns. While snuffing out the last flicker of press freedom, the government in March and April rearrested some of those who had been freed since mid-February including the poet Kim Chi Ha and 12 campus activists.

The poet Kim, upon gaining freedom earlier, published a three-part prison diary in the February 25-27 editions of the Tong-A Ilbo, in which he gave detailed accounts of the tortures of the prisoners whom he had come to know during his own incarceration. Kim wrote that the sentencing of the eight PRP members to death for allegedly being a Communist espionage ring was a frame-up fabricated out of the "confessions" of two of the condemned; and that the "confessions" had been extracted through tortures of the two, with whom the poet had a "chance" talk in jail. Because of these remarks, Kim was rearrested on March 14, only after 27 days out of prison.[60]

On April 8 President Park issued emergency decree Number 7, prohibiting all campus demonstrations and ordering armed troops to seize the Korea University, a center of the campus unrest. Within two days, eight more colleges were closed down by the order of the Ministry of Education or "voluntarily." On April 9, to the consternation of the public, the government executed the eight PRP men who had been on death row--less than 24 hours after their verdicts were upheld by the Supreme Court and without allowing them to exercise their legal rights to appeal to the President for clemency. An 11th-hour appeal for mercy by Cardinal Kim Su Hwan of Seoul Diocese on behalf of the eight was said turned down by the President, who was determined to "teach them a lesson."[61]

The student protests and other opposition rallies, however, did not subside. The government responded with unrelenting crackdowns, and the outburst of unrest showed signs of abating in the middle of the month. By then, about 20 universities had been closed down, more than 100

83

students had been expelled from schools, a number of
Christian clergymen had been detained, and three university presidents had resigned.[62]

Impact of the Indochina Debacle

While President Park and his domestic foes were locked
in confrontation, the situation in Indochina steadily
deteriorated: Phnom Penh fell to the Communists on April
17, 1975 and Saigon on April 30. These events rever-
berated in Korea causing nervousness among the South
Koreans, while elating the North Koreans who saw the
outcome of the war in Indochina as a harbinger of their
inevitable victory over South Korea. South Koreans were
particularly alarmed by North Korean President Kim Il
Sung's nine-day China trip, undertaken the day after the
fall of Phnom Penh and which was Kim's first journey to
China in 14 years.[63]

In Seoul throughout the month of April, President Park
Chung Hee issued a series of warnings about P'yongyang;
and finally on April 29 he addressed the nation with a
Special Message For Strengthening National Security.[64]
Reviewing the events in Indochina and President Kim's
return from Peking, Park stated that the danger of North
Korea "playing with fire against the South Korea is
greater than ever." Park hardened the tone of his
warning by asserting that the North would attack the
South within that very year. The North would strike,
according to Park, not only because of the events that
had just transpired in Indochina but also because under
the previous constitution the year 1975 would be a
presidential election year, when South Korea's strength
would be "at its nadir" due to "the social turbulence and
confusion" common in all previous election years. So,
"the time has already passed to raise pros and cons as
to whether there exists a danger of North Korea invading
the South," Park declared.

Park drew a lesson from the Indochina debacle. The
failure of the anti-Communist forces, as Park saw it,
resulted primarily from the "split of opinion" among
them. And he urged South Koreans to "unite" and build
a "total posture" in order to "destroy once and for all
the illusions of the North Koreans about conquering the
South." As if in reply, the South Koreans across the
country staged rallies against North Korea. The gatherings culminated in a mass rally in Seoul on May 10, which

was attended by more than a million people including some of Park's political adversaries. It passed a defiant anti-Communist resolution, excoriating Kim Il Sung and denouncing "any form of traitorous acts," apparently a reference to the activities of Park's political foes.[65]

While the nation was in the grip of mixed feelings of a fervor and nervousness, President Park on May 13 issued a ninth emergency decree, entitled the Emergency Measures for Safeguarding National Security and Public Order. Consisting of 14 points, the latest decree covered a wide field outlawing all opposition to the Constitution. It provided stiff penalties for violators—the minimum of one year imprisonment but with no ceiling on its length plus suspension of civil rights up to ten years. Specifically, Decree No. 9 forbade any act of "denying, opposing, distorting or defaming the Constitution," and outlawed unauthorized assemblies of students. It also prohibited the "spreading of falsehood," which included rumors and reports considered "detrimental to national security."[66]

The National Assemblymen were permitted to continue criticizing the government on the Assembly floor, but reports of their criticisms could not be printed or broadcast. Newspaper publishers, reporters, and university presidents violating the order could be removed from their jobs and arrested. The regulations governing the press so intimidated the South Korea press that no newspaper dared to carry the story disclosed in the U.S. Congress in May that Park's ruling DRP had demanded a "contribution" of $10 million from the Gulf Oil for the 1967 and 1971 elections but actually received $4 million.[67]

Other provisions in Decree No. 9 called for punishment of persons who sought to emigrate with false papers or by other illegal means or who tried to transfer assets overseas. They set stiff penalties for officials taking bribes or causing loss to the national treasury; convicted officials faced fines of ten times the amounts taken or lost, in addition to imprisonments.[68] Unlike the Presidential decrees issued early in 1974, the latest one did not provide for courts-martial. However, persons suspected of violation could be searched, arrested or detained without court warrants. All the measures in Decree No. 9 were claimed necessary in order to solidify "the national consensus" and build a "total posture" in the face of a real and imminent danger of attack from the

North. They were endorsed unanimously by the National Assembly at the end of its four-day special session on May 20.[69]

While the nation was still going through the trauma of the Indochina fiasco, the Park Administration on July 9 passed four stringent and highly controversial bills through the National Assembly. Though the bills were approved by the pro-government legislators alone, the proceedings--unlike in the past--were not hindered physically by the opposition NDP Assemblymen. The new legislation were a Defense Tax Law, a Civil Defense Corps Law, an Education Law, and a Public Security Law.[70]

The Defense Tax Law imposed a new defense tax of some $400 million annually. The Civil Defense Corps Law permitted the establishment of a civilian defense corps with a general mobilization of males aged from 17 to 50 to keep the country militarily alert. Under the Education Law, contracts of college professors had to be renewed every five to 10 years by screening committees-- by the government for the public institutions of higher learning and by the boards of foundations for the private colleges. Finally, the Public Security Law gave the authorities extraordinary powers to control political prisoners after the expiration of their prison terms. It was the very core of the controversy.[71]

The government continued to press on to further its own cause. On September 6, a Seoul court handed down prison terms against four Protestant pastors for alleged misuse of funds provided by the Bread For the World, a West German aid organization. The four were known activists for human rights and restoration of democracy. Among them was Kim Kawn Suk, the general secretary of the Korean National Council of Churches (KNCC). The prosecution accused Kim of having diverted U.S. $10,000 out of $48,700, which he had received from the Bread For the World to be used in slum areas, to his three codefendants to support the families of those who had been arrested under Park's 1974 decrees. The accused four did not deny the charges as such, but defended themselves stating that the money in question was not spent for their personal use but to help others.[72]

During the trial, the West German aid organization had sent an affidavit to the Ministry of Justice in Seoul, attesting to the defendants' good characters and stating that the money spent on prisoners' families was fully in keeping with the spirit in which the funds were provided. Its staff members even had come to Seoul to tell the court that the money in question had not been misspent and that there was nothing wrong or illegal in using the money for the families of prisoners. Nevertheless, the court found the four accused guilty of "misusing" the missionary funds and handed down six to 10 month jail terms to each man.[73]

The sentencing of the four dissident pastors was preceded by the sudden death on August 17 of President Park's liberal opponent Chang Chun Ha under mysterious circumstances. Chang, a courageous intellectual who had fought "against tyranny all of his adult life," was one of the organizers of the "Petition of One Million Signatures" that was launched late in 1973 for constitutional change. He was released in January 1975 from a 15-year prison term he had drawn for violating presidential emergency decree number 1. His death--officially explained as an "accidental hiking death"--robbed South Korea of "perhaps the only man who could have revived an effective opposition" to Park regime.[74]

Concerning the students, who had been a "thorn" in the side of the government, the authorities in the fall replaced the autonomous Students' Associations with new paramilitary National Students' Defense Corps. All students from high school up were obligated to join the Corps, and leadership positions in the Corps were filled by government-appointed students.[75] All other non-academic organizations were banned on campuses, and troublesome students were expelled and/or jailed.[76] The professors, who had been critical of or even suspected of wavering in their loyalty to the government, were removed.

As noted earlier, under the Education Law of July 1975 all college professors had to have their appointments renewed every five to 10 years by screening committees. In the first six months following the passage of the law, 376 of the country's some 10,700 to 10,900 academics had failed to renew their contracts, being labelled as "incompetent." By July 1976 the number had risen to 416.[77] Notably, many of the dismissed were "problem teachers," who were generally young and talented critics of the government including Dr. Han Wan Sang of Seoul National University. Professor Han, an American-educated professor of sociology, had earlier raised eyebrows of many people by his analysis of the widening gap between the haves and have-nots in South Korea. He also had pointed to the rise of "pseudo-religion," charging many of its leaders with exploitation of their worker-followers.[78]

The series of stringent measures, taken concerning the campuses in the aftermath of the Vietnam shock, helped the government put a break on political activism among the country's some 300,000 college students and enforce its own version of discipline upon the students. All this while, the main opposition New Democratic Party had remained in line with the wishes of President Park; and the party's earlier platform for constitutional reform and liberal rule had crumbled. Under the circumstances, the NDP's presence had been reduced to little more than a symbolic one.

So, the NDP was helpless when its woman legislator Kim Ok Son was forced to resign her assembly seat in October 1975 by pro-government lawmakers for her daring remarks on the National Assembly floor. Specifically, Ms. Kim had charged that the anti-Communist rallies conducted following the fall of Vietnam were "nothing but leverage to extend political power" by President Park and he was "a fascist."[79] As the opposition NDP became impotent, the National Council For the Restoration of Democracy (formed in November 1974 as a broad anti-government coalition) too was disbanded, thus further weakening the anti-government resistance movement.[80]

In the spring of 1974 President Park had narrowly survived the trauma of student challenge, but his position remained precarious. Another round of confron-tations seemed to be shaping up in the following spring. However, the failures of the anti-Communist regimes in Indochina were such a shocking experience for South Koreans that the beleaguered President found the ranks closing around him. This staved off the political crisis of his regime. Park moved quickly to squeeze the maximum political advantage from the fitful national mood of anti-Communist unity. In the process, Park's foes were sternly dealt with and his already virtually absolute power--enshrined in the Yushin Constitution--was es-tablished even more firmly.

Notes

1. Lee Sang Woo, "Yushin Chi'iha Chonggyoke'e Panch'eje Undong" (the Anti Establishment Movement of Religious Circles Under the Yushin Rule), Shin-Tong-A, No. 320, (May 1986), pp. 437-439.

2. New York Times, October 3, 4, 5, 26, 1973; and Vreeland, et. al., Area Handbook for South Korea, pp. 184-185.

3. Vreeland, et. al., Area Handbook for South Korea, pp. 184-185. The kidnapping of Kim Dae Jung was one of the most flagrant examples of the intimidation of its opponents by the Park regime.

4. Hanyang (Tokyo), No. 148, (May-June 1979), p. 34; and New York Times, November 10, 26, 28, 1973.

5. Kauh Kwang-man, "Problems Concerning Student Participation in Korean Society," Korea Journal (Seoul), VIII, No. 7, (July 1968), pp. 30-33.

6. Oh, "Students and Politics," in Wright ed., Korean Politics in Transition, p. 120.

7. Ibid.

8. During the war, most people were simply preoccupied with the problems of physical survival.

9. Korea may lack a democratic tradition, but it had not been a static society for the previous 100 years or so. From the latter part of the 19th century on, political ideals from Western democratic countries began to be introduced by pioneers such as Yu Kil Chun (1856-1914), So Chae P'il (1863-1951), and Yun Ch'i Ho (1864-1946). All three had studied in the United States. During the Japanese rule, Korean students had not been completely isolated from opportunities to imbibe democratic notions, thanks to the translated versions of Western literature which were abundant and readily accessible.

10. Kauh, "Problems Concerning Student Participation in Korean Society," pp. 32-33; and Kim Kyong-Dong, Man and Society in Korea's Economic Growth: Sociological

Studies, (Seoul: Seoul National University Press, 1985), pp. 163-164.

11. In the 1977 additionally there were 112 junior vocational colleges. The Economic and Social Modernization of the Republic of Korea, p. 348; and Maeda Yasuhiro, Seoul karano Hokoku: Tokyumento Kankoku 1976-1980 (Report From Seoul: A Document on Korea 1976-1980), (Tokyo: Diamond Kaisha, 1981), p. 59.

12. In 1965 some 63 percent of all college students were in Seoul; and in 1972 some 58 percent were there. Cole and Lyman, Korean Development, p. 67; and Vreeland, et. al., Area Handbook for South Korea, p. 131. Much of the population growth since the 1953 ceasefire had been concentrated in a few large metropolitan areas, especially in Seoul where the population had increased from 5.5 million in 1970 to 6.9 million in 1975. there were a series of problems associated with this fast urbanization: housing-shortage, congestion, pollution, and lack of adequate public services. Kim and Donaldson, "Dealing with Seoul's Population Growth," pp. 660-661, 663.

13. Kauh, "Problems Concerning Student Participation in Korean Society, "pp. 29-33.

14. Ibid., pp. 30, 31.

15. Gari Ledyard, "A Critical View of South Korea's Condition," in Kim and Halpern, eds., The Future of the Korean Peninsula, pp. 75-76; and Lee, Korea, pp. 180-181.

16. Hong Sung Chik, "Values of College Students, Professors, Businessmen, and Farmers," Journal of Social Sciences and Humanities, (Seoul), No. 24, (June 1966), pp. 32-42.

17. Ledyard, "A Critical View of South Korea's Condition," in Kim and Halpern, eds., The Future of the Korean Peninsula, pp. 74-76; and Frederick M. Bunge, ed., South Korea, A Country Study, (Washington, D.C.: American University Press, 1982), pp. 77-80. Because political favoritism has been a key factor for big business success in South Korea, the business elite have been beholden to the government and have stood on the side of government on major political issues.

18. Professor Ch'oe was said to have told on October 17, 1973 to his colleagues that "this time, we should stand on the side of [demonstrating] students and not punish them." Because of this remark, Ch'oe was arrested and found dead on October 20 at a KCIA building in Seoul. KCIA claimed that Ch'oe was a communist spy and committed suicide by "leaping out of a bathroom window." Sekai, ed., Kankoku karano Tsushin (Letters from South Korea), (Tokyo: Iwanami Shotten, 1974), pp. 71-73, 94.

19. Lee "Yushin Ch'iha Chonggyoge'e Panch'eje Undong," pp. 414-439.

20. Ibid., pp. 425-428.

21. Spencer J. Palmer, Korea and Christianity: The Problems of Identification with Tradition, (Seoul: Hollym Corporation, Publishers, 1967), pp. 37-96.

22. Lee Chae-Jin, "South Korea in 1984: Seeking Peace and Prosperity," Asian Survey, XXV, No. 1, (January 1985), p. 82; and Henry Scott Stokes, "Korea's Church Militants," New York Times Sunday Magazine, November 28, 1982, pp. 68-69.

23. Far Eastern Economic Review, November 9, 1979, p. 13.

24. Vreeland, Area Handbook for South Korea, pp. 104-105; Koreatown (Los Angeles), August 11, 1980; New York Times, December 26, 1979; and Stokes, "Korea's Church Militants," New York Times Sunday Magazine, November 28, 1982, pp. 68-69.

25. Stokes, "Korea's Church Militants," New York Times Sunday Magazine, November 28, 1982, p. 105; and Lee, "Yushin Chi'iha Chonggyoge'e panch'eje Undong," pp. 437-439.

26. Vreeland, Area Handbook for South Korea, p. 177.

27. New York Times, December 2, 4, 1973.

28. Far Eastern Economic Review, January 7, 1974, p. 14; and New York Times, December 30, 31, 1973.

29. The Sasangge was first published in 1953 by Chang Chun Ha as an intellectual magazine. Chong Chin Sok, Hanguk Ollon Kwange Munhon Saegin (An Index to Communication Studies in Korea: A Guide to Bibliography on Communication), (Seoul: National Assembly Library, 1978), p. 286.

30. Tong-A Ilbo, January 9, 1974.

31. New York Times, January 16, 1974.

32. New York Times, April 4, 1974.

33. Tong-A Ilbo, April 4, 1974.

34. Sakai, ed., Kankoku karano Tsushin, pp. 163-174; and Hanyang, No. 165, (March-April 1982), p. 74.

35. New York Times, August 2, 13, 1974; Far Eastern Economic Review, April 18, 1975, p. 27; and Hanyang, No. 165, (March-April 1982), p. 74.

36. Far Eastern Economic Review, September 19, 1975, p. 17.

37. Tong-A Ilbo, August 23, 1974.

38. New York Times, August 28, 1974; Sekai, ed., Zoku Kankoku karano Tsushin (The Second Series of Letters from South Korea), (Tokyo: Iwanami Shotten, 1975), pp. 79-81; and Far Eastern Economic Review, July 25, 1975, p. 22. Yu Chin San was called sakura by his critics; in

Japanese, sakura means cherry blossom but in South Korea, when used to describe a politician, it means an opportunist.

39. Lee, "Yushin Chi'iha Chonggyoge'e Panch'eje Undong," pp. 430-439.

40. New York Times, July 26, 1974; Hanyang, No. 165, (March-April 1982), p. 63; and Tong-A Yongam, 1975, p. 296.

41. New York Times, October 24, 25, 1974; and Lee Sang Woo, "Park Chongkwonha e Ollon T'anap" (The Suppression of the Press under the Park Regime," Shin-Tong-A, No. 325, (October 1986), pp. 314-315.

42. Vreeland, et. al., Area Handbook for South Korea, p. 139.

43. "The Press in Korea," in Marshall R. Pihl, ed., Listening to Korea: A Korea Anthology, (New York: Praeger Publishers, 1973), pp. 55-57; and Chong, Hanguk Ollon Kwange Munhon Saegin, p. 10.

44. Park, "Hanguk Ollon Sunansa," pp. 259-284.

45. Park, "Hanguk Ollon Sunansa," p. 270. English translation quoted from "The Press in Korea," in Pihl, ed., Listening to Korea, p. 60.

46. Lee, "Park Chongkwonha e Ollon T'anap," pp. 291-315.

47. New York Times, October 29, 1974.

48. Tong-A Yongam 1975, pp. 285, 296; and Hanyang, No. 165, (March-April 1982), p. 74. Yun Po Son, though had received a prison term in connection with the NFDYS incident, was placed on probation.

49. Tong-A Ilbo, January 22, February 5, 1975.

50. Tong-A Ilbo, February 13, 14, 1975.

51. Tong-A Ilbo, February 13, 1975.

52. In all, 203 dissidents were imprisoned under the two decrees, but 20 of them were released before the February 15 order. Tong-A Ilbo, February 15, 1975; and Far Eastern Economic Review, February 7, 1975, p. 20.

53. Tong-A Ilbo, February 18, 1975.

54. Tong-A Ilbo, February 14, 1975; and New York Times, February 13, April 4, 1975.

55. Boston Globe, March 30, 1975; and Washington Post, February 16, 1975.

56. New York Times, February 18, April 4, 1975; and Tong-A Ilbo, February 18, April 10, 1975.

57. Tong-A Ilbo, March 20, 1975.

58. Sakai, ed., Zoku Kankoku karano Tsushin, pp. 187-191; and Lee, "Park Chongkwonha e Ollon T'anap," pp. 314-315.

59. No less than 147 persons were sacked in March 1975 alone, 134 from Tong-A Ilbo and 33 from Choson Ilbo. New

York Times, August 24, 1975, August 24, 1979; and Hanyang, No. 149, (July-August 1979), p. 132.

60. Tong-A Ilbo, March 15, 1975.

61. Boston Herald American, April 10, 1975; Tong-A Ilbo, April 10, 1975; and Far Eastern Economic Review, April 25, 1975, pp. 23-24.

62. New York Times, April 16, 1975.

63. New York Times, May 31, 1975; and Boston Globe, May 25, 1975.

64. Tong-A Ilbo, April 29, 1975; and Washington Post, May 4, 1975.

65. Tong-A Ilbo, May 10, 1975.

66. Tong-A Ilbo, May 13, 1975. With the issuance of this order, Mr. Park lifted his order of April 8, thus permitting the Korea University and other colleges to return to normal operation.

67. New York Times, May 18, 1975; and Cho Dong Sung, "Incentives and Restraints: Government Regulation of Direct Investments between Korea and the United States," in Moskowitz, ed., From Patron to Partner, p. 52. For Koreans' squeeze of American firms doing business in Korea, see also William J. Bards, "The United States and Korean Peninsula," in Bards, ed., The Two Koreas in East Asian Affairs, p. 179; and Lee, "Park Chongkwon ha Kwollyokhyong Pup'ae e Chongch'e," pp. 279-295.

68. As to the transfer of assets, whenever President Park made a "war scare" statement, South Koreans withdrew money from banks and bought gold or converted money into dollars. New York Times, April 30, May 18, 1975.

69. Tong-A Ilbo, May 20, 1975.

70. Far Eastern Economic Review, July 18, 1975, p. 16, July 25, 1975, p. 24.

71. For the controversial public security law, see Maeda, Seoul karano Hokoku, pp. 28-29, 125-129; or Sekai, ed., Daisan Kankoku karano Tsushin (The Third Series of Letters from South Korea), (Tokyo: Iwanami Shotten, 1977), pp. 79-80.

72. New York Times, August 3, 1975; and Far Eastern Economic Review, July 11, 1975, pp. 22-23, September 19, 1975, p. 17.

73. Tong-A Ilbo, September 6, 1975; and New York Times, September 7, 1975.

74. Tong-A Ilbo, August 18, 1975; Pihl, ed., Listening to Korea, pp. 63-74; and Far Eastern Economic Review, September 12, 1975, p. 18. A lone article appeared in the August 19, 1975 edition of Tong-A Ilbo highlighting "suspicious" aspects of Chang's sudden death; the reporter who wrote the story was arrested on charge of

violating presidential decree No. 9. Sekai, ed., <u>Daisan Kankoku karano Tsushin</u>, pp. 21-28.

75. <u>Tong-A Ilbo</u>, May 20, 21, 1975; and Maeda, <u>Seoul karano Hokoku</u>, p. 15. It might be said that the corps was revived for the first time in 15 years. As members of the Defense Corps, the students--in addition to 360 hours of "general" military training annually--had to undergo 50 hours of "special" training yearly.

76. <u>Far Eastern Economic Review</u>, January 16, 1976, p. 20.

77. Maeda, <u>Seoul karano Hokoku</u>, p. 30; and <u>New York Times</u>, March 14, 1976.

78. Since his dismissal in 1976 and until his return to his old faculty position in March 1980, Dr. Han was arrested five times. <u>Washington Post</u>, March 13, 1980; and <u>Far Eastern Economic Review</u>, March 19, 1976, p. 30.

79. Ms. Kim Ok Son's troubles did not end with her resignation. She was subsequently tried for alleged violation of election law and was sentenced to one-year prison term with two-year probation. <u>New York Times</u>, October 11, 1975; and Sekai, ed., <u>Daisan Kankoku karano Tsushin</u>, p. 203.

80. <u>Far Eastern Economic Review</u>, January 16, 1976, p. 20, February 13, 1976, p. 20.

CHAPTER 5

THE CYCLE OF OPPOSITION AND REPRESSION

The Simmering Opposition

The turn of events in Indochina, met with consternation in Seoul, understandably made South Koreans more security conscious than ever before; and President Park's argument that the Western standards of human rights and democracy could not be strictly adhered to in Korea seemed to gain easy acceptance. Under the circumstances, criticisms of government became a highly risk art, and the various opposition forces remained subdued and mute by and large. Thus it looked as if President Park had made progress in dampening the opposition movement and forging a national unity.

However, the unity was one imposed from above, and the cooperation the government received from its foes was more apparent that real. Although Park's critics went along with his call for harmony "in principle," they did so more to avoid appearing out of step with the national concern over Indochina than out of genuine belief in his policies. They suspected that the President, in his attempt to still his foes, was converting the uneasiness over Indochina into a sense of crisis over a new Korean War; and they were convinced that Park's tough measures were creating internal dissension rather than unity.[1] Such suspicion and conviction were publicly expressed on May 10, 1975 by the NDP president Kim Yong Sam.

Agreeing with Park that South Vietnam suffered from divided national opinion, the NDP leader argued that the division was created by "Thieu's corrupt and repressive one-man rule which failed to earn confidence of the people." Kim admitted that a threat from North Korea existed, but pointed out that South Korea had some 600,000 men under arms and its 35 million people were strongly anti-Communist.[2] Furthermore, in line with Western analysis, Kim contended that Kim Il Sung's Peking visit in April had "not created a decisive crisis," since the North Korean leader was presumed to have been cautioned by his Chinese hosts against undertaking an overt military action against the South and was denied their military backing.[3] Invoking a crisis under the circumstances was simply a "tactics" on the part of President Park to threaten his opponents and to ensure the longevity of his regime, Kim declared.

The NDP head continued by asserting that Park had learned nothing from Vietnam because he called for national harmony but acted in ways that would weaken it. Declaring that Park might be able to "enforce a temporary stability" but "a genuine stability shall not be realized until democracy is restored," Kim demanded that for the sake of an "everlasting harmony" the government broaden its base of popular support with democracy.

Kims' statement, made during an interview with a Los Angeles Times correspondent could have brought a seven-year prison sentence under the law that forbade "slanderous or libelous remarks against the state" to foreign news media.[4] Be that as it may, Kim Yong Sam on June 5 defiantly renewed his criticism. He charged that the national security was under greater threat from Park's mode of rule than it was from the North and that any strengthening of the nation's security should be possible within a framework of normal constitutional politics. Therefore, Kim demanded that the government lift its recent emergency measures and "democratize itself."[5]

Students, too, despite the appearance of being subdued, were very much alive. On May 22--only nine days after the proclamation of the repressive decree No. 9--more than 1,000 students at Seoul National University dared to stage a full-blown anti-government rally. Leaflets scattered by the demonstrators read in part:

> How can we stand this situation anymore? Carry the torch of patriot Kim Sang Jin [the schoolmate who had committed suicide during the April 11th anti-government rally] and attack the stronghold of the dictator.[6]

Until dispersed with the arrival of riot police, the demonstrating students clashed with the faculty members who attempted to halt the rally. By the very next day, 77 demonstrators had been reportedly arrested and 25 expelled from the school, in addition to at least 100 who were in hiding. With this, a semblance of tranquility once again returned to the campus. Nonetheless, the disturbance, occurring despite decree No. 9 at the nation's most prestigious learning center, shocked the entire South Korean Establishment.[7]

It was apparent that President Park's tough post-Vietnam measures, though helped break significant pockets of resistance and keep them to a minimum, fell short of rooting out the opposition. What Park's draconian approach did achieve was merely to force the resistance movements underground, where they remained smoldering and stirring under the lid but sporadically surfacing. The political unrest manifesting even in the tense post-Vietnam "war scare" atmosphere foretold that in the days ahead the Yushin Constitution would continue to be the politically divisive issue causing social unrest, and might affect South Korea's ability to resist the subversion from the North.

Park's opponents felt that his post-Vietnam ruling style had disturbing echoes of the aspects of the P'yongyang regime, and that the measures enacted in the name of national security undermined the country's anti-Communist consensus by "blurring the differences" between the two Koreas. The Rev. Kim Kwan Suk contended that Park's governing style after the Vietnam fiasco was "the same" as that in P'yongyang, because it amounted to "a subtle worship of the idol," and that it had "a strong psychological effect on the people."[8]

The estrangement from and the resentment against Park's regime were not confined to its more vocal critics--the students, intellectuals, and the opposition politicians. From them the hostility had reportedly spread to other segments of the population eroding Park's popular support, apparent in the results of the 1975 February referendum. Even the farmers, the traditionally staunch supporters of President Park, were said to have been increasingly disillusioned with Park's harsh emphasis on "vigilance," which had moved their communities towards a society with striking similarities to the one they had been urged to oppose.[9]

Still more, the disclosure in May 1975 in Washington of the Gulf Oil Corporation's secret "contribution" of $4 million to President Park's ruling DRP had clouded the image of Park's rectitude, which had been cultivated by his regime. As a result, many analysts were uncertain as to the degree to which the South Koreans would resist North Korean subversion. Some observers even thought that Park's internal policy was doing more than Kim Il Sung to create a "receptivity" to P'yongyang's propaganda in the South.[10]

The Myongdong Incident

On March 1, 1976--the 57th anniversary of Koreans' uprising against the Japanese colonial rule--12 prominent dissidents signed and issued a "Declaration For Democracy and National Salvation" at Seoul's Myongdong Catholic Cathedral.[11] Claiming the Park regime was "a one-man dictatorship that tramples on human rights" and that "the people do not want obedience but want participation," the declaration demanded that the government rescind Emergency Decree No. 9, free political prisoners, and restore all of the shackled political freedoms as a prelude toward establishing democracy.

Secondly, the manifesto charged that the government's economic policy had placed materialistic development above human costs and that its export policy had been executed at the expense of the labor; and asked for more equitable distribution of wealth for the poor. Then, pointing to South Korea's growing foreign debt, in particular to Japan, the manifesto denounced that in the wake of the 1965 Japan-ROK Treaty South Korean economy had come under Japanese control and its industries and labor force had become "a victim of Japanese economic invasion." What's more, it urged that the government's fundamental "premise and the posture" concerning economic development be "thoroughly reexamined." Thirdly, the declaration asserted that the ending of the division of the country was "the supreme task" for all Koreans, and that the task had to be accomplished urgently and by the Koreans themselves, and pointedly questioned the government if it had any constructive policy concerning the issue.

The declaration went on saying that unless the government was willing to meet these demands, "there is no other way for the Park regime but to accept responsibility by stepping down." Considering harsh punishments meted out against President Park's critics, the issuance of this manifesto was a "daring act," which broke a 10-month old virtual "hiatus" in post-Vietnam anti-government activities.[12] It "startled" the authorities, who saw in the defiance an ominous potential of touching off another massive upheaval on the scale of that of the winter-spring of two years before.

On March 26 authorities in Seoul indicted the 12 signatories of the declaration and six of their supporters for violation of Decree No. 9. The indicted were all Christians, mostly active in the now outlawed National Council for Restoration of Democracy. Among them were Yun Po Son, Kim Dae Jung, Ham Sok Hon (a Quaker leader known as Korea's Gandhi), Dr. Chong Il Hyong, and Ms. Lee T'ae Yong. Ms. Lee, Korea's first woman lawyer and 1976 Magsaysay Award winner, was Chong Il Hyong's wife. At least three recently expelled professors, including Lee Moon Yong of Korea University were also indicted.[13]

As the 18 anti-government activists were brought to trial at the Seoul District Court for the first time on May 4, 1976, it was widely speculated that the principal target of the trial was Kim Dae Jung, who had the "temerity" to run against Park in the May 1971 election and had come close to beating him. Because of such an audacity, already in June 1975 during the Indochina jitters Kim was indicted for alleged 1971 election irregularity and was given a one-year prison term but remained free pending appeal.[14] The threat of jail did not silence Kim, however. He was rearrested on March 8, 1976--one week after the issuance of the anti-government manifesto at the Myongdong Cathedral.

Among the spectators at the court of the trial of Kim Dae Jung and the 17 others were Cardinal Kim Su Hwan of Seoul Diocese and Rev. Kim Kwan Suk, the general secretary of the National Council of Christian Churches.[15] Their presence at the court was a sign that South Korea's Christians were behind their 18 coreligionists put on trial. Outside the court and throughout the country many churchmen and churchwomen conducted demonstrations in support of the causes of the defendants.

At a protest mass held on March 15 at the Myongdong Cathedral, Cardinal Kim drew a parallel between the plight of the 18 accused and the sufferings of Christ on the Cross. The Cardinal declared that as long as oppression continued, the Catholic Church would not remain silent. The Protestants followed suit. In the name of the National Council of Christian Churches, they on March 25 issued a statement which denounced the government for blocking dissemination of the contents of the March First anti-government manifest to the public and for carrying out "one-sided" persecution of the 18 defendants who had fought for "anti-communism, democracy, and realization of justice."[16]

By now the locus of South Korean political dissent seemed to have shifted to and centered in Christian churches; and churches' already uneasy relationship with the government became tense. The prosecution of the 18 itself was even viewed by some as the government's attempt to dismantle the churches as such a source of opposition.[17] However, as the trials proceeded, lasting almost four months, the defendants took advantage of the occasion to denounce once again the very fundamentals of the government policies. In doing so, they turned the trials into "the most outspoken defense of democracy" in Korea.[18]

On August 28, 1976 the three-man court found all 18 defendants guilty of having violated Emergency Decree No. 9. Because the 18 had "grossly distorted" the political situation in South Korea by calling the government "repressive" and claiming that "there was no freedom" and denouncing the Constitution. And the court meted out prison terms ranging from eight to two years--the longest terms for Kim Dae Jung, Yun Po Son, Ham Sok Hon, and Moon Ik Hwan (a pastor and former professor).[19] The sentencings, coming on the heels of the ax-slaying of two American officers at Panmunjom by North Koreans ten days before, could hardly have been timed more meaningfully. Because the bloody incident made more palatable than otherwise the reproach of the chief judge of the court, who declared that the defendants had acted in disregard of the ever present military "threat from the North." And the sentences were believed tougher than they might have been without the gory incident.[20]

Incidentally, seven of the 18 convicts had been tried without actually being detained and were allowed to remain free even after their verdicts were rendered, a concession to old-age and the fair sex. Among the seven were Yun Po Son (79), Ham Sok Hon (75), Chong Il Hyong (72) and his wife Lee T'ae Yong (61), and Ms. Lee Woo Jong (53, formerly a professor and the president of a Protestant women's association).[21] The eight year prison term handed down to Kim Dae Jung was a culmination of President Park's efforts to avenge the temerity of this persistent opponent of his, who dared to run against him

100

in 1971 and who since then had not given up challenging him.

Kim's conviction was upheld on December 29 by the Seoul Appeals Court, as were the guilty verdicts of the 17 others. But the court reduced Kim's term to five years and shortened the sentences of most of the others, too. There was, however, a small surprise: the appeals court ordered the release of two of the 11 incarcerated with their remaining terms suspended.[22] Finally, on March 22, 1977, the Supreme Court in Seoul confirmed the lower courts' findings,[23] thus silencing some of the most articulate voices of dissent in South Korea.

The Opposition New Democratic Party

While the "Myongdong 18" were in the dock, the opposition New Democratic Party was gripped with debilitating intraparty squabbles. This threw the largest parliamentary opposition into total disarray, rendering it woefully ineffectual as opposition party. Much of the NDP's intraparty feuds was centered on controversies surrounding Kim Yong Sam, the party president since August 1974 who had engaged the party in a strident campaign against President Park's authoritarian leadership until the Vietnam fiasco.

While South Koreans were seized with jitters in the wake of Communist successes in Indochina, Kim on May 21, 1975 had a two-hour private talk with President Park.[24] Subsequently, when four bills (the defense tax bill, the civil defense corps bill, the education bill, and the public security bill) were put before the National Assembly, Kim uncharacteristically ordered his party floor leaders to reach a consensus with their pro-government counterparts on the pending legislation. The bills passed the Assembly on July 9 without the usual attempts at physical obstruction of proceedings by the opposition assemblymen.[25]

The passage of the package legislation without the usual fracas led many to believe that Kim had agreed on a measure of cooperation with President Park during their closed-door meeting in May. This ignited suspicion of "sell-out" among NDP ranks, especially the "militants" who nostalgically looked back on the days of street campaigns against government.[26] Thus as Kim's first year as party president drew to a close, his leadership came

101

under close scrutiny by the party ranks. It was especially so because Kim, like President Park, refused to disclose the details of what was said during the secret conference in question. Under the circumstances, the intraparty factional squabbles, that had been perennial in the NDP, intensified; and would-be contenders for the party's top post openly criticized Kim.

Late in October 1975 when Ms. Kim Ok Son was forced to resign her legislative seat after her scathing attack of President Park, Kim's intraparty opponents accused him of succumbing to government pressures, because Kim could not save Ms. Kim. This aggravated the intraparty bickerings, leading to brawls in April 1976 at several NDP's local offices over their reorganization between Kim's followers and his critics. Kim's opponents were led by Lee Ch'ol Sung, a five-times elected national assemblyman and deputy speaker of the Assembly.[27]

Kim's intraparty detractors denounced him as conducting a "zig-zagging struggle" against the Constitution, and contended that his "erratic" leadership had to be put to a stop. And they called for a collective leadership in lieu of the presidential system, then operant and under which Kim allegedly had run the NDP in dictatorial manner. Eventually on May 22 Kim's foes occupied the NDP headquarters, forcing Kim and other party officials to flee through a backdoor. The intruders held the building for several hours until dispersed by the police.[28]

On May 25 the NDP's internal wranglings flared up once again into open violence, very likely to the glee of the government. It occurred at the Citizen's Hall in Seoul, where the party's biennial national convention was to be held and where Kim Yong Sam was determined to seek re-election as party head. Kim's opponents stormed into the convention hall and barred Kim and his supporters from the place; then, they revised the party charter and elected a six-member "collective leadership," which did not include Kim Yong Sam. Kim and his followers, on the other hand, repaired to the party headquarters and held their own convention and elected Kim to a second term as party chief.[29]

With the NDP thus publicly split into two rival camps, each immediately sought the endorsement of its standing from the Election Management Committee. On June 9 the Committee handed down its findings declaring that neither convention was valid. Because one was held at a place

which had not been announced in advance, and the other
was conducted by those who were "not authorized." Also
the Committee noted that since the NDP had announced that
its new leadership would be chosen at its biennial convention in May, Kim Yong Sam's NDP presidential tenure
had expired in May.[30] The Committee's findings reportedly boosted the morale of Kim's rival camp, while
dismaying Kim's own supporters.

Meanwhile, in August Kim's group changed its position
and endorsed the collective leadership principle advocated by its opponents,[31] enabling the NDP to hold a
unified national convention on September 15-16. The
convention discarded the presidential "unitary leadership" principle, adopted a collective leadership, and
chose a six-member Supreme Council consisting of various
faction leaders. In a close contest with Kim Yong Sam,
Lee Ch'ol Sung was elected as the Representative Supreme
Councillor who was the party's top leader.[32]

Strains in the U.S.-South Korea Relations

As the Park government systematically deprived its
citizenry of what were generally considered human rights
in the West and employed draconian methods to silence the
dissidents, criticisms mounted in the United States--
especially at the Congressional hearings conducted inter-
mittently from 1974 through 1976 by the House Subcommittee on International Organizations. The Subcommittee
hearings, chaired by Representative Donald M. Fraser,
revealed a series of human rights violations by Park regime, which included intimidation by KCIA agents of the
Korean opponents of Park residing abroad. The disclosure
tarnished the image of the Seoul government internationally.[33]

When President Gerald Ford visited Seoul in late November 1974 en route to Vladivostok to meet Soviet Communist
Party leader Leonid B. Breshnev, he discussed the subject
of human rights with President Park underscoring the ser-
iousness of American concern over the issue.[34] During
the trial of the "Myongdong 18" the American press gave
it wide coverage, and many Americans frowned upon the
Seoul government's handling of the case.[35] The election
in November 1976 of Jimmy Carter, a friend of human
rights, as the U.S. President understandably disquieted
the Park government while delighting its foes.

If the Seoul government was disturbed by the American rebuke of its human rights record, it was confounded by President Carter's plan to withdraw the U.S. ground troops (33,000 men of the Second Division) stationed in South Korea. Carter's plan for troop pullout, promised during his presidential campaign in 1976, was in keeping with the Nixon Doctrine of July 1969, whereby the United States pledged its continued support to its Asian allies but expected them to do their own fighting on the ground.

President Carter's troop withdrawal plan--to be implemented by stages over a period of four to five years--was formally announced in Washington on March 9, 1977. The plan assumed that South Korea, given "the image of its dynamic economic growth," should in time be capable of repelling an attack from the North without the assistance of American ground combat forces, provided that the United States offered timely air, naval, and logistic support.[36] Thus the plan envisioned continued presence of the U.S. air force personnel (then some 7,000 men) in South Korea as well as American commitment of logistic and naval support.

However, the stationing of the American ground troops in South Korea, all just below the Demilitarized Zone (DMZ), had been regarded as a "trip wire" of automatic American involvement in ground combat in case of North Korean attack. As such, their presence along the area separating the two Koreas had been the highly "visible proof" of American commitment to defend the South against aggression from the North. Their pending removal meant the termination of such a guarantee and was a "shock" not only to the Seoul authorities but to their domestic opponents as well.[37] As the Seoul government was formally informed in May 1977 of the Carter Administration's decision on this crucial issue,[38] it slid into the same kind of the "mood of the neurotic anxiety" with which it had earlier greeted the collapse of the non-Communist regimes in Indochina.

The nervousness of the Park government increased because of North Korea's explorations of possible direct contact with the Carter Administration. Even before President Carter's inauguration in January 1977, P'yongyang had sent no less than three messages to the President-elect--twice through the Pakistani government that had helped the initiation of formal contact between the Nixon Administration and China in 1971, and once directly to Plains, Georgia. Some "signals" were also transmitted through scholars of Asian affairs and North Korean officials in Japan. And in the spring of 1978 President Kim Il Sung and President Carter reportedly exchanged letters through third parties such as President Ceaucescu of Rumania and the late Marshall Tito of Yugoslavia.[39]

The possibility of direct contact between P'yongyang and Washington pushed the Seoul government to the wall, because it feared that such a contact might lead North Korea and the United States to reach a "disengagement" agreement, reminiscent of the one between the Nixon Administration and Hanoi on the eve of the falls of the non-Communist regimes in Indochina.

The uneasy Seoul-Washington relations deteriorated following the reportings in the Washington Post on October 15 and 24, 1976 of alleged South Korean efforts to bribe U.S. Congressmen as well as other high American officials for favors. The stories were specific on the names of those who were allegedly involved as well as on the mode of Koreans' influence peddling operation. And they became an instant sensation for the American public, who already for more than a year had been reading reports in their newspapers suggesting suspicious activities of Koreans in the United States and bribe-takings of American high officials from them.[40] Thereafter for nearly two years a spate of stories appeared in the American press concerning the corruption scheme, popularly known as "Koreagate." By the spring of 1977 the scandal had spawned five separate governmental investigations in the United States.[41]

Seoul's covert influence-buying campaign in the United States started with the approval of President Park in 1970, the year President Richard Nixon announced his decision to withdraw the U.S. 7th Division from South Korea. The campaign aimed at preventing any further reduction of U.S. troops from Korea and assuring a continuous flow of U.S. military aid to South Korea. It was to be carried out by KCIA agents with some support from the Rev. Sun Myung Moon's Unification Church, and its major target was the U.S. Congress.[42] Following the promulgation of the Yushin Constitution, the favor-currying campaign expanded its field of activities in order to better cope with growing criticisms of the Seoul government abroad, especially in the United States.

As the Constitution went into force in December 1972 permitting President Park to rule by draconian decrees,

there were mounting internal disaffections in the coun-
try--even within Seoul's ruling circles themselves. They
were reflected in the defections and self-imposed exiles
of high-ranking governmental officials, including former
Minister of Foreign Affairs Ch'oe Dok Shin and former
KCIA director Kim Hyong Wook. Mr. Ch'oe left Korea for
ideological reasons, whereas Mr. Kim did so because of
complications stemming from his differences with President Park over distribution of power. Once abroad, they
disclosed diverse aspects of corrupt inner workings of
the Park regime.[43] There were also strong denunciations
in the United States of Park's dictatorial rule in the
news media, among intellectuals, and in the Korean com-
munity--indicating that the American public perception
of South Korea had changed from the Cold War days of the
1950's.

Under the circumstances, an entirely new dimension was
added to the influence-buying campaign, now aiming at
affecting no less than the whole political milieu in
which American policy debate over Korea was conducted.
The new plan, set forth by the spring of 1973, was designed to silence critics of the Yushin system and buy
American support by mobilizing additional manpower. The
people targeted were officials in the Executive branch,
media representatives, academicians, businessmen, religious leaders, members of the Congress, and Koreans in
the U.S.[44] The means utilized to achieve the goal included bribery and threat of physical violence.

The U.S. probings of this multi-faceted scandal were
facilitated by the defections of South Korean agents of
the illicit scheme stationed in the United States, who
offered information concerning their activities in exchange for the grants of asylum.[45] The testimonies of
these defectors about their activities to influence
American foreign policy were aired in the Congress and
courts; and they aroused resentment among a great number
of Americans. This aggravated the already tense U.S.-
South Korea relations, caused by the controversies over
the questions of human rights and troop pullout.

The scandal escalated into a major diplomatic crisis
when the Seoul government, already having lost face by
the defections of its influence-peddling agents, refused
to accede to U.S. demands that Seoul return to the United
States its agent Park Tong Sun as well as its former Ambassador to Washington Kim Tong Jo to testify. Park, a
middleman for U.S. rice sales to South Korea and a cen-

tral figure in Seoul's bribe-giving efforts, had left
the United States in September 1976 and returned to
Seoul. He was indicted in August 1977 by a federal grand
jury sitting in Washington to deal with the scandal. On
the other hand, Kim Tong Jo, while Ambassador in Washington from November 1967 to December 1973, reportedly fre-
quented Capitol Hill to pay U.S. Congressmen.[46]

The diplomatic impasse over Park Tong Sun was resolved
in the winter of 1977-1978, when Park came to the United
States under a grant of immunity from prosecution to
testify before Congressional Committees and courts probing the case.[47] The question of obtaining testimony from
the former Korean Ambassador Kim on his alleged lobbying
activities on the Capitol Hill too was resolved by an
agreement between Washington and Seoul, under which the
questioning of Kim would be done in writing. Kim returned the completed questionnaire to U.S. Congressional
investigators in mid-September 1978. Although his
answers were deemed less than satisfactory by the investigators, the Congressional Committees did not pursue the
matters further.[48]

The investigations of the Koreagate showed that 23 U.S.
Congressmen and four Senators were implicated in Seoul's
favor-currying scheme. But only two Congressmen were
indicted: Richard T. Hanna (a Democrat from California)
and Otto E. Passman (a Democrat from Louisiana). Hanna
pleaded guilty to a single count of conspiracy and was
given a two-and-a-half year prison sentence. Passman,
however, entered not guilty pleas to corruption and income tax evasion charges, and he was acquitted.[49]

The U.S.-Korea controversy over the Koreagate itself
had quieted down by October 1978 when the House Subcommittee on International Organizations issued its final
report on its findings of the affairs.[50] Thereafter, the
tensions between Seoul and Washington subsided.

Impact of the U.S.-Korea Tensions on Domestic Politics

Stories about the Koreagate, so prominently reported
in America and Japan, were understandably suppressed in
the South Korean news media. Nevertheless, information
in Washington concerning the uproar seeped into Seoul and
stirred the dissidents who had been ever sensitive to the
issues affecting U.S.-Korea relations.

On December 8, 1976, some 300 to 500 students at Seoul National University openly accused the Park government of having attempted to bribe U.S. Congressmen into supporting itself. Expressing their indignation at the influence-peddling activities, the students in their manifesto charged that "tens of millions of dollars" had been "stuffed into the pockets of Ford, Kissinger, and many U.S. Congressmen to ask them help support the present government," and that the affair had "brought to ground the self-pride of the Korean people." The students demanded that the Park government fully disclose the affair to the public.[51] For South Korea, whose population was still largely unaware of the furor caused by the scandal in the United States,[52] the student manifesto suggested a new trouble.

On March 22, 1977--the very same day the Supreme Court in Seoul upheld the lower courts' verdicts of the "Myongdong 18"--ten prominent dissidents, including Yun Po Son who had been under a suspended sentence, issued a "Charter For Salvation of Democracy" renewing the pressures on the government for democratization. The charter did not appear in the local newspapers as had been the case with most of the manifestoes released by dissidents, and most South Koreans were unaware of it. But it circulated clandestinely among dissidents and was quickly signed by more than 100 of them.[53] The signature-gathering was paralleled by a rash of anti-government protests from church pulpits, on college campuses, and city streets.

During a mass held at the Myongdong Cathedral in April, Cardinal Kim Su Hwan gave a sermon critical of the government. Referring to President Park's hackneyed rationale for retaining Emergency Decree No. 9 and other repressive measures, the cardinal commented that "communism is not stopped by guns and bayonets...or with massive agitation or sloganeering." Communism, the cardinal asserted, was spread through popular grievances such as a gap between the rich and poor and he urged the government to be tolerant of dissent as long as it stayed clear of ideology.[54]

Immediately, a group of Catholic priests issued a statement expressing their political conviction which was similar to that of Cardinal Kim. Echoing the sentiments of these church leaders, some 150 to 200 Catholic youths on April 24 marched out of a church in downtown Seoul, shouting anti-government slogans and clashing with police.[55] The government was vexed by the continuing challenge of Christian churches. However, its main worry was still the universities which had been the focal point of youthful discontent.

On March 28, 1977, some 400 to 500 students at Seoul National University staged a brief demonstration until they were dispersed by riot-police. Their demands included the ending of Park "dictatorship" and of the police surveillance of the campuses, the release of their imprisoned schoolmates, and the termination of the "industrialization" which had "no relevance to the domestic industry" and which had "degraded" South Korea.[56] Similar incidents occurred at other campuses in Seoul: Korea University in April and Yonsei University and Hanguk Divinity School in May. Three to five protestors were arrested at each of the three campuses.

The latest round of protests was not on the scale of the one during the winter of 1974-1975, but it was still a signal that the critics of the Park government had not given up their fight. On the other hand, the government, determined as ever to snuff out any signs of protests and concerned about the timing of their appearances,[57] moved to stem the rising tide of the opposition. And its security agents carried out a nationwide roundup of dissidents beginning April 14--only a few hours after the departure from Seoul of a four-member U.S. Congressional delegation investigating charges of human rights abuses.[58]

Once the crackdown got under way, the list of the arrested grew amidst speculations that the government was seeking evidence to build a court case of a Communist conspiracy. Eventually 40 people were known to have been taken into custody in the latest roundup (as of April 21); most of them were Protestants active in the human rights campaign conducted by the National Council of Christian Churches and were suspected of having signed the March 22 Charter.[59]

Following the latest crackdown on dissidents, a new level of nervous tension was injected into the South Korean political scene, which had already been fraught with fear and mutual suspicion. Even some of President Park's own aides reportedly began to express concerns about his policies; and one Seoul official told a <u>Newsweek</u> reporter that "everyone is afraid of everyone else. We do not dare discuss our true feeling with anyone except our wives."[60]

While many critics of President Park were being persecuted, the opposition NDP fell into renewed factional fights, this time over its new head Lee Ch'ol Sung. The new NDP leader Lee, elected in September 1976 as the party's Representative Supreme Councillor, was a political "moderate" and had been known for his "willingness to cooperate with the authoritarian government" of President Park. Thus to no one's surprise, Lee, as new party boss, advocated "an improvement of the system rather than a repudiation of it"[61]--a position suggestive of Lee's broad acceptance of the existing political makeup. Lee tacitly admonished the dissidents to cease their anti-government activities. He did so by declaring that "compromise and competition are always surer means of politics than the barricades and slogans" and that "we, faced with national crisis as we are, must seek a politics that transcends partisan spirit."[62]

While in New York City on March 7, 1977 during his two-week "fact-finding trip," Lee justified the restrictions of freedom in South Korea in the name of national security. He also denounced expatriate South Koreans critical of Park regime as "anti-state and anti-national," and warned the Carter Administration that "excessive public pressure" from United States for democratic reforms in South Korea might "provoke a strong nationalistic reaction" from "the Korean people."[63] Thus Lee set a new tone in the country's largest opposition party, that had been looked upon by many as a leading anti-Park government force.

Lee's openly accommodating--even ingratiating--stance with the government alienated many NDP members, particularly those who had not been reconciled with his assumption of the headship of the party. The party, a loose and uneasy coalition of factions, was once again drawn to the brink of renewed factional fighting that could wreck the NDP's effectiveness as opposition to the regime of Park. The NDP infightings surfaced at the party caucus held on March 24, 1977--two days after the Supreme Court had upheld the verdicts of the lower courts against the "Myongdong 18," among whom was the NDP assemblyman Chong Il Hyong.

Asked at the caucus about the fellow party member's conviction, which incurred automatic loss of his legislative seat, the Representative Supreme Councilor Lee sheepishly replied that he was "powerless" to save Chong. The response drew severe denounciations from every quarter. The strongest condemnation came from the faction led by Kim Yong Sam, who some 17 months before was castigated by his intraparty detractors because he could not save Ms. Kim Ok Son from losing her Assembly seat and who then lost the party's top post to Lee. Kim came straight to the point, demanding that Lee resign from the party's highest position.[64] Another faction leader Oh Se Ung assaulted Lee asserting that "some wonder if you want to go down with the Park government. If that is true, say so because we do not want to go down with you."[65]

In all appearance, the internal wranglings of the NDP intensified under Lee's tutelage of the party and the NDP looked hopelessly impotent. And the NDP legislators had made no significant attempts to open their own independent inquiry into the Koreagate in the one-and-a-half years since the scandal had erupted in Washington in the fall of 1976.[66] Especially worrisome for the NDP was its deteriorating public image since Lee had admonished his party members to accommodate themselves with the existing political order, which, carried out, would make the existence of the NDP as opposition superfluous.

Disillusionment of the public with the dissentious NDP and their alienation from the party head Lee's course of collusion with the government were so deep that not only the image of the NDP but also that of the country's whole political party system itself suffered a severe setback. It was so much so that in the by-elections held on June 10, 1977 in Seoul to fill two vacant National Assembly seats, neither the opposition NDP nor the ruling DRP fielded candidates fearing rejection by the voters and thus conceding the seats to the Independents.[67]

With the major opposition NDP hopelessly divided and its policies hardly distinguishable from those of the government, the anti-government movements were by and large carried on by extra-parliamentary forces, "the real opposition" centered on the students and politically active intellectuals and Christians. On October 7, 1977, about 1,000 students at Seoul National University demonstrated, demanding campus autonomy and freedom for imprisoned dissidents but skirting issues such as the Koreagate and the Constitution. During the rally, which began towards the end of a symposium at the school discussing the need for democracy in South Korea, the students attempted to march off the campus but were turned back by a 300-man tear gas firing riot squad.[68]

111

The disturbance, during which several protestors were arrested and at least one was injured, lasted for five hours until quelled by the police. For the next few days the school was closed. According to university officials, 23 students were expelled from school and 38 were prevented from attending class for at least one year.[69] Yet the students did not capitulate but rather braced themselves for another round of confrontations.

On November 11 some 2,000 Seoul National University students held a campus rally. They demanded sweeping democratic reforms in the country's political structure which was under the "one-man dictatorship" of President Park, and also asked for the release of the fellow students arrested in connection with the disturbance of October 7. Some of the demonstrators hurled stones at the riot-control police, who had entered the campus firing tear gas to break up the rally. After the melee, in which at least five students were arrested, the campus was closed for 17 days.[70]

The latest incident at Seoul National University was followed the very next day by similar protest gatherings at the campus of Sogang University, a Jesuit-run college, as well as several other universities in Seoul. Notably, the student demonstrations throughout the country in the fall were more widespread and more violent than those in the spring.[71]

Notes

1. Tong-A Ilbo, April 29, 1975; and New York Times, April 15, 1975.

2. Tong-A Ilbo, May 10, 1975; and Christian Science Monitor, May 13, 1975.

3. Reportedly, Kim Il Sung also unsuccessfully can-vassed Moscow early in May for support for military action against South Korea. Christian Science Monitor, May 27, 1975; and Washington Post, June 8, 1975. For Moscow's lack of receptivity to Kim's desire for military action against Seoul, see also Donald S. Zagoria and Kim Kun Young, "North Korea and the Major Powers," in Bards, ed., The Two Koreas in East Asian Affairs, p. 48.

4. Tong-A Ilbo, May 10, 1975; and Christian Science Monitor, May 13, 1975.

5. Tong-A Ilbo, June 5, 1975. The NDP head's criticism was mild compared with the assemblywoman Kim Ok Son's scathing attack upon President Park in October, which costed her her assembly seat.

6. Far Eastern Economic Review, June 20, 1975, p. 33.

7. Sekai, ed., Daisan Kankoku karano Tsushin, p. 6; and Far Eastern Economic Review, June 20, 1975, p. 33.

8. New York Times, June 30, 1979.

9. New York Times, March 5, 1976.

10. Boston Globe, May 25, June 1, 1975; and New York Times, May 12, 16, 18, 1975. South Koreans learned about the Gulf Oil's bribery case "indirectly" because of "a complete blackout of any news" about the affair in Seoul.

11. It was read toward the end of a mass commemorating the historical event of 57 years before. Time, March 22, 1976, p. 26; and New York Times, March 3, 1976.

12. Far Eastern Economic Review, March 19, 1976, p. 30.

13. New York Times, March 3, 5, 9, 1976; Time, March 22, 1976, p. 26; and Tong-A Yongam 1975, p. 301. The NDP assemblyman Chong on December 14, 1974 stated on the National Assembly floor that "now that President Park's leadership has arrived at a limit, I wonder if Mr.

President is prepared to step down." The statement instantly created a pandemonium in the Assembly, in which opposition legislators and their pro-government counterparts clashed.

14. Kim Dae Jung was charged, inter alia, with campaigning before official electioneering time, and also with claiming that Park, if reelected, would emasculate the existing constitution and take absolute power and govern for life (which was precisely what Park did after the election). New York Times, September 13, December 14, 1975; and Far Eastern Economic Review, January 2, 1976, p. 14.

15. Far Eastern Economic Review, May 21, 1976, p. 27.

16. Sekai, ed., Daisan Kankoku karano Tsushin, pp. 51-52. South Korean press, fearful of violating decree No. 9, reported the case for the first time on March 11, the day after the prosecution had disclosed the case. Tong-A Ilbo, March 11, 1976; and Time, March 22, 1976, p. 26.

17. Maeda, Seoul karano Hokoku, p. 13.

18. For the court testimonies of the defendants, see Sekai, ed., Daisan Kankoku karano Tsushin, pp. 80-106; and Maeda, Seoul karano Hokoku, pp. 18-21, 34-35.

19. Sekai, ed., Daisan Kankoku karano Tsushin, pp. 124-125; and New York Times, August 28, 1976.

20. Far Eastern Economic Review, September 10, 1976, p. 24; and New York Times, August 28, 1976.

21. South Korean courts automatically withheld physical detention of old people, and did so even after guilty verdicts. Easey and McCormack, "South Korean Society," in McCormack and Selden, eds., Korea, North and South, p. 86; and Far Eastern Economic Review, September 10, 1976, p. 24.

22. New York Times, December 30, 1976.

23. New York Times, March 22, 1977.

24. Tong-A Ilbo, May 21, 1975; and New York Times, May 22, 1975.

25. Tong-A Ilbo, July 9, 1975.

26. Haptong Yongam 1977, p. 83; and Far Eastern Economic Review, July 25, 1975, pp. 22, 24.

27. Kim's opponents were a coalition of three or four factions, of which one was headed by Lee. Haptong Yongam 1977, p. 36.

28. Far Eastern Economic Review, April 30, 1976, p. 12; and Tong-A Ilbo, May 24, 1976. The NDP president was vested with sweeping authority to run the party, including the right to pick party candidates for national assembly elections.

29. Tong-A Ilbo, May 25, 1976; and New York Times, May 26, 1976. Some 20 persons were injured in the fracas.

30. Tong-A Ilbo, May 26, June 10, 1976; and New York Times, June 8, 12, 1976.

31. New York Times, September 17, 1976.

32. Tong-A Ilbo, September 15, 16, 17, 1976. There were four or five major factions in the NDP, each striving to gain the party hegemony.

33. New York Times, March 20, 28, December 26, 1976; and Far Eastern Economic Review, January 14, 1977, p. 30.

34. New York Times, November 23, 1974; and Washington Post, November 23, December 5, 1974.

35. For instance, the admission of spectators to the court proceedings was limited to those who had received tickets issued by the court, and the spectators with tickets had to run the gauntlet of security agents before being admitted to the courtroom. The lack of free access to the courtroom also applied to foreign news media; and the Seoul Correspondents' Club, which represented foreign news organs in Seoul, issued on May 20 a statement charging the police with hampering foreign coverage of the trial. New York Times, May 21, 1976; and Maeda, Seoul karano Hokoku, p. 13.

36. Weinstein and Kamiya, eds., The Security of Korea, pp. 5-6; and Ho Lee Yong, "Military Balance and Peace in the Korean Peninsula," Asian Survey, XXI, No. 8, (August 1981), pp. 860-861.

37. The opposition to Carter's decision to withdraw U.S. ground troops was endorsed by the politicians of the opposition parties. New York times, April 28, 1978; and Time, June 6, 1977, p. 29.

38. The withdrawal decision was conveyed in Seoul to President Park by Carter's special envoys Philip Habib, Undersecretary of State For Political Affairs, and General George Brown, Chairman of the Joint Chiefs of Staff. New York Times, May 26, 1977; and Time, June 6, 1977, p. 28.

39. New York Times, April 11, 1978; Han Sungjoo, "South Korea and the United States: The Alliance Survives," Asian Survey, XX, No. 11, (November 1980), p. 1081; and Far Eastern Economic Review, May 6, 1977, pp. 26-27. In the United States and Japan too there were politicians who wanted direct contacts between Washington and P'yongyang. At a two-day gathering in September 1977 of liberal members of the U.S. Congress and Japanese Diet in Washington, where Senator George McGovern gave the keynote address, a resolution was passed urging President Carter to begin direct talks with North Korea for arms reductions and the ultimate pullout of all American military personnel from Korea. Far Eastern Economic Review, September 30, 1977, p. 22.

115

40. On June 10, 1975 Lee Jae Hyon, formerly a chief cultural and press attache at the Korean Embassy in Washington, testified before the Subcommittee on the House International Organizations describing Korean plan to bribe U.S. officials. Robert Boettcher and Gordon L. Freedman, Gifts of Deceit: Sun Myong Moon, Tongsun Park and the Korean Scandal, (New York: Harper and Row, 1980), pp. 241-242. Also on February 19 and 20, 1976 the Washington Post disclosed that two members of the House of Representatives were being investigated by the FBI for suspicion of accepting bribes from Korean government.

41. One of the five probing organs belonged to the Department of Justice, and the other four were Congressional Committees. Boettcher and Freedman, Gifts of Deceit, pp. 247-251.

42. Boettcher and Freedman, Gifts of Deceit, pp. 195-197, 213-236; and Lee, "Hanguk Kwa Miguk," p. 461.

43. Ch'oe Dok Shin, a retired three-star general, had served in the 1960's in various official capacities: head of the Seoul delegation to the United Nations, Ambassador to West Germany, and Foreign Minister. He left Korea for Japan in the mid-1970's, and then went to Canada via the United States. He eventually moved to North Korea in 1986 for good. Kim Hyong Wook, one of the army colonels who had come to power in the 1961 coup and who had headed the KCIA from 1963 to 1969, went into exile to the United States in 1973 after a break with Park. He was a key witness in the Congressional and Justice Department's investigations of the Korean scandal. In October 1979 while in Paris, he disappeared; at the time he was finishing a book intended to expose the seamy side of Park regime. Despite his disappearance--presumed murdered--Kim's book was published, entitled Kenryoku to Inbo (Power and Intrigue), (Tokyo: Kodo Shuppansha, 1980). New York Times, October 25, 1979; and Sekai, ed., Daisan Kankoku karano Tsushin, pp. 222-223.

44. New York Times, October 28, 1979; Sekai, ed., Zoku Kankoku karano Tsushin, p. 230; and Mark Selden, "Introduction: The United States and Korea at the Crossroads," in McCormack and Selden, eds., Korea, North and South, pp. 35-36.

45. In November 1976 Kim Sang Keun, the second highest KCIA officer in Washington, asked for asylum in exchange for information on the recipients of money from Korean agents. In September 1977 Sohn Young Ho, a KCIA officer at the Korean Consulate in the New York City, defected. He told U.S. officials about KCIA harassments of Korean critics of Park regime in the United States. Far Eastern Economic Review, December 24, 1976, p. 12, January 28,

1977, p. 21, October 7, 1977, p. 18; and New York Times, December 4, 1976, September 28, 1977.

46. The August 1977 indictment against Park contained 36 counts lobbying activities, spanning nine years of his political and social life in the United States. Far Eastern Economic Review, September 9, 1977, p. 28, October 7, 1977, p. 18.

47. New York Times, January 4, 1979; and Far Eastern Economic Review, October 14, 1977, pp. 31-32, November 11, 1977, p. 14. Grand jury indictment of a second Korean was issued in October 1977 against Hancho C. Kim for his alleged perjury and illegal attempt to manipulate the Congressional attitude.

48. Han, "South Korea and the United States," pp. 44-45.

49. Christian Science Monitor, April 3, 1979; and Boettacher and Freedman, Gifts of Deceit, pp. 267-272.

50. Han, "South Korea and the United States," p. 48. It should be noted that Representative Donald M. Fraser of Minnesota, who had been a persistent critic of Park regime, lost his bid for Senate seat in the Democratic primary in September 1978.

51. New York Times, December 9, 1976; and Sekai, ed., Daisan Kankoku karano Tsushin, p. 217.

52. The National Assembly in Seoul had discussed the charges in Washington of payoffs to U.S. Congressmen, but the discussion had not been reported in the Seoul press and the public had been kept in the dark.

53. New York Times, April 17, 22, 1977; and Far Eastern Economic Review, April 15, 1977, p. 29.

54. Far Eastern Economic Review, April 15, 1977, pp. 29-30.

55. New York Times, April 19, 25, 1977; and Sekai, ed., Daisan Kankoku karano Tsushin, pp. 196-197.

56. Sekai, ed., Daisan Kankoku karano Tsushin, pp. 173-176, 199-203. Ignoring domestic consumer demands, President Park initially mobilized national energies for the creation of a massive export industry. And as of late 1979 some 90 percent of leather goods, 78 percent of textile, 56 percent of metal wares, and 46 percent of electrical products were earmarked for foreign consumptions. Monthly Review of Korean Affairs, I, No. 4, (August 1979), p. 3.

57. For instance, on the day of President Jimmy Carter's inauguration on January 20, 1977, leaflets attacking President Park circulated in Seoul presumably by dissidents, who were apparently heartened by the election of Carter who had a strong commitment to human

rights. Far Eastern Economic Review, February 4, 1977, p. 24.

58. In addition, already on February 22 the police arrested 10 dissidents, including two journalists and a church pastor for violating Decree No. 9. New York Times, February 22, April 17, 20, 1977; and Newsweek, May 2, 1977, pp. 63-64.

59. New York Times, April 17, 22, 1977.

60. Newsweek, May 2, 1977, p. 64.

61. Tong-A Ilbo, September 21, 1976; and New York Times, September 17, 1976, January 15, 1977.

62. Sekai, ed., Daisan Kankoku karano Tsushin, pp. 147-148; and New York Times, January 15, 1977.

63. Tong-A Ilbo, March 9, 1977; and New York Times, March 8, 1977.

64. Tong-A Ilbo, March 24, 1977; and Far Eastern Economic Review, April 8, 1977, p. 22.

65. Far Eastern Economic Review, April 8, 1977, p. 22.

66. New York Times, April 10, 1977; and Far Eastern Economic Review, July 22, 1977, p. 24, September 9, 1977, p. 30. In October 1977, the NDP, however, proposed in the National Assembly the formation of a special committee to probe the influence-buying scandal. The proposal was defeated by pro-government legislators in the Foreign Affairs Committee of the National Assembly. New York Times, October 6, 29, 1977.

67. Tong-A Ilbo, June 10, 11, 1977; and Far Eastern Economic Review, June 24, 1977, p. 32. The by-elections were held to fill vacancies created by the death in April of former deputy premier Chang Key Yong and by the criminal conviction of Chong Il Hyong. In all, 15 candidates ran in the elections and all did so as Independents. Those with party backgrounds or previous political experiences were rejected by the voters, which was seen as a thumbs-down for the existing political party system.

68. Tong-A Ilbo, October 8, 1977.

69. New York Times, October 8, 9, 1977.

70. New York Times, November 12, 1977.

71. New York Times, November 13, 1977.

CHAPTER 6

THE STATE OF ECONOMY 1976-1979

The protesting voices of South Korean dissidents were not merely those of frustrated students and intellectuals, but included the voices of South Korea's many working men and women who had born the burden of the country's rapid industrialization. To a certain extent, the basic political issue, stemming mostly from President Park's political manipulation and symbolized by dissident movements, was rooted in economic problems which Park attempted to solve by repression but without appreciable results. When the economic problems, which had been overshadowed by the ostensibly spectacular industrial growth, had become serious, the country's intellectuals and Christians went beyond their normal discontent over the curtailment of political liberties and attacked Park's economic policies.

Division of Wealth and Labor Unrest

Under President Park, South Korean economy had surged tremendously and its structure had undergone a great transformation. From 1962 (the year the First Five-Year Plan was launched) to 1979 (the third year of the Fourth Five-Year Plan) the GNP rose at an average annual rate of more than 9.5 percent in real terms. The per capita income, which was merely $100 in 1962, had risen to over $800 by 1978.[1] The record was impressive, particularly so in the light of the economic difficulties experienced globally since the 1973-1974 "oil shock."

The growth was spurred by rapid export-oriented industrial development, mainly in light industrial goods. Exports, which were merely $54.8 million in 1962 when the economic drive began, rose to more than $450 million in 1968. They grew steadily exceeding $4.4 billion in 1974 and $5.0 billion in 1975 despite the world recession; and they reached over $12 billion in 1978, an

increase of more than 28-fold within ten years. Exports
accounted for no less than 60 percent of the economic
growth during 1971-1978.[2]

As a share of the GNP, exports increased from five
percent in 1960-1962 to 20 percent in 1970-1972, 25
percent in 1975, and 27 percent in 1978. The portion of
manufactured goods in total exports rose from approximately 13 percent in 1960 to nearly 53 percent in 1965
and over 86 percent in 1976.[3] All this while, the importance of manufacturing industry to the economy had
steadily risen, while that of agriculture had declined.
The share of the former in the GNP grew from 10 percent
in 1960 to 33 percent in 1979, and the latter dropped
from 39.9 percent to 19.2 percent during the same period.
This shift in production elevated South Korea's status
to one of the "newly industrializing countries."[4]

The South Korean economy, however, was not as robust
as the above statistics seemed to suggest. Although the
GNP grew fast once the economic drive got under way, the
tax burden of the people also increased sharply. Taxes
constituted 8.9 percent of the GNP in 1963, but it rose
to over 16 percent in 1975, 17.9 to 18.2 percent in 1978,
18.4 percent in 1979, and 18.7 percent in 1980. As a
source of national revenues, the share of taxes rose from
40.9 percent in 1963 to 80.5 percent in 1975.[5] The growing level of taxation was partly due to the new tax, the
Defense Tax introduced in July 1975. It supplied 32.7
percent of the national budget in 1976, 34.3 percent in
1977, and 35.4 percent in 1978.[6]

The problem, inherent in the rising taxation, was
compounded by wide gaps in the distribution of the fruits
of the economic growth, a phenomenon proved a constant
source of social unrest not only in Korea but elsewhere
in the world. For example, in 1963 some 30 percent of
manufacturing employment was in Seoul alone, and 57 percent in Kyonggi Province including Seoul and the Pusan-
centered South Kyongsang Province. The figures for 1972
were 33 percent and 63 percent, respectively. In 1974
nearly two-thirds of South Korea's total labor force,
excluding the farmers and miners, were in the Seoul-
centered Kyonggi Province and South Kyongsang Province.[7]

Thus the rapid economic growth not only changed the
overall economic structure and employment pattern, but
it also contributed to the increasing concentration of
economic activity and wealth in the country's two regions

centered around the two metropolises of Seoul and Pusan. The degree of the concentration was especially pronounced in Seoul; there in 1984 half of South Korean factories were located and 65 percent of all bank deposits as well as 52 percent of the passenger cars were found.[8]

Because the rapid industrialization was accompanied by spreading urbanization which was accelerated by migration of rural population, the sectoral imbalance was closely linked to the rural-urban imbalance in economic growth and income, a phenomenon commonly observed in other developing countries too. The income ratio between nonfarm and farming households widened in the 1960's, with the average rural household income in 1967 being only 60 percent of urban income.[9] The decline in the relative economic position of rural areas was sufficiently noticeable that the government became concerned, especially so because of the erosion of electoral support apparent in the 1971 presidential election.

Thus the Seoul government launched the New Village Movement (Saemaul Undong) during the winter of 1971-1972. It was intended to increase rural incomes by adding non-farm employment to the farming community and also to improve physical environment of villages (for example, the elimination of thatched roofs). These efforts, however, did not appreciably reverse the trend toward the concen-tration of wealth in urban areas, particularly in Seoul.[10] And the impact the New Village Movement had on the improvement of rural living standards was "marginal." For example, in 1973 the average rural per capita income was 71.2 percent of the urban counterpart, and in 1975 the figure was 76.9 percent.[11]

Gaps also existed in individual earnings. The use of the growing average per capita income as implicit evidence of rising consumption and welfare benefits for everybody was misleading and even "deceptive." Such an average conceals a wide variation in the size of personal incomes, and it obscures the impact of economic inequalities on the living standards of those at the bottoms of the economic heap. Indeed, as to the question of how the nation's wealth was distributed among its various income levels, there had been no regularly published information as late as midway through the Fourth Five-Year Plan (1977-1981).[12]

Yet, it was increasingly recognized that the wealthier elements had benefited "disproportionately" and the unskilled workers and farmers benefited only marginally. As the South Korean economy surged ahead, the inequality in income, hence the variation in consumption levels, was believed to have increased, once again an experience common among developing countries.[13] According to a study conducted by the Korea Development Institute (KDI), during the period of 1970-1976, the earnings of the top 20 percent income bracket increased by 24 percent, while those of the bottom 20 percent rose by only 17 percent; and only 0.3 percent of the population earned 43 percent of the GNP in 1976.[14] Another source in 1980 reported that one-third of the national wealth was concentrated in the hands of only one percent of South Korea's total families.[15]

Regarding the widening disparity in personal earnings, which was also noted by the World Bank, the KDI report concluded that the situation had reached a crisis proportion and that it would become a principal source of social instability unless alleviated quickly.[16] The concern about this potentially explosive issue was echoed in a similar vein editorially in Tong-A Ilbo on January 1, 1980:

> Because we have promoted high growth in a short span of time and dreamed of joining the rank of the economically advanced nations without our own domestic resources, it is most likely that the disparity in income distribution has widened, especially since the first oil crisis [of 1973-1974].

> Whether this state of affairs would continue to be tolerated by the people depends upon the interplay of political persuation and the psychology of people's expectation...Yet, the time has come to adopt positive measures in economic policies to improve the system of income distribution. From now on, we must change our sense [of priority] in deliberation of all policies so that income distribution would no longer worsen but improve for its fairness.

How the ordinary people fared can be adduced from the wages workers received. Between 1971 and 1976 wages had increased at the annual rate of 7.3 percent. But the average monthly wage in 1976, according to that year's March report of the Office of Labor Affairs, was $93, which was well below the $142 per month that the Economic

Planning Board had said was needed for an average family.[17]

Compared with its counterparts in the world's advanced industrial democracies, the figure was strikingly low. Given 100 points for South Korea, the wage ratio was as follows: 757 for Japan; 1,104 for the United States; 870 for West Germany; and 621 for England.[18] Although Korean wages increased at an average annual rate of 30 percent for three years from 1976, they were still relatively low, averaging less than $200 a month in 1979, which was one-fourth to one-eighth of the counterparts in industrially advanced non-communist countries.[19]

Furthermore, surveys conducted by the Korea Productivity Center and the Korea Trade Association disclosed considerable discrepancies in the 1976 earnings according to gender, educational levels, and the sizes and kinds of enterprises. The monthly average earning for a male junior high school graduate was $75 and for a female $60. A male high school graduate averaged $104 and a female $72, and the average entry level monthly salary for a college graduate was $290.[20]

The pay scales and working conditions at small firms, which usually hired less than a few dozen workers each, were inferior to those at large enterprises which generally had ready access to government-endorsed low interest loans. These small firms provided as much as three-quarters of the country's industrial jobs, that is, most of South Korea's industrial employment.[21] And according to statistics issued by the Office of Labor Affairs, 60.6 percent of all factory workers in 1977 earned less than $70 a month and as high as 80 percent earned less than $105. The same statistics revealed that the average labor cost amounted to only 10 percent of the unit price of manufactured goods, whereas it was 30 percent in Japan and 50 percent in the United States.[22]

Low wages were South Korea's weapon in the international market competition and "the key to the growth" of its economy.[23] This is because Seoul's exports were concentrated in light, labor intensive products such as basic textiles, elementary electronics, wigs, and plywood. Also because its export-led economic growth was based on its comparative advantage in producing labor intensive products and on the expansion of trade, principally with the United States and Japan. By basing her export competitiveness on low wages, Korea, in effect, exchanged her abundant low cost labor for its relatively scarce raw materials and capital.

In pursuing its low wage policy, the Seoul government was unimpeded by any significant trade union activism. Because of the availability of ready pools of labor and the government's hostility toward organized labor, trade unions in the Republic of Korea were weak. Indeed, they were so weak that their influence was minimal, and they seldom effectively articulated the needs of their members. Instead of being organizations concerned with the economic welfare of their members, the trade unions were instruments of labor control in the hands of the authorities.[24]

The initial efforts of the Park government to limit the scope of labor activities were embodied in the Special Measure Law on National Security and Defense, which was rammed through the National Assembly in the predawn session of December 1971. Article 9 of the law stipulated that the adjustment of all labor disputes that might harm "national security" and impede "national mobilization" be placed directly in the hands of government. It also made mediation by a government agency the precondition for labor's collective actions and negotiations.[25]

Article 9 was later incorporated virtually verbatim into the 1972 Constitution (Article 29), thus assuring that no constitutional challenge could be mounted against the restrictive measure. Its effect was to deprive the workers of the rights to act and bargain collectively, and to outlaw labor strikes regardless of the nature of grievances throughout the remainder of the Park presidency. These restrictions were supplemented by limitations placed upon the number of unions allowed in any single business enterprise and qualifications for union membership.

Only one union was permitted at one company and only "permanent" workers (apparently, those regularly employed) were permitted to join unions.[26] Given such restrictions, only 367,000 workers were unionized out of the total potential union membership of 1.37 million regularly employed non-farm workers toward the end of 1967. In 1974, out of about 4 million "manual and clerical workers," only 620,000 were unionized in 17 national labor federations affiliated with the Federation of Korean Trade Unions (Noch'ong).[27]

124

Furthermore, union leaders were generally picked by company managements or the government, and they exercised very little influence in the adjustment of labor-management relations. Unions' important matters were left to union presidents to deal with one to one with company presidents; such a practice impeded unions' development as democratic institutions.[28] Any attempt at organizing a self-governing union was deemed subversive by the authorities; should the attempt look promising it was surely broken by government agents.

Notwithstanding the government's surveillance and legal prohibition, labor disturbances erupted occasionally. On March 10, 1977 some 1,500 workers gathered at the Myongdong Cathedral in Seoul under the auspices of the Urban Industrial Mission, a Christian organization devoted to the betterment of the lot of the urban poor; and they issued a "Laborers' Human Rights Declaration" demanding improvements in wages and working conditions.[29] Following the incident South Korean labor scenes began to be marred by a series of outbreaks of violence.

In the very month the laborers' human rights declaration was issued, a major labor disturbance broke out among some 2,000 Korean construction workers at Jubail in Saudi Arabia. They rioted over the treatment they had been receiving from their Korean company, Hyondae that had employed them. Their main complaints were low wages and long work hours. The average wage for Korean workers in Saudi Arabia was $300 a month for unskilled laborers and $500 for skilled. Although more than the average wage in Korea, the wages were low by Middle Eastern standards for foreign workers. In order to settle the dispute and to apologize to the Saudi authorities, who were furious over the incident, not only Hyondae representatives but also Prime Minister Ch'oe Kyu Ha scurried to Saudi Arabia.[30]

Then in December, workers at an electric organ manufacturing shop in the city of Taegu seized the family of the company vice-president as hostages in protest against low wages and the violence to which they had been subjected at the hands of their company executives; and they clashed with police. In January of the following year, 1978, coal miners at Samch'ok County in Kangwon Province battled with police in the wake of their disputes over the company's labor policy, and many of the defiant miners were taken into police custody.[31]

The miners' strike was shortly followed in February by still another labor disturbance, this time at the Tong'il Textile Company in Inch'on. The company with some 1,300 girls and only 170 males, was unique because in 1972 the female employees rejected company endorsed union leaders and elected ones from among their own female coworkers. This breakthrough in South Korean labor history had been met over the years with unceasing harassments and threats from the KCIA-controlled National Textile Union which was bent on taming the union. The harassments culminated in a violent incident on February 21, 1978, when some 400 girls, who were about to vote to choose new union leaders, were set upon by a male gang hired by the company and forced to cancel the election. As the assault victims went on hunger strike in protest against the violent obstructionism, the company laid off 126 of them on grounds that they had absented themselves from work without permit.[32]

In all, there were 96 cases of labor-management disputes in 1977 and 105 in 1978. Yet, the nation's mass news media, fearful of government reprisals, hardly reported the disturbances.[33]

Foreign Dependency of the Economy

As the government-management imposed labor discipline was breaking down and worker unrest surfaced for all to see, the economy showed other signs of trouble which were less obvious but just as serious. They were trade deficits and dependency on foreign capitals as well as foreign raw materials.

The extraordinary high growth rate and modernization of the industrial structure were a matter of national pride, but exports were laden with a growing balance of trade deficits. The problem was compounded by the fact that south Korea was endowed with few natural resources, and that she lacked sufficient technology required for the production of sophisticated merchandise, and was dependent upon foreign raw materials as well as capital goods for production.

Much of Seoul's exports were manufactured using foreign raw materials and foreign semi-finished products. In 1979 almost as "high" as 60 percent of all raw materials used for exports was imported.[34] This ratio of import contents in the export goods was much higher than the ratio in the country's overall production, and some export items were simply assembled from imported components including those from Japan.[35] With such a built-in structure, Seoul's exports had been relatively unprofitable and incurred growing trade deficits.

The average annual deficit was $318 million in the 1960-1962 period, but it increased to $1.1 billion in 1970-1972. Specifically, it grew from $272 million in 1960 to $1.0 billion in 1971.[36] The balance of payment deficits worsened drastically in 1974 by hitting a record high of $1.9 billion amidst the worldwide recession in the aftermath of the abrupt rise in the prices of crude oil and other imported materials.[37]

Because South Korea was heavily dependent upon foreign raw materials, every increase in its exports had been generally achieved at the cost of a corresponding rise in imports. For example, between 1975 and 1979 exports grew at an annual rate of 27.5 percent from $5.0 billion to $14.7 billion; but during the same period imports grew at an almost equally rapid pace with an annual rate of 24.7 percent from $6.7 billion to $19 billion.[38] Thus, whenever Seoul tried to increase exports in order to close gaps in the trade imbalance, it was found that the efforts were in vain. The trade deficits thus accumulated for the 15 years from 1966 to June 1980 totalled more than $25 billion. Of the total, over $17 billion (or 70.1 percent) was incurred in the two-way trade with Japan, indicating that the Korea-Japan trade since the normalization of their relations in 1965 had been heavily lopsided in favor of the latter.[39]

Furthermore, analysts maintained that because of Seoul's heavy dependence upon imported components and raw materials, not only did exports fail to get much "value-added," but the economy fell short of acquiring significantly increased industrial skills and technologies.[40] When an export enterprise brings in already manufactured foreign components to assemble, taking advantage of low wages, it does not contribute much toward creating a "product cycle," whereby "ancillary" domestic industries develop to supply the enterprise with their own components.[41] Thus in the absence of a "product cycle" no new skills and technologies are acquired. In addition, there is a built-in necessity for Seoul to keep up a high rate of imports in order to sustain export growth, thus contributing to a steadily increasing trade deficit.

In order to make up the imbalance and obtain scarce capital, the Park government borrowed from abroad progressively larger amounts of money, which came neither cheaply nor without external strings attached. According to a report by the Ministry of Finance, external debt stood at $301 million in 1965 ($176 million public, the rest private). At the time Korea was considered creditworthy for foreign borrowing; so it was relatively easy for her to borrow abroad. Thus the total foreign debt tripled between 1965 and 1967, and in 1971 it was 10 times the amount of 1965.[42]

The outstanding foreign debt was over $3.5 billion in 1972, then increased to $5.9 billion in 1974, some $10.5 billion ($4.6 billion was commercial loans, the rest public loans) in 1976, and $14.9 billion in 1978. Toward the end of 1979 the foreign debt reached approximately $22 billion, nearly twice as much as that year's national budget or almost half of the year's GNP.[43] Naturally, the remittances abroad to service the accumulating debts grew. The yearly interest and principal payments on foreign loans in 1978 exceeded $2.1 billion and reached almost $2.5 billion in 1979; each sum represented about one-fifth of the year's national budget. Japan's share in the sums of the loans and credits was about 20 percent of the totals--second only to that of the United States, which accounted for some 28 percent.[44]

In addition to her preponderant role in South Korea's international trade and foreign borrowing, Japan made direct investments in South Korea, and here Japan overshadowed all other countries. Tokyo's direct investments, which had soared since the late 1960's, exceeded $600 million in late 1978, which was almost three times the American level or 53 percent of the total foreign investments in South Korea. In 1980 about 47 percent of the total foreign investments came from Japan and 29 percent from the United States. Especially, at the Masan Free Export Zone, established in 1970 modeled after such prototypes as Jurong Town in Singapore and the Kaoshiung Export Zone in Taiwan, over 90 percent of all the investments as of late 1975 was Japanese.[45]

Japan's economic presence in South Korea, with its GNP of over $1 trillion (as of 1978) compared with a mere $47.3 billion for the latter, was almost overpowering.[46] According to a South Korean banker's remark that appeared in the New York Times on October 16, 1979, through "loans, share exchange, technical agreements, trade missions," the Japanese "virtually control the Korean economy much as the Americans dominate the defense side."

The heavy Japanese presence in the South Korean economy and the burden of the multiplying external debt raised serious questions as to who really profited from Seoul's economic development and if the economic growth, based upon foreign dependency, really represented "progress." Because of the Koreans' deep-seated distrust of Japan, these doubts remained a sore point with many concerned South Koreans, especially intellectuals and scholars, and constituted a lingering political problem.[47]

What made the Japanese question so sensitive politically was not only Tokyo's ever growing presence in South Korea, but it was encouraged and exploited by the Park regime.[48] While the Japanese economic involvement in South Korea provided added employment opportunities for Koreans, Park's political operatives received slush funds from Japanese and other foreign firms doing business in Korea. And out of the existing economic setup emerged Korean nouveau riche, who were politically allied with the government and who had vested interests in the maintenance of status quo.[49] As the Japanese economic involvement mushroomed, so soon after Korea's bitter encounter with Japanese colonialism, Park's critics became more and more skeptical of his motive behind tolerating such a development.

The State of Agriculture

The Seoul government, engrossed as it was in the promotion of export-oriented industrialization, failed to take commensurate measures to invigorate agriculture. Except the land reform in the late 1940's and early 1950's, the attitude of the successive Seoul governments prior to the 1970's to the farmers had been "basically one of neglect." As such, agriculture, traditionally the backbone of Korean economy, had declined in the relative importance and since the mid-1960's had been overshadowed by the manufacturing industry.

As noted earlier in this chapter, the share of agriculture in the growing GNP dropped "precipitously" from 39.9 percent in 1960 to 19.2 percent in 1979, while manufacturing increased from 10 percent to 33 percent during the same period. In contrast to the rapid annual GNP growth rate of nearly 10 percent between 1965 and 1975, the agricultural sector registered a sluggish average growth rate of only 3.1 percent to 4.2 percent in the same period.[50]

As the ratio of agriculture in the GNP growth fell, so did the ratio of the farming population in the nation's total. It dropped from 61.9 percent in 1955 to 55.8 percent in 1965, to 38.2 percent in 1975, and continued to decline throughout the rest of the 1970's. Observers noted that the 1975 figure of 38.2 percent was "well below what one could expect given the still low level of per capita GNP then prevailing in Korea," which was $374 at 1970 prices.[51]

Behind this "aberrant" development, which resulted in the relative stagnation of agriculture, were the government's low price policy for farm products and allocation of meager capital to agriculture in the 1960's. For example, in 1965 just 11.5 percent of the total governmental capital investment went to agriculture, which was one-twentieth of that allocated to the manufacturing industry. The ratio declined to 5.4 percent in 1969.[52] On the other hand, the price of food grains, traditionally the key factor in the fluctuation of the prices of consumer commodities in Korea, was kept low in order to hold down the overall consumer price level and help keep wages low among the burgeoning industrial workers.

In pursuance of the low price policy for farm products and in view of the inability of domestic agricultural production to meet rising domestic consumption,[53] the Park government imported low-cost American foodstuff. The volume of food imports had risen significantly since the mid-1960's, perpetuating South Korea's dependency on foreign grains. It rose from an annual average of 600,000 metric tons in 1956-1965 to about 1,400,000 metric tons in 1966-1970, and to over 2,600,000 metric tons during 1971-1975. All this while, South Korea's self-sufficiency in food steadily fell. It dropped from 94 percent in 1965 to 80 percent in 1970, and in 1976 it stood at 75 percent.[54]

The grain purchases abroad drained off Seoul's foreign currency reserves: $450 million in 1974, $689 million in 1975, and $459 million in 1976; and they contributed to the worsening international balance of payments.[55] Moreover, the importation of increasingly larger quantities of low-cost food grains dampened farmers' efforts to raise productivity and even forced many of them off their lands, thus widening the income gap between rural dwellers and their urban counterparts and leading to rural decay.[56]

Concerned with the rural conditions, the government, along with the launching of the New Village Movement in the winter of 1971-1972, adopted a policy of improving the terms of trade in favor of agriculture by adjusting food prices upward by more than 20 percent. The government did so hoping the measure would help boost agricultural production and raise rural incomes.[57] Though it reduced the disparity between rural and urban incomes, the price support measure had by and large a "polarizing effect" on rural income distribution. This is because the measure benefited principally one-third of the farm households with more than one hectare of land each and did little to help the small landholders who comprised the bulk of the farm population.[58] The program failed in reversing the shortage of food grains or the income disparity between the rural and urban sectors.

Under the circumstances, many peasants abandoned their old profession and migrated to cities in search of a better life, leaving farm villages in a destitute state. According to a statistics issued by the Ministry of Agriculture and Fisheries, in 1977 alone some 480,000 people left their villages and in 1978 some 780,000 did so. The mass desertion of decaying farm villages resulted in a decrease in the absolute number of rural population since the mid-1960's and throughout the 1970's, despite the national average annual population growth rate of about two percent.[59] By the late 1970's the plight of the farm villages had become so dire that many of those who were leaving were unable to sell their lands and had to abandon them.[60]

In the ten years until early 1984, the rural population had dropped by 34 percent. This meant that on the average half a million people had left their villages and moved to cities each year. Most of them had gone to Seoul, where the accommodation facilities and employment opportunities by no means matched the size of their influx.[61]

The 1978-1979 Recession

The South Korean economy took a sharp downturn in 1978-1979, and floundered in combined difficulties of severe

131

inflation and recession. Inflation--an indicator of shortage of goods and a sapper of economic foundation--had been rampant in South Korea. For two decades since the end of the Korea War in 1953, consumer goods prices had increased at an annual rate of 16 percent; and from 1973 until 1979 the country had experienced a much higher rate of 20 percent annually on the average. Inflation in 1977 and 1978 was officially 10.1 percent and 14.4 percent, respectively; but most observers agreed that the actual rates were about 27 and 30 percent.[62]

The double-digit inflation since 1973-1974, coinciding with the worldwide oil crisis, posed a serious problem for the country's economy. Because the rampant inflation not only stalled the improvement of living standards for ordinary people, but it also weakened the country's export competitiveness in the international market by boosting the prices of Korean manufactured products.[63]

Contributing to the high rates of inflation were the government's policy of easy money and credit in its intensive drive for exports, its "excessive" money supply in 1978 to develop capital intensive heavy and chemical industries,[64] and increased remittances from Korean workers in the Middle East since 1973-1974.[65] More, under the export-oriented economy, the growth in the domestic supply of food, housing, and other consumer items had lagged behind the domestic needs. Indeed, the more than a decade long emphasis on exports had produced a shortage of consumer goods at home, shooting up prices, which was aggravated by rising wages granted to appease the increasingly militant workers.[66]

Still more, poor weather in 1978 adversely affected the farming as well as the fishing, driving up the costs of all foods. Furthermore, the government in June raised fees of all public transports by more than 20 percent, adding another factor to the inflationary spiral.[67] With another surge in international oil prices in 1979, South Korea entered even harder times. As South Korea paid for its oil imports at 41.7 percent higher than in 1978, and the average price for all imported commodities increased by 27 percent over the year 1978, inflation in 1979 ran at a rate of 20-32 percent in consumer prices.[68] This hyper-inflation virtually wiped out any increases in salaries and wages.

To cope with the rampant inflation and to cure its associated ills, the government in December 1978 introduced "stabilization" measures, which entailed lowering of the growth rate of the economy and a tight money policy. These measures, however, produced an instant recession, leading to growing delinquencies of loan repayments and widespread bankruptcies among business enterprises and increasing unemployment.[69] For example, during the first six months in 1979, as many as 349 business and industrial concerns in South Korea were unable to pay their employees a combined total of $3,000,000 in wages and salaries, which represented a 625 percent increase in delinquent payments over the entire previous year. The total amount in 1979 subsequently crept up to nearly ten times the one in 1978.[70]

As the government's tight money policy held on, even many of the nation's leading industrial groups operated precariously, mostly being deep in debt. Startling were the bankruptcies of the Chese industrial group in the fall of 1978 and of the Yulsan in the spring of 1979. Both were among the rapidly rising new major industrial conglomerates, which took advantage of the governmental concessional rate of loan interests for production or sale of exports.[71]

Given Seoul's heavy reliance on exports for economic well-being and the worldwide recession, especially the doldrums in the U.S. and Japanese economies, the prospects for a quick recovery from "stagflation" which gripped the economy appeared slim. Under the circumstances, many South Koreans wished to leave the country in search of a better life in foreign lands.[72]

Notes

1. Asian Wall Street Journal, June 29, 1983; and
Princeton Lyman, "Economic Development in South Korea:
A Retrospective View of the 1969's," in Wright, ed.,
Korean Politics in Transition, p. 250.

2. Paul W. Kuznets, Economic Growth and Structure in
the Republic of Korea, (New Haven: Yale University Press,
1977), pp. 51-52, 156; and Monthly Review of Korean
Affairs, I, No. 9, (January 1980), p. 2. The export-
promotion program initiated in 1962 replaced the previous
strategy of importing only those goods which domestically
could not be produced. And in the 1970's about one-
quarter of Korea's manufactured output was exported. Ho
Samuel P.S., "South Korea and Taiwan: Development
Prospects and Problems in the 1980's," Asian Survey, XXI,
No. 21, (December 1981), p. 1176.

3. The Economic and Social Modernization of the
Republic of Korea, p. 137; and Ho, "South Korea and
Taiwan," p. 1176. The shares of exports in GNP in 1975
and 1978 were computed from statistics of GNP and exports
in New York Times of November 25, 1979 and Tong-A Ilbo
of January 15, 1980.

4. Ho, "South Korea and Taiwan," p. 1175; and The
Economic and Social Modernization of the Republic of
Korea, p. 211.

5. Gavan McCormack, "The South Korean Economy: GNP
versus the People," in McCormack and Selden, eds., Korea,
North and South, p. 101; Haptong Yongam 1977, p. 528; and
Haptong Yongam 1980, p. 620.

6. Maeda, Seoul karano Hokoku, pp. 109-113.

7. Ho Samuel P.S., "Rural-Urban Imbalance in South
Korea in the 1970's," Asian Survey, XIX, No. 7, (July
1979), p. 646; and Kuznets, Economic Growth and Structure
in the Republic of Korea, pp. 168, 172.

8. Far Eastern Economic Review, May 3, 1984, p. 30.

9. Weinstein and Kamiya, eds., Security of Korea, p.
9.

10. Kim, Man and Society in Korea's Economic Growth, pp. 81-104.

11. Ho, "Rural-Urban Imbalance in South Korea in the 1970's," p. 648; and Economic and Social Modernization of the Republic of Korea, pp. 648, 656-657.

12. Tong-A Ilbo, January 1, 1980; and Kuznets, Economic Growth and Structure in the Republic of Korea, pp. 62, 95.

13. New York Times, March 20, 1976; and Weinstein and Kamiya, eds., Security of Korea, p. 9.

14. Monthly Review of Korean Affairs, I, No. 4, (August 1979), p. 3.

15. Time, September 8, 1980, p. 36. According to still another source, 40 percent of South Koreans received 90 percent of the country's total earnings in 1975. Sekai, ed., Daisan Kankoku karano Tsushin, pp. 160-161. Personal income in 1978 of Mr. Chong Chu Yong, Chairman of the Hyondae Chaebol (financial conglomerate), was 6.3 times larger than in the previous year. The rate of increase was about twice that of Mr. Uehara Masayoshi, Japan's richest man and Chairman of the Taisho Pharmaceutical conglomerate. Maeda, Seoul karano Hokoku, p. 142.

16. Monthly Review of Korean Affairs, I, No. 4, (August 1979), p. 3.

17. New York Times, March 20, 1976.

18. Hanyang, No. 176, (January-February 1986), p. 53.

19. New York Times, June 30, 1979.

20. New York Times, March 1, 20, 1976.

21. Since 1972 South Korean economy has been a command economy and not a free one; and in 1978 there were some 30 chaebol which, together with government, controlled South Korean economy. Maeda, Seoul karano Hokoku, p. 14. Among the small business firms widely publicized for deplorable working conditions were the sweat shops at the P'yonghwa Market garment industrial district in Seoul. New York Times, March 1, 1981.

22. Maeda, Seoul karano Hokoku, p. 103; and New York Times, June 30, 1979, March 1, 1981.

23. Kuznets, Economic Growth and Structure in the Republic of Korea, pp. 151-152, 156.

24. Frank, et. al., Foreign Trade Regimes and Economic Development, pp. 226, 242. The influences of other non-governmental associations in South Korea were not different from that of the labor unions.

25. Full text of the Special Law on National Security and Defense is in Haptong Yongam 1977, pp. 492-493.

26. Sekai, ed., Daisan Kankoku karano Tsushin, p. 130.

27. Kuznets, Economic Growth and Structure in the Republic of Korea, p. 122, Vreeland, et. al., Area Handbook for South Korea, p. 276.

28. Kuznets, Economic Growth and Structure in the Republic of Korea, pp. 121-122; and Ledyard, "A Critical View of South Korea's Condition," in Kim and Haplern, eds., The Future of the Korean Peninsula, pp. 76-77.

29. Maeda, Seoul karano Hokoku, p. 119. The Urban Industrial Mission had been active since early 1960's for the improvement of living standards of the urban poor.

30. Far Eastern Economic Review, August 27, 1987, p. 16; Nigel Disney, "Korea and the Middle East," in McCormack and Selden, eds., Korea, North and South, pp. 200-204; and Maeda, Seoul karano Hokoku, pp. 119-120. South Korea's export of labor originated in the construction contracts awarded to Korean companies in Vietnam following Seoul's decision in 1965 to deploy its troops there; and it became an important source of the inflow of foreign exchange. At the time of the incident in Saudi Arabia, Seoul's overseas work was overwhelmingly concentrated in the Middle East, where there were some 20,000 to 34,000 South Koreans; and most of them were in Saudi Arabia.

31. Maeda, Seoul karano Hokoku, pp. 119-120.

32. Sekai, ed., Daisan Kankoku karano Tsushin, pp. 12-20; and Monthly Review of Korean Affairs, I, No. 3, (July 1979), p. 4.

33. Maeda, Seoul karano Hokoku, pp. 120-122; and Sekai, ed., Daisan Kankoku karano Tsushin, pp. 12-20.

34. Tong-A Ilbo, January 15, 1980.

35. Kuznets, Economic Growth and Structure in the Republic of Korea, p. 159; and Harrison, the Widening Gulf, p. 227. The import intensity of the South Korean general production in 1970 was 14.2 percent and that of the exports in 1969 was 41.7 percent. The annual average of the import contents of the exports for the years from 1967 to 1973 was 42.5 percent. Frank, et. al., Foreign Trade Regimes and Economic Development, pp. 81-83.

36. Lee, "Major Achievements and Problems of the South Korean Economy, " in Kim and Halpern, eds., Future of the Korean Peninsula, p. 30; and Kuznets, Economic Growth and Structure in the Republic of Korea, p. 160.

37. Lee, "Major Achievements and Problems of the South Korean Economy," in Kim and Halpern, eds., Future of the Korean Peninsula, pp. 18, 30.

38. Computed by the author from statistics in Tong-A Ilbo of January 15, 1980.

39. Sekai, ed., Gunsei to Junan: Daishi Kankoku karano Tsushin (Military Rule and Tribulation: The Fourth Series

of Letters from South Korea), (Tokyo: Iwanami Shotten, 1980), pp. 37-38; and Maeda, Seoul karano Hokoku, pp. 156-159. During the 15 years from 1966 to June 1980, about 23.4 percent of Korea's exports went to Japan, while 35.8 percent of her imports came from Japan. Korean imports from Japan exceeded her exports to Japan by 1.9 times in 1975, then 1.8 times in 1976, and 2.4 times during the first six months of 1978.

40. Sunoo Harold Hakwon, American Dilemma in Asia: The Case of South Korea, (Chicago: Nelson-Hall, 1979), pp. 167-168; Weinstein and Kamiya, eds., Security of Korea, pp. 6-7; and Kim Kee Young, "American Technology and Korea's Technological Development," in Moskowitz, ed., From Patron to Partner, p. 82. It should be noted that between 1968 and 1982 Seoul imported a total of 972 cases of foreign technologies, of which 24 percent came from the United States and 52.3 percent from Japan.

41. Suh Sang Chul, "Development of A New Industry through Exports: the Electronics Industry in Korea," in Hong Won Tack and Anne O. Kreuger, eds., Trade and Development in Korea, (Seoul: Korea Development Institute, 1975), pp. 103-123.

42. Economic and Social Modernization of the Republic of Korea, p. 14.

43. Tong-A Ilbo, February 16, 1980; New York Times, October 16, 1979; and Sekai, ed., Gunsei to Junan, pp. 37-38.

44. Tong-A Ilbo, January 15, 1980; Monthly Review of Korean Affairs, I, No. 5, (September 1979), p. 5; and Maeda, Seoul karano Hokoku, p. 159.

45. New York Times, October 16, 1979; Park, "An Analysis of the Trade Behavior of American and Japanese Manufacturing Firms in Korea," in Moskowitz, ed., From Patron to Partner, p. 28; and Choe Boum Jong, "An Economic Study of the Masan Free Trade Zone," in Hong and Kreuger, eds., Trade and Development in Korea, p. 229. Korea was one of the few countries in which direct foreign investments from Japan were greater than those from the United States, which was by far the largest foreign investor in the world. In July 1974 a second free trade area was opened at Iri, a town about halfway down the west coast of Korea from Seoul.

46. Koreatown, December 31, 1979; and New York Times, October 16, 1979.

47. Harrison, The Widening Gulf, p. 225.

48. New York Times, October 16, 1979.

49. Harrison, The Widening Gulf, p. 227.

50. Economic and Social Modernization of the Republic of Korea, pp. 212, 241. As a matter of fact, three times

during the years from 1965 to 1972 agriculture, together with forestry and fishery, registered minus growth. Frank, et. al., Foreign Trade Regimes and Economic Development, p. 11.

51. Economic and Social Modernization of the Republic of Korea, p. 211.

52. Lee, "Major Achievements and Problems of the South Korean Economy," in Kim and Halpern, eds., Future of the Korean Peninsula, p. 27; and Economic and Social Modernization of the Republic of Korea, pp. 100-101, 230-231.

53. Over the years domestic production increased somewhat, but it was hardly enough to feed the growing population. Given Korea's poor land endowment (only 22 percent or 23 percent of land surface cultivatable), there was not much land left that could be developed. The rise in domestic output came about mainly through increased use of chemical fertilizers. Christian Science Monitor, March 17, 1981; and Economic and Social Modernization of the Republic of Korea, pp. 219, 222.

54. Gavan McCormack, "The South Korean Economy: GNP versus the People," in McCormack and Selden, eds., Korea, North and South, p. 103; Lee, "Major Achievements and Problems of the South Korean Economy," in Kim and Halpern, eds., Future of the Korean Peninsula, p. 27; and Economic and Social Modernization of the Republic of Korea, p. 213. South Korea, a net exporter of food under the Japanese colonial rule, had been a net importer since 1945.

55. McCormack, "South Korean Economy," in McCormack and Selden, eds., Korea, North and South, p. 103; and Moskowitz, "Limited Partners," in Moskowitz, ed., From Patron and Partner, pp. 154-157. Pressure from the growing imports of food stuff on the balance of payments became heavier after around 1966 when the virtually free imports from the U.S. under the PL 480 program began to be replaced by commercial imports. The free imports under PL 480 program ceased in 1975.

56. Tong-A Ilbo, January 1, 1980. For example, on December 27, 1979 representatives from agricultural and fishing industries met with the Minister of Agriculture and Fisheries and urged the minister to curb the imports of foreign agricultural and marine products.

57. Ho, "South Korea and Taiwan," p. 1180.

58. Vreeland, et. al., Area Handbook for South Korea, p. 248. Roughly two-thirds of the South Korean farms in the early 1970's were smaller than the average size of 2.2 acres.

59. The absolute number of rural population decreased by 882,000 between 1966 and 1970, and by 593,000 between

1970 and 1975. In 1978 there were 120,000 less people in the countryside than the previous year. Maeda, Seoul karano Hokoku, p. 184; and Monthly Review of Korean Affairs, I, No. 3, (July 1979), pp. 3, 5.

60. As a result of the exodus, farm labor became scarce and many plots were left uncultivated. Meanwhile, the rural household debt doubled between 1976 and 1978; and as of the mid-1980's the average farm family's debt stood between $2,875 and $3,750. Maeda, Seoul karano Hokoku, p. 184; and Ch'oe Il Nam, "Nongch'on un so'oe tang'hako itta" (Farm Villages are Being Alienated), Sing-Tong-A, No. 322, (July 1986), pp. 315-317.

61. Far Eastern Economic Review, May 3, 1984, p. 30. For the two decades that ended in early 1984, the population of Seoul had quadrupled to 9.5 million, which was almost a quarter of the country's 40 million people.

62. Haptong Yongam 1980, pp. 74, 214; Ho, "South Korea and Taiwan," p. 1183; New York Times, June 30, 1979; and Far Eastern Economic Review, October 13, 1978, p. 25.

63. For five years since December 1974 wholesale prices in South Korea went up 113.6 percent; but they rose only 18.5 percent in Taiwan, 49 percent in the United States, and 24.7 percent in Japan. Tong-A Ilbo, January 15, 1980; and Ho, "South Korea and Taiwan," p. 1183.

64. Han Sungjoo, "South Korea 1978: The Growing Security Dilemma," Asian Survey, XIX, No. 1, (January 1979), p. 48; and Kim, "American Technology and Korea's Technological Development," in Moskowitz, ed., From Patron to Partner, p. 78. The Seoul government moved into heavy industry in the late 1970's because South Korea was losing its competitive advantage in the labor intensive light industry in the international market. In addition, the government began to shift from labor intensive manufacturing to heavy and chemical industries to establish the foundation for a viable defense industry at a time when the United States was considering a troop withdrawal from Korea.

65. Lee Chong-Sik, "South Korea 1979: Confrontation, Assassination and Transition," Asian Survey, XX, No. 1, (January 1980), p. 65; and Ho, "South Korea and Taiwan," p. 1183.

66. Wages went up 35 percent annually for three years until the summer of 1979. New York Times, August 28, 1979.

67. Haptong Yongam 1980, pp. 174-175.

68. Koreatown, December 31, 1979; New York Times, October 28, 1979; and Tong-A Ilbo, January 2, 9, March 24, 1980. As of 1979-1980 oil fuel accounted for 60 percent of South Korea's industrial power source. And

South Korea's crude oil import bill in 1979 hit $3.1 billion, which was 15.6 percent of her $20.3 billion total import bill of the year and by far the biggest item among the imports. Koreatown, March 17, August 11, 1980; and Tong-A Ilbo, January 31, 1980.

69. In 1978 those who were officially "completely unemployed" were 3.2 percent of the total work force. But as of September 1979, the rate crept up to 4 percent of the total work force or 552,000 men. New York Times, August 28, October 28, November 25, 1979; and Haptong Yongam, 1980, pp. 175, 252.

70. Monthly Review of Korean Affairs, I, No. 4, (August 1979), p. 3; and Haptong Yongam 1980, p. 252. The number of the firms which went bankrupt in 1979 after issuing bad checks totaling $41,500 per firm was 164, of which only four firms were saved by the government. Tong-A Ilbo, February 16, 1980.

71. New York Times, November 25, 1979; Hanyang, No. 149, (July-August 1979), pp. 110-112; and Far Eastern Economic Review, April 27, 1979, pp. 104-105. The president of the Chese, which began its operation in 1974, was arrested following its collapse on suspicion of illegal concealment of company funds abroad. The president of Yulsan, which was established in 1975, was arrested on charge of embezzlement of company money. It led to resignations or arrests of the presidents of four banks that had business dealings with Yulsan.

72. New York Times, February 20, 1979.

CHAPTER 7

GATHERING POLITICAL STORM, 1978-JUNE 1979

The economic downturn, coming at the time of rising labor unrest, could not help but have political repercussions. It was especially so because President Park, lacking any credible nationalistic claim for his political leadership, had substituted economic development for it and actively utilized the high economic growth of the 1960's and 1970's as a weapon against the critics of his authoritarian rule. Thus the economic crisis brought about a crisis of the legitimacy of Park's political leadership.[1]

The Politics of 1978

It was amidst the growing social unrest that presidential as well as National Assembly elections were held in 1978. While the elections were approaching, the South Korean society seemed enveloped in despair and fear, and the country appeared to be drifting aimlessly.[2] Be that as it may, on May 18 South Korean voters (78.5 percent of the electorate) elected 2,583 deputies to the NCFU, the presidential electoral college. Interestingly, the candidates running for the NCFU (twice the number of deputies to be selected) had neither expressed their political views nor been asked of them by the voters, even though the country was faced with serious internal and external problems.[3]

On July 6 the newly elected NCFU deputies gathered at the Changch'un Gymnasium in Seoul to choose the new President. Like the first Presidential elections under the Yushin Constitution six years before, Park was the only candidate and the meeting too was chaired by Park in his capacity as the NCFU Chairman. Before the balloting, Park delivered a short speech, once again stressing the importance of what he had been saying: the "strengthening of the national power" to grapple with the threat from the North through political stability and economic growth. Following the speech, all the NCFU deputies present but one endorsed Park for another six-year presidential term, a result which hardly surprised anyone. During the entire proceedings no debates were permitted, and the whole affair was over in two hours.[4] Park was inaugurated for his second presidential term under the Yushin Constitution on December 27 amidst growing sociopolitical disturbances.

The mounting problems faced by the government were compounded by the public's lingering suspicion of the integrity of their social and political leaders because of a series of corruption scandals involving public figures. The latest of such instances was the illegal purchase by scores of influential people of apartments and the resale of some of them at large profits. The existence of this corruption had been suspected by the public since before the July presidential elections; and it was a subject of widespread gossip even while the voting was going on at the Changch'un Gymnasium.[5] Because the public were keenly interested in the affair and also because much of the substance of the scandal had already been exposed through gossips, the prosecution, unlike in earlier cases of corruption involving public figures, was able to conduct a thorough investigation of the affair and publicize the finding on July 14.[6]

The apartments, totalling 950 units, were originally built in Seoul by the Hyondae business conglomerate for its homeless employees. However, only 300 units were awarded to the company's employees; the remaining 650 units, each costing a minimum of U.S. $100,000, were turned over by Hyondae's president Chong Chu Yong to 265 influential people. Among the 265 individuals were five former or incumbent cabinet ministers, a deputy mayor of Seoul, eight national assemblymen including President Park's brother-in-law, and 24 judges and state prosecutors.[7]

To make the matter worse, these influential purchasers not only jumped the official buying queue for the Hyondae apartments but 56 of them sold their newly acquired apartments, which amounted to 40 percent of the illegally acquired, on an open market at profits of up to US $60,000 per unit. As the scandal was officially disclosed, revealing the extent of corruption in the country's Establishment, the public, though generally accepting of corruption involving their public figures with cynical calmness, were said to be stunned by the brazenness of the people implicated in the scandal. An opposition NDP assemblyman denounced it as "a bribe on a massive scale" that threatened to "pollute the very heart" of the nation.[8]

Meanwhile, the dissidents continued to castigate the government. Already in April, referring to the upcoming elections of new NCFU deputies, a critic of President Park anonymously told a New York Times reporter that the whole affair was "a sham" which was "all part of the democratic veneer that Park had laid across Korea."[9] On the eve of the July 6 presidential election by the NCFU members, the ever resolute former President Yun and his fellow dissidents announced the formation of the "National Association For Democracy" (Minju Kungmin Yonhap), while issuing in its name a manifesto severely critical of the government:

> Aiming at making the one-man rule absolutely permanent, a criminal act called "presidential election game" is being unfolded, in which competition is stirred up among the [NCFU] deputies by the use of grafts as baits and the people are stupefied and corrupted through power and money. And the consequences of such deeds are about to reveal themselves.[10]

All this while, indeed throughout the year 1978, the students, though closely watched by the police, sporadically staged anti-government demonstrations demanding political liberalization and resignation of the Park government.[11] By now the students had been aroused not only because of the usual political repression and corruption in high places but also because of the growing number of labor disputes.

The labor unrest drew the attention of students to the plight of the working people, leading them to make attempts to form a common front with the workers and farmers. The students' object was expressed in November by the Seoul National University students, who stated that "we, of the same mind as the workers and farmers, have set the goal of our struggle upon the liberation of the masses who are oppressed by the anti-national politicians and capitalists."[12] A dissident poet Ko Un, while praising the combative female workers at Tong'il Textile Company, wrote that:

143

> Now you are the teachers, leaders and pioneers.
> Neither Mr. Ham Sok Hon or Cardinal Kim Su Hwan
>   is our leader.
> You are the leaders who would lead our people.
> I too will follow you.[13]

The open voicing of such a sentiment, when the country
was troubled by a series of politico-economic strifes,
raised before the eyes of the Establishment the spectre
of a political alliance between intellectuals and laborers.

The feeling of the public toward their government
manifested itself formally in the national assembly
election held December 12, 1978. It was to choose two-
thirds of the assemblymen (154 of them) in the nation's
77 two-man electoral districts and was the second of the
kind since 1973. Because criticisms of the government
were prohibited under the Yushin Constitution, and the
scope of campaigning was narrowly circumscribed, including the airings of political views by candidates, the
election was one of "the most lackluster" in South
Korea.[14]

Despite the usual advantages of the party in power in
South Korea, the governing Democratic Republican Party
suffered a major loss. The DRP captured 68 seats with
30.9 percent of the popular vote--a decline of five seats
from 1973, despite an increase of the Assembly seats by
14 to 231, and a decrease of 7.8 percent in popular vote
from the previous election. The opposition New Democratic Party won 61 seats with 34.7 percent of the votes
cast, an increase of nine seats as well as 2.2 percent
in electoral popularity from 1973. This was the first
time in the South Korean electoral history that an opposition party outpolled the ruling party, and it was a
"shocker."[15] Independent candidates captured 22 seats
with 27.2 percent of popular vote, an addition of three
seats and 8.6 percent in voter support from 1973. The
splinter Democratic Unification Party won only three
seats, one more from the previous floor strength, but
suffered a loss of three percent in popular vote.[16]

The electoral returns made it clear that the majority
of South Koreans were dissatisfied with their government.
It was particularly so with the urban dwellers who, as
acknowledged even by President Park, were discontented
with "high consumer prices and tax burdens."[17] In the
country's six metropolitan centers the DRP candidates

garnered only 26.7 percent or only one vote out of approximately every five in contrast to 41.9 percent won by the NDP candidates. In Seoul, many of whose inhabitants were recent arrivals from the countryside and became members of an urban mass, Park's party obtained 26.6 percent of the popular votes, whereas the NDP won 60.3 percent of them. In Pusan, the former received 29.7 percent of the ballots cast and the latter 52.0 percent.[18]

Though thrashed by the opposition NDP, the ruling DRP was able to retain its dominant status in the National Assembly because of the presidential prerogative to appoint one-third of the assemblymen. And it was on December 21 that 78 Yujonghoe members were selected to serve as assemblymen, which gave the government 146 supporters in the new 231-man single chamber legislature.[19]

Park's Proposal of January 19, 1979 to P'yongyang

As he smarted under the election verdict, President Park called upon P'yongyang for an inter-Korea dialogue during his New Year press conference on January 19, 1979. Specifically Park proposed to hold a meeting of "the authorities of the South and the North at any time, any place, and any level" in order to discuss "all problems relating to...a peaceful reunification" of the divided peninsula "without any preconditions."[20] Four days later, P'yongyang countered with a proposal of its own in the name of the Central Committee of the Democratic Front For the Unification of Fatherland (DFFUF). It called for the convening of a "pan-national congress" that would bring together representatives of all political parties, social organizations, and "patriotic" individuals from the North and South to discuss the problems relating to the reunification.[21]

For the Seoul government, determined as ever to hold the dialogue only with "the responsible authorities" of the North (presumably North Korean government officials), the response from the DFFUF could not be construed as an "official" answer of the North. In addition, the DFFUF's counterproposal to conduct talks through a broadly composed pan-national congress was unacceptable to Seoul authorities.[22] Yet strangely enough, meetings of a sort took place at P'anmunjom on February 17, March 7 and 14.

The four-man delegation from the North claimed that it represented the DFFUF and reiterated its demand to hold a pan-national congress. The four men from Seoul, on the other hand, insisted that they represented the North-South Coordinating Committee (NSCC)--set up under the accord of July 4, 1972--and refused to deal with the DFFUF and opposed the holding of an all-Korea conference.[23] With neither side yielding on its own proposal just like during the Seoul-P'yongyang contacts in 1972-1973, the bizarre meetings at P'anmunjom floundered.

Furthermore, the P'yongyang representatives during the second contact on March 7 denounced the joint U.S.-South Korea military exercise--held below the Demilitarized Zone between March 1 and 17 involving 140,000 to 150,000 personnel--as an "unbearable insult" and a "provocation."[24] Under the circumstances, the latest round of Seoul-P'yongyang contacts for reunification collapsed after the third meeting on March 14.

Notably, unlike in 1972 when they had welcomed the July 4th accord with euphoria, this time the people in South Korea were apathetic to the news of the Seoul-P'yongyang talks and even cynical about the motives of President Park's overture to the North. As a matter of fact, the majority of South Koreans perceived in Park's January 19 proposal a desperate attempt to boost his sagging popularity,[25] the feat he was able to accomplish for a brief span of time in the summer of 1972.

On March 4 three prominent dissidents--Yun Po Son, Ham Sok Hon, and Kim Dae June--jointly announced the formation of National Coalition For Democracy and Unification (Minjuju'i Minjok T'ong'il ul wihan Kungmin Yonhap), while issuing a manifesto in the name of the coalition, which was composed of 14 regional organizations along with an unspecified number of individuals. The manifesto declared that the national unification was "the supreme goal" of the entire nation and that it had to be accomplished by a "democratic government" and by "relying upon the people." It denounced all the "schemes" aimed at abusing "the debates about unification" for prolonging the tenure of a regime or for any other ulterior motives.[26]

Broadening and Emboldened Opposition

146

The latest waves of the anti-government protests by the campus activists and the series of labor disputes and the NDP's strong electoral showing in 1978 all indicated that the opposition to Park's prolonged rule was spread widely among the general public. Indeed, the elderly former President Yun, while attacking the government following the start of the latest talks between the two Koreas, boasted increased strength of the opposition:

> Two or three years ago, park was on the attack and was victoriously pressing down on his opponents on human rights issues. But the boot is on the other foot now. It is we who are gathering support, and Park only imprisons and tortures unfortunate and unknown individuals and people who have no way to defend themselves.[27]

On the other hand, Kim Dae Jung, released on parole from prison in December 1978, risked another imprisonment by assailing Park's Yushin Constitution as "illegal" and insisting that "unless democracy is fully and quickly restored," South Korea might "go the way of South Vietnam and now Iran."[28] The renewed outspokenness of Kim and Yun and other dissidents at the time of socio-political tension suggested that South Korea might have reached "the beginning of a new stage in the political scene."

Further indication that South Korea was once again at "a political crossroads" was the reassertion of independence from governmental interference by certain reporters in the news media, that had been cowed by the memory of the 1975 massive layoffs of journalists as well as by Decree No. 9. Indeed since 1975 the press had studiously toed the governmental line and had been generally reticent about reporting socio-political topics frowned upon by the authorities. Under the circumstances, the press was less than fully trusted by the public as a source of information, and the prestige it was used to hold in the society was forfeited.[29]

It was this situation that finally aroused in June 1978 the reporters of the daily newspaper Chung-Ang Ilbo and its affiliates Tongyang Broadcasting Company and Tongyang Broadcasting Company-TV to issue a statement demanding editorial independence from the management. The statement asserted that "the journalists' mission and their spirit of criticism are perishing under business calculations" and that unless the news media broke away from the control of financial conglomerates, it would be unable

147

to safeguard the freedom of speech.[30] Ironically, the Chung-Ang Ilbo (carried the largest circulation in Seoul) and its two sister organs were managed by no other than Samsong Chaebol, one of the three major financial conglomerates in South Korea; and the three had been "pro-government" media.

The spirit of press independence was upheld on June 14 of the next year, 1979, by editors and reporters of the Choson Ilbo, who dared to affront the authorities by printing in the paper an article "The Wandering Farming Villages" which depicted South Korean countryside pessimistically.[31] Several days later, young reporters at the daily Kyong-Hyang Shinmun confronted their editors; they did so because they were incensed by the appearance of an article "Today's Farming Villages At a Turning Point Uplifting Korea" in the June 16 edition of their paper. To the young journalists, the article appeared to be written by their editors in order to offset the negative image projected by the Choson Ilbo article. It was a distortion of the facts; the journalists protested and exacted an apology from those responsible for the publication of the article.[32]

The incidents occurring at Seoul's major dailies and other news media indicated that the old tradition of the press as a critic of government and guardian of public morality was by no means completely dead. Rather the traditional independent spirit was still alive and well, thanks to the dedication of some journalists who were not reconciled with the status quo.

While the political storm was brewing in 1978-1979, the government was unable to express a new vision for the country's future that could have defused the situation. Instead, it continued to rely on the twin method of coercion and justification of repression in the name of the national security. Among those the government imprisoned in 1978-1979 were seven teachers of the Korean Christian Academy and 10 former reporters at the Tong-A Ilbo.[33]

The 10 journalists were among those who were discharged by the management of Tong-A Ilbo in the spring of 1975. In October 1978 they were arrested and tried for printing "illegal underground literature" concerning student demonstrations, labor disputes, and the human rights movement of the Christian activists--the subjects which were taboo for the "Establishment press." In addition, the ten asked for the "abolition" of the emergency decree No. 9, the "release of people in prison, and a guarantee of freedom of the press." For these transgressions, in August 1979 they were given prison terms up to two and a half years.[34]

The Korean Christian Academy, like the Urban Industrial Mission, was an organization devoted to helping workers and farmers, and run by "a tiny minority of Christians." Headquartered in the outskirts of Seoul and financed mainly by the West German church group, Bread For the World, the academy from 1974 on conducted seminars among farmers and workers to "raise" their "consciousness" in line with political ideals of various Social Democratic parties in Western Europe.[35]

However, the authorities--wary of the looming spectre of an alliance between intellectuals and laborers-- arrested in March 1979 seven "Christian teachers" of the academy who had been helping poor people in the crowded industrial suburbs of Seoul. The prosecution charged the seven with violation of the Anti-Communist Law, under which "giving aid and comfort to the enemy" was a crime calling for jail terms of up to seven years. In September all seven were found guilty of breaking the law because they had read "illegal" political writings and acted just like "covert Communists" sympathizing with North Korea, and were given prison terms ranging from 18 months to seven years.[36]

The New Democratic Party On the Offensive

As the resistance to Park's rule swelled amidst the severe economic downturn, the main opposition New Democratic Party went on a new anti-Park offensive. The NDP's latest assault was to be led by Kim Yong Sam, who was to regain the party's top post from Lee Ch'ol Sung at the party convention in May 1979.

As noted already, under the guidance of the Representative Councillor Lee, the NDP had been more compliant with--than critical of--the government on major political issues. Lee's outlook on key issues such as the Koreagate and national security was hardly distinguishable from that of President Park's. Lee's posture earned him the wrath of many party members, who were eager to push the party into confrontation with the government and urged Lee to toughen the party into an instrument of struggle against President Park or face ouster.[37] Indeed, Lee was ousted at the May 1979 party convention.

During the weeks preceding the party convention, Kim Yong Sam, intent on recapturing the top party post, pledged that, if elected, he would invigorate the NDP's critical spirit that had been dormant under Lee's steering. He campaigned under the slogan of "Clear-Cut Opposition Party," while contending that South Korea could face a violent unrest unless President Park softened his tight and repressive rule. Kim received support from dissidents outside the National Assembly as well as the NDP such as Yun Po Son and Kim Dae Jung, both of whom had quit the NDP in disgust with the Representative Councillor Lee's cooperation with the government.[38] The incumbent party leader Lee, on the other hand, reminded his audiences that it was under his leadership that the NDP had accomplished the unique feat of outpolling the governing DRP in the National Assembly elections of the previous December. Lee extolled the way he had led the party, and promised that he would continue to seek sociopolitical changes through "gradual reform and painstaking persuasion."[39]

When the two-day NDP congress opened on May 30, it was agreed that the party would abandon the collective leadership principle which was adopted in September 1976, and revert to the old "unitary" rule. Then the convention chose Kim Yong Sam over Lee Ch'ol Sung as the new party president by a vote of 378 to 367, an eleven vote margin out of a total of 751 ballots cast. It should be noted that because 376 votes constituted the minimum majority of 751, Kim won by a margin of only two votes over the required minimum majority.[40] Nonetheless, emerging jubilant from the successful election, Kim declared that it was "a victory of the people's rights" over "the repressive government." And he vowed to stand up and fight the Park government both inside and outside the National Assembly and to transform the NDP into "the channel" for the expression of "general public opinion."[41]

As he had repeatedly pledged, the new NDP president made his presence felt immediately by launching an intensive campaign against the Park government, and the party picked up considerable fire and strength. On June 11, during his first post-reelection policy speech addressed to foreign correspondents in Seoul, Kim declared that Park's "dictatorship" had been perpetuated under the "pretext" of preserving "national security" and of achieving "unification" and "economic growth." Denouncing Park's harsh rule as "security dictatorship," Kim implicitly stated that such a rule, far from increasing nation's security, had instead provoked widespread repugnance among the populace, thereby making the country growingly vulnerable to infiltration from the North and leaving the domestic resistance little alternative but insurrection.[42]

Kim continued saying that "genuine national security" could be founded only upon a truly democratic government to which the people could freely give their support. Kim further stated that Park's domestic governing strategy required maintaining a tension by exaggerating the danger from the North, and that Park's anti-Communist crusade was the very core of that strategy. He declared that such tactics were incompatible with--even could adversely affect--the goal of the national unification. Finally, Kim offered to meet with the P'yongyang authorities to discuss the problems relating to unification.

Kim's overture to the North received a favorable response from P'yongyang three days later; and it touched off a sharp controversy in the National Assembly between the NDP legislators and their pro-government counterparts. The pro-government assemblymen maintained that any negotiations with the North should be conducted through a single government-controlled channel. They charged that Kim's conduct was "irresponsible," implying that Kim was a Communist sympathizer, and demanded that Kim retract his proposal to P'yongyang. At about the same time, "Anti-Communist" youths assaulted the NDP headquarters inflicting injuries and damages;[43] however, Kim refused to yield. Under the circumstances, the relationship between the NDP and the government became highly tense leading to a series of clashes.

Notes

1. Ironically, shortly before the onslaught of the 1978-1979 recession, international businesses showed euphoria over the Korean economic performance. The Foreign Affairs, Business Week, Fortune, New York Times Magazine, Asian Wall Street Journal, and the World Bank issued uniformly glowing reports on South Korea's economic vitality and prospects in the summer and fall of 1977. Selden, "Introduction," in McCormack and Selden, eds., Korea, North and South, p. 38.

2. New York Times, April 18, 20, 1978.

3. Tong-A Ilbo, May 19, 1978.

4. Tong-A Ilbo, July 6, 1978; and Washington Post, July 7, 1978.

5. Ibid.

6. Tong-A Ilbo, July 15, 1978.

7. Tong-A Ilbo, July 8, 10, 14, 15, 1978.

8. Far Eastern Economic Review, July 21, 1978, p. 23; and Tong-A Ilbo, July 6, 15, 1978.

9. New York Times, April 20, 1978.

10. Maeda, Seoul karano Hokoku, p. 144.

11. New York Times, June 27, 1978; Hanyang, No. 165, (March-April 1982), pp. 65-66; and Far Eastern Economic Review, July 21, 1978, p. 23.

12. Hanyang, No. 149, (July-August 1979), p. 11.

13. Ibid.

14. Kim C. I. Eugene, "Significance of Korea's 10th National Assembly Elections," Asian Survey, XIX, No. 5, (May 1979), pp. 531-532; and New York Times, December 14, 1978. In all 72 percent of the eligible voters or some 12.9 million people cast their ballots.

15. Kim, "Significance of Korea's 10th National Assembly Elections," p. 527.

16. New York Times, December 14, 1978.

17. Maeda, Seoul karano Hokoku, p. 169.

18. New York Times, December 14, 1978; and Seoul karano Hokoku, p. 169. The six metropolitan areas were: Seoul, Pusan, Taegu, Inch'on, Kwangju, and Taejon.

19. Korea Annual 1981, p. 331.

20. Tong-A Ilbo, January 19, 1979.

21. Nodong Shinmun, January 24, 1979.

22. New York Times, February 7 and 16, 1979; and Far Eastern Economic Review, March 2, 1979, p. 24. The DFFUF was organized in P'yongyang in June 1949 as a united front organization. Concerning the DFFUF, a high-ranking Seoul official said:

> [It is] a suspicious organization which we can in no way regard as responsible authorities of the P'yongyang side and thus which we can never accept as a counterpart in a serious dialogue with us.

23. New York Times, February 21, March 14, 1979; and Far Eastern Economic Review, February 23, 1979, pp. 16-17, March 23, 1979, pp. 20-21, April 20, 1979, pp. 33-34. After the futile third contact, a highly placed Seoul official commented that "our position that inter-Korean talks should be conducted between delegations appointed by the authorities of two sides remains unchanged and is final."

24. Far Eastern Economic Review, March 23, 1979, p. 21; and Lee Chong-Sik, "Normalization of Sino-American Relations and the Korean Peninsula," in John Bryan Starr, ed., The Future of U.S.-China Relations, (New York: New York University Press, 1981), p. 103.

25. Sekai, ed., Gunsei to Junan, pp. 34-38; and Maeda, Seoul karano Hokoku, pp. 179-180.

26. Boston Globe, October 27, 1979, July 5, 1980; Sekai, ed., Gunsei to Junan, pp. 38-40; and Far Eastern Economic Review, March 23, 1979, p. 20. Kim Dae Jung, who had been serving a five-year prison term for his involvement in the anti-government manifesto of March 1, 1976, was released on parole under the general amnesty granted on December 27, 1978, which was the day of Park's inauguration for another six-year presidential term.

27. New York Times, February 20, 1979.

28. Robert Shaplen, A Turning Wheel: The Decades of the Asian Revolution As Witnessed by a Correspondent for the New Yorker, (New York: Random House, 1979), p. 275; and New York Times, February 20, 1979.

29. Lee, "Park Chongkwonha e Ollon T'anap," pp. 307-314.

30. Maeda, Seoul karano Hokoku, pp. 130-133.

153

31. Lee, "Park Chongkwonha e Ollon T'anap," p. 316; and Hanyang, No. 149, (June-August 1979), pp. 129-130. Originally Choson Ilbo planned a serial on the rural communities, but the plan was abandoned after the appearance of the first issue on June 14 due to pressures from the government.

32. Hanyang, No. 149, (July-August 1979), pp. 128-129; and Lee, "Park Chongkwonha e Ollon T'anap," p. 318.

33. Boston Globe, October 27, 1979; and New York Times, October 28, 1979. During the 10 months immediately preceding President Park's death in October 1979, some 200 opinion makers and students were arrested under Decree No. 9.

34. New York Times, August 24, 1979; Hanyang, No. 149, (July-August 1979), pp. 132-136; and Maeda, Seoul karano Hokoku, p. 132.

35. New York Times, August 26, 1979; and Sekai, ed., Gunsei to Junan, pp. 45-48.

36. New York Times, August 26, 1979; Haptong Yongam 1980, p. 265; and Sekai, ed., Gunsei to Junan, pp. 45-47, 144. In January 1980 four of the seven successfully appealed their cases and were released.

37. Haptong Yongam 1980, p. 161; and Far Eastern Economic Review, February 24, 1978, p. 23.

38. Hanyang, No. 149, (July-August 1979), p. 61; Maeda, Seoul karano Hokoku, pp. 167-169; and Sekai, ed., Gunsei to Junan, pp. 51-54.

39. New York Times, May 28, August 28, 1979; and Hanyang, No. 149, (July-August 1979), p. 61.

40. Sekai, ed., Gunsei to Junan, p. 51; and Haptong Yongam 1980, pp. 125, 161.

41. Far Eastern Economic Review, June 8, 1979, p. 13; and Sekai, ed., Gunsei to Junan, p. 50.

42. Full text of Kim Yong Sam's speech is in Hanyang, No. 149, (July-August 1979), pp. 54-59.

43. Far Eastern Economic Review, June 22, 1979, pp. 22-23; and Hanyang, No. 149, (July-August 1979), p. 133.

CHAPTER 8

DEMISE OF THE AUTHORITARIAN REGIME, JUNE-OCTOBER 1979

Carter's State Visit to Seoul

It was amidst another confrontation between Mr. Park and his critics that American President Jimmy Carter paid a two-day state visit to Seoul from June 30 to July 1, 1979.[1] While the furor over the Koreagate scandal had subsided, the thorny issues of human rights and the withdrawal of the U.S. ground combat troops--especially the latter--remained highly sensitive matters between Seoul and Washington. However, by the time he arrived in Seoul, Mr. Carter had already backtracked considerably from his original plan of phasing out all ground combat soldiers stationed in Korea by 1981-1982, amidst controversies surrounding the plan in the United States as well as among America's Asian allies abroad. The plan had been in suspense after withdrawal of a token number of troops.

President Carter's original pullout plan was unveiled at his press conference in Washington on March 9, 1977. It immediately created discomfort and even consternation in Seoul as well as among America's other East Asian allies, while causing American Congressmen and military leaders to express serious misgivings.[2] Throughout the remainder of the year and into the next, American public opinion was unfavorable to the Carter plan; and it became the object of persistent attacks from influential Congressional leaders and remained the target of "a strong and stubborn resistance from both the military and civil bureaucracy."[3] The opponents of troop pullout doubted the validity of Mr. Carter's premise that South Korea--with its image of a booming economy that would "outdistance" the North--would in time be able to repel an attack from the North without the assistance of American ground troops, provided the United States offered timely aid and naval and logistical support.

In South Korea itself, following Carter's March 1977 announcement, people expressed misgivings about U.S. air and naval aid as a sufficient deterrent against an attack from the North in view of the failure of American air and naval power to stem the tide of the Communist victory in Vietnam. And there were some reports of declining morale among South Korean soldiers stationed along the DMZ, while the tension on the Korean peninsula heightened, rather than the reverse.[4]

The lack of self-confidence and the low morale among the South Koreans, according to Korea watchers, was rooted in Seoul's "dependency" upon foreign powers for its survival and in the fact that such dependency had "eroded its will and its capacity for disciplined resistance." The same observers maintained that this "psychological malaise" was caused principally by Seoul's foreign-dependence economy that had brought on "an international demonstration effect" in which a privileged minority with foreign connections acquired a living standard that could not be reached by the majority of the population. As the disparity in the standards of living grew, it was argued, the nationalistic spirit eroded.[5] This view was echoed by former KCIA director Kim Hyong Wook during his U.S. Congressional testimony on June 22, 1977:

The North Korean people do not suffer from a high degree of international demonstration effect. The international demonstration effect in South Korea is extremely high. There are no visible gaps between the haves and the have-nots in North Korea. Therefore, I feel that the North Korean population most likely feel less relatively deprived than their southern counterparts.

I estimate that the standard of living of the ordinary people in North Korea is higher than in South Korea. Even though the average standard of living in North Korea may be lower than the standard of living of South Koreans, I believe that the people of North Korea live with a greater sense of satisfaction.

The discipline and ideological zeal of the North Korean Communists is much stronger than that of the South Koreans. In fact, I feel that there is no comparison; the will of the North Koreans is almost 100 times stronger than the will of the South Koreans.[5]

It was apparently with this comparative situation between the South and the North in mind that Major General John Singlaub, the third-ranking U.S. officer in Korea, made on May 19, 1977 the highly controversial statement to a Washington Post reporter that the withdrawal would "lead to war."[7] The statement triggered hot debates among political and military circles in the United States.

Faced with opposition from Capitol Hill as well as from his military advisers--which was rather unexpected so soon after the bitter experience of Vietnam--Mr. Carter on April 21, 1978 announced that the number of troops scheduled to be withdrawn from Korea in that year would be reduced by two-thirds. The revised timetable called for the pullout of one, instead of three, combat battalion of 800 men and 2,600 non-combat personnel in 1978. They were brought home by the end of the year despite grumblings of the opponents of the pullout.[8]

As if to send out another signal that he was rethinking his pullout decision, Carter, in his July 20 letters to Senator Majority Leader Robert Byrd and House Speaker Thomas O'Neill, stated that the withdrawals were not intended to "follow a rigid timetable not subject to modification in the light of changing circumstances" but that "our plan will be adjusted if developments so warrant."[9]

While Carter was thus wavering about his pullout plan, a new U.S. Army intelligence report--purportedly the product of a three-year study to reassess the military situation in Korea--was released early in January 1979. The report stated that North Korea, though with only half of the South's population and with one-quarter of South's GNP, had a "substantially larger military capability now" than did South Korea and had "a clear military superiority." The report concluded that the military strength of the North was "far greater" than "the earlier estimates" upon which Carter allegedly had based his initial withdrawal plan.[10]

President Carter's initial reaction to the new intelligence "re-evaluation" was one of hesitation. But then he "suddenly accepted" it and gave it as his main reason to announce on February 9 that he would be "holding in

abeyance" any further reduction of combat elements from
Korea until 1981. A Western analyst, however, claimed
that "a change" in political attitudes of the American
public (from their post-Vietnam skepticism of U.S. involvement in an Asian military conflict) rather than
military realities was a decisive factor for Carter's
decision to halt the troop pullout. The same observer
further stated that the Army intelligence report in
question provided a face-saving device for Carter, who
had long been trying to find one for shelving his idea
of a troop withdrawal.[11] Be that as it may, in May there
was a report in the American press, attributed to "a
senior White House official," that the Carter Administration had finally determined to "freeze further troop
withdrawal from South Korea."[12]

Then on July 1, in a U.S.-South Korea joint communique
issued at the end of his two-day "summit conference" with
President Park in Seoul, Carter pledged that "American
forces will continue to be stationed in Korea" and would
be prepared against "the increasing threat to peace emanating from North Korea's augmentation of its military
might" and would "solidify peace and security" in
Korea.[13] In the same communique, Carter and Park jointly
called on P'yongyang to agree to hold a three-way talk
with them in order to explore the possibility of reducing
tension on the Korean peninsula.[14]

North Korea rejected the proposal on July 10 because
it was "utterly infeasible," did not "stand to reason,"
and was "a confused proposal," while demanding that only
P'yongyang and Washington discuss the question of withdrawal of the U.S. troops from South Korea in conjunction
with replacing the 1953 Korean Armistice Agreement with
a peace treaty.[15] Finally on July 20, exactly 10 days
after the North's flat refusal and less than three weeks
after his meeting with Park in Seoul, President Carter,
through his national security advisor Zbigniew Brzezin-
ski, announced a halt to the troop withdrawal that had
been in suspense since the spring.[16]

While Carter relieved anxieties of the South Koreans
by reversing himself on the troop withdrawal plan, his
commitment to human rights problems in South Korea, as
demonstrated in July 1 joint communique, was less than
satisfactory to South Korean dissidents.[17] Although
Carter showed his concerns about individual rights during
his brief sojourn in Seoul by meeting the NDP president
Kim Yong Sam and a dozen religious leaders active in

human rights issues, Park's critics were disappointed because the question of human rights was dealt with only "lightly" in the joint communique. Only one of out of a total of 21 articles in the communique touched upon the human rights issue, mentioning briefly that the Presidents of the two countries would "pay heed to the fact that the dignity of human rights is important in all the nations."[18] Otherwise, Carter praised President Park in the communique for his leadership and Seoul's economic accomplishments, by stating that the United States would "continue to support the efforts of the Korean government to maintain peace and stability in Korea and to further its economic and social development."[19]

Apparently, President Park got all he wanted from his "summit conference" with President Carter: the halt of the troop withdrawal, which the Seoul government called "virtual nullification"[20] of Carter's original goal; and U.S. backing of the Park regime, which had been seriously eroded because of the Koreagate scandal and Park's trampling of the human rights of his critics. Indeed, Carter's Seoul visit could not have come at a more opportune time for Park, who had received a jolting blow in the National Assembly elections of the previous December.

Y.H. Incident and the Escalating Political Crisis

After Carter's departure from Seoul, the South Korean political scene, which had been relatively quiet during the American President's sojourn in Seoul, was punctuated with a series of clashes between the government and the opposition NDP. And the already tense political situation turned critical while the public's uneasiness over economic difficulties and Park's mode of rule reached an explosive point.

If Park had been buoyed by Carter's Seoul visit, he was once again vexed with the challenge of the NDP leader Kim Yong Sam, who on July 17 severely criticized the Yushin Constitution before a gathering of Catholic priests in the city of Chonju in North Cholla Province.[21] As if provoked, Park two days later warned his political foes not to question the legitimacy of the Yushin structure; and derided the persistent clamors of his critics for democratization as Chongjaeng, a derogatory term referring to factional strife among scholar-officials during the Yi Dynasty and which had an enervating effect on the stability of the dynasty. And Park accused the dissidents of indulging in "unproductive, time-wasting, and undemocratic politics."[22]

Ignoring Park's warning, NDP leader Kim on July 23 delivered from the floor of the National Assembly a scathing attack against the government.[23] Declaring that Emergency Decree No. 9 had stifled people's freedoms and that the suppression of human rights had brought on international condemnation, Kim demanded an expansion of freedom as the requisite condition for national security, called for an examination of the Constitution, and denounced the economic policies of the government. Kim asked that people should be permitted to choose their own President through direct elections, that they should be allowed to live without fear, and that a fair distribution of wealth should be permitted without interference from the authorities.

Further asserting that the strongest weapon against communism was not the restriction of freedom and that Park had been discredited by the election results of the previous December, Kim called for "a restoration of democracy" and urged Park to resign. Finally, Kim charged that the government had colluded with hoodlums to assault the NDP headquarters and harass him, an apparent reference to the incident following his June 11 speech before foreign correspondents. The speech was "a stronger public challenge to the authorities of Park than has previously been allowed."[24]

While the authorities did let the NDP president have his say in the parliament, they quickly retaliated and reaffirmed the limit of dissent that would be tolerated by arresting on July 31 Moon Pu Shik, editor of the NDP organ Minju Chonson (Democratic Front) that had printed Kim Yong Sam's speech, for violation of Decree No. 9.[25] With Moon's arrest, the government made its point clear: opposition in the National Assembly might be "tolerated to an extent not previously allowed," but there could be "no leeway" in taking that opposition to "the street" by printing critical remarks made in the National Assembly for public distribution.[26] The relations between the government and the NDP "crashed to an all-time low" following a police raid in August on the NDP headquarters, where laid-off employees of the Y.H. Industrial Company had been staging a protest demonstration over the closure of their factory.

The Y.H. Industrial Company, located in Seoul, was one of the numerous textile-apparel manufacturing plants which were the "mainstay" of South Korea's export goods and where the overwhelming majority of the workforce were young women often working in "Dickensian sweatshop" surroundings.[27] In the early 1970's the Y.H. concern had as many as 4,000 employees, but the firm soon experienced financial difficulties and continued to do so. In 1978 the company retrenched operations by reducing its workforce to only a few hundred, but it still could not overcome the problems.[28]

Early in August 1979 the plant went bankrupt and closed down, despite the protest of the employees, mostly teenage females, who insisted that they could run the shop. To make matters worse, while the company was experiencing financial troubles leading to its closure, company bills collected on its sales in the United States since the early 1970's were pocketed by the company president Chang Yong Ho, who had since gone to the United States. This infuriated the Y.H. employees, while confirming the cynical saying widely circulating in South Korea: "Enterprises may collapse but not entrepreneurs."[29]

On August 9, more than 190 former female Y.H. employees, who had earlier been forced to end their protest at the factory against its shutdown, betook themselves to the NDP headquarters to enlist assistance from the party in regaining their lost jobs. Once in the NDP building, the laid-off females staged a sit-in hunger strike. On August 11, the third night of their strike, some 1,000 steel-helmeted riot policemen stormed the NDP headquarters and dragged out the protesting women to waiting police buses, causing pandemonium.[30] In the fracas, which lasted for half an hour during the midnight-to-4 A.M. curfew, one woman protestor died. About 100 people, including NDP National Assemblymen and reporters, were injured, and the building itself was considerably damaged.[31]

The police storming of the NDP headquarters served to confirm, like the arrest of the editor of the NDP press organ Moon, that "the government would not tolerate street action even when that action was not directly related to the political system."[32] The police blamed the NDP and the female workers, who had held the "illegal meeting," for the whole incident and demanded that the NDP head Kim apologize for "provoking" the clash by providing the unemployed workers with a shelter at the party building and for drawing public attention to their plight. Subsequently, the authorities charged the "Communist-inspired" Urban Industrial Mission with having instigated the sit-in protest, and detained two clergymen, Professor Lee Moon-Yong, and the poet Ko Un.[33]

According to the government "investigation" completed on September 14, certain "impure elements" in the Urban Industrial Mission had infiltrated the young industrial workers and had taught these "impressionable" and "malleable" people about "illegal means for combat" while trying to "foster and instigate class struggle."[34] It is true that the Urban Industrial Mission was a thorn in the side of the government, for the Mission conducted classes for the workers on their rights and exposed illicit practices of employees, thereby creating strains in labor-management relations.

The police storming of the NDP headquarters created outrage in the NDP. "Park has gone out of his mind," a NDP member commented, "not all the harassments and arbitrary actions without redress in the last 18 years match up to this onslaught." Kim Yong Sam, on the other hand, stated that "this is Park's gravest act to date, [and] it is a clear contradiction to democracy."[35] Finally, on august 28, the NDP published its findings on the police raid, denouncing it as "the last-ditch writing" of the Park regime to hang onto power and contending that Park had lost "moral power" to remain in power.[36] After the Y.H. incident, the NDP broke off all its contacts with the governing DRP, bringing a total rift between the two political camps and helping precipitate South Korea's political crisis.

Political analysts were in general agreement with the NDP's appraisal of the South Korean political situation. One of them noted that the attack on the NDP building was not only a demonstration of Park's fury at his persistent critic Kim Yong Sam, but was "a much more drastic sign of Park's disquiet" about his apparently slipping grip on power due to the faltering economy that threatened to divest him of his only claim to continuing his repressive rule. Another analyst commented that the midnight police assault was an indication that Park was "out of touch with public opinion" and that he no longer knew "the limits to his powers" and could "force himself out of office by clumsy actions."[37]

While the relations between the NDP and DRP were turning bitter, three disgruntled NDP members on August 13 filed a lawsuit in the Seoul Civil District Court, asking for nullification of Kim Yong Sam's recent election as party president as well as removal of four party vice-presidents appointed by Kim. The three men, all close to Lee Ch'ol Sung and relieved of their branch party chairmanships after Kim's election, contended that Kim's victory over Lee by a margin of 11 votes (or with only two votes more than the required minimum majority) should be voided because the election was conducted improperly.[38]

Specifically, the suit argued that 22 of the 751 delegates at the NDP convention in May were ineligible to participate, because the civil rights of 16 of them were under suspension as a result of their earlier criminal convictions and the remaining six were nominated as convention delegates by one of the 16. The suit maintained that had these 22 delegates been barred from participating in the election, Kim's narrow victory over Lee might have been reversed.[39]

The court acted amazingly fast. On September 7 it upheld the suit and issued a "temporary" injunction prohibiting Kim from acting as NDP head and voiding Kim's appointments of four vice-presidents, pending a full hearing of the case. In place of Kim, the court appointed a veteran party member and the May convention chairman Chong Woon Kap as the acting head of the NDP.[40] This ruling was made by the court despite the fact that, given the secret balloting employed for the selection of the NDP president, one could not automatically assume or prove that all or any of the 22 delegates voted for Kim. In addition, the election result was accepted by the delegates of the entire convention as well as by the NDP apparatus.[41]

As early as August 17, Kim Yong Sam declared that the three NDP members were induced by the government to file the lawsuit and that it was a "conspiracy to force me out." When the court issued its injunction against Kim on September 7, Kim rejected it claiming that it was "political revenge," which was carried out "under the supervision of the Administration in an immoral effort to perpetuate the present Park regime," and he vowed to resist the injunction and continue to act as party chairman.[42]

163

Indeed, many South Koreans questioned the independence of the Seoul court that had heard the case and assumed that the government had organized the lawsuit behind the scenes.[43] They believed that it was the latest in a series of government schemes to undermine Kim, which included the detention of the NDP editor on July 31 and of the party's chief secretary on September 7, and the forcible removal of the striking girls from the party building on August 11. The government's plan to deflate Kim's spirit and muzzle him backfired. Instead of fading into silence and obscurity, Kim became more vocal in his denunciation of President Park and was catapulted into the symbol of the persecuted leader of the anti-government movement.

On September 10, just three days after the court had issued the injunction against him, Kim demanded once again during a press conference held at the NDP headquarters that the Park regime resign. Otherwise, Kim said, he would rally whatever forces he could to overthrow the Park government.[44] If there was any doubt whether he was calling for street action against the government, it was dispelled when Kim warned that it would be "their own choice," should there be a "repetition of such a tragic incident as the April 19 Student Revolution." Denouncing "the Park regime's political terrorism" as well as its "one-party dictatorship," Kim declared that he would do whatever he could "to defeat the Park regime and to save the country from terrorist politics."[45]

For some time, it had been widely speculated that the NDP chief was on the verge of arrest because of his unceasing outspoken criticism, but he continued to speak out. Kim made another sweeping anti-government remark, this time at his home, to a New York Times reporter; Kim's statement appeared in the September 16th issue of that paper. Asserting that "the time has come for the United States to make a clear choice between a basically dictatorial regime and the majority who aspire to democracy," Kim called upon the Carter Administration to end its support of Park's "minority dictatorial regime." Referring to Carter's recent Seoul visit, Kim stated that it gave Park not only "a big present" but also "the courage to wipe out the opposition by boosting his prestige." Kim also criticized the U.S. Embassy in Seoul because it was "seemingly incapable of widening its horizon and its contacts." Iran was "America's supreme diplomatic disaster," Kim asserted, in a reference to the failure of

the U.S. Embassy in Teheran to warn the Carter Administration of the pending disaster faced by the Government
of Sha Mohammed Riza Pahlev less than a year before. Kim
went on:

> Whenever I tell American officials that only by
> public and direct pressure on Park can U.S. bring
> him under control, they say that they cannot
> interfere in the domestic politics of South
> Korea. This is a phony theory. Doesn't U.S.
> have 30,000 ground troops here to protect us?
> What is this if not interference in domestic
> affairs?[46]

Within days after Kim's remarks had appeared in the New
York Times, the authorities mounted a news media campaign
to depict Kim as an American "flunkey" amidst speculations that it was only a matter of time before Park had
Kim thrown out of the National Assembly and into jail.[47]
Indeed, on October 4, pro-government Assemblymen unanimously voted for a resolution to "reprimand" Kim by
stripping him his assemblyman status. While the pro-
government legislators were voting on the resolution in
the assembly chamber, police blocked the opposition legislators from entering the chamber.[48]

The reason for Kim's expulsion was that, since his re-
election as NDP head in May, Kim had committed a series
of "rash" acts, which had brought shame on the country
and were "country-ruinous." Among Kim's "impudent" acts
were his condemnation of Park's regime as "a basically
dictatorial regime," his call on the United States to
"pressure" Park on behalf of human rights, and his declaration of his readiness to meet Kim Il Sung of North
Korea to discuss reunification.[49] And Kim lost his assembly seat; this was "the first time" in South Korea's
parliamentary history that a lawmaker was deprived of his
parliamentary seat by the National Assembly.

The months-long political crisis headed toward a new
climax when the entire body of opposition legislators
resolved to relinquish their National Assembly seats in
protest against Kim's ouster. Apparently, such a mass
protest was not anticipated by the government, given the
deep rifts within the NDP and so soon after the elections
of the previous December. Thus despite speculations by
observers that some Kim "loyalists"--perhaps as many as
40 assemblymen--might boycott the parliament, a govern-

ment spokesman had predicted that "only a few hopeless cases will resign with Kim Yong Sam, the marginals."[50]

President Park and his advisors miscalculated. On October 13, all of the 69 opposition legislators (66 of the NDP and three of the small Democratic Unification Party) tendered their resignations to protest Kim's expulsion.[51] This move on the part of the opposition lawmakers, too, like Kim's ouster, was unprecedented in the history of the South Korean National Assembly. Among the resigned were, of course, those who had been critical of Kim's leadership including his old rival Lee Ch'ol Sung and the new caretaker president Chong Woon Kap, both of whom had reportedly been looking forward to Kim's departure from the political scene since he was stripped of his NDP chairmanship by court injunction. The resignations of these men, who were personally hostile to Kim, along with the Kim "loyalists," were said to have reflected the deep disenchantment of the general public with Park's 18-year-old rule.[52]

As the political crisis in Seoul deepened, the Carter Administration repeatedly expressed displeasure with Park's handling of the opposition along with his record on human rights, which had been worsening since Carter's Seoul visit. The U.S. government condemned the forcible dispersal of the female protestors from the NDP headquarters as "excessive and brutal." Washington also showed its disapproval of Kim's ouster from the National Assembly by temporarily withdrawing its ambassador in Seoul, William H. Gleysteen Jr., for "consultations"--the first time an American ambassador had ever been recalled from South Korea in protest.[53]

The End of A Regime

The National Assembly had been an arena--indeed the only place--in South Korea under the Yushin system where criticism of the government was by and large tolerated. However, now that the opposition assemblymen had relinquished their seats and with Emergency Decree No. 9 still in force, South Koreans were completely deprived of institutionalized outlets for political grievances. This, in conjunction with the public's frustrations over the economic difficulties, made the country's political situation suffocating and explosive.

166

Already, immediately following the Y.H. incident, which could not help but agitate the college students, virtually all major universities in the country were once again rocked by massive demonstrations. On September 3, some 800 students at Kangwon University in Ch'unch'on staged an anti-government rally on the college campus until they were dispersed by the police. Notably, this was the very first such rally ever held on the premises of the university.[54] Then on September 4, approximately 2,500 students at Kyongbuk University, 2,000 students at Kemyong University, and 2,500 students at Yongnam University--all in Taegue--held anti-government rallies on their respective campuses. The Kemyong students managed to march off their campus and clashed with the police, while demanding that the government "solemnly apologize to the entire nation" for the death of the young Y.H. woman. During the same month of September, students at the elite Seoul National University held three on-campus anti-government rallies and battled the police sent to quash their gatherings.[55]

The student demonstrations of September were contained more or less within college premises by the police. However, the student demonstrations of the following month in the port city of Pusan--250 miles southeast of Seoul and the home of Kim Yong Sam--erupted into full-scale anti-government riotings engulfing virtually the entire city. The student flare-up in Pusan began on October 15, two days after the mass resignation of the opposition assemblymen, when students at Pusan University held a campus rally denouncing the lack of academic and political freedoms. The gathering was broken up by the police. The following day, there was a similar but larger demonstration again on the university grounds with some 5,000 students participating. Once again it was put down by the local police.[56] In the early evening, however, some 1,000 students from the university managed to gather in the downtown area and march through the streets.

The marching students chanted anti-government slogans such as "Remove government agents from the campus" and "Restore freedom of the press and freedom of the campus." The marchers also called for the ouster of President Park, while protesting Kim Yong Sam's expulsion from the National Assembly. Soon the students were joined by a large number of citizens. The students and citizens together battled tear-gas-firing riot police and attacked government offices far into the night with rocks and firebombs. The disturbance ended with the arrests of some of the rioters. On the evening of October 17, there were similar but even more violent riotings, in which 1,000 students from the city's Tong-A University joined forces with the Pusan University students and non-students.[57]

During the two night uprisings, 21 police booths and 18 police vehicles were destroyed and 56 policemen and an unknown number of demonstrators were injured. Also damaged and attacked by the rioters were newspaper and television offices whose reports on the demonstrations had been pro-government and biased. At the height of the melees, some 5,000 protestors were involved and at least 200 of them were arrested, of whom half were "ordinary citizens."[58] This was the most serious outbreak of anti-government demonstrations in South Korea since the student uprising of April 1960 that had brought down the government of the octogenarian Syngman Rhee after a 12-year rule.

In the wake of the massive uprisings, the government declared martial law in Pusan early in the morning of October 18, and appealed to the public to cooperate against "unruly movements threatening the foundation of constitutional rule." This was the first imposition of martial law since the Yushin Constitution had gone into effect in December 1972. Despite the martial law, a crowd estimated at 3,000 demonstrated in front of city offices on the night of October 18. On the following night, too, protestors took to the streets, now for the fourth consecutive night. The rallies of these two nights were peaceful for the most part, in contract to the violence of October 16 and 17.[59] But the continuing mustering of protestors on the streets in defiance of martial law represented an extraordinary challenge to the government.

While the police and soldiers were quelling the demonstrations in Pusan, pressures mounted on the Seoul government from Washington, which had earlier re-called its ambassador to Seoul "for consultations." President Jimmy Carter himself remonstrated against President Park's continuing suppression of political freedom and human rights, and urged Park to ease the repression. Carter did so in a letter delivered to Park on October 18 by his Secretary of Defense Harold Brown, who had arrived in Seoul the day before for a three-day ROK-U.S. annual conference on defense issues.[60]

Meanwhile, the disturbances in Pusan spread to the nearby industrial port city of Masan, 36 miles west of Pusan and with a population of 450,000 people. There, on the nights of October 18-19, approximately 2,000 people--students from the city's Kyongsang University and other residents--staged violent demonstrations. As in Pusan, the demonstrators in Masan attacked a variety of government offices including police-posts with rocks and firebombs, while battling tear-gas-firing police. The anti-government tone of the uprisings became even more poignant when one group of rioters attempted to break into the office of the ruling Democratic Republican Party in the town. After the second night of unrest, the government placed Masan and its smaller sister industrial city of Ch'angwon under "garrison decree," a form of military control similar to martial law but retaining the authority of the civil courts.[61]

The outbreaks of the disturbances in Pusan and Masan were "spontaneous" with "no evidence" that the opposition NDP had instigated them, despite Kim Yong Sam's agitations and even though his expulsion from the National Assembly helped create the bloody situations. Notably, during the riotings in the two cities the public at large gave outright support to the demonstrators by sheltering or providing drinks. This was one of the most unsettling aspects of the incidents for the government.[62] Indeed, President Park faced a crisis of magnitude, especially so because the disturbances showed signs of spreading to other cities including Seoul, and also because the pressures from the United States were unabating. For example, the New York Times, in its October 20th editorial "Karate Politics in Korea," excoriated the Park government for the series of crackdowns on the dissidents since Carter's Seoul visit several months before and condemned them as "open contempt for American public opinion."

In Seoul over 200 students at Seoul National University held a brief on-campus rally on October 19, demanding reinstatement of the students who had been expelled or suspended because of their anti-government activities. Following this latest rally, 23 participants received suspension from the university authorities. Almost simultaneously, anti-government leaflets were distributed on campuses in Taegue and Ch'ongju (75 miles southeast of Seoul). Other cities throughout the country, too, were rocked with outbreaks of, or were on the verge of outbreaks of, anti-government demonstrations.[63]

As the political tension mounted and discipline among the public broke down throughout the country, South Korea appeared to be declining into the same kind of chaos and bloodshed which had preceded the downfall of the Shah regime in Iran in January of the very same year.[64] At this critical juncture President Park was shot to death by the KCIA head Kim Jae Kyu. Park's sudden death momentarily defused the tension and halted the downward spiral of the country.

The Death of A President

Kim Jae Kyu, born in 1926 in North Kyongsang Province, was a classmate of Park's in the South Korean officers' training class that graduated in December 1946. Known as President Park's close friend and having retired from the Army with the rank of lieutenant general, Kim since 1976 had headed the KCIA, which was Park's personal instrument of political control.[65] Sometime before Park's assassination, however, Kim decided to turn against Park for a combination of personal and political reasons. Kim was apparently not the only one who was moving against Park in South Korea's ruling circles.

Indeed, as the country descended into total chaos, certain high-ranking officers in the Army, which was Park's ultimate source of power, revealed to American officials their dissatisfaction with Park's recent handlings of his critics.[66] These Korean officers reportedly said that the expulsion of Kim Yong Sam from the National Assembly had turned him into a hero, and that the way Park had tackled the riotings in Pusan and Masan had alienated the populace from the government and was not in the best security interest of the country. The Korean officers wanted more flexibility on the part of the government on human rights as a safety-valve for the release of popular frustrations, and thus, as a practical measure, for the government to retain the support of the people.[67] As if to reflect the feelings of these officers, a discord was believed to have developed within President Park's own inner ruling circle.

The political power, devolved on the President to an unprecedented degree under the Yushin Constitution, was actually exercised by a small group of still surviving former army officers who had taken part in the 1961 coup. When confronted with serious political or economic problems, these men typically attempted to divert or

170

isolate the problems rather than solve them. This very pinnacle of the government was insulated from political pressures, usually by artificial repression. This state of affairs was facilitated by the fact that the Judiciary under the Yushin Constitution was made even more subservient to the Executive than it had been, and that the role of the Legislature was relegated to a level lower than the Administration.

Eventually, a situation developed in which power was exercised not through formal political processes but rather at will by individuals, especially by those who were in day-and-night contact with the President and had his ear. The power of those who were in maximum and intimate touch with Park increased after the tragic death of Mrs. Park in 1974, as the bereaved man, suspicious of outsiders and weary of political intrigues, withdrew more and more into himself and retreated into his own entourage for advice.[68] Three men were at the center of this surrogate power structure during the last couple of years of Park's reign. They were Kim Jae Kyu, the KCIA director; Kim Ke Won, the chief of the Blue House secretariat since 1978; and Ch'a Chi Ch'ol, the head of the presidential security service since 1974.

Kim Ke Won, born in 1923, became the army chief-of-staff in 1966 and retired from the service in 1969 with the rank of four-star general. He headed the KCIA for a year (1969-1970). On the other hand, Ch'a Chi Ch'ol, born in 1934 and the youngest of the survivors among the 1961 coup makers, reached the rank of lieutenant colonel before retiring from the service in 1962. From 1963 to 1973 he served in the National Assembly as a member of the governing DRP and was Chairman of the Assembly's Home Affairs Committee for a year before being named as head of the presidential bodyguards in 1974. While serving as the president's chief bodyguard, Ch'a also played a role of confidant and policy advisor to the President.[69]

Mr. Ch'a was an intemperate and obstreperous man, who used to go to the extent of "grabbing his superiors by their necks" who disagreed with him. Thus he was "a maverick amid Korea's Confucian notions of hierarchy" and was hated by most officials who had dealings with him.[70] Especially, the personal relationship between the abrasive Ch'a and the KCIA boss Kim Jae Kyu was said to be very poor. It became worse in the final months of Park's life, as the reclusive President turned for advice more and more to Ch'a and spurned Kim's "soft" policy recom-

mendations. Reportedly, it was ch'a who had persuaded
the President to launch the head-on assault on the NDP
headquarters, to expel the NDP head from the National
Assembly, and to crack down on the demonstrators in Pusan
and Masan against "moderation" recommended by the KCIA
director. Under the circumstances, Kim felt that his
access to the President was limited and his advisory
functions nullified by Ch'a.[71]

In the wake of the Pusan riots, President Park and Ch'a
berated the KCIA chief for not forestalling the disturbances in Pusan and Masan by foreseeing them, and for his
being "soft" on the rioters.[72] Kim was said to have defended himself, explaining that the hardline approach of
Park and Ch'a had intensified the discontent of the public with the government rather than containing it, and
that a more tolerable attitude would have defused the
situation that had erupted in the uprisings in Pusan and
Masan. But the KCIA head justified himself in vain.
Under the circumstances, it was said that Kim Jae Kyu--
and probably Kim Ke Won, too--felt that Park could not
be weaned away from his habit of a hardline approach,
which aroused in the minds of many a spectre of even
greater violence, except by his removal from the political scene.[73] It was these policy disputes along with
rivalry for power as well as clashes of personalities
which led to the slaying of Park.

The place and time of his death were unwittingly set
by Park himself, who in the afternoon of October 26 had
his chief bodyguard Ch'a phone KCIA head Kim to tell that
he wanted to dine with Kim that evening. The place
picked for the meal was a small dining room at a KCIA
annex in the Blue House compound. The dinner started at
about 6:20 P.M. and was attended by the four most powerful men in South Korea: Park, Ch'a Chi Ch'ol, Kim Ke Won,
and Kim Jae Kyu who was the host. Additionally, two
young women--one a model, the other singer--were at the
gathering.[74]

As the party got under way, Ch'a poured out scathing
criticisms against the intelligence chief for his alleged
mishandling of political unrest in the southeastern port
cities. In silence, Kim listened to the abuses, but left
the room, to return shortly. Then at about 7:30 P.M. Kim
pulled out a gun and shot Ch'a, then turned the gun on
Park, killing both men. On hearing the shots, five of
Kim's KCIA agents, armed and waiting outside the room,
fired at five other Presidential guards who had accom-

panied the President, killing four and seriously wounding one. Then Kim Jae Kyu met with Army-Chief-of-Staff General Chong Sung Hwa who, by prior arrangement with the KCIA head, was dining at a restaurant close to the scene of the shootings. The two men drove off together in the same car to the Armed Forces Headquarters.[75]

Kim Ke Won, who was present at the fateful dinner and witnessed the killings, did not try to prevent them. Nor did he immediately inform the authorities of what had transpired. It was only at about 11:30 P.M.--some four hours after the killings--that he appeared at the Armed Forces Headquarters, and told Army Chief-of-Staff Chong and Minister of National Defense, Ro Jae Hyon, that the KCIA chief had slain Park. It was only then that Chong and Ro had the intelligence chief arrested.[76]

At the trials of himself and seven co-defendants before a martial law court, which began on December 4, 1979, Kim Jae Kyu claimed that he had killed Park for the sake of a "national revolution to restore liberal democracy." The prosecution, on the other hand, charged Kim and six co-defendants with the slayings of Park and five of his bodyguards as well as with attempted sedition, and the seventh co-defendant with concealment of evidence. It demanded death penalties for Kim and the six, and a prison term for the seventh. On December 20, the martial law court found all the accused guilty as claimed by the prosecution, and handed down sentences again as demanded by the prosecution. All of the death sentences except one were subsequently carried out.[77]

Notes

1. Carter arrived in Seoul in the evening of June 29, 1979.

2. Newsweek, June 6, 1977, pp. 49, 51; New York Times, April 27, 1978; and Larry A Niksch, "U.S. Troop Withdrawal From South Korea: Past Shortcomings and Future Prospects," Asian Survey, XXI, No. 3, (March 1981), pp. 328-332.

3. Ho, "Military Balance and Peace in the Korean Peninsula," p. 862; and Han, "South Korea and the United States," p. 1079.

4. Weinstein and Kamiya, eds., Security of Korea, pp. 71, 89-90; and Lee "Normalization of Sino-American Relations and the Korean Peninsula," in Starr, ed., The Future of U.S.-China Relations, p. 99.

5. Weinstein and Kamiya, eds., Security of Korea, p. 73.

6. Ibid., pp. 73-74.

7. Time, May 30, 1977, p. 14.

8. New York Times, April 22, June 30, July 21, 1979.

9. Ho, "Military Balance and Peace in the Korean Peninsula," p. 862.

10. New York Times, January 4, July 4, October 27, 1979. In 1978 the North Korea's population was 17 million and the South's population was 36.9 million, and the North's GNP was $10 billion ($570 per capita) and the South's GNP was $46 billion ($1,242 per capita).

11. Ho, "Military Balance and Peace in the Korean Peninsula," p. 862; and Far Eastern Economic Review, February 13, 1979, pp. 16-17.

12. Ho, "Military Balance and Peace in the Korean Peninsula," p. 862.

13. Haptong Yongam 1980, p. 575.

14. The proposal for tripartite conference was sent to North Korean Foreign Minister by Secretary of State Cyrus R. Vance, who accompanied Carter to Seoul. It was "the

first political communique" between Washington and P'yongyang in the 1970's. New York Times, July 4, 1979.
15. Haptong Yongam 1980, p. 129. The Armistice Agreement was signed at P'anmunjom on July 27, 1953 by China and North Korea on one hand, and the U.N. Command on the other. South Korea refused to sign the agreement.
16. New York Times, July 21, 1979.
17. New York Times, May 13, June 22, 30, 1979.
18. Hanyang, No. 149, (July-August 1979), pp. 64-65; New York Times, August 20, 1979; and Haptong Yongam 1980, p. 575.
19. Haptong Yongam 1980, p. 575.
20. Boettcher and Freedman, Gifts of Deceit, p. 330.
21. Haptong Yongam 1980, p. 161.
22. Monthly Review of Korean Affairs, I, No. 4, (August 1979), p. 1; and New York Times, July 21, 1979.
23. Lee, "South Korea 1979," pp. 62-63; and Far Eastern Economic Review, August 24, 1979, p. 13.
24. Far Eastern Economic Review, August 24, 1979, p. 13.
25. Tong-A Ilbo, December 19, 1979; and New York Times, August 24, 1979.
26. Far Eastern Economic Review, August 24, 1979, p. 13.
27. According to a study published in 1980 by the Korea Exchange Bank, the textile industry, which had served as the initial driving force behind the economic growth of South Korea since the mid-1960's, "remains one of the nation's most important industries in terms of the number of employment and the volume of exports. In 1980 the textile industry accounted for one-third of the country's total export earnings. Christian Science Monitor, March 17, 1981. According to the August 31, 1982 issue of the Asian Wall Street Journal, textiles were 30 percent of South Korea's total exports and were still the country's largest export item.
28. New York Times, August 15, 1979.
29. Sekai, ed., Gunsei to Junan, pp. 43-44, 65.
30. New York Times, August 15, 17, 20, 28, October 7, 1979; and Haptong Yongam 1980, p. 126.
31. Sekai, ed., Gunsei to Junan, pp. 65-66.
32. Far Eastern Economic Review, August 24, 1979, pp. 12-13.
33. New York Times, August 15, 20, 1979; and Haptong Yongam 1980, pp. 126-127.
34. Tong-A Ilbo, September 17, 1979; and Haptong Yongam 1980, p. 573.
35. New York Times, August 17, 1979.

36. New York Times, August 29, 1979; Tong-A Ilbo, December 19, 1979; and Sekai, ed., Gunsei to Junan, pp. 70-71. The authorities held NDP's chief secretary responsible for the publication of the findings, itself a violation of Decree No. 9, and arrested him on September 7. At the same time, the police confiscated copies of the written findings before distribution to the public, even though the Y.H. incident had been given "unprecedented" media coverage in Seoul.

37. New York Times, August 17, 1979.

38. New York Times, August 20, 1979.

39. Monthly Review of Korean Affairs, I, No. 5, (September 1979), p. 1; Sekai, ed., Gunsei to Junan, pp. 74-75; and New York Times, September 9, 1979.

40. Full text of the court injunction is in Haptong Yongam 1980, pp. 569-571.

41. Monthly Review of Korean Affairs, I, No. 5, (September 1979), p. 1.

42. Far Eastern Economic Review, September 21, 1979, p. 16; and New York Times, August 20, 1979.

43. New York Times, September 23, 1979.

44. Far Eastern Economic Review, September 21, 1979, p. 16.

45. Ibid.

46. New York Times, September 16, 1979.

47. New York Times, October 5, 1979.

48. Tong-A Ilbo, October 4, 1979.

49. Ibid.

50. Sekai, ed., Gunsei to Junan, pp. 82-83; and New York Times, October 5, 14, 1979.

51. New York Times, October 14, 15, 21, 1979. One of the NDP Assemblyman submitted his resignation from prison cell.

52. New York Times, October 15, 1979.

53. New York Times, August 15, October 7, 1979.

54. Sekai, ed., Gunsei to Junan, pp. 76-81.

55. Hanyang, No. 165, (March-April 1982), p. 66; and Monthly Review of Korean Affairs, I, No. 6, (October 1979), p. 3.

56. Sekai, ed., Gunsei to Junan, pp. 109-111; and New York Times, October 17, 1979.

57. Far Eastern Economic Review, November 2, 1979, p. 24; and New York Times, October 18, 1979.

58 Korea Annual 1981, p. 335; and Maeda, Seoul karano Hokoku, p. 192.

59. Time, October 29, 1979, p. 60; and New York Times, October 19, 20, 1979.

60. Far Eastern Economic Review, November 2, 1979, p. 26; and New York Times, October 18, 19, 1979. Ambassador

Gleysteen returned to Seoul on the same plane with Mr. Harold Brown.

61. Haptong Yongam 1980, pp. 127, 169; and New York Times, October 20, 21, 1979.

62. Maeda, Seoul karano Hokoku, p. 191; and Far Eastern Economic Review, November 2, 1979, p. 24.

63. New York Times, October 20, 21, 28, 1979; and Maeda, Seoul karano Hokoku, pp. 192-193.

64. Robert Graham, Iran: The Illusion of Power, (New York: St. Martin's Press, 1980), pp. 208-241.

65. New York Times, October 28, November 2, 7, 1979.

66. New York Times, October 28, November 2, 4, 5, 1979.

67. New York Times, November 4, 5, 1979.

68. Robert Shaplen, "Letters From South Korea," The New Yorker, November 17, 1980, p. 180.

69. Hanguk Inmyong Sajon (A Korean Biographical Dictionary), (Seoul: Haptong T'ongshinsa, 1977), pp. 35, 233; Far Eastern Economic Review, November 9, 1979, p. 15; and New York Times, October 28, December 16, 1979. During his trial for his alleged involvement in Park's assassination, Kim Ke Won testified that Ch'a routinely overstepped his legal duty of protecting the President and meddled in political decision-makings.

70. Monthly Review of Korean Affairs, I, No. 7, (November 1979), p. 13; and Shaplen, "Letters From South Korea," p. 180.

71. Far Eastern Economic Review, November 9, 1979, p. 15, December 21, 1979, pp. 20-21.

72. Once Ch'a was said to have talked about "running over" dissidents "with tanks." Newsweek, November 5, 1979; and New York Times, November 7, 1979.

73. Shaplen, "Letters From South Korea," p. 180; and New York Times, October 28, 29, December 16, 1979. On the eve of Park's death, a large number of students in Seoul secretly planned a nationwide students' strike on October 29. Park's death was believed to have aborted the planned uprising, which might have developed into a popular revolutionary upheaval. Boston Globe, October 27, 1979; and Kamiya Fuji, "The Korean Peninsula After Park Chung Hee," Asian Survey, XX, No. 7, (July 1980), p. 746.

74. Newsweek, September 1, 1980, p. 17; and New York Times, October 29, 1979.

75. New York Times, October 29, 31, November 7, 1979.

76. Maeda, Seoul karano Hokoku, p. 119; and Far Eastern Economic Review, November 9, 1979, p. 16.

77. Tong-A Ilbo, January 17, 1980; Boston Globe, December 13, 1979; and Washington Post, December 19, 1979. Kim Jae Kyu's seven co-defendants were Kim Ke Won

and six KCIA employees, of whom one received a three-year prison term for concealing evidence. The original sentences were all upheld by higher military tribunal on January 28, 1980. But the very next day, Kim Ke Won's death sentence was commuted to a life term.

CHAPTER 9

POLITICS OF INTERREGNUM, OCTOBER 1979-APRIL 1980 (1)

Political Limbo

Upon Park's death, an emergency cabinet meeting, held at the Defense Ministry at dawn on October 27, 1979, declared martial law throughout the country except the southwesternmost island province of Cheju, and appointed the army chief-of-staff Chong Sung Hwa as the martial law commander. The new martial law commander immediately issued Martial Law Decree No. 1, whereby imposing prior censorship of press, closing universities and colleges and banning all indoor and outdoor gatherings.[1] The same cabinet meeting named Ch'oe Kyu Ha (60), the late President Park's Prime Minister since 1975, as Acting President under the Yushin constitutional line of succession.

On December 6, again in accordance with provisions in the Yushin Constitution, Acting President Ch'oe was selected by the NCFU as the 10th president (or the fourth person to occupy the presidency) of the Republic of Korea. Ch'oe, the sole candidate, received the endorsement of an overwhelming majority of the electoral college (2,465 out of 2,560 votes), and was inaugurated on December 21 as the new President of South Korea.[2]

Although elevated to the very pinnacle of the highly centralized power structure erected under the Yushin Constitution, there was little to suggest in the experience of the new president that he would be a strong leader exercising fully the presidential authority. That was because President Ch'oe was a long-standing bureaucrat and had never been a politician with an independent power base. In formulating policies since becoming Acting President, Ch'oe, unlike the late President Park, typically entered into rounds of consultations with leading national figures. This opened a political vacuum in the country that had been accustomed to the late Park's 18-and-a-half years' tight reign.[3]

Notably, the KCIA, one of Park's main political instruments, had been "disgraced" and greatly declined in
prestige and power after the arrests of its director Kim
Jae Kyu and its other officials implicated in Park's
assassination.[4] Park's other pillar of power, the head
of the presidential security service, Ch'a, was killed
with Park. Also the DRP, that had been headed by Park
himself and served as a political vehicle for him, was
thrown into confusion and weakened following his death.[5]

Still more, the National Assembly--with one-third of
its members appointed by the late Park and whose role had
been no more than that of rubber stamp--had no sufficient
popular support to be able to upstage other political
institutions in the country and lead the nation. Only
the Army, a long time political rival of the now demoralized KCIA and whose position had been enhanced with the
imposition of the martial law, confronted the various
dissident groups for political supremacy.[6]

Meanwhile, the highly controversial Yushin Constitution
remained intact, even though it became clear that opposition to it was not limited to "a small group of
Westernized, Christian intellectuals," as Park's apologists had often claimed, but was widespread among the
general population.[7] According to various national
opinion surveys, conducted within the six months after
Park's death and the first polls of its kind since 1972,
an overwhelming majority of South Koreans (between 62.3
and 72.8 percent of those interviewed) favored wholesale
political reforms for the sake of "democratization."
Specifically, they wanted a presidential system of government coupled with direct elections of president and
reduction of his powers, the independence of the legislature and judiciary, and local autonomy. They hoped
that the reforms would be completed within six to nine
months.[8]

Acting President Ch'oe himself, in his nationally
televised speech on November 10, stated that the constitution would be "amended" in order to "promote democracy" and promised general elections under a new
constitution. Ch'oe reaffirmed the need for a new basic
law in his inaugural address on December 21, promising
that a new fundamental law approved by a majority of
people would be adopted within a year or so and that
general elections would be held soon thereafter.[9] Thus
for the first time since 1971, the prospects opened for

free and direct presidential elections, and it looked as if a democracy would be given a new lease on life.

Even before his inauguration on December 21, Acting President Ch'oe had removed certain repressive measures. On November 6, he released former president Yun Po Son from home arrest. On December 8, as a gesture of "national reconciliation," Ch'oe revoked Emergency Decree No. 9 and freed several hundred individuals serving prison terms for, or detained on suspicion of, violation of that decree.[10] As a result, 687 individuals won back their civil rights on February 29, 1980. Among them were 373 students, 24 professors, 42 religious leaders including Ham Sok Hon, 22 opposition politicians including Kim Dae Jung, and nine journalists.[11]

Another sign of easing political tensions was the rejection on November 5 by the National Assembly--convened by the DRP Assemblymen and their parliamentary allies Yujonghoe members only--of the mass resignation motion of the 69 opposition legislators and the immediate resolution of the opposition lawmakers to return to the Assembly.[12] On December 4 the National Assembly, according to the public demands for reforms, established a bipartisan 28-member National Assembly Special Committee on Constitutional Revision. Though the former Park's supporters dominated the Assembly, they divided the seats on the Committee equally with the opposition: seven to DRP members, seven to Yujonghoe, 13 to NDP, and one to DUP.[13] If these were hopeful signs for making a break with the vestige left behind by the late Park, there were other signs which suggested that the repressive order established by Park might outlive him.

While the majority of political prisoners had been freed with the revocation of Decree No. 9 and their civil rights restored, the fates of those held under the Anti-Communist Law and the National Security Law--both dealing with alleged Communist elements--still remained unchanged. Among them were the nation's best-known poet Kim Chi Ha who had been held under the former law, and Rev. Moon Tong Whan who had been detained under the latter law for helping the Y.H. company workers strike during the summer of 1979.[14] Also because the country was under martial law and the martial law was liberally invoked by the authorities to restrict dissident activities, the lifting of Decree No. 9 did not appreciably enhance the legal basis for human rights and, thus, did not represent significant political liberalization.[15]

As a matter of fact, despite its gesture of national reconciliation, the Ch'oe government was as relentless as the late Park government in the persecution of its critics, and the former looked increasingly like the latter. For example, the Martial Law Command on November 28 announced the sentencings of prison terms against 20 students and workers, who were arrested during the Pusan and Masan uprisings some six weeks before.[16] Similarly, Ch'oe's government continued the arrests, begun in October 1979 shortly before Park's murder, of members of the "South Korean National Liberation Front," allegedly a pro-North Korean spy ring. Late in December, the authorities charged 73 men and women of the group with hatching a plot to overthrow the government.[17]

The trials of the front members began in secret in February 1980. Early in May four of the accused were sentenced to death and the rest to various prison terms for what the authorities claimed was involvement of the condemned in one of the largest underground communist activities uncovered in South Korea. Among the four condemned to death were a former reporter and a former college professor. Many of the 69 who received prison terms were former college students who had been expelled from schools because of their activities opposing the rule of the late President Park.[18]

Notwithstanding the guilty verdicts, analysts believed that the alleged subversive scheme of the liberation front existed only in the minds of the authorities and that the only reason for the punishment of most of the over 70 people--if not all of them--was that they had fought for democratization of their country. And in the persecution of these individuals, the observers noticed a continuity in repressive political practice between the Park and Ch'oe Administrations.[19] Under the circumstances, the opponents of the still remaining Yushin order continued to be restive. They were even suspicious of the intention of the Ch'oe government concerning its promised adoption of a democratic constitution, which was very much the political focus of the day.[20]

As described already, Acting President Ch'oe promised a new constitution in his TV address of November 10. In the same speech, however, Ch'oe stated that the selection of the next president (to be done on December 6) would be conducted "according to the [Yushin] constitutional procedure," that was to say, by the NCFU (whose deputies were chosen in 1978) to prevent "suspension of the constitution" and ensure "national security" and "social stability."[21]

The government plan then meant that the choice of the new president, in which the Acting President was considered a heavy favorite, would precede constitutional change and not vice versa. It was quickly denounced by the foes of the Yushin system. Ch'oe's proposal was attacked even though he had told his national television audience that the next president should not serve out the remaining five years of late Park's presidential term but hold the office only to prepare the way for democratic elections under a new constitution. And Ch'oe's proposal became the focus of opposition to the government.[22]

Already on November 4, the NDP head Kim Yong Sam called for replacement of the Yushin Constitution with a democratic constitution within three months, and direct elections of the new President as well as the entire National Assembly members by April of 1980. Immediately after Ch'oe's November 10 TV address, the NDP issued a statement accusing the government of having "not shaken off its bad habit of making unilateral decisions and then ordering the people to follow them" under the pretext of ensuring political stability. The NDP also condemned the forthcoming pro forma presidential election by the NCFU as deliberate moves on the part of the government to guarantee the election of Ch'oe, who had been a loyal supporter of the Yushin structure created by the late Park.[23]

On November 12, the National Coalition For Democracy and Unification also--the umbrella organ for democratic movements formed in March 1979 by Kim Dae Jung and other democratic figures--issued a manifesto critical of Ch'oe's November 10th TV address. That manifesto declared that upon hearing Ch'oe's announcement, they became "greatly despondent and indignant," because it amounted "almost to a declaration that Mr. Ch'oe would virtually continue the present system in the name of maintaining order and stability" and it represented "the betrayal of the national passion for a democracy." The manifesto demanded, among other things, the abolition of martial law and the adoption of a democratic constitution within three months.[24]

Now the South Korean political scene, which had been relatively calm in the wake of Park's murder, began to heat up. On November 24, some 400 people in Seoul defied the martial law fiat forbidding unauthorized public assembly and demonstrated in support of the November 12 manifesto issued by the National Coalition For Democracy and Unification. The rally, staged under the pretext of holding a wedding ceremony at the Y.W.C.A. building in Myondong district, was the largest protest meeting held under the latest martial law. It was also the first major challenge to the authorities. The gathering was broken up by police in half an hour, and 96 participants were arrested, including the Quaker civil rights activist Ham Sok Hon and two DRP lawmakers.[25]

Three days later, again in Seoul the police took into custody another group of people, some 100 mostly Christian students, who were gathering at another downtown Christian building. On November 28, the martial law authorities in the southwestern city of Kwangju picked up 18 Christian activists, who were about to hold a clandestine anti-government meeting at a downtown Y.W.C.A. building. Among the 18 was a well-known young novelists Hwang Sok Yong.[26] The incident in Kwangju was an indication that anti-government unrest was by no means confined to Seoul. Amidst these growing anti-government agitations and swelling undertow of political tensions Acting President Ch'oe on December 6, despite the opposition protests, was elected unopposed by the NCFU to the presidency.

During his inaugural address on December 21, Ch'oe once again promised a "political evolution," stating that his government would revise the Yushin Constitution by the end of 1980 and that free elections would follow within six months thereafter. Ch'oe, however, added that the programs for "political development" would be implemented only "barring exigencies," which was construed by observers as "an ominous hedge to his promise."[27] Furthermore, Ch'oe warned against:

> internal confrontation and schisms [which] will create disorder and confusion and thus certainly result in impairing our defense capabilities and may lead to the North Koreans into miscalculation and provocative actions against the South.[28]

Analysts believed Ch'oe's warning was directed in part at the domestic opposition not to agitate for quick elimination of the remnants of the Yushin order. As such, Ch'oe's inaugural address did little to assuage the suspicion of the dissidents, who regarded Ch'oe's elec-

tion just as more "rigged politics" and perceived in his
Administration's treatment of its critics a "certain
familiarity" with the previous Park Administration.[29]

In a deliberate gesture of their dissatisfaction with
the new national leadership, the opposition NDP and DUP
boycotted Ch'oe's inauguration ceremony. The NDP denounced Ch'oe's timetable for political reforms and
called on the government to adopt a new constitution
quickly and turn over the government to the popularly
elected president by August 15, 1980, the date which was
one year sooner than the government planned.[30] Thereafter, the opposition politicians and dissidents focused
their attacks on the government's timetable for constitutional change. They were now feeling the kind of anger
they had formerly felt toward the Park government.[31]

The December 12th Intra-Army Putsch

The uncertainty concerning the direction of political
course under Ch'oe's presidency was largely due to the
attitude of the South Korean Army leaders--the ultimate
arbiters of political conflicts since the 1961 coup and
who, now that the country was under martial law, were
playing a major role in running the government. Indeed,
the "high military men," among whom were the Chairman of
the Joint Chiefs of Staff Kim Chong Hwan and the Army
Chief of Staff Chong Sung Hwa who was also the Martial
Law Commander, attended daily cabinet meetings presided
over by Acting President Ch'oe.[32]

Under the circumstances, even though the military men
were technically responsible to Acting President Ch'oe,
who ran the civilian government which was in theory in
control of the country, their political influence was
strongly felt in the power vacuum created by Park's sudden death.[33] Mr. Ch'oe's decisions about the "political
evolution" themselves were said to have been reached
after his talks with army leaders. As a matter of fact,
since Park's death generals had dominated the political
scene and had been effective rulers of the country behind
the facade of Ch'oe's civilian government.[34] The military, however, was divided over the question of the current relevancy of the Yushin system. Reportedly, the
split cropped out at the meeting of key army generals,
which was held in secret on October 29-30, 1979 at the
Ministry of National Defense.[35]

185

The "mainstream group," led by senior general officers including Martial Law Commander Chong Sung Hwa (53), expressed a "moderate" political view favoring genuine civilian rule based on a "moderate" constitution in place of the Yushin Constitution.[36] On the other hand, the "non-mainstream group"--consisting mainly of younger generals who were in their 40's and were favored by the late Park--were less tolerant of civilian rule and democracy; and they did not want to see the Yushin Constitution abandoned "precipitately" and viewed Ch'oe's proposed liberalization with skepticism. Consequently, the meeting on October 29-30 ended without reaching any decision concerning the future course of the country.[37]

Among the young "hawkish" officers was Major General Chun Doo Hwan (47). Chun was one of the fastest rising officers of the Korean Military Academy (KMA) class of 1955 (the 11th class), which was the first four-year and "competently" trained KMA class. Representative of the younger hardline officers, Chun was "a devoted disciple" of Park's authoritarian ways and was said to have owed his fast military promotion to his "fierce loyalty" to Park.[38] Notably, like many other generals, Chun came from Kyongsang Province which was also the home province of the assassinated President who personally had promoted all senior military officers.[39]

At the time of Park's murder, Chun was the head of the Defense Security Command, a military intelligence body set up by Park in the late 1960's. It was the Defense Security Command that led the official inquiry into Park's assassination. As the man in charge of the investigation of the killing of Park, which was potentially full of political implications, Chun suddenly rose to prominence. Indeed, Chun's sudden prominence was such that he occasionally appeared to "outshine" his superior and politically "moderate" General Chong Sung Hwa, who himself had been catapulted into limelight since the declaration of the martial law. It was also Chun's Army Security Command that oversaw the press censorship under the martial law, and it exercised that authority "with severity."[40]

All this while, there had been persistent speculations among political observers concerning possible motive for General Chong Sung Hwa's presence near the scene of Park's assassination. Gen. Chong, also a native of Kyongsang Province, was an old friend of Park's confessed assassin Kim Jae Kyu. He became the army-chief-of staff

186

in February 1979 on Kim's recommendation despite the opposition of Ch'a Chi Ch'ol, Park's hardline chief bodyguard who was shot to death with Park by Kim. On the eve of Park's death, Chong, like "some of the most powerful generals," developed misgivings about Park's uncompromisingly repressive policies that not only aggravated the already tense domestic political situation but also strained the relations with the United States.[41]

When President Park and his bodyguards were shot by KCIA director Kim Jae Kyu and his agents, the politically "moderate" General Chong was dining at a restaurant that was only 50 yards from the scene of the shootings and was close enough to hear the shots. General Chong had come to the restaurant at the invitation of the KCIA head who already had a dinner appointment with President Park.[42] Upon killing Park and Ch'a, Kim sped off to see General Chong in the dining room, and the two men left together in an automobile. They arrived at the Military Command Bunker, then moved to the Defense Ministry next door, where the KCIA head was arrested.

Thus from the moment of Park's death, which though catapulted him into prominence, General Chong came under suspicion. People wondered how he had come to dine so close to the assassination scene and was picked up by the assassin right after the killings. It was even speculated that General Chong was involved in a conspiracy against President Park. It was even rumored that other senior generals--all belonging to the military's politically moderate mainstream group--were also implicated in the conspiracy.[43] Such lingering suspicions provided an all too convenient pretext for the officers of the hardline non-mainstream group to make a clean sweep of their rivals in the armed forces.[44]

On the evening of December 12, 1979--barely six weeks after Park's sudden death--Major General Chun Doo Hwan and a few other younger generals discreetly commandeered some 7,500 troops from various units. They did so despite resistance by some unit commanders and also in disregard of U.S.-South Korea Combined Forces Command stipulations requiring approval from the Command for troop movement in South Korea.[45] At about 7 P.M., a force under Maj. Gen. Chun surrounded the official residence of Gen. Chong Sung Hwa. After a brief gun battle with Chong's force, the attacking troops arrested Gen. Chong unharmed. Several hours later, about 2 A.M. on December 13, Chun's rebel troops stormed the Defense

Ministry and the nearby army headquarters, subduing forces under generals allied to Gen. Chong.[46]

During the night shootouts, at least 23 combatants were wounded and 16 generals were arrested by the insurgents.[47] In addition to Gen. Chong, among the detained generals were Lt. Gen. Lee Kon Yong, Commander of the Third Army deployed between Seoul and the DMZ; Maj. Gen. Chang T'ae Wan, Commander of the Capital Garrison; and Maj. Gen. Chong Pyong Chu, Commander of the Special Forces.[48]

A terse government announcement on the morning of December 13 stated that Gen. Chong and several other unnamed generals had been detained for questioning "on new evidence" uncovered "in connection with the plot" against the late President Park. It further stated that Gen. Chong had been dismissed from the posts of army-chief-of-staff and martial law commander and that the military command structure had been reorganized.[49] Notwithstanding the official explanation, the whole affair on the night of December 12-13 was the first mutiny in the South Korean army since the pro-Communist army putsch in the Yosu-Sunch'on area in October 1948. It also revealed a serious breach of army discipline, perhaps the most shocking one in the 31-year history of the Republic of Korea.

Immediately, the victorious insurgent generals flexed their "political muscle" by winning from Ch'oe's civilian government three powerful cabinet posts--Defense, Home, and Justice--in the new 18-member cabinet, whose formation was made public on December 14. For the post of the Defense Minister, President Ch'oe was said to have originally planned to keep the incumbent minister Ro Jae Hyon who had worked closely with Ch'oe since Park's assassination. Instead, the position went to Gen. Chu Yong Bok, the former air force chief of staff who was the choice of the leading insurgents. President Ch'oe's original choice to head the Home Affairs Ministry, which controlled the national police force and provincial governments and administered election law, was dropped in favor of Gen. Kim Chong Hwan, who had been the chairman of the joint chiefs of staff.[50] Neither Chu nor Kim was involved in the coup by the generals who were their juniors in rank and years of service, and it was believed that their old positions would be filled by representatives of the newly ascendant military chiefs.

188

The Minister of Justice could order prosecutions of all lawbreakers including anti-government demonstrators when martial law was not in effect. That post was awarded to Paek Sang Ki, formerly a prosecutor and a close ally of the late Park.[51] Meanwhile, President Ch'oe, "shaken" by the December 12 insurgency, remained silent about the bloody incident; he had no comments when the list of the new cabinet was made public by a spokesman on December 14.[52]

Indeed, the authority of the Ch'oe government, which had been weak from its inception, was further diminished by the rise of the aggressive hardline younger generals through the insurrection. More than anything else, that single army rebellion revealed the weakness, or even the impotence, of the civilian government under Ch'oe.[53] It also raised serious doubts about the ability and/or willingness of the government to scrap the Yushin Constitution; it was so because the younger generals sprang the surprise move on the night of December 12-13, not only for their suspicion of the complicity of high military officers in Park's murder but also because of their aversion to dis-mantle Park's legacy.[54]

On December 18, the new military leaders issued a manifesto, providing the first glimpse into their thinking and suggesting their determination to play a decisive role in politics. It was issued in the name of the new martial law commander Gen. Lee Hee Song,[55] considered a figurehead for Gen. Chun Doo Hwan, who had emerged as the new "strongman" but had been maintaining a low profile and public silence. While maintaining that the bloody action on the night of December 12-13 was a "legal course" and thus did not disrupt "constitutional order," the manifesto conveyed a strong sense of military "Big Brother" by urging the general population to "Trust the Military" and to get on with their everyday duties. It gave the impression that the new military chiefs saw themselves as "purer" than the older generals whom they had purged.[56]

The statement demanded a thorough purification of South Korean society in order to remove the "deep-rooted obstacles" to its well-being such as the self-serving "terminologies and methods of agitation" utilized by the dissidents and the "flunkyism to curry favor with foreign elements in total oblivion to the national pride," apparently a reference to the opposition politicians who frequently had appealed for American support in fighting

189

the repression of the Park regime. Also denounced as "obstacles" were the practices of public officials who "try to rise above the people or bring about distrust" and of rich businessmen who harmed "the public interest" by violating "business ethics."[57]

Notably, in their manifesto the new military leaders stated that South Korean armed forces "should not meddle in politics" and pledged that they would return to their "original military duties" upon completion of their objectives. But such a verbal assurance to keep out of politics was contradicted by the generals' insistence that politics had to be left to "politicians who have patriotic minds and good intelligence."[58] Such an assertion revealed that the generals had their own ideas about with whom politics should be entrusted and what should be the political future of the country.

As noted earlier, the core of the new military leaders, whom some sardonically called the "Yushin generals," were graduates of the 1955 KMA class; and they banded together around the then 47-year old head of the Defense Security Command Chun Doo Hwan. Chun had received exceptional preference from the slain president, and his democratic instincts were believed not to run any deeper than those of the late Park's bodyguard Ch'a Chi Ch'ol.[59]

Not surprisingly, Chun and his cohorts opposed a dilution of the centralized power that had been Park's legacy, and were "furious" about the "political evolution" taking place under the Ch'oe government with apparent endorsement by "moderate" senior military officers. With these new "Yushin generals" now in control of the military, the prospects for democratic evolution of the country's politics appeared bleak and a ground seemed to have been laid for future conflict between the armed forces and the people who opposed Park's heritage.[60]

Realignment in Political Parties

Following the intra-army putsch of December 12, the perplexing south Korean political scene became even more so and the already uncertain path for democratization was in even greater jeopardy. Nevertheless, the country's attention was still fixed on how it would politically evolve under President Ch'oe Kyu Ha's stewardship. And

190

the debate continued on constitutional revision, the debate which was revived with the lifting of Decree No. 9.

Following the Interim President Ch'oe's November 10th announcement of his plan for political reform, both the ruling DRP and the major opposition NDP began to maneuver to strengthen their ranks for the free elections they saw ahead. While Park's sudden demise disarrayed and demoralized the DRP, it broke the chains that for many years had shackled the NDP and kept it as the perennial opposition party. Indeed, in sharp contrast to the DRP which was dispirited following its leader's ignominious murder, the NDP found itself suddenly resurging and riding the waves of public support. And for the first time since 1971, when the last popular presidential election was held, the NDP, buoyed by the prospect that the country would return to democracy, perceived a realistic chance of coming into power.[61] The NDP's optimistic estimate of its future was encouraged by its success in the 1978 national assembly elections in which the party had outpolled the ruling DRP.

The NDP earned its public support through its long struggle for the "restoration of democracy," and the party was expected to win the promised democratic elections by a wide margin.[62] Under the circumstances, the NDP, led by Kim Yong Sam, tried to avoid an extended period of finding the new leader for the country, because such an eventuality might undercut the party's popular support. Still worse, a long delay in popularly electing the new president might provoke social unrest and give the military, that was leery of turning the government over to a liberal force, an excuse to clamp down on the democratization movement then afoot. Thus the NDP demanded adoption of a new constitution and popular election of the next president by August 1980.[63]

Meanwhile, the late Park's DRP moved to recover from its initial shock and demoralization. On November 12 the party's "Steering Committee" unanimously voted Kim Jong P'il, a longtime associate of the late Park, as the party's new president in succession to Park. Prior to Kim's election, however, the Steering Committee had revised the party charter which entrusted the selection of party president with a national convention, and made it possible for the Steering Committee to choose one. The revision was approved by a "plenum" of the DRP's national assemblymen in time for the election of Kim as the new party head.[64] Obviously, Kim took advantage of the tur-

moil in the DRP which followed Park's murder and quickly
established himself as the leader of the party. Be that
as it may, the new DRP president immediately positioned
himself as a candidate in the country's presidential
election.

Because of his longtime association with the regime of
late Park, Kim Jong P'il's ascension to the country's
presidency was thought to bring very few changes and
would be the least tampering with Park's political lega-
cies. Kim appeared to be the only credible candidate
available to those who had vested interests in blocking
the transfer of power to the opposition NDP. As such,
Kim was considered by political analysts as a contender
to be reckoned with for the nation's presidency.[65]

However, as a presidential aspirant at the time when
the public mood was for change, Kim Jong P'il was not
unaware of his liability stemming from his close ties and
public's identification of him with Park's repressive
rule. Even more politically damaging, Kim--only a colonel with no independent financial means at the time of
1961 coup--had since become a wealthy man, so rich that
he had become the "incarnation" of "rags to riches"
through corruption in the minds of the public.[66] As such
and also in view of the likelihood of the opposition NDP
to win elections in case they were held soon, Kim needed
time to improve the public's perception of him and also
to revamp the dejected DRP. Thus "timing is crucial" and
it was "in Mr. Kim's interest for the whole thing to be
delayed and spun out."[67]

On December 20, 1979 Kim Jong P'il stated that it would
require more than a year before the Yushin structure
could give way in favor of a new political order. The
statement sharply contrasted with the position of the NDP
which demanded elections under a new constitution no
later than August 1980.[68] Then despite the aftermath of
the December 12th army putsch, Kim on January 22, 1980
said that the "political development is proceeding
smoothly," and admonished "the people belonging to the
party which opposes us" not to scheme a "social unrest"
to expedite political reforms. Kim now proceeded to
exonerate his ties with the Yushin system which was
introduced while he was the Premier. He claimed that it
was "an inevitable measure to overcome the difficulties
we then faced" and argued that it "is too early" to make
the ultimate judgment about the system.[69] Furthermore,
in contrast to the dissidents as well as the NDP head who

had called the killing of Park "a revolution," the DRP leader on January 28 claimed that it was "an accident."[70]

Though posed as a presidential contender, Kim Jong P'il understandably was not willing to face the test of direct popular judgment. He disclosed his preference for forgoing a popular election of president in a news conference on January 7, 1980. Kim admitted that he was "well aware that the media and the majority of the people have been demanding direct elections." Yet, as if to conjure up the late Park's hackneyed arguments, Kim asserted that such a mode of presidential selection, repeated periodically, would entail "waste" and "enormous confusion" and might even shake "the very foundation of the nation." He also declared his support for indirect election of president by the National Assembly.[71]

While endorsing an indirect presidential election by the National Assembly, Kim campaigned to generate public support for the abandonment of the current electoral system for the National Assembly (two lawmakers from each electoral district) in favor of a multi-member electoral district system. A multi-member district system could enhance the electability of DRP candidates in the urban areas where they had experienced defeats throughout Park's years in power, while fragmenting the various democratic forces. Thus a multi-member district system could lead to a DRP majority in the National Assembly, a prerequisite for Kim's election as the next president of South Korea.[72]

While Kim tried to absolve himself from the conflict of his past with his attempt to survive in a potentially democratic future with procrastination and equivocation, his DRP was convulsed with internal dissensions. The intra-party convulsion started on December 24, 1979, when 17 of the party's young national assemblymen submitted to Kim Jong P'il a resolution calling for purification (Ch'ong-P'ung) of the party. The Young Turks, all apprehensive that Kim's corrupt image might jeopardize their reelection chances, proposed that the DRP purge itself of those who had abused their positions for pecuniary and other gains and thus were morally bankrupt. The targeted purgees numbered about 10 leading DRP members including Kim Jong P'il himself.[73] The DRP leadership reacted icily to the proposal of the young "rebels," and urged them to regain their party discipline and loyalty for the sake of "party unity."[74] Yet the intra-party wranglings continued.

The dissensions in the DRP widened and multiplied when Lee Hu Rak, himself a target of the Young Turks' purification campaign and former KCIA director, fell out publicly with the DRP head Kim. During his press conference on March 24, 1980, Lee denounced Kim for occupying the party presidency without following proper procedure and for betraying President Park after his death, and demanded that Kim resign from the party presidency. Lee's remarks created a "live volcano" in the DRP.[75] However, Kim, aided by his loyal supporters, managed to head off the growing intra-party opposition. By April 7, Kim had duly expelled several of his critics from the party, including Lee and young "purificationists," thereby consolidating his grip on the party. Kim's position as the DRP leader became secure, especially so since the party had no alternative leader who could build support quickly enough to run for the presidency of the country.[76]

Not only the DRP was plagued by intra-party strife but so was the opposition NDP. Indeed, the troubles afflicting the NDP were more complex. As the leader of the major opposition party that was expected to win popular elections in the wake of Park's death, Kim Yong Sam suddenly found himself thrust onto the center stage of political scene. It was a quick change of political fortune for Kim, who had been stripped of his party presidency and ousted from the legislative chamber only a short while before. Riding on the crest of the public mood for change, Kim Yong Sam campaigned for the nation's topmost political office with the principal theme of "peaceful transfer of government," that is, the change of power through democratic elections.[77] This catch phrase had been on Kim's lips throughout the years of his fight against the late Park and reflected public sentiment that had been grated by the political violence that had toppled all previous governments in the country.

There were, however, a number of challenges Kim Yong Sam had to weather before he could be nominated as the presidential candidate of the NDP. One of them stemmed from Kim's less-than-complete control of the NDP, which could be surmised by the fact that he had won only narrowly in the election for the party presidency in May 1979. As noted already, the NDP was composed of several warring factions, the formation of which was based upon personal and/or regional ties rather than upon clear ideological stances. Some factions were led by opportunists, who had previously been prepared to cooperate with the late Park avoiding confrontation and who were now waiting to see if Kim Yong Sam could muster enough support to win the party's nomination as the presidential candidate.[78]

Under the circumstances, the chance for Kim Yong Sam to win the party's nomination was less than assured. It became even uncertain when the NDP's 1971 presidential standard-bearer Kim Dae Jung returned to active politics with his civil rights restored on February 29, 1980. Already Kim Dae Jung had indicated that he would seek the nation's highest political office and had expressed his wish to rejoin the NDP, which he spurned in 1978 disgusted with the then party leader Lee, and to seek the party's nomination.[79]

It was true that the incumbent NDP head Kim Yong Sam himself had gained political stature through his parliamentary struggle for political reforms and by helping bring about the end to the Park regime. Yet, Kim Dae Jung's political standing was also formidable, thanks to his endurance of years of Park's persecution and his uncompromising posture toward Park's repression. Particularly, because of various detentions he had been put under since the KCIA's kidnapping of him from Tokyo in 1973, Kim Dae Jung had become a symbol of "martyrdom" for political liberty. Thus, though out of active politics for some seven years, he commanded a considerable political following, and his reappearance in active politics galvanized his supporters in the NDP.[80]

While the NDP head Kim Yong Sam held to the "moderate center line" in the basically conservative NDP, Kim Dae Jung maintained the "left-of-center" views. The latter also represented the hope of "the forces in the field" (Chaeya Seryok)--the dissidents who had engaged in the "direct" struggle against the regime of the late Park and had incurred dismissals from their positions and even suffered imprisonments.[81] Thus Kim Dae Jung's plan to rejoin the NDP set the stage for potential alteration of the power configuration within the NDP, which would inevitably affect the choice of the party's standard-bearer in the anticipated presidential election.

Preliminary to his reentry into the NDP, Kim Dae Jung pressed the party to increase the membership of its 300-man Central Standing Committee, which determined party policies, by admitting about 100 new members, mostly from among the Christian dissidents and professors and lawyers

195

who had represented "the forces in the field" and for whom Kim Dae Jung had been their rallying point. The NDP president Kim was prepared to accept 100 new members on the Central Standing Committee, provided the "mainstream faction" under him nominated half of them.[82] At stake in the negotiations of the conditions for Kim Dae Jung's re-instatement was the presidency of the republic, because the NDP was expected to win the forthcoming elections. Neither side yielded on this crucial point.

The competition between the two Kims erupted into violent clashes between the followers of the two men in March 1980 at various local party conventions held to choose branch party leaderships.[83] As the delegates of the two Kims confronted and clashed, regional animosities were aroused--the animosities which had been a bane of the Korean society for centuries. Kim Yong Sam was from Kyongsang Province which was also the home province of the late Park, and Kim Dae Jung's native province was Cholla Province. The late President Park, in order to "divide and rule," had actively fostered discrimination against Cholla Province by filling his government with people from his native region and neglecting to indus-trialize Cholla area.[84]

The rivalry between the two Kims was further compli-cated by hostile remarks made by the army high command about Kim Dae Jung. Generals in the army claimed that Kim had engaged in left-wing political activities late in the 1940's and was unsuitable for the nation's pres-idency.[85] The army leaders' chilly view of Kim Dae Jung appeared to convince Kim Yong Sam that the military would never allow his rival a chance to run in presidential race; this seemed to enable the NDP head to campaign on a "positive note."[86]

Meanwhile, with neither Kim willing to step down to back the other, the negotiations for Kim Dae Jung's entry into the NDP remained deadlocked. Finally, on April 7, 1980, Kim Dae Jung declared that he would no longer seek to join the NDP. He now moved to build and consolidate his political following outside the NDP and primarily among "the forces in the field" in preparation for pres-idential elections. Kim's campaign strategy was revealed at Tonguk University on April 18, 1980, during his speech in commemoration of the April 1960 Student Uprising. He stated that "the forces in the field" represented "the very center" of "the democratic forces" in contrast to

Kim Yong Sam for whom the NDP was the focal point of democratic movement."[87]

With the failure of the two Kims to strike a compromise which might have led to the selection of a single opposition presidential candidate, the spectre loomed of the two opposition candidates competing against the DRP head Kim Jong P'il, who represented the old order, thereby leaving the field open to him.

Notes

1. New York Times, October 28, 1979; and Boston Globe, October 27, November 6, 1979. The martial law decree No. 1 was proclaimed early in the morning of October 27.

2. Tong-A Ilbo, February 26, 1980; and New York Times, December 7, 1979. It should be noted that these 2,560 NCFU deputies were among the 2,563 elected on May 8, 1978 for six-year terms.

3. Time, November 19, 1979, p. 49; and New York Times, October 27, 1979.

4. At least 80 KCIA men including all departmental heads were rounded up for questioning, and the agency became "a rather demoralized outfit." Newsweek, November 12, 1979, p. 55.

5. Far Eastern Economic Review, November 9, 1979, pp. 11-12, and December 7, 1979, p. 28.

6. Newsweek, November 5, 1979, pp. 60-61; and Time, November 19, 1979, p. 49.

7. Edward J. Baker, "Politics of South Korea," Current History, April 1982, p. 173.

8. Kang Song Chae, "80 Nyon Pom Kuk'hoe Kaehon Tuk'i e Chwajol" (The Collapse of the 1980 Spring National Assembly Special Committee on Constitutional Revision," Shin-Tong-A, No. 322, (July 1986), pp. 265, 269-270, 281; Tong-A Ilbo, January 3, 7, 1980; and Baker, "Politics in South Korea," p. 173.

9. Tong-A Ilbo, December 25, 1979.

10. Tong-A Ilbo, December 19, 1979; and Boston Globe, November 9, 1979.

11. Washington Post, March 1, 1980; and New York Times, February 29, 1980. The five-year sentence Kim Dae Jung had received in connection with the 1976 Myongdong Incident was suspended in December 1978. Since then, Kim had been under house arrest.

12. Boston Globe, November 6, 1979; and Washington Post, November 10, 1979.

13. Haptong Nyongam 1980, p. 127.

198

14. Washington Post, March 1, 1980; and New York Times, December 2, 8, 9, 1979.

15. Boston Globe, December 23, 1979.

16. New York Times, November 29, 1979. A church leader, concerned over orders by the martial law command prohibiting prayer meetings and other joint activities, said that "the government plans to restore democracy" but "its intentions have not yet penetrated down the lower-level police, the military, and the KCIA types." New York Times, November 16, 1979.

17. Sekai, ed., Gunsei to Junan, pp. 108-109.

18. Tong-A Ilbo, May 3, 12, 1980; and Sekai, ed., Gunsei to Junan, p. 163.

19. New York Times, April 16, 17, May 3, 1980.

20. New York Times, November 16, 1979, April 17, 1980.

21. Tong-A Ilbo, November 10, 1979.

22. Tong-A Ilbo, November 10, 1979; and New York Times, December 2, 1979.

23. New York Times, November 11, 23, December 2, 1979.

24. Newsweek, November 12, 1979, pp. 56, 61; and New York Times, November 13, 1979.

25. Tong-A Ilbo, December 31, 1979; and New York Times, November 25, 27, 1979. Of the 400 people who demonstrated in Seoul on November 24, 96 were apprehended and 17 of them were brought to trial before a military tribunal. On January of 1980, all 17 drew prison terms for violation of the martial law decree banning indoor and outdoor meetings. Among the convicted were the 83-year old Yun Po Son and the 78-year old Ham Sok Hon. The convicted had the right to appeal to a higher military court. Tong-A Ilbo, January 16, 28, February 1, 1980.

26. New York Times, November 25, 29, December 4, 7, 1979; and Tong-A Ilbo, February 1, 1980. Of the 100 arrested in Seoul on November 27, at least four were tried by a military court and found guilty of violating martial law decree.

27. Far Eastern Economic Review, January 4, 1980, p. 14.

28. Tong-A Ilbo, December 21, 1979.

29. Far Eastern Economic Review, January 4, 1980, p. 14; and Newsweek, December 31, 1979, p. 46.

30. Tong-A Ilbo, December 25, 26, 1979.

31. Newsweek, December 17, 1979, p. 68; and Time, December 31, 1979, p. 36.

32. New York Times, October 29, November 4, 1979.

33. Sekai, ed., Gunsei to Junan, pp. 102-103.

34. For example, the New York Times reported on October 29, 1979:

Mr. Ch'oe's office in the Capitol Building was almost deserted during the weekend and the Acting President had few callers yesterday. By contrast, the Ministry of Defense in the Yongsan section... bustled with cars and new arrivals.

35. New York Times, November 2, 1979. The conference on the second day was attended by over 50 army generals.

36. Newsweek, November 2, 1979, p. 56.

37. New York Times, October 31, November 2, 4, 1979.

38. Kamiya, "Korean Peninsula After Park Chung Hee," p. 747. At the time of Park's death, 11 of the 20 South Korean army divisions were commanded by Chun's KMA classmates. Sekai, ed., Gunsei to Junan, pp. 100-101.

39. There were over 300 generals and admirals in the armed forces, and as high as 75 percent of them were from Kongssagg Province.

40. Tong-A Ilbo, April 16, 1980; Washington Post, October 23, 1980; and New York Times, December 16, 1979.

41. Newsweek, November 12, 1979, p. 55; and New York Times, October 28, 30, November 3, 1979.

42. New York Times, November 4, 5, December 13, 1979.

43. Time, December 24, 1979, p. 39; and New York Times, December 13, 1970. Observers were surprised to learn that Chong had left at once with Kim without pausing to investigate the barrage of shots from the building where Park had been dining. They claimed that Chong supported "the plot" against Park but did not bargain for assassination.

44. Over 80 individuals were questioned in the official inquiry into the murder of Park. Among them were not only KCIA agents but also elements of the South Korean army. Newsweek, November 12, 1979, pp. 55-56.

45. Tong-A Ilbo, December 27, 1979; and Washington Post, December 24, 1979. The U.S.-South Korea Combined Forces Command was established on November 7, 1978.

46. Time, December 24, 1979, p. 39; and New York Times, December 13, 15, 16, 1979. The Defense Minister Ro Jae Hyon was trapped in his office by the attacking force but managed to escape to the U.S. Eighth Army compound across the street through a secret tunnel.

47. Three of the 23 wounded died eventually. Tong-A Ilbo, December 27, 1979; and New York Times, December 14, 15, 1979.

48. In March 1980, Gen. Chong Sung Hwa was found by a military court guilty of "tacitly" helping Kim Jae Kyu in his "insurrection" and was sentenced to a 7-year prison term. Washington Post, March 6, 1980. Major Gen. Chong Pyong Chu was said to have been wounded by one of his officers when he refused to comply with request from

Chun Doo Hwan to mobilize troops on behalf of the insurgents.

49. Boston Globe, December 13, 14, 1979; and Time, December 24, 1979, p. 39. Reportedly on December 8 or thereabout, Kim Jae Kyu gave a secret testimony at his trial implicating Chong Sung Hwa in his assassination of Park.

50. Tong-a Ilbo, December 19, 1979; and Boston Globe, December 15, 1979.

51. Tong-A Ilbo, December 19, 1979; and Washington Post, December 15, 1979. For the selection of the rest of the 18 cabinet ministers, Ch'oe was said to have been able to exercise his own authority.

52. Tong-A Ilbo, December 18, 19, 1979; and Boston Globe, December 15, 1979.

53. Chun Doo Hwan was said to have arrested Chong Sung Hwa and other generals without authorization from Ch'oe Kyu Ha, who was elected the president on December 6 and was to be inaugurated on December 21. Boston Globe, December 14, 16, 1979; and Washington Post, December 15, 1979.

54. Far Eastern Economic Review, January 4, 1980, p. 14.

55. Lee Hee Song--a 55-year old Lt. Gen. and deputy army chief of staff and also the acting head of the KCIA--was promoted to the rank of full general and appointed to the posts held by Chong Sung Hwa. Sekai, ed., Gunsei to Junan, pp. 139-140.

56. Tong-A Ilbo, December 20, 1979; and Washington Post, December 19, 1979. The new military chiefs were relatively free of business connections which were prevalent at high levels in the armed forces, and they resented the corruption and "softness" of senior generals.

57. Tong-A Ilbo, December 20, 1979; and Washington Post, December 19, 1979.

58. The December 12th coup was reportedly opposed by U.S. representatives in Seoul. The Americans were particularly upset because Gen. Chun flouted guidelines for the movement of South Korean troops under the Combined Forces Command. And the promise to stay out of politics was said to be a response to American pressure upon the generals not to interfere with reform programs of the Ch'oe Administration. Washington Post, December 19, 21, 1979; and Newsweek, December 31, 1979, p. 46.

59. Monthly Review of Korean Affairs, II, No. 1, (January 1980), p. 3; and Time, December 24, 1979, p. 39.

60. Boston Globe, December 16, 23, 1979; and Newsweek, December 31, 1979, p. 46.

61. Boston Globe, November 9, 1979; and Newsweek, November 12, 1979, p. 61.

62. Newsweek, November 12, 1979, p. 61.

63. New York Times, November 3, 6, 1979.

64. Haptong Yongam 1980, p. 159; and New York Times, November 11, 13, December 4, 1979.

65. Lee Kyong Chae and Park Ki Chong, "'Sam Kimssi' rul Umjikinun Saramdul" (The People Who Move the 'Three Kims'), Shin-Tong-A, No. 190, (June 1980), p. 138; and Far Eastern Economic Review, December 7, 1979, p. 28.

66. Monthly Review of Korean Affairs, II, No. 4, (April 1980), pp. 3-4.

67. Boston Globe, December 16, 23, 1979; and New York Times, November 13, 29, 1979.

68. Tong-A Ilbo, December 25, 1979.

69. Tong-A Ilbo, January 25, 1980.

70. Tong-A Ilbo, January 31, 1980.

71. Tong-A Ilbo, January 10, 1980.

72. Monthly Review of Korean Affairs, II, No. 1, (January 1980), p. 1; Tong-A Ilbo, March 27, 1980.

73. Tong-A Ilbo, December 28, 1979.

74. Tong-A Ilbo, December 31, 1979.

75. Tong-A Ilbo, March 21, 27, 1980; and Hanguk Ilbo, March 27, 1980.

76. Tong-A Ilbo, April 29, 1980; and Sekai, ed., Gunsei to Junan, pp. 173, 176.

77. Lee and Park, "'Sam Kimssi' rul Umjikinun Saramdul," pp. 139-141.

78. Tong-A Ilbo, March 1, 1980; and Far Eastern Economic Review, February 22, 1980, p. 21.

79. Tong-A Ilbo, March 1, 5, 1980; and Washington Post, March 1, 1980.

80. Lee and Park, "'Sam Kimssi' rul Umjikinun Saramdul," p. 145; and New York Times, March 2, 1980.

81. Im Ch'un Ung, "Chae-ya Seryok iran Nuku inga" (Who are the Forces in the Field?), Shin-Tong-A, No. 190, (June 1980), p. 160; and Washington Post, September 29, 1980.

82. Sekai, ed., Gunsei to Junan, p. 176; and Lee Chong-Sik, "South Korea In 1980: The Emergence of A New Authoritarian Order," Asian Survey, XXI, No. 1, (January 1980), p. 127.

83. Tong-A Ilbo, March 6, 21, 29, 1980; and Hanguk Ilbo, March 21, 27, 1980.

84. No industries received government encouragement to locate in Cholla Province during Park's rule. Park also gave few promotions to Cholla-born officers in the armed forces, as he surrounded himself with officers from his Kyongsang Province. Tong-A Ilbo, April 4, 1980; Washing-

202

ton Post, May 22, 1980; and Time, June 2, 1980, pp. 36-37.

85. New York Times, December 11, 1979; and Far Eastern Economic Review, April 11, 1980, p. 31.   In November 1979 the then martial law commander Chong Sung Hwa told reporters that Kim Dae Jung had a communist background and should not be considered for the post of a future head of the state.   Gen. Chun Doo Hwan and his associates too made similar spiteful comments about Kim.   Yet, when asked why Kim was allowed to compete against Park in the 1971 presidential election, they lamely replied: "Well, the situation then, with Park alive, was much different." Kim rejected the charges as "totally groundless" and added that if some of the charges were true, "how could President Park, my political enemy, not have used them against me?"

86. Far Eastern Economic Review, April 11, 1980, p. 31.

87. Im, "Chae-ya Seryok iran Nuku inga," p. 160; and Tong-A Ilbo, April 21, 1980.

CHAPTER 10

POLITICS OF INTERREGNUM, DECEMBER 1979-MAY 1980 (2)

Procrastination of the Government

While politicians were gearing up for the anticipated free elections, doubts lurked in the minds of many obser-vers concerning the ability and/or willingness of the Ch'oe Kyu Ha government to overhaul the Yushin Constitu-tion and hold elections as it had promised.

Despite his repeated pledges for "political develop-ment," President Ch'oe's commitment to liberal democracy remained as much "an unknown quantity" in Seoul's polit-ical circles as his presidential position was considered to be tenuous. This was because Ch'oe was a conciliatory career bureaucrat with some 30 years of public service, including four years as appointed Prime Minister of the late Park, and also because he was an active apologist for the Yushin system.[1] When caught between conflicting demands of the dissidents who wanted to dismantle Park's legacy quickly and the "conservative generals" who were determined to move "slowly," Ch'oe proved to be more amenable to the influence of the latter group--even to the extent of appearing that he was merely their figure-head acting out their wishes.[2]

In addition to his suspected empathy with political views of army leaders, Ch'oe was too "cautious" a man to ignore the wishes of generals, especially after the De-cember 12 putsch which had exposed the impotence of his government vis-a-vis the military for all to see. Con-sequently, the future of democratization of South Korea appeared threatened. Commenting on the political situ-ation of the time as if to make predictions of coming events, an unnamed observer said that "Korea stands be-tween the choice of 20 years of democratic rule or a return to 20 years of military rule."[3] As time went by and the Ch'oe Administration made more policy announce-ments, it became increasingly clear that the government was more disinterested than interested in altering the existing social order. Among other things, such a posture revealed in the government's economic policy statements dealing with the country's business world.

⊂ South Korean business world--long in symbiosis with Park's regime--was shaken by his assassination. Rumors flourished that several rich businessmen would be forced to "retire" because of their profiteering at the public's expense. It was believed that such developments would find a support among the majority of South Koreans who were struggling with high inflation and were angry at the sight of those individuals who were getting rich quickly because of their government connections.⁴ In response to these rumors, high government officials made a series of statements denying them.

At afternoon press conference on December 27, 1979, Lee Hahn Been, then Deputy Premier and the Chairman of the Economic Planning Board, said that "at the present moment when stability is of the utmost importance, it is the firm policy of the government not to question how business firms expanded in the past." Then in the evening appearing before a gathering of foreign businessmen in Seoul, Lee announced that a decision had been reached not to punish those businessmen who had "illicitly amassed fortunes" under the Park regime. According to Lee, the decision was made in order not to disrupt foreign credits of those entrepreneurs concerned, and it was not only his own expressed "intention" but was also in accordance with "instructions of the Prime Minister and the President."⁵ The following day a similar statement--this time reassuring not only businessmen but also public officials who had accumulated fortunes through corruption--was issued by the then Minister of Culture and Information, Lee Kyu Hyon:

> Recently, certain foreign news media have reported that rumors flourish that government agencies concerned have been preparing lists of those entrepreneurs and government officials who accumulated wealth illicitly and that they would be punished. However, I state categorically that the reports are totally groundless.⁶

While the government exonerated unscrupulous profiteers and corrupt officials of the Yushin days, President Ch'oe Kyu Ha on January 28, 1980, expressed his view on the

principle of socio-economic parity before a group of
government officials:

> As discussions have been under way recently con-
> cerning 'political development,' many people seem
> to think parity as arithmetical one or even sit-
> uational one, but this is a dangerous notion.
> What parity means is that if we work honestly and
> diligently with just minds, we shall live pros-
> perously, that is to say, parity is 'parity of
> opportunity.'

> Why do I have to live in a single-story house
> when that fellow occupies a two-story dwelling?
> Why can't I ride in a car when other people can?
> If we think the notion of parity like this, dem-
> ocratic society is bound to become an intoler-
> able place to live.[7]

Implicit in Ch'oe's assertion was that his economic policy would not be different from that of the late Park's
and that he would reject the notions of redistribution
of wealth in favor of working people that had been urged
by dissidents.

Meanwhile, concerning the constitutional amendment--
the focal point of public discussions of the time--[8]
Ch'oe announced on January 15 that he would dispatch two
constitution-study teams to Europe within a week or so.
The teams were to be composed of government officials and
constitutional scholars, and they were to go to Europe
to conduct on-the-spot examinations of the workings of
basic laws there.[9] Then during his New Year press conference on January 18, Ch'eo stated that his Administration would develop its own draft constitution and that
he had already set up a working-level panel consisting
of some 20 college professors and lawyers for the purpose.[10]

Thus the Ch'oe Administration became a late entrant
into the constitution-writing, the task which had been
carried on by the National Assembly's bipartisan Special
Committee on Constitutional Revision established in December of the previous year. On March 14, the Ch'oe
government entered "the second stage" of its program for
revision of basic law by establishing a 68-man Constitutional Amendment Deliberation Committee. The new organ,
a presidential advisory body headed by Prime Minister
Shin Hyon Hwack, was to draft the Administration's

version of constitution based on the findings of the working-level panel.[11]

The lengthy constitution-writing process proposed by the Ch'oe Administration fuelled suspicions among analysts that the government was attempting to delay reforms of the power structure which had evolved under the late Park and was still largely in place. Observers were especially suspicious because the National Assembly's Special Committee on Constitutional Revision had been working on a new basic law and the Committee was expected to complete its draft by the end of April 1980. In addition, the National Assembly had all along assumed that it was its sole prerogative to rewrite the constitution, and a spokesman of the Ch'oe Administration had also conceded such a privilege the previous fall.[12]

The skepticism about the government's willingness to carry out constitutional overhaul was editorially voice in the Tong-A Ilbo on January 18 in conjunction with the government's decision to dispatch two constitution research teams abroad:

> According to the Assembly's Special Committee Chairman Kim Su T'aek, his committee is expected to finish its draft by the end of April; so we wonder to what extent the Administration has coordinated with the Assembly's Special Committee in dispatching its study teams abroad. It would create a problem should a time gap develop between the Assembly's work on a new basic law and government's preparation of its draft based on the future researches of the study teams to be sent out.

> Secondly, we wonder if the constitutional systems of the countries where the government is about to send the study groups--such as France, West Germany, Finland, et. cet.--[13] are so unfamiliar to our specialists in the field that the teams have to be dispatched. We can't help wondering why they have to be sent at this point in time.

> We are not quite sure if the government wants to say that a place like the National Assembly's Legislative Research Bureau has no materials on the subject or has them but not sufficiently, or our own academic circles on constitutions and

political sciences have no knowledge on the subject.

Also we question the efficacy of the study teams
whose sojourn abroad would of necessity be of
short duration. We urge the government to avoid
this kind of noisy research method and find a new
one by reconsidering its decision to send study
teams abroad.

While the Ch'oe Administration's posture concerning the
constitutional change caused many raised eyebrows, the
77-man Yujonghoe National Assemblymen began to behave
"counter to political development." For the Yujonghoe,
the end of the Yushin system would mean the termination
of its own existence depriving the 77 parliamentarians
of their posts, including salaries of about $3,000 a
month plus perquisites.[14] For a few months following
Park's death, they had kept quiet; then, however, some
of them started saying "outrageous" things, showing their
"sensitivity" about the future of the over 2,500 NCFU
deputies.[15]

Yujonghoe members said that even though under a new
constitution the NCFU might lose its privileges of choosing the President of the country and "electing" one-third
of the National Assemblymen, it should be kept until June
1984 when the six-year term of its deputies elected in
1978 would expire so that the NCFU could continue to
carry out its "sacred mission of the unification of the
fatherland" as entrusted under the Yushin Constitution.[16]
They also demanded that a provision to that effect be
written as a supplementary rule of the new constitution.[17]

Dismayed and appalled, the Tong-A Ilbo on February 22,
1980 editorially denounced the contention of the Yujonghoe members:

The political evolution for liberalization and
democratization has been proceeding cautiously
and gradually, and presently a pan-nation debate
is under way to adopt a new constitution.

Although the various contentions revealed in this
process of debates are mutually different or vary
in emphasis, one thing is crystal clear: the very
consensus concerning the course of ours toward
liberalization and democratization.

From this point of view, the argument that the NCFU has to remain as a constitutional organ or other similar assertions...are...of little use. To repeat, we must realize that the NCFU or...the Yujonghoe, etc. are the very targets of obliteration in the process of constitutional revision.

[Indeed,] we can't help asking to what extent the NCFU in its seven-year existence has participated in the 'deliberation or decision concerning unification policy' other than selecting the President twice and the Yujonghoe members thrice.

In the future, the 'deliberation and decision concerning unification' should be left to the organ of people's representatives, the National Assembly, and to the President who would be elected directly by the people. As far as the issue [of unification] is concerned, the NCFU has existed in nothing but name.

The Tong-A Ilbo on February 27 once again editorially stated that "the NCFU is an organ incongruous with new constitution," and urged the Yujonghoe to "control itself" for the sake of a "smooth proceeding of the constitutional revision and the stability of political situation."

It was obvious that the Yujonghoe--like other beneficiaries of the Yushin system such as the DRP, the top military leadership, high governmental officials, etc.-- were discomforted over the prospect of a change of power, which was the likely outcome in the event of quick popular elections under a new democratic constitution. Not unlike other beneficiaries of the late Park regime, the Yujonghoe attempted to delay or minimize democratic evolution, showing how tenacious were the "remnants" of the Yushin forces in trying to retain their privileges acquired under the late Park. This left the future political course of the country in a murky and perplexing state.

The baffling state of affairs was compounded by remarks made by Prime Minister Shin Hyon Hwack, who had served as Deputy Premier and head of the Economic Planning Board under Park. On March 10, commenting on a constitutional amendment during press interview with the Sankei (a daily) in Tokyo, Premier Shin stated that "only inappropriate features [in the Yushin Constitution] should

be eliminated and appropriate ones must be retained."[18]
Mr. Shin conveyed a similar message on April 3 through
the Foreign Minister Park Tong Jin at the meeting in
Geneva, Switzerland, of the heads of Korean diplomatic
and consular officers in Africa and the Middle East.[19]
On the other hand, already at the inauguration ceremony
of the government's Constitutional Amendment Deliberation
Committee on March 14, President Ch'oe had recommended
that South Korea adopt the "binary system of government"
practiced in Finland and West Germany by choosing an
"eclectic" form of government "seasoned with presidential
system and parliamentary cabinet system."[20]

The latest statements by President Ch'oe and Premier
Shin added to the already widespread uncertainty about
what the future would hold for the country, and it was
reflected in the humorous greetings exchanged by politicians at their informal gatherings in downtown Seoul. One
would ask "What do you see ahead?" and the frequently
heard reply was that "My visibility is zero." Indeed,
for some time, the complaint that had been frequently
heard in Seoul was that "It is all very mysterious and
confusing; we do not know what is happening, or where we
are going, or why we are moving so slowly." The NDP
Chairman Kim Yong Sam himself was moved to remark that
the high officials in the Ch'oe Administration, most of
whom were prominent in the late Park regime including
President Ch'oe and Premier Shin, "haven't awakened to
the meaning of Park's tragic end."[21]

While the country's future political course remained
"opaque," an unnamed high Administration official on
April 22 issued a statement concerning government's
decision on "the timing" of a constitutional amendment
that had attracted "an extraordinary attention at home
and abroad." The anonymous official's statement, however, was issued indirectly through a high-ranking
National Assemblyman, and it was the first "concrete"
comment made by any Administration official on the subject. According to the announcement, Ch'oe's government
was resolved to hammer out a new basic charter and hold
a referendum on it by the end of October, conduct a Presidential election by March-April 1981 and a National
Assembly election by May-June, and inaugurate a new government by mid-August 1981.[22]

However, the announcement--conveyed anonymously and
circuitously--failed to address the crux of the issue:
how and by whom the constitution would be rewritten,

211

whether future Presidents would be elected directly by the people, and how elections would be conducted in a free atmosphere. Thus, the announcement did not erase the public's puzzlement over the government's intention concerning political reforms and did not change the sour mood of the country, into which it had already been driven.

Student and Labor Unrest

While the government was wavering in its promises for democratic reforms, the college students, who had seen in Park's death a rare opportunity for liberalization, became restive and stirred. They demonstrated sporadically against the legacy of the Yushin system in defiance of the martial law. Student activism was expected partly because of the reinstatement of politically active students who had been released from prisons after the abolition of Decree No. 9 and whose civil rights were restored.[23]

The nation's universities and colleges, closed or on vacation since Park's death except for a few weeks of examinations, began their new semester in the first week of March 1980. The returning students found the campus atmosphere less repressive under the direction of the new Minister of Education Ms. Kim Ok Gil, president emeritus of Ehwa Women's University and who was regarded as one of the more reform-minded members of the Cabinet. Police and the KCIA agents--placed since 1973 on campuses to monitor activities of professors and students--were removed along with riot squads; and the autonomous students' associations were revived, which had been dissolved in the aftermath of the Vietnam shock.[24]

A bureau was abolished that had funneled money to certain professors and student groups, whom the dissidents had long believed to be paid government informants. The students were also permitted to assemble and demonstrate on campuses. In another area of contention, the National Students' Defense Corps, which had been resented by students as an instrument of government control, students failed to abolish it altogether or rename it at least. However, they were permitted to elect their own officers in the corps. Perhaps, the most visible sign of revived campus liberties was the return of the professors and students who had been freed from incarceration and granted amnesty.[25] These signs of reform-measures, however, were not enough--indeed far from being sufficient--to placate the students who resented the residue of the Yushin system still remaining in the society at large.

Students held rallies on campuses initially confining their protests to school affairs and off-campus military training. The military training in question was a 10-day drilling at army bases, which was required of all male freshmen and had been controversial since its inception in 1976. Now students--freshmen as well as others--defied its continuation on the grounds that it took time from their studies, especially since they were already receiving military training on campuses.[26] In addition, students at many private universities and colleges denounced "nepotism in university foundations" and demanded resignations of the owner-presidents of these schools who had amassed fortunes by operating their academic institutions. Also clamored for by the students was the ouster of, or apologies from, the "professors of violence" and "incompetent professors," because the intellectual integrity of these professors had been compromised due to their close ties with the Park regime.[27]

The on-campus protests began in March 1980 at major universities in Seoul and Kwangju; immediately these protests spread to other colleges in the two cities as well as others, paralyzing normal operations of the schools. According to a report released by the Ministry of Education on April 18, 1980, four college presidents and deans had resigned under the waves of student pressures, another 10 presidents and deans had expressed willingness to step down, 19 universities had gone into untimely recess, and at 24 universities all-night sit-in demonstrations were being staged.[28] The campus unrest showed no sign of abating short of complete acceptance by the authorities of the students' demands: adoption of liberalizing measures on campuses along with rectification of the administration of private university foundations.

Concomitant with the nationwide student demonstrations, there broke out a series of labor-management confrontations. Demands for higher wages in the face of soaring inflation were one of the causes for the labor disputes.[29] According to statistics released by the Office of Labor Affairs on May 1, 1980, there were 809 labor protests during the first four months of the year--seven times the number in the same period of the previous year.

A rundown of their causes was: 560 delinquent payments of wages, 77 demands for wage increases, nine unfair layoffs, 37 inadequate or questionable union representations, and 126 other miscellaneous reasons. Of the protest forms resorted to by angry workers, 35 cases were walkouts, 39 sit-ins, nine demonstrations at worksites, and 726 petitions.[30]

This series of labor troubles, occurring on the heels of the campus disturbances, was virtually "unprecedented" in its "scale," shocking business leaders and government officials alike and serving to increase the edginess of the already nervous military leaders. Yet, the government, unlike during the Park's days, could not or would not actively intervene in the disturbances on behalf of management, thus in effect permitting the strikes which were still illegal. Most of the strikes were settled without serious violence largely because employers had granted wage increases as demanded by strikers. In at least one of the reported cases, a union president deemed subservient to management was ousted in addition to a pay hike.[31] However, two disputes were marked by widespread violence: one at the coal mining town of Sabuk in Kangwon Province, and the other at the Tonguk Steel Mill in Pusan.

The flare-up in Sabuk was touched off by the failure of miners to obtain a hefty 40-percent wage increase as well as to force their union president to resign who had accepted the company's offer of a 20-percent pay hike. Frustrated in their attempts to win their demands concerning the two issues, on April 21, 1980 the miners--numbering over 700--turned into an angry mob. The riot quickly escalated into a siege of the mining town as the miners repelled the police and occupied the town, and the rioters unleased their pent-up ire on the union president's family who failed to escape the siege. The incident--in which one policeman was killed and more than 50 miners and policemen were injured--came to a conclusion four days later, when the company agreed to accept the miners' demands.[32]

Then in Pusan about 1,000 workers of the Tonguk Steel Mill, who had been staging a sit-in strike at the mill asking for a 40-percent wage hike, clashed with local police for three days from April 28 on. During the skirmish, the rioters smashed or burned company property and 12 persons (one worker and 11 policemen) were seriously injured.[33] At still another company in Pusan--this time at the Tongmyong Timber Company which had gone bankrupt leaving liabilities of $106 million--some of its 3,000 former employees demonstrated early in May demanding their unpaid wages and clashing with the police.[34]

Faced with the outbursts of disturbances among laborers and students, President Ch'oe and the Martial Law Command issued a series of warnings, repeatedly stating that an "overheated political atmosphere" or "democracy's excesses" would not be tolerated. This sort of caveats, first issued no later than in January 1980, indicated that the government would not allow the country to return to pre-Park days of free wheeling street politics, namely, the tumultuous days during the short-lived Chang Myon regime.[35]

By the way, it was amidst the growing labor and campus unrest that the prosecution in Seoul was reported on April 14 to have demanded penalties against the 73 defendants of the "South Korean National Liberation Front," who in May received a variety of sentences including death sentences (as described in the previous chapter).[36] On the very same day the prosecution's demand for punishments against the 73 was reported in Seoul newspapers, Head of the Defense Security Command Chun Doo Hwan was appointed by President Ch'oe to serve concurrently as Acting Director of the KCIA.[37]

Chun's new position was an "Acting" one because the KCIA regulations not only forbade a military man on active duty from becoming its director but also prohibited its incumbent chief from holding another position. Apparently, Chun--risen to prominence after the December 12th putsch and promoted to the rank of lieutenant general in March--was unwilling to relinquish his position in the military.[38] Chun's latest appointment was "extraordinary."[39] Chun now held two extremely powerful post concurrently: one in the Defense Security Command that watched over the South Korean armed forces for political loyalty and also maintained law and order under the martial law, and the other in the KCIA, which conducted massive surveillance of political activities of civilians.

This concentration of power in the hands of one man alarmed not only the critics of the Ch'oe government but also some of its supporters. It increased the fear, first risen in the wake of the December 12 coup, that the powerful army under Chun's control, taking advantage of his twin civilian and military security roles, might force the shaky Ch'oe government to delay or even shelve the timetable for "political development."⁴⁰ Unsure of what lay ahead, presidential candidates Kim Dae Jung, who had been running as an Independent, and Kim Jong P'il either slowed down or cancelled their campaigns.⁴¹ As the public's suspicion of the future political role of the army grew, professional politicians took a backseat and college students moved to the forefront.

Indignant over government's footdragging on political reforms and alarmed by Chun's new appointment, early in May the students, who had until then largely confined their protests to intra-campus affairs, broadened their demands by including political issues. They challenged the government and the army by calling upon them to lift the martial law immediately, to abolish the controversial military drill conducted at army bases, and to abandon the Ch'oe Administration's plan to draft a new constitution and to leave the job to the National Assembly.⁴² The students rejected the assurance made on April 22 by the unnamed administration official that elections would be held in the spring-summer of 1981, because the time-table was too slow and its content too vague. They also pressed for immediate "removal" of the "remnants of the Yushin system," including Chun Doo Hwan, and for accelerated political changes. The students further demanded a guarantee of the rights of the workers and farmers and the eradication of "comprodore capitalism."⁴³ The students' concern with socio-economic issues was made more pungent because of the unprecendented wave of the labor strikes.

As they broadened their demands, the students, who hitherto had held rallies on campuses, made attempts to move into the streets to back their demands in defiance of the martial law authorities. Beginning May 1 in Seoul and several provincial capitals, students spilt into the streets in growing numbers despite the attempts of riot police to curb them.⁴⁴ Thereafter, the illegal street demonstrations were staged almost daily by students of most of the nation's colleges and universities until May 13. During the demonstrations, the students asked, among other things, for the martial law to end by May 14.⁴⁵

As if endorsing the students' demands, the major political parties, the DRP and the NDP, on May 12-13 adopted separate resolutions calling for a 20-day special session of the National Assembly beginning May 20 in order to vote for the termination of martial law. The National Assembly had the power to lift martial law by a simple majority vote. If such a motion passed, which was likely under the circumstances, President Ch'oe either had to lift martial law or present precise reasons for keeping it, something the government had been unwilling to do.[46] Meanwhile, the country's journalists too showed signs of restiveness, and some of them staged sit-in strikes between may 19 and 28 against the Martial Law Command's censorship of the press.[47]

As the strains and conflicts intensified between the government and its foes and things appeared heading toward a new climax, the government at midnight on May 13 placed troops at major government buildings and newspaper offices in Seoul amidst rumors of a North Korean attempt to take advantage of the disturbances and step up infiltration into the South. The appearance in downtown Seoul of soldiers carrying rifles engendered fear that the government might resort to tougher measures to maintain social stability. The rumors concerning the North Korean move, however, were immediately denied by American officials in Seoul, who said that they were unaware of any evidence of a new infiltration campaign on the part of P'yongyang. On the other hand, student activists charged that the rumors were started by the government to frighten them into halting their agitation.[48]

Student demonstrations erupted with renewed force on May 14, the deadline set by the students for lifting martial law. Their deadline was ignored by the government. On that day, some 50,000 to 60,000 students swarmed through the heart of Seoul and of six other major cities in the biggest turnout since the off-campus protests had broken out two weeks before. The protestors chanted anti-government slogans including the "resignation" of Chun Doo Hwan, while fighting riot police who attempted to curb the demonstrations by swinging clubs and firing tear-gas canisters. According to the police, over 600 individuals were either arrested or injured. The worst clash of the day occurred in the city of Kwangju, where students had previously been involved in bitter disputes with their college administrators over campus reforms.[49]

On the following day, May 15, the eve of the 19th anniversary of the 1961 military coup, even a larger number of students demonstrated in order to "make the day an unforgettable anniversary for the government," in the word of a student. In Seoul along, some 60,000 students packed and marched downtown streets, which drew a government tear-gas response, and fought pitched battles with policemen late into the night. During the melee, scores of students and policemen were injured. Miraculously, only one man (a policeman) was killed. Elsewhere in the country, some 40,000 students carried out protest marches.[50]

The massive demonstrations on May 15 were conducted despite news, announced by the Defense Ministry on the day, that an unknown number of North Koreans had intruded into the southern half of the DMZ early in the day and then had fled.[51] This series of student uprisings, one of the most serious in South Korea, posed the gravest challenge thus far to the government of President Ch'oe Kyu Ha. There was no way for the government and the army leadership to accede to the students' demands and still remain in power.

Confronted with the mounting crisis, Premier Shin Hyon Hwack appeared on television on the evening of May 15 to address the nation. At the time, President Ch'oe was on a week-long Middle Eastern tour to secure oil supplies.[52] Mr. Shin announced that the government would try to quicken the pace of constitutional reform "to the maximum degree to respond to the aspirations of the people." However, like previous government pledges on the issue, the Premier's promise of political concessions was vaguely worded, with no specifics provided. Also, the Premier's offer was coupled with a warning that the government would not put up indefinitely with any attempts to "destroy law and order." Asserting that the persistent violence was "paralyzing the social order" and could thwart plans for lifting martial law, Premier Shin appealed to the students and their parents to end the turmoil and restore order.[53]

Shin's television address was greeted with derision by some of the students. But it also generated speculations and even hints in Seoul that the government was preparing a package of political concessions, which would be shortly announced by President Ch'oe upon his return from the Middle Eastern trip. Many of the student leaders, who once again met in Seoul late on the night of May 15, thought that their desire for quick democratic reforms had been sufficiently conveyed to the government. They called off further street agitations, pending a government response to their demands for a firm schedule for constitutional revision and free elections. On May 16 the students returned to their campuses.[54]

It was believed that most South Koreans sympathized with the goals of student demonstrators. However, there were many who feared that the growing unrest, seemingly leading to a new social convulsion, might prompt the military to intervene openly in governmental affairs and wrest power completely from the precarious Ch'oe government, leaving unfulfilled the government's promises of transition toward democratic rule. Even some of the die-hard dissidents urged the students to go slow, while still agreeing with their aims to liberalize campus surroundings and the country's political structure.[55]

In March, Yonsei University Professor Kim Tong Kil, who had served a prison term under the late Park and was widely respected by students, said that "we should not provide an excuse for the military to come in."[56] Similar concern about the military was expressed on April 18 by Kim Dae Jung at a gathering of students in Seoul. While demanding that Ch'oe's "interim government" be ended quickly, Kim admonished his audience: "We must not present a pretext to those who do not want democracy by engendering confusion and thus jeopardizing national security."[57] It was such apprehensions that brought together on May 16 Kim Dae Jung and Kim Yong Sam, the two feuding opposition presidential candidates who had not spoken to each other for more than a month, and had the two men issue a joint communique. While endorsing the objectives of the campus agitators, the communique called on them to exercise "maximum self-restraint."[58]

The uneasiness was particularly acute in view of the students' demands, as well as the resolutions by the NDP and DRP, for the dissolution of the Martial Law Command, a vehicle whereby the army under Chun held a tight reign on the country behind Ch'oe's civilian government. It was not long before these misgivings were materialized. Indeed, the systematic and speedy actions taken subsequently by the army appeared to reveal that generals had been ready with a well-laid plan of their own concerning the basic direction of the country.

On the night of May 17, a squad of 300 riot police, backed by armed troops, launched a surprise raid against a gathering of 110 student leaders at Ehwa Women's University. The student leaders, representing 55 colleges

219

and universities, had come to the Ehwa campus to plan new
tactics pending a government response to their earlier
demands. Over 50 of them were arrested on the spot by
the police. Simultaneously, other detachments of police
and troops apprehended and jailed a number of intellectuals and professors as well as prominent politicians
including Kim Dae Jung and his associates.[59]

To the surprise of many, among the arrested politicians
were South Korea's 10 most prominent pro-government
political figures during the days of Park regime. They
included DRP chairman Kim Jong P'il, former KCIA director
Lee Hu Rak, and "pistol" Park Chong Kyu who was a chief
security officer for the late Park. Their arrests surprised many people because Chun Doo Hwan--the prime mover
behind the midnight crackdown--had been just as loyal a
follower of the late Park as these 10 individuals. Cur-
iously, NDP president Kim Young Sam was spared in the
dragnet. According to his aides, this was a calculated
move on the part of the army leaders to discredit Kim.[60]

As the army-backed government rounded up dissidents and
others on the night of May 17, the entire nation was
placed under martial law effective midnight of the same
day. Simultaneously, Martial Law Decree Number 10 was
promulgated. With the imposition of martial law throughout the country, the military, the real power behind the
precarious civilian government, became even stronger.
Under the limited form of martial law, proclaimed after
Park's death, the Cabinet headed by Premier Shin Hyon
Hwack had the "authority to run the country," and it was
to the Cabinet that the Martial Law Command made its reports through the Defense Minister.[61]

However, now under full martial law, the Martial Law
Command--headed by full general Lee Hee Song but controlled by his nominal subordinate Lieut. General Chun
Doo Hwan--was responsible directly and solely to the
President who was also the Commander-in-Chief. Thus now
the Martial Law Command in effect cut the Cabinet out of
the decision-making role of President Ch'oe and acquired
"full powers to govern" granted under Decree No. 10.[62]

The text of Decree No. 10 was reportedly presented on
the evening of May 17 to President Ch'oe without prior
consultation, who had cut his Middle Eastern trip short
and returned to Seoul the previous evening. Ch'oe had no
choice but to go along with its promulgation.[63] The
decree barred the "spreading of groundless rumors" and

"desertion" of one's own workplace and banned political meetings of any kind. Furthermore, it shut down all universities and colleges in the country and closed down the headquarters of both major political parties. The decree also closed down the National Assembly, which had been expected to open its special session on May 20 to vote on the lifting of martial law.[64]

The sudden and broad midnight crackdown led to augmentation of the power of the young generals who had taken control of the armed forces the previous December. Indeed, these young officers now gained all but the official control over the country's political life.[65] Notably, the roundups purged the South Korean political scene of prominent politicians who could impede the aspiration of Chun Doo Hwan, South Korea's behind-the-scene ruler and who was widely expected to run for the presidency of the country.[66] In retrospect, Chun's midnight crackdown of May 17-18 was his "second coup," the first being carried out some five months before; and it confirmed the worst of the fears of the dissidents that the government's promises of transition toward democratic rule would never be fulfilled.[67]

The Kwangju Uprising

The army's sweeping crackdown immediately led to a nine-day bloody uprising in the city of Kwangju, the capital of Kim Dae Jung's home province, South Cholla Province, and which in 1980 had a population of some 800,000 people. As noted in the previous chapter, during the late Park's 18-year rule, South Cholla Province was systematically neglected by the government along with North Cholla Province. The two provinces had not reaped the obvious benefits of the industrial growth enjoyed by the rest of the country.[68]

It was early in the afternoon of May 18, 1980 that students from Chonnam University and Choson University in Kwangju, angry with what had transpired in the country the previous night, began non-violent demonstrations in defiance of the new martial law edict. The protestors called for an immediate ending of martial law and a speedy implementation of democratic reforms. They also demanded the release of their detained local hero Kim Dae Jung and the ouster of the country's offstage military ruler Chun from his official posts. Quickly, the ranks of demonstrators swelled from a initial few hundred to several thousand, and they overwhelmed the police who had attempted to disperse them.[69]

Because the police were unable to control the crowd, Special Paratrooper Forces, "trained for brutal combat behind North Korean lines," were dispatched to the city late in the afternoon. Wielding bayonets, the paratroopers arrested all the students in sight who were unarmed and subjected them to an excessive, violent show of force, including public beatings with rifle butts and rippings of clothes off coeds.[70] The brutality inflamed the townspeople, leading them to join the students and turning the turmoil into an open insurrection. Using vehicles and rifles and other weapons seized in raids on local armories, the enraged student-led insurgents battled the paratroopers and the police. They also burnt down two broadcasting stations, which had given distorted reportings of the event, demolished a local tax office, and destroyed or damaged a number of police stations and government vehicles.[71]

The round of fightings reached a peak on May 21, when the special forces withdrew during the night from the city and left it in the hands of the rebels numbering more than 100,000. By then, many police officers had exchanged their uniforms for civilian clothes and vanished into the crowds. A number of bodies were lying in the streets, casualties of the four-day destructive confrontation.[72] By now, the citizens' insurrection in Kwangju had spread to the rest of the province including the town of Mokpo, 44 miles southwest of Kwangju and the birthplace of the jailed Kim Dae Jung.[73]

Once in control of Kwangju city, the rebels set up the student command post at the provincial government building; there, they stockpiled most of the captured weapons and erected barricades around the building with trucks and buses. Meanwhile, army troops dug into hills around the city presumably in preparation to retake it.[74] As the two opposing sides thus faced each other, negotiations got under way beginning May 22 to solve the crisis between the militant students in control of the city and the local martial law authorities. No sooner had the talks started than they foundered because the two sides were irreconcilable in their mutual demands. The martial law command all along insisted that the rebellion must end and the captured weapons be turned in before a serious negotiation could get under way. The rebels, on the other hand, demanded an end to martial law, immediate ouster of Chun, release of the detained students, and withdrawal of army troops from points around the city.[75]

The denouement to the civil turmoil in Kwangju came on May 27. In a predawn action, some 17,000 army troops, spearheaded by tanks, launched an attack against the city which was then held by some 200 students holed up in the provincial capital building. After three-hours of light skirmishes with the holdouts, the troops squashed the resistance ending the rebellion and bringing the troubled city under military control. Shortly thereafter, the revolts in other parts of South Cholla Province were also brought to a halt.[76] The price paid during the nine days of clashes in Kwangju was heavy. An uncounted number of people were dead or wounded along with property damages. At least 1,740 civilians were arrested by the army, and 730 of whom, mostly students, were detained for investigations, according to the authorities.[77]

The civil upheaval in Kwangju was the most serious domestic uprising in South Korea since the Korean War because, among other things, citizens had never taken up arms against their government even in the most repressive days of Syngman Rhee or Park Chung Hee. Many older Koreans could not recall civil disorders of this scale since the October 1946 revolts, which were led by leftists and directed against the American Military Government.[78] Also the Kwangju incident was the first time since the end of the Korean War for South Korean troops to turn guns against their own civilians under government order. Because the people's animosity toward the army deepened after the army's sweeping crackdown of May 17 and intensified following the reign of terror that had descended upon the city of Kwangju, analysts of Korean politics pointed out that the tragedy aggravated antagonisms already existing between the army and the people since around the December 12th putsch.[79]

Still more, the nine-day bloody confrontation in Kwangju was believed to have intensified the regional animosity that had existed between Kyongsang Provinces and Cholla Provinces because of the protagonists involved in the incident.[80] Furthermore, the suppression of the uprising brought to an end the public debate on a new constitution and ground the moves towards democratization to a complete halt. Thus the Kwangju incident marked an important landmark in the ever fluctuating political scene of South Korea.

Notably, the aftermath of the Kwangju upheaval witnessed the rise of overt anti-American sentiment among
the general South Korean population for the first time
since the Korean War.[81] Such an ill-feeling arose in
conjunction with the controversial U.S. role in mobilization of the army troops which retook Kwangju from the
rebels and were part of the over half a million-man South
Korean force under General John A. Wickham, Commander of
the U.S.-South Korea Combined Forces Command. When Chun
Doo Hwan asked for immediate release of the troops for
assault against the insurgent-held city, General Wickham
quickly acceded to the request.[82]

It was while the nation's attention was riveted on the
uprising in Kwangju that Kim Jae Kyu and his four code-
fendants--all implicated in the slayings of President
Park and his bodyguards--were executed by hanging at a
Seoul prison on May 24, only four days after rejection
by the Supreme Court of their appeals against their death
sentences. Ironically, after his assassination of President Park, the former KCIA chief Kim was portrayed as
a hero and patriot by students and other critics of
Park's authoritarian rule. Up to the time of his death,
there had even been a mercy campaign, led by former President Yun Po Son, to spare his life.[83]

Notes

1. <u>Tong-A Ilbo</u>, January 2, 1980; and <u>Boston Globe</u>, December 16, 23, 1979.

2. <u>Time</u>, December 17, 1979, p. 48; <u>Washington Post</u>, March 26, 1980; and <u>Far Eastern Economic Review</u>, January 4, 1980, pp. 14-15.

3. <u>Newsweek</u>, December 17, 1979, p. 68.

4. <u>New York Times</u>, November 25, 1979; and <u>Washington Post</u>, December 19, 1979.

5. <u>Tong-A Ilbo</u>, January 1, 1980.

6. <u>Ibid.</u>

7. <u>Tong-A Ilbo</u>, January 31, 1980.

8. According to the result of public opinion survery that appeared in the <u>Chung-Ang Ilbo</u> on December 22, 1979, about 83 percent of the respondents said that the most important task facing the Ch'oe Administration was constitutional revision and that "the faster" the task was completed, "the better" it would be. Kang, "80 Nyon Pom Kuk'hoe Kaehon Tuk'i e Chwajol," p. 165.

9. <u>Tong-A Ilbo</u>, January 17, 1980.

10. <u>Tong-A Ilbo</u>, January 21, 22, 1980.

11. <u>Tong-A Ilbo</u>, March 17, 1980; and <u>Korean Newsletter</u>, (Washington, D.C.), III, No. 3, (March-April 1980), p. 2.

12. <u>Far Eastern Economic Review</u>, February 22, 1980, p. 15; <u>Tong-A Ilbo</u>, January 18, 1980; and <u>New York Times</u>, November 18, 1979.

13. England and the United States were excluded from the list of target countries ostensibly because of Seoul's familiarities with these two countries. <u>Tong-A Ilbo</u>, January 17, 1980.

14. <u>New York Times</u>, November 6, 1979.

15. <u>Tong-A Ilbo</u>, February 26, 1980.

16. <u>Ibid.</u>

17. <u>Tong-A Ilbo</u>, February 22, 27, 1980.

18. <u>Tong-A Ilbo</u>, March 13, 1980.

19. <u>Tong-A Ilbo</u>, April 4, 1980.

20. Kang, "80 Nyon Pom Kuk'hoe Kaehon Tuk'i e Chwajol," pp. 273-275.

21. Far Eastern Economic Review, April 11, 1980, pp. 30-31; and Claude A. Buss, The United States and the Republic of Korea, (Stanford, CA: Hoover Institute Press, 1982), p. 16.

22. Tong-A Ilbo, April 23, 1980.

23. According to the March 13, 1980 issue of the Washington Post, the Ministry of Education in Seoul announced that about 800 students had been expelled and 39 professors ousted since 1973, and that 639 students were reinstated and 25 professors rehired.

24. Washington Post, March 13, May 3, 1980; and Tong-A Ilbo, March 3, 1980.

25. Tong-A Ilbo, March 5, 6, 7, 1980; and Washington Post, March 13, May 3, 1980.

26. Tong-A Ilbo, April 19, 1980.

27. Maeda, Seoul karano Hokoku, pp. 207-208; Sekai, ed., Gunsei to Junan, pp. 168-172; and New York Times, May 5, 1980.

28. Tong-A Ilbo, April 19, 1980.

29. Tong-A Ilbo, January 11, 1980. According to a January 1980 government guideline, the wage hike ceiling for that year was 15 percent in private industries, while the annual inflation rate (as of November 1979) was 31 to 36 percent.

30. Tong-A Ilbo, April 29, May 2, 1980; and Maeda, Seoul karano Hokoku, p. 209.

31. Washington Post, May 1, 19, 1980.

32. Tong-A Ilbo, April 25, 26, 1980.

33. Tong-A Ilbo, May 1, 1980.

34. Time, June 2, 1980, p. 37.

35. Tong-A Ilbo, January 21, February 12, 1980; Washington Post, March 10, 1980; and Far Eastern Economic Review, April 11, 1980, p. 31.

36. Tong-A Ilbo, April 15, May 3, 1980.

37. Tong-A Ilbo, April 16, 1980.

38. New York Times, March 2, 1980.

39. New York Times, April 16, 1980.

40. Washington Post, April 30, 1980; and Sekai, ed., Gunsei to Junan, pp. 179-180.

41. Far Eastern Economic Review, April 25, 1980, p. 24; and Kang, "80 Nyon Pom Kuk'hoe Tuk'i e Chwajol," pp. 278-279.

42. Tong-A Ilbo, May 3, 5, 1980; and Time, May 26, 1980, p. 32.

43. Tong-A Ilbo, May 5, 1980; and Far Eastern Economic Review, May 23, 1980, p. 9.

44. Tong-A Ilbo, May 3, 5, 6, 1980; and New York Times, May 11, 1980. Persuaded by the "moderate" Education Minister Kim Ok Gil, most of the college freshmen in Seoul by May 6 had dropped their boycott of the military drill at army bases. The government, on the other hand, cancelled the public hearings on its draft constitution, which were planned to start on May 12. Shaplen, "Letters From South Korea," p. 192; Tong-A Ilbo, May 12, 1980; and Washington Post, May 14, 1980.
45. Tong-A Ilbo, May 8, 9, 1980; and Washington Post, May 14, 16, 1980.
46. Kang, "80 Nyon Pom Kuk'hoe Kaehon Tuk'i e Chwajol," pp. 281-282; Boston Globe, May 20, 1980; and Newsweek, May 26, 1980, p. 54.
47. Economist, (London), May 24, 1980, pp. 47-48; and Washington Post, July 31, 1980.
48. Washington Post, May 14, 1980; and New York Times, May 11, 15, 1980. While South Korean censors banned any mention of the American disclaimers, many South Koreans suspected the government of having planted or at least encouraged the rumors. Economist, May 24, 1980, p. 48.
49. New York Times, May 15, 1980; and Far Eastern Economic Review, May 23, 1980, p. 9.
50. Boston Globe, May 16, 1980; and Washington Post, May 16, 1980.
51. New York Times, May 16, 1980.
52. Tong-A Ilbo, May 10, 1980.
53. Washington Post, May 16, 1980; New York Times, May 16, 1980; and Tong-A Ilbo, May 16, 1980.
54. Washington Post, May 17, 1980; New York Times, May 17, 1980; and Tong-A Ilbo, May 17, 1980.
55. New York Times, May 16, 1980.
56. New York Times, March 17, 1980.
57. Tong-A Ilbo, April 21, 1980.
58. New York Times, May 17, 1980; and Washington Post, May 17, 1980.
59. Time, May 26, 1980; and Economist, May 24, 1980, pp. 47-48.
60. Boston Globe, May 19, 1980; and Far Eastern Economic Review, May 23, 1980, p. 10. Kim Yong Sam, however, found himself under virtual house arrest on the morning of May 18. New York Times, May 21, 1980.
61. New York Times, May 18, 19, 1980.
62. New York Times, May 18, 19, 1980; and Boston Globe, May 19, 1980.
63. Boston Globe, May 19, 1980; and Economist, May 24, 1980, p. 47.
64. New York Times, May 19, 1980; Boston Globe, May 19, 1980; and Tong-A Ilbo, May 19, 1980.

227

65. Concerning the May 17 crackdown, one U.S. official in Seoul said that "[t]here's no question that a coup has occurred. There is no more civilian government. It looks pretty ugly." Newsweek, May 26, 1980, p. 54.

66. The arrests of Park's cronies, who were among the wealthiest in South Korea, were a shrewd move on the part of Mr. Chun. Because the wealth accumulated by these men, who had been junior army officers of no independent financial means before the 1961 coup, and their network of political power could have impeded Chun's further pursuit of power.

67. New York Times, May 19, 21, 1980; Washington Post, May 19, 1980; and Newsweek, May 26, 1980, p. 54. The government claimed that the crackdown was carried out in response to "North Korean [troup] movements on the northern side of the DMZ." The U.N. Command in Seoul, however, once again stated that it had no evidence of unusual North Korean troop movements.

68. Washington Post, May 22, 1980; and Time, June 2, 1980, pp. 36-37.

69. New York Times, May 20, 22, 1980; Washington Post, May 22, 1980; Sekai, ed., Gunsei to Junan, p. 194; and Maeda, Seoul karano Hokoku, p. 212.

70. Gregory Henderson, "The Politics of Korea," in John Sullivan and Robert Foss, eds., Two Korea--One Future ?, (Lanham, MD: University Press of America, Inc., 1987), p. 105; Boston Globe, May 20, 22, 1980; and Sekai ed., Gunsei to Junan, pp. 194-195, 206-208.

71. Washington Post, May 22, 1980; and New York Times, May 20, 21, 22, 1980.

72. Far Eastern Economic Review, June 4, 1987, p. 21; Newsweek, June 2, 1980, p. 42; and Sekai ed., Gunsei to Junan, pp. 195, 204, 208.

73. The rebels in Mokpo burnt at least one police station and a factory between May 21 and 25; and on May 25, a defiant crowd of 50,000 people burnt an effigy of chun Doo Hwan. Boston Globe, May 22, 25, 1980; and Newsweek, June 2, 1980, p. 42.

74. Boston Globe, May 23, 1980; and New York Times, May 24, 25, 27, 1980.

75. Boston Globe, May 23, 26, 1980; and Washington Post, May 24, 27, 1980.

76. Sekai, ed., Gunsei to Junan, pp. 208, 210; Time, June 9, 1980, p. 40; Washington Post, May 27, 29, 30, 1980; and Boston Globe, May 30, 1980. The anti-government demonstrations in Mokpo lasted at least until May 29 despite the presence of soldiers.

77. Benjamin Patterson, "South Korea's Time of Testing," America, October 17, 1981, p. 214; and New York

<u>Times</u>, June 1, 10, 1980. Because of the tight press censorship as well as the closure of traffic and telephone lines into and out of the rebellious areas, information concerning casualties was sketchy. While the martial law command estimated the number of dead rebels in Kwangju at less than 200, dissidents claimed that more than 1,000 protestors were killed in the city.

78. The revolts in October 1946 started when railway workers in Seoul, failing to win their demands for better working conditions from the U.S. Military Government, went on strike and were instantly joined by other workers in the city as well as in other places. Henderson, <u>Korea</u>, pp. 144-147.

79. A <u>Newsweek</u> reporter, who visited the besieged Kwangju before the army's final assault, found it a "surprisingly united city." After the army's takeover, he returned to a very different scene: "a climate of fear and resentment" in the city. <u>Newsweek</u>, June 9, 1980, p. 23.

80. Lee, "South Korea in 1980," p. 132; and <u>Economist</u>, May 31, 1980, p.12.

81. Kim Sang Chun, "Panmi nun odiso onunga" (Where From Is the Anti-Americanism Coming?), <u>Shin-Tong-A</u>, No. 322, (July 1986), pp. 409-410.

82. Henderson, "The Politics of Korea," in Sullivan and Foss, eds., <u>Two Koreas--One Future ?</u>, p. 105.

83. <u>Tong-A Ilbo</u>, March 10, 1980; and <u>Boston Globe</u>, May 24, 1980.

CHAPTER 11

EMERGENCE OF A NEW MILITARY-DOMINATED REGIME
MAY 1980-MARCH 1981 (1)

In the aftermath of the bloody Kwangju incident, the shock of which had snuffed the hope for liberalization, the military came forward to jettison the vestiges of still remaining civilian rule and openly to take full command of national affairs.

The Special Committee For National Security Measures and Its Standing Committee

Already on May 20 amidst the Kwangju upheaval, the military abruptly prompted Premier Shin's cabinet to resign en masse, which anyway had been merely a front for generals and of which only the "shell" had remained.[1] However, in order to save face, the Shin cabinet tendered their resignation ostensibly as a gesture of accepting responsibility for the continuing violence, stating that they were "holding themselves accountable for the unprecedented unrest" and were taking the blame for "failing to maintain domestic calm"[2] The very next day, a new cabinet was formed, whose members represented the choices of the military. It was headed by Acting Prime Minister Park Choong Hoon, a retired air force major general who since 1973 had been president of the Korean Trade Association, which represented most of South Korea's large trading companies. Mr. Park carried the title of acting premier because the appointment of a regular premier required approval of the National Assembly, which the martial law authorities had forbidden to meet.[3]

The military were not fully satisfied with the rehuffling of cabinet alone. They reinforced and broadened their already strong grip on power by forming on May 31 a 25-man military-dominated Special Committee For National Security Measures (SCNSM). The SCNSM was officially described as "an advisory and assisting body to the president" and would function as "the coordinating mechanism" between the Cabinet and the Martial Law Command. The new committee, however, was to take over almost all the functions of the cabinet and legislature, making the barely two-week old civilian cabinet of Premier Park superfluous.[4]

The SCNSM was made up 14 active service generals and 11 civilians (of whom three were retired generals). Among the 14 active duty generals were Chun Doo Hwan, Commander of the Defense Security Command; Lee Hee Song, the Martial Law Commander and the Army Chief of Staff; Yu Byong Hyon, Chairman of the Joint Chiefs of Staff; the heads of the navy and air force; and the Deputy Commander of the U.S.-South Korea Combined Forces Command. Of the 11 civilians, eight were cabinet members and two were staff members of the presidential secretariat.[5] Notably, President Ch'oe Kyu Ha was made Chairman of the newly created organ, suggesting that the generals were still publicly deferring to him as the head of state.

The day-to-day handling of the SCNCM's business was entrusted to its 30-man Standing Committee, whose formation was announced on June 5.[6] Headed by Chun Doo Hwan, the standing committee was composed of 18 military officers on active duty and 12 civilian government officials. Interestingly, four members of the SCNCM served concurrently on the Standing Committee. They were Lieut. General Chun; Maj. General Ro T'ae Woo, Commander of the Capital Garrison Division; Maj. General Chong Ho Yong, Commander of the Special Forces; and Lieut. General Ch'a Kyu Hon, Deputy Army Chief of Staff. Notably, Ro and Chong were from Chun's native Kyongsang Province, as they were his classmates at the Korean Military Academy.[7]

The Standing Committee, in turn, spawned 13 subcommittees, which were mostly headed by generals loyal to Chun and to which Chun personally appointed 108 field-grade officers, government officials, and professors. These subcommittees--each comprised of seven to nine staff members including one or two colonels or lieut. colonels--exercised authority over the government ministries and directed operations of all phases of government. In doing so, they bypassed the Cabinet and reported directly to the 30-man Standing Committee.[8] Thus with the help of its 13 subcommittees, the Standing Committee in effect ran the government. Indeed, many Korean specialists likened the Standing Committee to the Supreme council For National Reconstruction set up by the late Park after the

1961 coup; that is to say, the Standing Committee was the law unto itself.' Thus, though ostensibly subordinate to the 15-member SCNSM that was headed by President Ch'oe, the Standing Committee was the supreme organ of power in the country and its chairman Chun was in effect the most powerful man in South Korea.

The Purges

The presence of the Special Committee For National Security Measures was awesome and intimidating for the population, because one of the 13 subcommittees under it, the "social purification committee," was charged with the task of "cleansing" society and polity. The social purification subcommittee pushed its crusade of weeding out corruption and corrupt elements with zeal and audacity. And on June 18 the Martial Law Command announced the result of the purification committee's one-month long investigation into abuse of power by former Prime Minister Kim Jong P'il and nine other close associates of the late Park, all of whom were arrested on May 17.[10]

According to the announcement, these 10 top former politicians had amassed a total of U.S. $147 million during their services with the Park regime that had lasted 18 years. The methods used to accumulate such a huge sum included coercion of businessmen to make "campaign contributions" and collection from them of "cooperation fees" in exchange for promises to put pressures on government to further their business interests. It had for long been known among South Koreans that many of their officials were venal; still they were stunned by the enormity of the wealth misappropriated by these 10 underlings of Park's. However, the announcement from the Martial Law Command stated that the authorities were dropping criminal prosecutions in exchange for promises from the offenders to surrender their ill-gotten riches to the state and to retire from public life.[11]

The scope of the cleanup drive was sweeping and its targets included virtually every public institution. For example, on June 20 the KCIA, which had involved itself heavily in domestic politics as a tool of political repression, announced that over 300 of its agents had been fired for being "corrupt or incompetent" or high-handed. Among the ousted agents were those who had been connected with "outside" political influences, namely, the supporters of previous KCIA directors. The shakeup, "the most extensive purification" of the KCIA in its 17-year history, was the second purge of the agency since Mr. Chun's takeover of it in April.[12]

The ax of purification continued to fall. On July 9 the SCNSM announced that its "anti-corruption squad" had removed 232 senior officials from various branches of the government on suspicion of sundry malfeasances. Among the dismissed were one cabinet minister, five vice-ministers, and three provincial governors; 11 purgees were from the secretariat of the National Assembly and another 11 from the Judiciary.[13] By now the purification drive had gone into full swing. On July 16 the government announced that it had sacked no fewer than 4,760 middle-to-lower level officials and other employees in various ministries, in state-run cooperations, and in other business institutions under government control.[14]

On July 19 the Martial Law Command announced a second "major" roundup of venal public figures stating that 17 politicians had been taken into custody on suspicion of influence-peddling and other corrupt practices during the Park era. Three were "former" cabinet ministers and six were DRP members who had served as parliamentary aides to the late President Park.[15] The remainder were senior legislative leaders of the opposition NDP, which was said to contain a fair number of corrupt politicians who had secretly worked for President Park in exchange for political funds. Observers in Seoul speculated that these 17 figures too would "voluntarily" retire from politics, or they would risk further public disgrace along with likely legal sanctions.[16]

The series of purges and rumors of pending ones sent down shivers through the whole bureaucracy; and officials and other public employees, intent on knowing who were leaving and who were staying, were nervous and deeply worried. The purges of those who were on public payrolls were completed around late July. By then, some 8,650 persons had lost their jobs including school teachers. As a result of such extensive firings, the central Administration had lost some 12 percent of its "top echelon." When lesser grade bureaucrats were counted, the total of officials ousted was said to be enough to staff a major ministry. Notably, not all those fired were accused of corruption or incompetence; some were just asked to leave "to make room for a new generation."[17]

The "cleanup campaign" extended to the mass media, a predominantly private domain and a major source of information for the South Koreans, who had a keen desire to keep up with what was going on around the world. On July 31 the authorities cancelled the registration of 172 weekly and monthly magazines deemed unworthy of publication, forcing as many as 10,000 writers and workers out of their jobs.[18] Some of the banned periodicals dealt with "immoral themes" and were "obscene and vulgar." However, a number of others were prestigious intellectual journals, which fomented "class awareness or social uneasiness" by criticizing government and "instigating social confusion."[19] The daily newspapers were not affected by this purge, but they had already knuckled under an earlier government pressure.

It was on July 30 that the Korean Newspaper Association, accepting a suggestion of the Standing Committee of the SCNSM, adopted a resolution pledging that it would "voluntarily" eliminate "impure elements" from among its own members by "giving priority to the national interest."[20] The very next day, the Korean Broadcasters' Association followed suit. When the deadline for the completion of this stage of "cleanup" came on August 10, well over 400 editors and reporters from both branches of the news media--about 10 percent of the nation's total--were out of work.[21]

Admittedly, some of the dismissed newsmen were corrupt. But many were simply "guilty" of having attempted to report facts while protesting the press censorship of the martial law command; and their oustings went far beyond the occasional dismissals on government orders of journalists unpopular with the authorities during the late Park's reign. Indeed, the scale of the latest purges of reporters, which came on the heels of "purification" carried out earlier in July among newsmen working for government-owned mass media, was unprecedented in South Korea.[22]

The government's "suppressive and intrusive actions" against the press created "an underlying sense of fear and uncertainty" that was "probably more pervasive" than during "all but the worst days" of the late President Park.[23] The situation was a far cry from the spring of that year, when the press under "modest" censorship routinely printed statements by opposition politicians and prominently reported on the striking students and workers and enjoyed "a brief burst of freedom."[24]

The systematic emasculation of the news media was preceded by punitive actions meted out against those involved in the spreading of news deemed undesirable by the authorities. For instance, on June 9 the Martial Law Command announced that eight journalists were being questioned on suspicion of spreading "vicious" rumors related to the Kwangju incident. This was the first official announcement of questioning of any reporters since full martial law was imposed on May 17. Then on July 12, the government made it known that six Roman Catholic priests and a nun had been detained for spreading "wild, malicious rumors" that government troops had used brutality in quelling the Kwangju uprising.[25] In August the Martial Law Command announced that it had meted out jail sentences to four journalists and 13 others who had been found guilty of spreading "unfounded rumors" and of holding "illegal meetings" and demonstrating.[26]

In other developments, the Martial Law Command on August 6 announced that it had rounded up nearly 17,000 "hooligans" in a sweeping two-day crackdown on "social evils."[27] On August 15, a government spokesman said that about 30,000 "racketeers" and "procurers" and other "hoodlums" had been detained since the 11th of the month. The majority of these detained "social miscreants" were freed after questioning and/or following several weeks' "purification education," which included lectures and physical labor at military camps. The rest went to prisons.[28] Meanwhile, the purification campaign reached even popular singers and other entertainers, leading to the prohibition in September of all the performances deemed by the authorities as "unhealthy" or "degrading."[29]

The firing of many officials and roundup of tens of thousands of others were "unprecedented" in the then 32-year history of South Korea, even though bribery and other dishonest dealings had been endemic since 1948 and this was not the first time a Seoul government had been forced to clean them up.[30] Only big business interests were left unscathed. Despite its repeated threats of purge of the businessmen who had "accumulated great wealth through illegal means," the government simply excluded them from the "social and political cleanup." According to an announcement of the Martial Law Command on June 18, the authorities "had exercised restraint" even about identifying "unethical businessmen" in order to avoid possible adverse effects on the economy. The

business concerns were simply asked to "cleanse themselves"; and businessmen agreed to "behave more moder-
ately" by avoiding the "overexposure" of their wealth.[31]

The massive shakeup, affecting virtually every segment
of the society, served more than the single purpose of
"purifying" the society. Because of the prevalence of
official corruption and built-up popular resentment a-
gainst venal public figures, most South Koreans conceded
that some cleansing of the officialdom and other segments
of public life was necessary. Thus the purges reportedly
elicited some popular support, while making the military-
dominated government appear as social reformers in the
eyes of the public.[32]

As noted already, however, it was not only the venal
who suffered in the anti-corruption campaigns; rather,
those who were affected by the cleanup of public life
were "a clever mix of corrupt politicians and genuine
members of the opposition." Similarly, the move against
journalists and other intellectuals included removing
from public life those who had openly defied authoritarian controls. Thus the crackdowns on the politicians
and intellectuals were aimed not only at weeding out
corruption but also destroying the power bases of established political figures as well as quelling dissent.
On the whole, the purification drive appeared more
interested in politics than in honesty and morality.[33]

Having cleared the political arena of all resistance,
Chun Doo Hwan, still officially only Head of the Defense
Security Command and Acting Chief of the KCIA, proceeded
openly to take over the presidency by assuming some of
President Ch'oe's ceremonial chores. Chun inspected
flood damages in Ch'ung-ch'ong Province on July 23.[34] He
was the principal guest on August 6 at an annual inter-
denominational Christian prayer meeting in Seoul, which
was traditionally attended by the President of the country. On August 11 Chun fired off a cable congratulating
the first South Korean swimmer to spatter successfully
across the Korea Strait to the Japanese Island of Tsu-
shima.[35]

Perhaps in an even "bolder move," Chun, who had received his third star only in March, had President Ch'oe
and a presidential aide fasten four-star shoulder boards
to his uniform in a short ceremony on August 6. This
made Chun one of the seven highest-ranking officers in
the South Korean army.[36] Chun's promotion to full gen-

eral, the rank held by the late Park before shedding his uniform to become president in 1963, was made in anticipation of his retirement from the army late in the month. It was a signal that he was ready to emerge from a behind-the-scenes role and assume the nation's very top political post. Already on June 2 Chun submitted his resignation from the KCIA, which by then had been transformed into his "fiefdom."[37] The agency's vacant directorship was taken over on July 18 by General Yu Hak Song, a graduate of Officers' Candidate School and who had endorsed Chun's December 12th putsch.[38]

Meanwhile, a concerted propaganda campaign had been launched to whip up the public's acceptance of Chun as the president. Already since early June the heavily censored newspapers had been allowed to run front-page photographs of Chun in civilian garb.[39] And early in August an article in the press, from which all "impure elements" had been removed, hinted that a military officer should be the chief executive of the country. It was followed by the publication, in Seoul's major dailies, of Chun's press interview held on August 8, in which Chun intimated that he was of presidential material because he could provide "a strong leadership" that could control the military.[40]

In spite of all efforts, however, there were serious doubts concerning the "strongman" Chun's electability to the presidency in a direct popular election. Thus propaganda efforts had been mounted since July to pave the way for the public's acceptance of indirect presidential elections by an electoral college, as had been practiced since 1972. The reason given was that direct elections would produce "adverse side effects" by creating "divisions of opinion" at a time when the whole nation had to face the northern enemy with one mind.[41] This was a carbon copy of the late Park's justification of indirect presidential elections under the Yushin Constitution.

Meanwhile, an opportunity presented itself for Chun and his associates to seize on a chance timing of an interview held on August 7 between General John A. Wickham, the Commander of the U.S. forces in Korea, and a visiting American correspondent to link publicly Chun's name with the presidency. Wickham's remarks made during the interview were quoted the very same day in the Associated Press, without revealing the general's name but attributing the remarks to an unnamed U.S. military officer. According to the AP wire service, the anonymous American

officer said that the United States would support Chun
as president if he came to power "legitimately," demonstrated "a broad base of support," and did not "jeopardize the security" of South Korea.[42]

On August 8 and 9, all the dailies in Seoul printed
stories based on the AP report but leaving out the qual-
ifying remarks of the unnamed American for U.S. support
of Chun's ascent to the presidency. The banner headline
carried by these papers read that "a top U.S. military
officer" had said that Washington was prepared to support
Chun "if he consolidates his near total power by taking
over the presidency." Wickham was identified as the
source and his name was widely quoted in the controlled
press.[43] The story, as slanted as it was and quoted out
of context, was given orchestrated prominence to give the
impression that Chun was the American choice for the
South Korean presidency.

This was the first authorized suggestion that Chun
would seek the presidency; and it marked the start of a
whirlwind public campaign for the Chun presidency. Now
government officials and the military-censored newspapers
openly endorsed Chun as president, claiming that he was
the strong leader South Korea needed to end the period
of confusion and drift that followed Park's death.[44] On
August 16, the figurehead president Ch'oe Kyu Ha, whose
civilian administration was in tatters, "abruptly" resigned after 36 weeks in office to make room for Chun.[45]

Now events moved swiftly. On August 21, Chun won
strong endorsements for his presidential bid from former
president Ch'oe and the military leaders who provided
Chun with his power base.[46] The following day Chun, all
but certain to be named president, resigned from the
army. The resignation ceremony, held near the demarcation line north of Seoul, was attended by the members of
the military who had been ruling South Korea under the
martial law since May 17, the entire cabinet members, and
32 retired generals. Businessmen too attended, as did
three American officials including a lieutenant general.[47]

Chun quit the service because the constitution forbade
a military officer from becoming president. Already he
had taken steps to assure his continued control of the
military by naming on August 21 his close associate
Lieut. General Ro T'ae Woo as Head of the Defense Security Command that monitored the armed forces for loy-

alty.⁴⁸ All that remained for Chun now was to take
formal steps to move into the presidency. Finally on
August 27, Chun, the sole candidate, was made president
by 2,524 of the 2,525 votes cast by the NCFU, the indirect presidential election mechanism under the Yushin
Constitution and whose members were selected in May 1978.
The single ballot, which was cast against, was ruled invalid for some unknown reason.⁴⁹

On September 1, Chun took the oath as the 11th president of South Korea (fifth person to hold the office).
In his inaugural address, President Chun asserted that
his ultimate goal was the construction of a "democratic
welfare state."⁵⁰ To create such a society, Chun emphasized the necessity of transforming "the political
climate" fraught with "corruption" into one in which
justice and "mutual trust" could prevail along with "new
values." Among the corrupt practices Chun cited were the
"evil habits" of seeking "unearned incomes" and "concessions through improper means" and of "expecting money
to open every door." And Chun promised to uproot them.

Chun also promised that his government would prepare
"an efficient constitution" and it would be submitted to
the people in a referendum "in October at the latest,"
and that presidential and legislative elections would be
held in the first half of 1981. Until a new presidential
election was held under a new constitution, Chun was to
govern as the "interim president." Needless to say, Chun
was expected to run again to seek a "regular term."⁵¹

Interim President Chun brought in many civilians into
his administration. On August 27, he named American-
educated civilians to key posts on the presidential
staff: Kim Kyong Won as the chief of staff, and Kim Pyong
Hun as the chief of protocol as well as the chief inter-
preter.⁵² Of the new 20-man cabinet appointed by the
president on September 2, all but two were civilians
including the American-trained Prime Minister Nam Duck
Woo, who was an architect of South Korea's high economic
growth under the late Park.⁵³ The placing of these
civilians in the positions of high visibility, however,
was largely a "window-dressing." All the real power lay
in the hands of military men, specifically the staff
colonels brought into the presidential office and the
commanders of vital military units in and around Seoul.
They were said to make key decisions concerning government policies.⁵⁴

Indeed, President Chun's power rested upon the support provided by his staff which, though headed by a civilian, was dominated behind the scenes by the colonels on the staff. The presidential staff, in turn, was backed by the armed forces along with the KCIA.[55] Ultimately, President Chun's rise to supremacy stemmed from his grip on the armed forces--the grip effected through Chun's massive turnovers of personnel in the military, his close personal connections with commanders in key military units, and monitoring of the loyalty of the servicemen by the Defense Security Command. President Chun's hold on power was "completed" by his concurrent holding of the chairmanship of the Standing Committee of the SCNSM.[56]

The New Constitution and the Legislative Council For National Security

On September 29, 1980, the government presented the nation with the official draft of a new constitution,[57] which was written by a government-appointed committee. The new draft constitution abolished the presidential electoral body, the NCFU, and did away with the presidential right to appoint one-third of the national assembly members. It also made it more difficult for the president to declare an emergency in order to curb protest activities, the authority abused by the late President Park to muffle opposition and prolong his rule.

Additionally, the proposed charter limited the president to a single seven-year term, a move designed to prevent a repetition of the prolonged rules of Presidents Rhee and Park. The draft charter gave the National Assembly somewhat more power than under the Yushin Constitution. It also granted the Chief Justice of the Supreme Court--not the President as was the case under the 1972 basic law--the right to appoint all judges other than the Supreme Court justices, who would continue to be appointed by the president.

Despite all the changes, the revision contained elements which did not figure in democratic constitutions elsewhere and were controversial. One of them was the provision for an indirect election of the president by an electoral college composed of more than 5,000 members elected by the people.[58] Even more controversial were the "supplementary provisions," set out in 10 articles and tacked onto the end of the draft constitution. Under these riders the National Assembly and all the existing

241

political parties would automatically dissolve upon the approval of the new draft constitution by a simple majority in a referendum and its promulgation.

Thereafter, legislative functions would be exercised by a Legislative Council For National Security (LCNS) (Kukka Po'ui Ippop Hoe'ui) until the election of a new National Assembly under the new constitution. The LCNS was to be established shortly, with all of its members appointed by President Chun; any actions taken by it were to be final and not subject to retroactive appeals or litigation.[59]

On October 22, the draft constitution was submitted to a national referendum. This was a fifth constitutional referendum in South Korea. It was conducted without lifting the martial law and without public debate, just as the late Park had done with his 1972 charter. According to the Central Election Management Committee's announcement, 95.5 percent of the 20.3 million eligible voters cast their ballots and 91.6 percent voted in favor of the proposed basic law.[60] However, it should be noted that the result was neither surprising nor meaningful, because the voters know that the new constitution was sponsored by the government and that the alternative to it was the retention of the discredited Yushin Constitution.[61] Be that as it may, on October 27 the newly approved basic law was promulgated. It was the eighth revised constitution or the ninth constitution of the Republic of Korea founded in 1948.

As the new fundamental law went into effect on October 27, the National Assembly and all the existing political parties disbanded. The next day the LCNS came into being to serve as the interim legislature. While consisting of 81 members appointed by President Chun, it was a revamped and expanded body of the military-dominated SCNSM, and it sat in the National Assembly building.[62]

The very first legislative action of the interim legislature was the passage on November 3 of a Political Climate Renovation Law, which banned from politics anyone "responsible...in bringing about political and social corruption or fomenting confusion."[63] A Political Renovation Committee--a nine member screening committee established under the Political Climate Renovation Law and whose members were appointed by President Chun--issued blacklists disqualifying 567 politicians and intellectuals from playing any role in politics until June 30,

242

1988 in order "to open a new era and a new political style."[64]

The 567 purgees included virtually every politician of note, including most of former President Park's aides. Among them were Kim Dae Jung, who was now under a death sentence (as will be explained); Kim Yong Sam, former head of the disbanded opposition NDP; and Kim Jong P'il, the late Park's close associate and former president of the defunct DRP. The length of the ban--seven and a half years--was particularly significant, because it would cover the next two presidential elections; and the first, in which Chun was expected to run for a "regular" term, was anticipated in the spring of 1981. Thus the lengthy restriction would prevent the blacklisted from taking part in any elections during Chun's presidential terms, including one that would determine Chun's successor.[65]

This was not the first time a retroactive law was used in South Korea to castigate political enemies. Indeed, this was the fourth time an ex post facto legislation was resorted to in order to chastise political opponents. The first such political purge law was the National Traitors' Law, enacted in September 1948 to punish the Koreans who had actively collaborated with the Japanese during their occupation of Korea from 1910 to 1945. The second law, which was legislated in December 1960, was designed to suspend the civil rights for five to seven years of the "traitors of democracy": namely, the core members of Sygman Rhee's Liberal Party.[66]

The third was the Politics Purification Act of March 1962, which prohibited politicians who had been active in the previous Liberal and Democratic regimes from engaging in political activities until August 15, 1968 (described in Chapter 2).[67] Thus, the removal of the 567 individuals was an extension of South Korea's "dreaded" tradition of political revenge and of the habit of blaming all problems on former politicians.

The second item that received the attention of the Legislative Council was the Political Party Law, which was enacted on November 19 and which preferred a multi-party formula to the previous two-party system. The official rationale was that a multi-party system would prevent the kind of confrontation and tension between two major parties that had been characteristic of much of the previous history of the Republic of Korea.[68] But the critics pointed out that a multi-party system would split the opposition and make it easier for the government to deal with it.[69]

Meanwhile, on November 22 the Martial Law Command partially lifted the ban on political activities by permitting indoor political meetings to organize political parties.[70] By late January 1981, no less than 15 new political parties had emerged. Among them were the army-backed Democratic Justice Party (DJP), which was headed by President Chun himself; the "main opposition" Democratic Korea Party (KDP), established by former members of the old opposition NDP led by Yu Ch'i Song; the Korea National Party (KNP), organized by the late Park's parliamentary supporters who had belonged to the disbanded DRP; the Democratic Socialist Party (DSP), led by an old-time "democratic socialist" Ko Chong Hun; and the Civil Rights Party (CRP), headed by "a top party official" of the defunct opposition NDP Kim Ui T'aek.[71]

It was widely assumed that the government allowed these miscellaneous parties to be formed not as rivals to it, but rather to supply a facade of popular political participation "with the actual strings being pulled by persons of unquestioned loyalty" to President Chun. In particular, the appearance of the legal Democratic Socialist Party--the first appearance of a leftist party in South Korea with official sanction since the 1961 army coup--was believed to have stemmed from the government's hope to make itself more acceptable to Western Europe where many center-leftist parties were in strong positions. In addition, it could have been aimed at countering North Korea's propaganda charges that Seoul government was a "fascist clique" bent upon suppressing leftist forces.[72]

All this while, the already tight government control of the news media had become even tighter through massive mergers and takeovers, which were undertaken according to realignment plans based upon two separate resolutions adopted on November 14 by the Korean Newspaper Association and the Korean Broadcasters' Association.[73]

Under the plans, two privately operated major broadcasting companies--the Tongyang Broadcasting Company and the Tong-A Broadcasting System--along with a few privately-run provincial radio stations were merged with the state-run Korean Broadcasting System. The Christian Broadcasting System, an independent network established in 1945 and which had acquired a reputation for outspoken political comments, ceased general news broadcasts and confined its programs to information of a purely religious nature.[74]

Most of the major newspapers in Seoul continued to remain in private hands, but three financially ailing minor papers were merged into other publications. In addition, two dailies that had been in competition in the city of Pusan were merged into one, as was the case with two other papers in each of three provinces. This left only one paper in Pusan and each of South Korea's nine provinces.[75]

Probably, the biggest change in the media was the alteration of news gathering by establishing a unified news service. The two general news agencies--the Orient Press and the Haptong News--and three small wire services dealing in specialized topics were integrated into a single channel called the Yonhap News Agency, which was established on January 1, 1981. Now newspapers and broadcasting stations in Seoul had to withdraw their correspondents from their provincial bureaus; thence they had to rely on the newly established wire service for all information emanating from outside of Seoul.[76] Thus the Yonhap News Agency, with its nationwide news distribution networks, became the dominant source of both domestic and foreign news for all newspapers and broadcasters across the country.

Government officials claimed that the massive realignment of the mass media was proposed "voluntarily" by leaders of the news industries themselves. The officials claimed so, because the execution of restructuring was based upon the two separate resolutions of November 14 by the Korean Newspaper Association and the Korean Broadcasters' Association. The same officials justified the realignment as necessary not only to ease competition among news companies and preserve some financially shaky ones but also raise journalistic standards and to reduce media domination by a few private companies.[77]

Observers, however, claimed that the restructuring had been forced on owners of the news industries by the government and that attempts to resist or modify the government plan had been rejected.[78] The same analysts saw the government move as an attempt to insure that news organizations would stay under government control when martial law would be lifted before presidential and legislative elections in the spring of 1981. All in all, the aftermath of the realignment found South Korean journalists "in shock."[79] Be that as it may, the drastic changes had been frozen in the Press Law passed on December 26, 1980 by the Legislative Council For National Security.[80]

By the way, the legislature pro tempore LCNS, during its lifetime of five and a half months until its dissolution on April 10, 1981 (the day before the opening of a new National Assembly), passed over 200 bills--23 of them in its last plenary session on March 31, 1981--affecting virtually every segment of society. Indeed, the Legislative Council was a tool in the hands of President Chun to exercise "constitutional dictatorship," changing the nation's political landscape as he chose.[81]

Notes

1. Boston Globe, May 21, 22, 1980; and New York Times, May 22, 1980.
2. Tong-A Ilbo, May 21, 1980.
3. Korean Newsletter, III, No. 4, (June 1980), pp. 1, 7; and Washington Post, May 22, 1980.
4. Tong-A Ilbo, May 31, 1980; and Washington Post, June 3, 1980.
5. Far Eastern Economic Review, June 6, 1980, p. 12; and Economist, June 7, 1980, p. 39.
6. Tong-A Ilbo, June 5, 1980.
7. Washington Post, June 3, 5, 6, 1980; New York Times, June 8, 1980; and Maeda, Seoul karano Hokoku, pp. 215, 216.
8. Far Eastern Economic Review, June 6, 1980, p. 12, June 20, 1980, p. 32.
9. Time, June 9, 1980, p. 41; New York Times, June 5, 17, 1980; and Lee, "South Korea in 1980," p. 133.
10. Tong-A Ilbo, June 18, 1980.
11. Tong-A Ilbo, June 18, 1980; and New York Times, June 19, 22, 1980.
12. New York Times, June 21, 1980, January 4, 1981; Far Eastern Economic Review, July 4, 1980, p. 32; Boston Globe, July 16, 1980; and Economist, June 28, 1980, p. 32. The first KCIA head Kim Jong P'il was said to have built a "hidden mountain of supporters" in the agency as his personal political bulwark. Upon his assumption of the acting directorship of the KCIA in April 1980, Chun dismissed 33 senior officials from the agency.
13. Tong-A Ilbo, July 10, 1980; and New York Times, July 10, 1980.
14. New York Times, July 16, 20, 1980.
15. Tong-A Ilbo, July 19, 1980.
16. New York Times, July 20, 1980; and Washington Post, July 25, 1980.
17. Boston Globe, August 3, 1980; Washington Post, August 16, 1980; and New York Times, July 20, 1980.

18. <u>Tong-A Ilbo</u>, July 31, 1980; and <u>New York Times</u>, September 22, 1980.

19. <u>Christian Science Monitor</u>, August 1, 1980; and <u>Boston Globe</u>, August 25, 1980.

20. <u>Tong-A Ilbo</u>, July 30, 1980; and <u>Washington Post</u>, July 31, 1980.

21. <u>Christian Science Monitor</u>, July 31, 1980; and <u>Far Eastern Economic Review</u>, August 15, 1980, p. 16.

22. No previous Seoul government had ever ordered every news organization all at once to purge its employees considered undesirable by the government. <u>Washington Post</u>, July 31, 1980; and Maeda, <u>Seoul karano Hokoku</u>, p. 134.

23. Shaplen, "Letters from South Korea," p. 207.

24. <u>Washington Post</u>, December 10, 1980.

25. <u>Boston Globe</u>, July 13, 1980; and <u>New York Times</u>, June 10, July 13, 1980.

26. <u>Boston Globe</u>, August 15, 1980. The draconian measures to control information reached foreigners too. The government on June 2 ordered Japan's Kyodo News Service to close down its Seoul bureau because the bureau had made "ill-intended, distorted, and false reporting" on events in South Korea. Then on June 27, two U.S. representatives of the United Presbyterian Church were detained by police as they were leaving for the U.S. after a two-day fact-finding visit to Kwangju where troops had just crushed the rebellion. The two persons were arrested for possession of documents which contained "unfounded rumors." Their "report" and photographs were confiscated, and they were freed the next day. <u>Washington Post</u>, June 3, 1980; and <u>New York Times</u>, June 29, 30, 1980.

27. <u>Tong-A Ilbo</u>, August 6, 1980; and <u>Boston Globe</u>, August 7, 1980.

28. <u>Washington Post</u>, August 16, 1980; and <u>New York Times</u>, August 31, 1980.

29. Maeda, <u>Seoul karano Hokoku</u>, p. 107; and <u>Boston Globe</u>, August 25, 1980.

30. <u>Boston Globe</u>, August 7, 1980; and <u>New York Times</u>, July 16, August 24, 1980. Discussing the causes of the corruption, an official in the summer of 1980 said that his salary had risen fivefold during the previous decade whereas the cost of living had gone up sevenfold.

31. <u>Tong-A Ilbo</u>, June 18, 1980; and <u>New York Times</u>, June 19, 1980. The hands-off attitude of the government concerning business community led some analysts to suspect that the business community had backed behind the scenes the moves of the general on May 17, and that it was willing to put up with the policies of these gen-

erals. _Time_, August 25, 1980, p. 40; and Shaplen, "Letters from South Korea," p. 200.

32. _New York Times_, August 24, 1980; _Washington Post_, June 5, 1980; and Patterson, "South Korea's Time of Testing," p. 215. A similar "corrupt" situation had existed before the 1961 coup, which brought Park and his younger officers to power, and one of Park's six "revolutionary pledges" was to end graft. Yet some of Park's own officials who had handled that job now themselves became purgees of Chun's anti-corruption drive.

33. Patterson, "South Korea's Time of Testing," p. 215; and _New York Times_, September 22, 1980.

34. _Tong-A Ilbo_, July 24, 1980.

35. _Tong-A Ilbo_, August 12, 1980.

36. _Tong-A Ilbo_, August 6, 1980; and _New York Times_, August 7, 1980.

37. _New York Times_, July 10, September 8, 1980; and _Economist_, June 7, 1980, p. 39.

38. General Yu retired from the army to take the KCIA job as the agency's ninth head. In September President Chun appointed his KMA classmate Kim Song Jin as the deputy director of the KCIA. _New York Times_, July 15, September 8, 1980.

39. _New York Times_, June 13, 1980; and _Boston Globe_, August 17, 1980.

40. _Tong-A Ilbo_, August 11, 1980; and _Far Eastern Economic Review_, August 22, 1980, pp. 8-9.

41. _New York Times_, June 13, 1980; _Far Eastern Economic Review_, August 8, 1980, p. 12; and _Korean Newsletter Special_, III, (September 1980), p. 6.

42. _New York Times_, August 9, 1980; and _Washington Post_, August 16, 1980.

43. _Tong-A Ilbo_, August 8, 9, 1980; and _New York Times_, August 13, 1980. Wickham's remarks supporting Chun, though conditional, were out of step with the policy of the Carter Administration that had for months expressed displeasure over the military-dominated leadership in Seoul; and his comments were disavowed by the State Department. _New York Times_, August 29, 1980; and _Boston Globe_, August 19, 1980.

44. _Washington Post_, August 1, 22, 23, 1980; and _New York Times_, August 22, 1980.

45. _Tong-A Ilbo_, August 16, 1980. Acting Premier Park Choon Hoon took on interim functions of Acting President, which lasted less than two weeks.

46. _Tong-A Ilbo_, August 21, 22, 1980.

47. _Boston Globe_, August 25, 1980; and _Washington Post_, August 22, 23, 1980. Chun's retirement from the service

entailed relinquishment of his position as head of the Defense Security Command.

48. Washington Post, August 23, 1980.

49. Tong-A Ilbo, August 27, 1980.

50. Full text of Chun's inaugural address is in Tong-A Ilbo, September 1, 1980. In view of the fact that the hope for democratization had faded away with the ascendancy of Chun, his remark concerning "a democratic welfare state," which Chun had uttered as early as on August 22, reminded Korea watchers of the statements by late Park's apologists that South Korea under Park had pursued "Korean-style democracy." New York Times, August 23, 1980.

51. Far Eastern Economic Review, October 3, 1980, p. 22. With Chun's assumption of the presidency, South Korea had succeeded in having three presidents in less than a year.

52. Tong-A Ilbo, August 28, 1980.

53. Tong-A Ilbo, September 2, 1980.

54. New York Times, August 28, September 3, 1980.

55. New York Times, August 28, September 3, 8, 22, December 1, 1980.

56. New York Times, August 27, September 3, 1980. According to the December 12, 1980 issue of the Far Eastern Economic Review (p. 22), Chun had ousted some 70 generals during "the past year", and "the latest annual promotion list" showed that 53 colonel-grade field officers had become brigadier generals.

57. Full text of the draft charter is in Tong-A Ilbo, September 29, 1980.

58. Tong-A Ilbo, September 29, 1980. Unlike the 1972 charter, the new draft allowed political parties to participate in the selection of a president by permitting them to put up candidates for the electoral college.

59. The law concerning the establishment of the LCNS was promulgated on October 28, 1980, and its text is in Tong-A Ilbo, October 28, 1980.

60. Tong-A Ilbo, October 23, 1980.

61. It should be recalled that the Yushin charter was endorsed twice in national referendums, but an overwhelming majority of South Koreans disowned it as soon as Park died.

62. Tong-A Ilbo, October 28, 1980. Among the 81 Legislative Council members were 20 politicians; and of these 20 politicians, 13 were members of the dissolved National Assembly. And of the 13, five were from the DRP, another five from the NDP, and three were former Yujonghoe parliamentarians. Korea Annual 1981, p. 79.

63. Tong-A Ilbo, November 3, 1980.

64. Tong-A Ilbo, November 12, 15, 1980; and Korea Annual 1981, p. 15. The first purge list, announced on November 3, carried 811 names; but the names of the second batch, made public on November 15, added 24 more names to the roster. Subsequently, 268 individuals had been reprieved by President Chun by December 5, the last day for filing applications by the blacklisted for review of their cases.

65. Washington Post, November 4, 8, 13, 1980; and New York Times, November 4, 13, 1980.

66. Oh, Korea, pp. 86, 88; and Kim, Divided Korea, pp. 123-124. The collaborators, who entrenched themselves in Syngman Rhee's bureaucracy and police and who were a source of political support for Rhee, hindered the implementation of the National Traitors' Law; and the attempt to purge the police and the bureaucracy came to an end in February 1950. Under the second purge law, about 600 political supporters of Syngman Rhee were found guilty of associating with his dictatorial regime. But the law was quickly overturned by Park's army coup the following year.

67. Washington Post, November 13, 1980; and Kim, Divided Korea, pp. 123-124.

68. Tong-A Ilbo, November 19, 1980.

69. Far Eastern Economic Review, December 12, 1980, p. 24; and Time, November 3, 1980, p. 63.

70. New York Times, November 22, 1980; and Boston Globe, November 22, 1980.

71. New York Times, January 14, 18, 1981; Washington Post, February 13, 1981; and Korea Annual 1981, pp. 81-84.

72. Christian Science Monitor, January 30, 1981; and Far Eastern Economic Review, March 13, 1981, p. 30.

73. Boston Globe, November 14, 1980; and Tong-A Ilbo, November 15, 1980.

74. New York Times, December 12, 1980; and Korea Annual 1981, pp. 262-264.

75. Washington Post, December 10, 1980; and Patterson, "South Korea's Time of Testing," p. 216.

76. Tong-A Ilbo, November 15, 1980; New York Times, December 12, 1980, February 1, 1981; and Korea Annual 1981, pp. 261-262.

77. Tong-A Ilbo, November 15, 17, 1980.

78. In this conjunction, it should be noted that on October 9, 1980 the Martial Law Command announced that Kim T'ae Hong, a former president of the Korean Journalists' Association, would be tried by a military court on charge of sedition and violation of martial law decrees. According to a spokesman of the Martial Law

Command, Kim was accused of taking part in the alleged anti-government plot for which Kim Dae Jung was sentenced to death (as will be described). *Washington Post*, October 10, 1980.

79. *Washington Post*, December 10, 1980; and *New York Times*, December 12, 1980.

80. *Sekai*, No. 424, (March 1981), p. 225; and *New York Times*, February 1, 1981.

81. *Korea Annual 1981*, pp. 79-80; *Washington Post*, March 1981; and Lee, "South Korea In 1981," p. 134.

CHAPTER 12

EMERGENCE OF A NEW MILITARY-DOMINATED REGIME
MAY 1980-MARCH 1981 (2)

The South Korean military hierarchy, while consolidating its hold on power in the summer of 1980, was deeply concerned about the continuing popularity of Kim Dae Jung, a proponent of democracy and the foremost critic of the late President Park.

As Kim maneuvered to run in the free presidential election promised by President Ch'oe Kyu Ha in the brief hiatus of political relaxation that followed Park's death, military leaders became apprehensive that Kim's political ability and public support might vault him into the presidency with damaging effects on their career.[1] The abhorrence of Kim Dae Jung's political ascendancy was not confined to the generals only. The entire South Korean ruling circles, nurtured under the late Park and still remaining virtually intact, felt antipathy toward Kim. Indeed, Kim was an anathema for the whole South Korean Establishment.[2]

Thus the arrest of Kim Dae Jung on May 17, when the country had just been convulsed by massive anti-government demonstrations, was a logical sequence. It was the crux of the campaign conducted by the military under Chun to wipe out opposition along with corruption. The subsequent trials of Kim and his 23 supporters became perhaps the best known and the most controversial of political issues of the period in the country.

The Trials of Kim Dae Jung and Others

The Martial Law Command began to pave the way for Kim Dae Jung's trial by publishing on May 22, 1980 an "interim report." It stated that Kim was in custody "on positive proof" that he had instigated the student demonstrations that had erupted in the country's major cities earlier. Kim had done so, according to the report, in the hope of coming into power through a violent overthrow of President Ch'oe Kyu Ha's government.[3] Then in another announcement--this time issued on May 31 concerning the just ended nine-day Kwangju uprising--military investigators charged that Kim had "manipulated and agitated" the militant students in Kwangju.[4]

The reference to Kim's purported role in the Kwangju incident was made, even though Kim had already been under arrest when the student-led demonstrations began on May 18 in Kwangju. Thus, the charge that Kim had encouraged Kwangju students to spark the open revolt against the government was flimsy. Rather, it reinforced the public's conviction that the military, led by Chun, was determined to end the political career of Kim Dae Jung.

On July 4, the Martial Law Command issued its full report on its probe into the alleged crimes of Kim Dae Jung and his colleagues. The report portrayed Kim as a dangerous revolutionary who was sympathetic to North Korea and who, aided by his associates, had manipulated the nationwide students' uprisings earlier in the year to topple the government. It claimed that Kim had "engineered the origins of the Kwangju turmoil" and said that he, along with other culprits, would be referred to a general court martial.[5] The politically damaging descriptions in the July 4th report about Kim Dae Jung were subsequently reinforced by other publications released by the heavily censored news media.[6]

The trial of Kim Dae Jung and his 23 codefendants-- among whom were pastors, professors, and opposition party politicians--opened its first session on August 14 in the compound of the Ministry of National Defense.[7] The key charges against them consisted of a conspiracy to commit sedition to install Kim Dae Jung in the country's presidency through student-led violence (for which the maximum punishment was a life imprisonment) and of the violation of martial law decrees banning political activities (which could risk three years' imprisonment). In addition, Kim was accused of having been associated with leftists immediately after Korea's liberation in 1945, being a pro-Communist aligning himself with the North Korean line, and having founded an organization called the Hanmint'ong (The National Congress For the Restoration of Democracy and Promotion of the Unification of Korea) in Tokyo during his stay there in 1973 and led it until 1980.[8]

The allegation that Kim had ties with the Hanmint'ong in Japan was the most serious of the charges leveled against him. This was because the group in question was declared a pro-P'yongyang "anti-state organization" by the South Korean Supreme Court in 1978 and Kim's association with the group constituted a violation of Article 1 of the National Security Law, which could incur the maximum penalty of death. Indeed, the prosecution demanded death for Kim, because "such an opportunist agitator politician must be eliminated from this land for good."[9]

The Hanmint'ong had been obscure to most Koreans until the prosecution in Seoul brought it out. It was a relatively small organization with about 10,000 members among the deeply divided Korean population of some 600,000 in Japan--some of whom supported Seoul and others P'yongyang. Its leaders were drawn from the "mainstream" of pro-South Korean community in Japan--not from North Korean sympathizers, as alleged by the prosecution. Indeed, the Hanmint'ong was a splinter group from the anti-Communist Mindan (The Korean Residents Association in Japan).

The Mindan was organized in October 1946 in opposition to the leftist-dominated Choryon (The League of Korean Residents in Japan), which had existed between October 1945 and 1949. The Mindan also fought against the pro-P'yongyang Ch'ongryon (The General Federation of Korean Residents in Japan), which was organized in May 1955. It was early in the 1970's that some of these anti-Communist Mindan members seceded from the organization and formed the Hanmint'ong as a vehicle to crusade against Park Chung Hee's newly installed Yushin system. And since its formation, the Hanmint'ong had spearheaded the anti-Park movement among non-Communist Koreans in Japan.[10]

According to observers, however, the political "activity" of the Hanmint'ong was only "marginal" and its annual budget was about $50,000, collected in Japan but not from North Korean sources. And Kim's own supporters as well as Japanese officials in Tokyo said that the Hanmint'ong was not pro-North Korea, even though the Supreme Court in Seoul had ruled it as a subversive organization sympathetic to P'yongyang. Kim's followers in Japan claimed that the Hanmint'ong's programs consisted of first restoring democracy in South Korea and then tackling the problem of reunification.[11]

During his court testimony, Kim himself stated that he first formed the Hanmint'ong in July 1973 in San Francisco, where he had arrived via Japan in self-imposed exile, in order to oppose "the dictatorial regime of Park Chung Hee." Then Kim returned to Tokyo, where he stayed from July 10 until August 8, the day he was kidnapped by KCIA agents to be forcibly returned to Seoul. While in Japan, Kim had worked with his Korean friends to organize a second Hanmint'ong group, which was inaugurated on August 15, 1973--one week after his abduction.[12]

Meanwhile, in Seoul on September 17, 1980, the general military court found Kim and all of his 23 codefendants guilty and sentenced Kim to death and the others to various prison terms of up to 20 years, "almost exactly as the prosecution had demanded."[13] The sentences would go to a military appeals court for review and then to the Supreme Court, which was the highest civilian court but also had jurisdiction over military tribunals. On November 3, the military appeals court in Seoul confirmed the rulings of the lower military tribunal against Kim Dae Jung and 16 others while reducing prison terms of the remaining seven. Within less than a week, Kim and 11 others, who had received long prison terms, appealed to the Supreme Court.[14]

As the first round of the trials of Kim and his associates concluded on September 17, other trials by military tribunals got under way in or near Seoul and Kwangju, the two main centers of the anti-government activities of the spring and summer. Unlike the trials of Kim and his codefendants which were "open" to diplomatic observers and local and foreign journalists, these trials were held in secrecy. Concerning the secret trials at the embittered city of Kwangju, however, it was revealed early in September that 172 to 175 persons had been arraigned because of their involvement in the May insurrection in the city. The following month, five of them were sentenced to death and the majority of the remainder received jail terms ranging up to life.[15] In addition, in Seoul and other cities at least another 200 persons were believed to have been imprisoned as a result of the spring disturbances.[16]

In South Korea the immediate reactions to the court verdicts against Kim Dae Jung and his associates were mute, even though the sentences were understood to have evoked a good deal of hard feelings. Abroad, the sentences, particularly Kim's death penalty, drew a storm

256

of protests, especially in the United States and Japan, Seoul's closest allies and where Kim had been well known as a democratic figure.[17] Even before the original verdicts were handed down on September 17, various countries around the world had expressed their misgivings about the Seoul government's handling of the case. For instance, the Washington Post on JUly 23 reported that at least 10 countries had expressed concerns about Kim's fate through diplomatic channels or public statements, and other countries were prepared to do so.

For the governments of these foreign countries, the charges leveled against Kim and 23 others were flimsy because, among others, the government accused Kim of having helped plan and finance the Kwangju rebellion, even though he had already been placed under confinement when the insurrection broke out. As the trials progressed, these foreign governments--like other observers--saw in the indictments hardly anything but a fact that a group of staunch foes of late Park's authoritarian system had worked to further Kim's chance of winning the presidency in the unsettling conditions following Park's assassination. As a matter of fact, from the very beginning, knowledgeable sources viewed the trials more as a political charade, than an exercise of justice, aimed at exterminating any vestiges of political opposition by eliminating Kim from the political scene.[18] International focus on the whole trials was on Kim, and the major question was whether he would be sentenced to death and be executed.

Already on May 18, the day after Kim's arrest, the Carter Administration, that had been alarmed by the rise of military rule in South Korea, voiced its concern for Kim in a meeting between the U.S. Ambassador in Seoul William H. Gleysteen and President Ch'oe Kyu Ha. And on July 7, the State Department characterized the charges against Kim as "farfetched" and "hardly amount to anything more than that Kim Dae Jung was campaigning to be president."[19] Subsequently, the State Department time and again warned the Seoul government against sentencing Kim to death, while repeating its earlier characterization of the trial.[20] In Japan too, where public opinion had become highly critical of the Seoul government in the aftermath of Kim's kidnapping from a Tokyo hotel seven years before, Prime Minister Suzuki Zenko and other high officials made known their concern about Kim's fate.[21]

257

Following the handing down of its verdicts on September 17 by the general military court despite the international pleas and warnings, the Japanese government proved itself the first among foreign governments to react angrily. Within hours of sentencing, the Foreign Ministry in Tokyo, amazed at the death penalty, suggested that relations between Japan and South Korea could suffer if it was carried out.[22] On September 22, the Japanese Prime Minister Suzuki Zenko stepped up the pressure on Seoul government by publicly stating that there could be a "serious restraint" on Tokyo's economic and technological aid to Seoul if Kim was executed.[23] As Kim's appeal was rejected by the military appeals court and the case went before the Supreme Court in November, Tokyo government reiterated the warnings while questioning the judicial procedure in the case.[24]

The officials in Japan--the country that had keen geopolitical interests in the political stability of South Korea--were anxious to save Kim's life, because they were apprehensive that Kim's execution might ignite domestic uprisings in South Korea which could lead to political instability on the peninsula. The Suzuki government's worry about Kim's fate also reflected its concern over rising public opposition within Japan to the trial and conviction of Kim. The Japanese public, like their government, believed that the trial was not only unfairly conducted but also violated the spirit of the "political settlement" reached orally in 1975 between the Tokyo government and its Seoul counterpart over the earlier KCIA's abduction of Kim from Tokyo.[25]

The agreement was said to have centered on the premise that the Tokyo government acknowledged that the Seoul government was in no way involved in the spiriting of Kim back to Seoul, while the latter promised not to punish Kim for his activities carried out during his stay in Japan.[26] Yet the most serious of the charges leveled against Kim in the trial was that he had organized the once obscure group Hanmint'ong in Japan during his stay there in 1973 and led it since. It was on account of this that Kim was condemned to die. The Japanese private citizens, along with their government officials, viewed Kim's trial as "a gross miscarriage of justice on Japan's doorstep," while fearing that Kim's execution would compound the offense committed by the KCIA agents on the Japanese soil seven years before.[27] As their government expressed anxiety and displeasure over Kim's sentence, concerned Japanese citizens greeted the verdict with a series of protest demonstrations, in which they clashed not only with police but also with pro-Seoul government elements in Japan.[28]

All this while, the U.S. government--that had been appalled at the power play by Chun Doo Hwan--also expressed dismay at the verdict in Kim's case. This was because the entire original sentencings against Kim and 23 others lasted only six minutes, and American officials, like their Japanese counterparts, felt the charges in Kim's case were "vague" and did not know how the statutes concerning sedition were applied against Kim, even though U.S. government representatives observed the court proceedings in Seoul.[29]

However, unlike the Japanese whose protests were "open," officials in Washington adopted a "restrained" approach to avoid charges of outside interference from Seoul. Thus despite the State Department's earlier denunciations that the Seoul prosecution's charges against Kim were unsubstantiated, Secretary of State Edmund M. Muskie simply voiced a "deep concern" and "strong feelings" the day after the original sentences were handed down in Seoul and avoided further comments at the time. Other American officials too made pleas to President Chun on behalf of Kim; in keeping with State Department's advice, however, most of these communications were conveyed in private rather than in public.[30] Kim's fate now became the major political issue between Washington and Seoul.

The foreigners' incomprehension of the legal bases of the guilty verdicts was not surprising. For one, as noted already, the Japanese branch of the Hanmint'ong was not inaugurated until August 15, 1973--one week after Kim's Tokyo abduction. Once dragooned back to Seoul, Kim never visited Japan. Instead, he spent his time in incarceration or other state of political limbo, hardly an ideal condition to lead the "anti-state" Hanmint'ong. Furthermore, had Kim had ties with any "anti-state" organization, many foreign and domestic analysts wondered, how these points escaped the attention of President Ch'oe Kyu Ha when he restored Kim's civil rights.[31] Above all, the Seoul government did not make public the text of the original verdicts against Kim and his associates; nor the military appeals court gave the reasons why it upheld the findings of the lower court and why it reduced the jail terms of seven of Kim's codefendants.[32]

American and Japanese officials pleaded with Seoul authorities for clarification of the verdicts, in particular the legal ground for Kim's death penalty. The clarification of Kim's death sentence was especially warranted because, among others, the general public initially were under the impression that Kim had received the death sentence because of his "crime of insurrection." The foreign pleas, however, were met with "ill-defined" responses from Seoul, including one which said that Kim was given the death penalty because he had "assumed chairmanship of the Hanmint'ong upon his return to Korea [in 1973]."[33] And American and Japanese officials were convinced, as they had been, that "Kim's real crime" was that he was "the most popular opposition leader when President Chun [was] trying to tighten his grip."[34]

The American and Japanese feelings were virtually uniformly shared abroad where Western forms of democracy were practiced, including West Germany and Australia. The governments of these countries barraged the Seoul government with clemency pleas for Kim. Groups such as the International Commission of Jurists and the Amnesty International also denounced the trial as unfair.[35]

The Geneva-based International Commission, an independent body of notable jurists, reproved Kim's trial as "a mockery of the process of democratization which South Korean government claims to be pursuing" and asked President Chun to commute the death sentence.[36] The Amnesty International, the London-based human rights organization, similarly condemned the trial as "failing to meet internationally accepted standards of fairness," and on December 9 appealed to the 43 governments on the United Nations Human Rights Commission on behalf of Kim Dae Jung.[37]

After Kim had appealed his death sentence to the Supreme Court in November 1980 (as did his 11 co-defendants), the Court, which had just been reconstituted along "pro-Chun lines," was widely expected to confirm the death penalty.[38] That was to leave Kim's fate to President Chun, who had the power to grant clemency and who already must have been weighing the potential damages and gains that could result from his handling of the case.

The South Korean military elite, who were composed largely of relatively young army officers and who consti-

260

tuted President Chun's power base, were believed to be
strongly in favor of Kim's execution. They believed that
sparing Kim's life would run against the rationale of
their seizure of power, namely, delivering the country
from the political and social anarchy that Kim had
threatened to unleash. These young hard-line army officers were also said to be loath to give the impression
that they were yielding under international pressure,
because that would be seen as a sign of weakness of
Chun's military-backed regime.[39] Thus in order to eliminate Kim permanently as a source of embarrassment and
challenge to them, President Chun's young army officers
sought Kim's execution. Likewise, with Kim still alive,
President Chun too appeared to be "unsure of himself in
his new post" as the President.[40]

Killing Kim, however, would perpetuate his image as a
rallying point for the democratic protests against repression and turn him into "a martyr." It was so because
Kim had a broad nationwide political following stemming
from his long-standing struggle for democratic causes,
and his popularity was evidenced as early as in the last
open presidential election held in 1971. Indeed, a continued political threat posed by Kim to the late Park
regime was responsible for his kidnapping in 1973 from
Tokyo. Given Kim's popularity at home and his reputation
abroad, his execution could plunge South Korea into a
fresh political turmoil, whipped up by the "dissident
fire brands," while bringing a storm of international
protests on the Chun regime.[41]

Publicly, the Seoul government spurned outcries from
abroad against Kim's death sentence, declaring that the
trial was conducted in accordance with "the pertinent
South Korean laws" and that Kim's case was "entirely an
internal affair" of no concern to foreigners.[42] However,
despite such public posture, the Korean government was
understood to have been shocked by the instantaneous
worldwide flood of protests against the death penalty.[43]
It was especially so, because among the countries most
offended by the sentence were South Korea' friends in the
international arena as well as her important trading
partners such as Japan and the United States. Ignoring
the sentiments of these countries, which saw Kim's death
sentence as a political revenge, could be costly. It
would damage Seoul's international standing, worsen the
image of Chun who already had earned a reputation as an
oppressor, and could touch off international sanctions
against Seoul.

Thus the final disposition of Kim's case was a serious challenge, perhaps "the first real political test" confronting the newly installed President. Indeed, it was "a nasty decision" to make, in the words of a Western diplomat in Seoul.⁴⁴ As Mr. Chun was pondering the potential damage Kim's execution could do to his regime against that clemency could have on his power base in the army, many observers at one point saw "signs of a shaky president who seemed to change directions sharply."⁴⁵

Meanwhile, the sentencings on September 17 by the general military court were followed by conjectures among observers that President Chun might eventually commute Kim's death sentence to life in order to dampen the anticipated adverse foreign reactions in case Kim was put to death. Even though Kim's appeal was rejected by the military appeals court and the case was pending before the Supreme Court, there were indications that after all the death sentence might not be carried out.⁴⁶ Both foreign and Korean analysts speculated that Chun, beneath his public posturing of spurning the foreign pleas, was planning to use Kim's fate as leverage in dealing with the Carter Administration,⁴⁷ which had been angered by Chun's rough-and-tumble way of coming to power.

Indeed, by the time the general military court handed down its verdicts on September 17, delicate behind-the-scenes bargaining had already been underway between Korean and American officials.⁴⁸ It was to avoid endangering the talks, held in Washington as well as Seoul, that Secretary of State Muskie and other American officials refrained from severe condemnations of the death sentence other than reiterating the oft stated "concern." They were particularly careful because they were "cautiously" optimistic about getting Chun, who had the final say, to spare Kim's life and did not want to jeopardize the chance by remarks that could be irritating to South Korean authorities.⁴⁹

As the U.S.-South Korea negotiations got under way, Chun was believed to have sought a "whole hearted support" of his regime from the Carter Administration. Specifically, Chun wanted the United States to avoid the kind of critical comments which it had previously made about Chun.⁵⁰ If Chun could win his demands, he would be able to grant clemency without seeming to cave in under U.S. pressures. The task for the American negotiators was to point to the risk ensuing from the execution of Kim for Chun's prospects of building "a democratic welfare society" and to convince Chun that sparing Kim's life was "in Korea's own interest."[51]

Among the final efforts of the Carter Administration on behalf of Kim were those made in December 1980--only several weeks before its departure from the seat of power as the result of Carter's defeat in the November presidential elections. These last minute efforts included two private calls made on the 4th and the 6th of the month by the American Ambassador Gleysteen on the Acting Foreign Minister Kim Tong Hui,[52] and the visit to Seoul on December 13 of the then Defense Secretary Harold Brown.

Defense Secretary Brown arrived in Seoul for a seven-hour stopover on his way home after visiting Tokyo for defense talks. Leading a delegation of 10 including onetime CIA chief in Seoul Donald Gregg, the Defense Secretary spent 90 minutes in a private meeting with President Chun. Although neither Brown nor any other American or Korean officials publicly mentioned Kim Dae Jung's name, the diplomatic sources in Seoul assumed that Brown had conveyed American concern over Kim's fate during the meeting.[53] Brown was the highest ranking official of the outgoing Carter Administration to visit Seoul since Chun had become the president, and his face-to-face plea with Chun in Seoul on behalf of Kim was "one of the weightiest" of the expressions of concern by the United States over the condemned dissident.[54]

The incoming administration of Ronald Reagan joined the outgoing Carter's in making the case for clemency for Kim. Shortly after the November elections, the President-Elect Reagan had his foreign policy advisor, Richard V. Allen, make an unattributed statement that the incoming president opposed Kim's execution and that he believed it would strain U.S.-South Korea relations. And on November 19 a news report quoting "a senior aide" to that effect appeared on the front page of the New York Times, but it "did not do the trick."[55]

Since then throughout December, Allen held a series of private talks in Washington with high South Korean officials including Gen. Yu Byong Hyon, then Chairman of the Joint Chiefs of Staff, and Kim Yong Shik, then Korean Ambassador in Washington, and showed them that the position of the President-Elect Reagan reported in the New York Times was not a propaganda gesture but an expression of serious concern. The message evidently had an effect on the Seoul government--especially so because it was reinforced by similar remarks made in other places including Japan and Western Europe.[56]

However, President Chun could not be asked to give or expected to give, even in private, a pledge to spare Kim's life without being reciprocated. Chun needed a leverage whereby he could mollify the hard-line army officers in case he showed mercy to Kim. Thus during his meetings with South Korean officials, Mr. Allen discussed a possibility of President Chun's visit to Washington after Reagan's inauguration, and he extended Reagan's invitation to that effect. Chun accepted the invitation around Christmastime. Nothing was to be said as yet publicly.[57]

The talks between Seoul officials and Reagan's representatives were facilitated by the fact that Reagan was elected President on "a new tone" for America and that the Seoul government was pleased with the Reagan's election victory on that account. President Chun himself in an interview on December 15 praised Reagan for "his willingness to understand" the problems of allies such as those of South Korea, and contrasted Reagan's "encouraging" attitude with what he described as the American practice of punishing and weakening its allies whose actions "do not meet with your approval."[58] Though he was not specific and did not mention anyone by name, Chun was obviously referring to the Carter Administration's criticisms of Seoul's handling of its political opposition.

Chun must have been still more pleased with the President-Elect's new Korea policy, which was revealed in a remark made on January 12, 1981 by Secretary of State-designate Alexander M. Haig during his confirmation hearing before Congress. Referring to the Carter's plan for "phased withdrawal" of American ground troops from Korea, which had been bitterly opposed by South Korean leaders, Haig told the Senate Foreign Relations Committee that he was against any further pullout of American soldiers from Korea under the then existing circumstances.[59] Such an assertion, coming from a man of Haig's position, could be construed as a public repudiation by the incoming President Reagan of the outgoing Carter Administration's pullout plan, which had been suspended by Carter but never completely abandoned. Haig's remark, which a Seoul newspaper termed "an utterance deserving of attention," must have been a great relief for the South Korean government.[60]

The secret Chun-Reagan negotiations through their proxies reached the denouement on January 21, 1981. On the day, which was the day after Reagan's inauguration, official announcements both in Seoul and Washington said that President Chun would visit Washington on February 2 for talks with President Reagan on "bilateral political, economic, and security aspects as well as regional issues affecting Northeast Asia."[61] It was widely assumed that Chun would not have asked to be received in Washington unless he was prepared to resolve Kim's case to the satisfaction of the White House. It was also considered inconceivable that the just inaugurated Reagan Administration would be willing to receive Chun as a guest without some assurance that Kim's life would be spared.[62]

Indeed, it was announced in Seoul on January 23 that at the direction of President Chun the State Council had commuted Kim's death sentence, which had been confirmed by the Supreme Court only hours before, to a life imprisonment. The State Council did so in consideration of the appeals for leniency from "friendly nations and persons at home and abroad" and in the interest of "national reconciliation." The presidential mercy also shortened the prison terms of the 11 co-defendants of Kim's by two to five years.[63]

Then on January 24, in another gesture expected to soften his image, President Chun lifted the martial law stating that "the foundation for social stability" had been "restored," while pointing out that the need for social order was as great as ever. This ended 456 days of partial or total military control of the country, which was the longest period of martial law in the history of South Korea. The termination of martial law was portrayed by the Seoul government as a major transition back to "normality."[64] In the announcement, which lifted the martial law, Chun also stated that the two-step presidential election would be held on February 11 and 25, and National Assembly election about a month later.

Chun's U.S. Visit and the Elections

On January 28, 1981, President Chun Doo Hwan embarked on an 11-day tour of the United States. Following several days' stopovers in Los Angeles and New York City, Chun met President Reagan in Washington on February 2.[65] Chun was the first foreign head of state to meet the new President at the White House, where the reception accorded to Chun was "cordial."[66] The meeting between the two leaders lasted for 80 minutes, at the end of which a joint communique was released.

The communique stated that Reagan had assured Chun that the United States "has no plans to withdraw [its] ground combat troops from the Korean peninsula"; instead, the communique suggested that there could be an increase in the American forces stationed in Korea. The communique went on saying that Reagan and Chun had "pledged to seek to strengthen the U.S.-Korean cooperation in deterring and defending against aggression." Furthermore, the communique affirmed the Carter Administration's policy that ruled out any direct bilateral discussions between Washington and P'yongyang, which the latter had unsuccessfully sought; and it stated that Seoul would be "a full partner" in any Washington's face-to-face talks with North Korea.[67] Now the South Korean president publicly received what he had wanted from Mr. Reagan, namely, an official reaffirmation of American security commitment to South Korea, including the retention of U.S. ground troops there.

With the formal reassurance of the American security blanket provided for, the Seoul's recent suspicions of American reliability as an ally were dispelled--the suspicions which had risen largely because of the Carter's ill-fated troop withdrawal policy. A further sign of improved Seoul-Washington relations was complete reticence of the joint communique about the question of human rights, whose violations in Seoul had been soundly denounced by the Carter Administration. Nor were the human rights issues mentioned in the farewell speeches of the two presidents.[68] All in all, Chun's cordial reception at the White House signified that the Korean-American relations, which had been strained during the Carter presidency, were restored to normalcy.

By being warmly received by the American President, Chun showed South Koreans that he had clout with the White House, a crucial factor in the effort of South Korean leaders to win power and preserve it. It inevitably strengthened Chun's position at home. The cordial White House reception was especially important for Chun, because he had defied the U.S.-Korea accord governing movement of troops in South Korea on the night of December 12, 1980. In particular, Reagan's promise of firm U.S. military support was a big boost for Chun's prestige as the leader of South Korea, a country that postulated the preservation of its security upon American military and economic backing. All told, Chun's American tour was a "politically triumphant" one.[69]

In Seoul, comments about the trip from government officials and reporters were euphoric. They labelled it as "the Chun-Reagan summit meeting" that marked the beginning of a "new era" in U.S.-Korean relations, and cited it as an international accord of legitimacy to the Chun regime.[70] For the average South Korean who saw the scenes of Chun's reception in Washington via a satellite newscast, Reagan's message of military and diplomatic support for South Korea, which implied the American president's endorsement of Chun, could not be lost. Thus the reception of President Chun at his homecoming, who had already declared his candidacy for the forthcoming presidential election, was "more like a coronation than a simple welcome home."[71]

Even before his visit to the United States, Chun had been widely believed to be the sure winner in the presidential election set for February, and that his Democratic Justice Party (DJP) would emerge victorious in the National Assembly election the following month. It was so assumed because of the exclusion by law of most of the serious opposition from politics, and also because of the country's politically restrictive atmosphere, in which freedom of the press and other civil right remained carefully regulated even after the lifting of martial law on January 24.

After Chun's return home from his "political pilgrimage" to Washington, the results of the forthcoming elections became all but a foregone conclusion: "a walkover for President Chun and the party he headed, the DJP."[72] Thus even though the South Korean voters would shortly choose the new president and the new legislature, there was "curious lack of the sort of speculation" rampant normally in the previous elections. And the election campaigns themselves were an insipid affair, lacking "the animation" which had often accompanied the earlier election campaigns.[73]

On February 11, 1981, almost 78.12 percent of the nearly 21 million South Korean electorate went to the polls to choose 5,278 electoral college members among approximately 9,300 candidates. The candidates from the DJP, of which Chun was the presidential candidate, seized 3,676 seats with 69.64 percent of the total ballots cast; the Independents followed with 1,123 seats won with 21.27 percent of the popular vote; and those belonging to three opposition parties lagged far behind, capturing only 479 seats altogether with a total of 9.07 popular vote.[74]

Since all that Chun needed was a simple majority of the 5,278 electoral college deputies when they make the final selection of the president--Chun was assured a new seven-year term as the head of state, not that there was any doubt as to who would win. Thus the final and second step of the presidential election was now a mere formality, especially so because most of the electoral college deputies elected as Independents were understood to be supporters of Chun's latest presidential bid.[75] On February 25, the presidential electoral college convened to choose the president. The DJP's candidate Chun received 4,755 votes (90.23 percent) of the total valid votes; and candidates of the three opposition parties won only 515 votes altogether.[76]

On March 3, 1981 Chun, for the second time in six months, was sworn in as the president, pledging to lay the foundation of a "a viable democracy" as well as of "a welfare state" and "a just society."[77] With Chun's new presidential inauguration, the Fifth Republic was officially launched, formally putting an end to the turbulent transition period that had begun with the assassination of Park about one and half years before.

In the ensuing National Assembly election of March 25, a total of 276 seats was at stake. The mode of the allocation of seats was skewed in favor of President Chun's DJP. Of the total assembly seats, two-thirds (184) were to be filled through popular voting in the nation's 92 electoral districts. Each district was assigned two seats, with each voter restricted to one choice and with no single party allowed to take both seats in one constituency. Of the remaining 92 seats, which were the "proportional representation seats," two-thirds (61) were to be awarded to the party that would win the largest number of district seats, regardless of its actual share of the votes. The rest (31) were to be distributed among all other parties that would have won at least five seats in the district elections in strict proportion to the popular votes garnered by these parties.[78]

Analysts contended that this formula for allocating the parliamentary seats was devised to favor Chun's DJP and to insure its "victory." Due to the financial and organizational resources of the President's party complemented by a split opposition, it was anticipated that not very many DJP candidates would finish lower than second in the contested district elections and that the party would emerge as the largest vote-getter.[79] Besides, the election campaigns were "tightly controlled" by the Central Election Management Committee (CEMC)[80] and were virtually "devoid" of issues--other than pork-barrel ones--to the advantage of the DJP.[81]

The outcome of the National Assembly election confirmed the optimistic predictions about the DJP. It won 90 seats with 35.6 percent of the votes cast and was allocated 61 "proportional" seats. Thus the DJP held 151 seats altogether in the 276-member single chamber parliament, a clear although not an overwhelming majority. The nearest rival, the opposition Democratic Korea Party had 57 candidates of its own elected with 21.6 percent of the vote, which accorded the party 81 parliamentary seats in all; and the Korea National Party won 18 elected seats with 13.3 percent of the popular vote and acquired a total of 25 seats. The remaining 19 elected seats were divided among five minor parties and Independents, with none of the groups able to claim "proportional" seats.[82]

Had a pure proportional representation system been in effect, under which all the 92 seats in question would be distributed in strict proportion to the popular votes won by the parties, the DJP would have won far fewer seats (well below a simple majority), while the DKP and KNP would have substantially increased their shares of seats. On the other hand, none of the parties would have controlled a majority in the National Assembly.

Finally on April 11, 1981, the new National Assembly--the 11th one in South Korea and elected for a four-year term--opened its session; henceforth, the Legislative Council For National Security ceased to exist.[83] With this, the political experimentation under martial law, which was marked by uncertainty and haphazardness, was done away. Now changes were to take place within a predictable institutional framework under the newly elected President Chun and his coterie, who had already run the country in effect for a year or so and who, thanks to their landslide victories in the latest two elections, appeared to have been secured in their newly acquired positions.

1. In the spring of 1980, a senior general in the inner group of the military hierarchy said that "Kim was going to seize power" that spring and that it was "a real crisis" for the "survival" of his group. Washington Post, July 23, 1980.

2. For example, those involved in the KCIA's kidnapping of Kim from Japan in 1973 could have feared that Kim's presidency would reveal more of the plot than serve their interests.

3. Tong-A Ilbo, May 22, 1980.

4. Tong-A Ilbo, May 31, 1980.

5. Tong-A Ilbo, July 4, 1980. In all, 37 persons were accused of breaking the law in the July 4th report.

6. New York Times, August 17, 1980; and Newsweek, August 23, 1980, p. 44.

7. Tong-A Ilbo, August 14, 1980.

8. Full text of charges against Kim Dae Jung and 23 associates is in the Supplement to the August 14, 1980 edition of Tong-A Ilbo.

9. New York Times, August 19, 1980; and Boston Globe, September 13, 14, 1980. Kim was arraigned on five counts including violation of the Foreign Exchange Control Law. Kim was alleged to have breached the foreign exchange control law, because he possessed and used foreign currency (U.S. dollar and Japanese yen) which was illegally brought into the country to finance students' demonstrations.

10. Lee and De Vos, Koreans in Japan, pp. 123-127; and New York Times, August 17, 19, 1980.

11. New York Times, August 19, 1980; and Far Eastern Economic Review, August 29, 1980, p. 15.

12. Kim was in the United States and Japan between October 11, 1972 and August 8, 1973. Park had avoided prosecuting Kim on account of his connection with the Hanmint'ong perhaps because the overseas group, with few members and little following in South Korea, was not

regarded as a serious threat to him. New York Times, August 17, 19, December 7, 1980.

13. Tong-A Ilbo, September 17, 1980; and Boston Globe, September 17, 18, 1980. Kim was convicted on all the five counts.

14. Nihon Keizai Shimbun (Tokyo), November 4, 1980; and Boston Globe, November 11, 1980.

15. Boston Globe, September 21, 29, 1980; New York Times, November 4, 1980; Maeda, Seoul karano Hokoku, p. 231; and Shaplen, "Letters From South Korea," p. 20.

16. New York Times, October 26, 28, November 10, 1980.

17. Time, September 29, 1980, p. 39; and Boston Globe, September 21, 1980.

18. Far Eastern Economic Review, August 29, 1980, p. 15; Boston Globe, September 14, 1980; and Washington Post, August 20, 22, 1980.

19. Monthly Review of Korean Affairs, II, No. 7, (July 1980), p. 3; and Washington Post, July 23, 1980.

20. New York Times, August 18, 1980; and Boston Globe, September 14, 1980.

21. Far Eastern Economic Review, August 29, 1980, p. 16.

22. Nihon Keizai Shimbun, September 18, 1980; and New York Times, September 18, 1980.

23. Washington Post, September 23, 1980; and Nihon Keizai Shimbun, September 22, 1980.

24. Nihon Keizai Shimbun, November 22, 26 (evening edition), 1980; and New York Times, December 26, 1980. During their court testimonies, the defendants said that they had been unable to obtain the lawyers of their own choice because over 50 lawyers they had contacted, fearful of governmental reprisal, had refused to represent them. They further stated that their proposal to introduce witnesses from Japan and the United States had been turned down. Also during the trial, government officials in Seoul freely made prejudicial comments about Kim. New York Times, September 18, 29, 1980; and Time, September 29, 1980, p. 39.

25. Nihon Keizai Shimbun, July 10, August 14 (evening edition), 1980.

26. Far Eastern Economic Review, August 29, 1980, pp. 15-16, September 19, 1980, p. 12. The Japanese cabinet of Premier Tanaka Kakuei was in no mood or position to come down hard against the regime of Park Chung Hee on the issue of territorial integrity or sovereignty. And it settled the controversy with Park's government in favor of political expediency and failed to expose the crime committed against Kim Dae Jung by the KCIA.

27. New York Times, September 28, 1980.

28. New York Times, November 10, 30, December 6, 11, 26, 1980; and Washington Post, November 5, 1980. For example, on December 4 about 40 protestors invaded the South Korean consulate in Yokohama.

29. Boston Globe, September 17, 1980; and New York Times, October 25, 1980. State Department legal officer Jeffrey H. Smith spent four and a half weeks in Seoul observing the trial.

30. New York Times, December 19, 1980; and Washington Post, December 19, 1980, January 27, 1981.

31. Far Eastern Economic Review, July 11, 1980, p. 8.

32. Nihon Keizai Shimbun, November 4, 1980.

33. Ibid.

34. Time, September 29, 1980, pp. 39-40; and Newsweek, September 29, 1980, p. 41.

35. Far Eastern Economic Review, September 26, 1980, p. 11.

36. Washington Post, September 18, 1980.

37. Boston Globe, December 9, 1980; and Washington Post, January 27, 1981.

38. Five of the Supreme Court's 16 justices were replaced in August by "hardliners." Sources claimed that four of the five dismissed justices had supported the bid of the confessed Park's assassin Kim Jae Kyu to have his case transferred to a civilian court. Kim lost and was put to death. Thus the removal of the five justices was viewed by sources as a purge by the military of lenient justices on the Court before Kim Dae Jung's case could reach it. New York Times, August 12, November 10, December 14, 26, 1980; and Newsweek, August 25, 1980, p. 44.

39. New York Times, December 1, 1980; and Far Eastern Economic Review, December 12, 1980, p.24.

40. New York Times, December 7, 1980; and Newsweek, February 9, 1981, p. 48. Toward the end of the year, the then head of the Defense Security Command Ro T'ae Woo said to a visitor that "the army would lose confidence in President Chun if he showed mercy to Kim." New York Times, December 26, 1980.

41. Boston Globe, September 14, 1980, January 24, 1981; New York Times, November 10, 1980; and Newsweek, February 9, 1981, p. 48. A religious leader, long sympathetic with the cause of Kim Dae Jung, said that "General Chun is in power and everything seems stable. But if Kim is executed, he will be a national hero, and people will dare to fight in his name." Another Christian dissident said that "there will be a severe reaction if he is hanged. There will be another Kwangju--not just in a single city but elsewhere." Boston Globe, July 29, September 21, 1980.

42. *Nihon Keizai Shimbun*, July 10, November 4, 26, 1980; and *Tong-A Ilbo*, December 15, 1980, January 5, 1981.

43. *New York Times*, October 25, 1980; and *Boston Globe*, September 21, 1980.

44. *New York Times*, December 1, 1980.

45. *Washington Post*, January 29, 1981.

46. *Nihon Keizai Shimbun*, November 4, 1980; and *New York Times*, December 7, 1980.

47. *Far Eastern Economic Review*, September 19, 1980, p. 13, September 26, 1980, p. 11.

48. *Washington Post*, August 22, 28, 1980; and *Nihon Keizai Shimbun*, November 4, 1980. The day before Chun resigned from the army on August 22, "a top Korean emissary" Ch'oe Kwan Soo made the rounds of policy makers in Washington explaining the political situation in Seoul.

49. *New York Times*, December 7, 1980; and *Washington Post*, January 27, 1981. As noted, State Department legal officer Jeffrey H. Smith spent four and a half weeks in Seoul observing Kim's court martial. But Smith's report was not permitted to be published on the grounds that it would complicate the task of winning clemency for Kim. And the Carter Administration's reaction to the death sentence was uncharacteristic of its previous attitude to Chun's handling of dissidents, which was "hyperbolic" in castigating Chun.

50. *Washington Post*, August 28, 1980; and *Boston Globe*, September 21, 1980.

51. *Far Eastern Economic Review*, September 26, 1980, p. 10; and *New York Times*, December 7, 1980.

52. *New York Times*, December 7, 1980.

53. *Boston Globe*, December 14, 1980.

54. *Far Eastern Economic Review*, December 19, 1980, p. 10; *Washington Post*, December 19, 1980; and *Boston Globe*, December 14, 1980.

55. *New York Times*, November 23, 1980; and *Washington Post*, December 10, 19, 1980, February 4, 1981.

56. *New York Times*, November 10, 23, 1980; and *Washington Post*, January 27, February 4, 1981. The right-wing government of President Chun, that had been irked by Carter's human rights policy, was jubilant at Reagan's landslide election victory in the belief that the Reagan administration would be less concerned with human rights issues than Carter's. Thus "the colonels" in Seoul were said to have interpreted the *New York Times* story of November 19 as political posturing for Reagan to avoid being blamed for Kim's death.

57. *New York Times*, December 10, 1980; and *Washington Post*, December 16, 1980, January 27, February 4, 1981.

58. Washington Post, December 16, 1980; and US News and World Report, February 2, 1981, p. 8.

59. Washington Post, January 13, 1981; and New York Times, January 13, 1981.

60. Tong-A Ilbo, January 13, 1981; Far Eastern Economic Review, January 30, 1981, p. 20; and Boston Globe, January 24, February 2, 1981. Even though Carter had suspended the pullout plan after his meeting with President Park in Seoul in the summer of 1979, Korean leaders continued to see him with bitterness and suspicion.

61. Tong-A Ilbo, January 22, 1981; and Christian Science Monitor, January 23, 1981.

62. Christian Science Monitor, January 23, 1981; and New York Times, January 24, 1981.

63. Tong-A Ilbo, January 24, 1981. Incidentally, the dissident poet Kim Chi Ha, who had been serving a 20-year prison term, was freed on December 11, 1980 along with seven other dissidents. Washington Post, December 12, 1980; and New York Times, December 11, 1980.

64. Tong-A Ilbo, January 24, 1981; and Boston Globe, January 25, 26, 1981.

65. Chun's visits to the three cities sparked protests from Korean and Korean-American critics of Chun in the United States. Chun's official visit to Washington lasted from February 1 to 3, 1981. This was the first trip to the United States by any Korean president since Park had met President Richard Nixon in San Francisco in 1969; and it was also the first meeting of the leaders of the two countries since President Jimmy Carter's visit to Seoul in the summer of 1979. Washington Post, January 29, 1981; and Boston Globe, February 2, 1981.

66. Jamaican Prime Minister Edward Seaga arrived at the White House on January 28, 1981, and he was the first foreign leader to visit Reagan after inauguration.

67. Full text of the joint communique is in the Tong-A Ilbo, February 3, 1981.

68. Boston Globe, February 3, 1981; and New York Times, February 3, 1981. Since 1977, reports on human rights practices in various countries had been annually delivered by the State Department to the Congress. The report for the calendar year 1980, which contained some 160 countries and was prepared by the Carter Administration's State Department, was said to include a section highly critical of Seoul's human rights violations. The Reagan Administration quietly asked the Congress to delay the publication of the report in order to avoid embarrassing Chun during his stay in Washington; otherwise, it would have been made public on February 2, 1981--the day of Chun's meeting with Reagan.

69. Far Eastern Economic Review, February 20, 1981, p. 21.
70. Tong-A Ilbo, February 3, 1981.
71. Christian Science Monitor, February 13, 1981.
72. Christian Science Monitor, February 6, 1981.
73. Far Eastern Economic Review, February 20, 1981, p. 12; and Sekai, No. 424, (March 1981), pp. 225-226, No. 425, (April 1981), p. 192.
74. Tong-A Ilbo, February 12, 1981. The new constitution, unlike the Yushin charter, allowed candidates for the electoral college to affiliate themselves with political parties and campaign for the presidential candidates of their parties during their own election campaigns for the electoral college (text of Presidential Election Law is in Tong-A Ilbo, December 26, 1980). The three opposition parties were the Democratic Korea Party, the Korea National Party, and the Civil Rights Party; and each fielded its own presidential candidate, not because they thought they could win but to gain prestige.
75. Washington Post, February 12, 1981.
76. Tong-A Ilbo, February 26, 1981. Yu Ch'i Song of the Democratic Korea Party received 404 votes, Kim Jong Ch'ol of the Korea National Party 85, and Kim Ui T'aek of the Civil Rights Party 26.
77. Text of Chun's inaugural address is in the Tong-A Ilbo, March 3, 1981.
78. Text of the National Assembly Election Law is in the Yonhap Yongam 1981, pp. 513-525.
79. Washington Post, March 27, 1981; and New York Times, March 25, 26, 1981.
80. The CEMC regulated virtually every aspect of campaign activities. For example, candidates were prohibited from making door-to-door visits or holding individual rallies or using campaign trucks. Candidates could state their positions at joint gatherings sponsored by the CEMC, with a time limit on their speeches. The CEMC also regulated campaign expenditures as well as the sizes of posters. Yonhap Yongam 1981, pp. 513-525.
81. Far Eastern Economic Review, March 27, 1981, p. 35. Many of the South Korea's about 21 million voters, who had given up the hope of instituting a fully democratic parliament along the line of those of Western Europe or Japan, were said to be more than willing to be swayed by the government's promises for local development projects or actual delivery of them.
82. Tong-A Ilbo, March 26, 1981.
83. Tong-A Ilbo, April 11, 1981.

CHAPTER 13

SOUTH KOREA UNDER A NEW REGIME (1)

As General Chun and his fellow officers rose to power during 1980-1981, it appeared to many that they were playing the same tune familiar since the days of the late Park: a stern authoritarian rule based upon the control of a large military force and ever watchful security and intelligence networks. If any, Chun's regime was even more stringent than Park's, as if he were committed to restoring "a purified version of the late Park's dicta-torial rule."[1]

Government's Grip on the Society in Ideological Vacuum

On January 3, 1981, President Chun renamed the much feared KCIA the Agency For National Security Planning (ANSP), entrusting it with the responsibility of main-taining "internal security" and conducting "investigation of those involved in treason."[2] Thus despite the change in the name, the ANSP was to continue to carry out such works as the surveillance and suppression of the domestic critics of government, which had been undertaken thither-to by the KCIA.

Concerning university students who had been troublesome for the successive governments in Seoul, the Special Com-mittee For National Security Measures adopted several restrictive measures aimed at curbing their political activism. Among them were regulations concerning the permissibility of student demonstrations. For several months until the army's seizure of power in May 1980, protest actions by students had been permitted so long as they had remained on campus. However, new directives issued by the Ministry of Education on June 11 prohibited all students' demonstrations on or off campus.[3] Then in July a "large" number of students and professors, who had been active in the demonstrations of the spring, were ex-pelled from schools as part of the campaign for the "purification of educational circles." Some of the expelled even went to prisons. In the same month, the autonomous students' associations, that had sprung up earlier in the spring, were replaced by the old students' national defense corps.[4]

A further brake was applied to the students' anti-government activism by means of a quota system which restricted the number of college graduates. Under this quota sys-tem, announced on July 30 by the SCNSM, beginning with the incoming 1981 freshmen classes, about a third of all students would be failed and dismissed from schools before graduation. Observers believed that this policy was designed by the authorities to heighten the already intense competition for grades and to compel students to surrender their more idealistic aspirations for the sake of sheer academic survival.[5]

Another area to receive a close attention of the Chun regime was labor activism. To restrict the activities of the workers and to keep the lid on labor disorder, the Legislative Council For National Security on December 30, 1980 passed five "basic" labor laws: the Labor-Employer Council Law, the Labor Standard Law, the Labor Union Law, the Labor Dispute Settlement Law, and the Labor Committee Law.[6] With the adoption of the new labor legislation, which went into effect on January 23, 1981, the handling of labor-employer relations became the responsibility of the Labor-Employer Council, instead of the old labor union mechanism. "Outside forces"--such as the Urban Industrial Mission or even the tame Federation of Korean Trade Unions--were forbidden from helping workers to organize themselves or assisting them in settling labor disputes.[7]

Thus under the new labor laws, national unions became little more than weak liaison boards, because collective bargaining processes were reduced to the level of local factories and the initiative of national unions was eliminated on even such basic matters as wages and working conditions. All this while, the union officials democratically elected before the Army's seizure of power were forced to "retire."[8]

As the Chun regime tightened its hold on the society, it came to control more areas of the country's life than any other Seoul regime, while swiftly and thoroughly putting down any signs of protest. Under the circumstances, even though the martial law was lifted and Chun's military regime was compelled to "civilianize" itself, South Koreans continued to live "under martial law without martial law."[9] Yet, Chun asserted that the political structure he was erecting would lay the foundation for a "democratic welfare state." This is like Park's claim that the Yushin system, installed in the wake of the destruction of democratic institutions, would assure "Korean-style democracy."[10]

It is obvious that the Chun regime was ambiguous in the enunciation of its fundamental political creed (or rather devoid of it), as had been the case with the Park regime. As Park had substituted economic growth along with the threat from the North as an apology for the way he had ruled, Chun used slogans--such as "the realization of a just society" or a "reformation of the way of thinking"[11] --as a surrogate to political ideology. This poverty of political ideologies was characteristic of successive governments in Seoul, with the possible exception of the short-lived Chang Myon regime.

Under the Republic's first President Syngman Rhee the guiding principle centered around two dominant themes: anti-Communism and anti-Japanism (even though Rhee harbored in his administration many Korean collaborators of Japanese colonial rule). Such themes were not only "negative" in nature but mere political slogans. They remained so without being crystallized into a positive moral and political philosophy, which could have provided the country with a long-term direction and rallied the population around their government, while fully unleashing their energy in the nation-building endeavors undertaken since 1948.

Instead of a basic political and moral principle, the successive regimes in Seoul resorted to, among others, the issue of national security and/or regionalism as major devices for political manipulation to stay in power. While invoking national security in time of domestic turbulence, the Seoul regimes, from Syngman Rhee's time on, often equated themselves with the state itself and branded their opponents as "anti-state." With regard to regionalism, it was the late President Park who for the first time in South Korean politics played it up, especially the traditional prejudices between Kyongsang and Cholla Provinces, as a tool for political manipulation.[12] The abuse or misuse of the national security issue and the instigation of regional animosity for self-centered political gains engendered skepticism, even cynicism, among the public about the integrity of their political leaders. When combined with the widespread political corruption in the country, such a public attitude generated an intense moral turpitude both in the public and private lives of the country.

The Old and New Fissures

The seizure of power by Chun Doo Hwan had given rise in its wake to worrisome trends. The Chun regime, like the late Park's, was immediately dominated by the people from Kyongsang Province to the extent that it too came to be labelled by the public as the "Kyongsang Province regime."[13] Basing its public support upon a parochial allegiance rather than a nationwide one, the new Chun regime sowed seeds of further inter-provincial hostility. As he relied upon the regional support, the general public in Seoul showed "little excitement" over Chun's presidential inauguration in September 1980. And on the day of his second presidential inauguration in March of the next year, all the roads leading from the Blue House to the ceremonial site were "heavily guarded by armed soldiers and policemen."[14]

Moreover, the bloody December 12th intra-army putsch was said to have created "fissures" in the military, especially since the ousted generals still had many followers in the armed forces, and it was believed that the rifts would widen in time. Under the circumstances, observers speculated that the putsch, one of the most shocking breaches of discipline in the South Korean army, might cause endless conflicts among officers, erode the chain of command, and interfere with Seoul's defense capability.[15] Indeed, when military intervention in civil politics is hitched to the service of soldiers' career aspirations, as was the case with Chun and his fellow officers, it could create a frightening possibility of revolving military coups to the detriment of the general well-being of the society.

Still more, Chun's relentless drive to seize power and hold onto it was said to have generated distrust between the people who had been weary of the late Park's 18-year authoritarian rule, on one hand, and the army that acted as the instrument of the suppression of the democratization movement in the spring of 1980, on the other.[16] Especially, the killings of insurgents by government troops in Kwangju engendered resentment against the troops that had made assault upon the city, while stunning the whole nation. The incident saddled Chun with sobriquets such as a "cutthroat" or "the butcher of Kwangju," and "Kwangju became the albatross around Chun's neck." After Kwangju, there was seemingly no looking back for the army-backed Chun regime, because many "heads were at stake including Chun's."[17]

Furthermore, the aftermath of the Kwangju tragedy witnessed the surfacing of anti-American sentiments in South Korea for the first time since the Korean War. A sizable segment of the population was aggrieved by the U.S. role in the mobilization against Kwangju of the assault troops, which were part of the U.S.-South Korea Combined Forces Command then under General John A. Wickham.[18] Perhaps even more germane to the initial stirrings of anti-Americanism was Gen. Wickham's statement made early in August 1980, purported to express a conditional U.S. support for Chun's presidency. It was so because Wickham's remark--made in the aftermath of the Kwangju tragedy but immediately preceding Chun' accession to presidency--had given the impression that the United States was backing Chun's drive at presidency. Or, at least, it was interpreted by Korean intellectual circles as an American acquiescence in Chun's rise. The domestic foes of Chun were further chagrined at the American President Ronald Reagan's reception of Chun at the White House in February 1981, which made it appear that Washington was reinforcing--if not legitimizing--Chun's position.[19]

The incipient grudge against the United States manifested itself in Seoul during anti-government campus rallies, which recurred throughout the fall and winter of 1980. As the campus disturbances continued throughout the year 1981 in the capital, students in provincial centers followed suit. While calling the Chun regime a "military fascist," the demonstrating students "for the first time almost universally condemned the U.S." for what they considered American complicity in the birth and the policy of the Chun government.[20] The surge of the overt anti-Americanism[21] was an extraordinary development even among the students who had been the most persistently active anti-government force. Not only because South Korea had been known as "the most anti-Communist, most pro-American nation in Asia" but also because her existence itself had been predicated upon her firm alliance with the United States.

From the fall of 1980 and throughout the next year, in all 74 campus disturbances (47 rallies and 27 cases of scatterings of "seditious leaflets") were reported. These disturbances were by and large confined to campuses, and they were a far cry from those of the spring 1980 in terms of frequency and intensity. Nonetheless, they made it clear that college students would not be reconciled with or even acquiesce in the political supremacy claimed by the Chun regime, which, the students believed, would not survive in power without American support.[22]

The aspect of anti-Americanism--growing out of the political struggle between Chun's regime and its foes--was highlighted by the firebombing of the Pusan branch of the United States International Communications Agency (USICA) on March 18, 1982 by three youths. The arson gutted the ground floor of the building, and a student trapped inside died and three people were injured. Leaflets scattered at the burnt U.S. mission accused the United States of having "supported the military regime which refused democratization, social revolution, and development"; and they called on the United States to "leave this land" or, they warned, there would be more anti-American attacks.[23]

Thitherto, this had been the most violent outburst of fury against the United States in the post-Korean War era in South Korea. However, this was not the first such incident. In December 1980 a fire was set in the office of the USICA in Kangju, about which the government controlled South Korea news media did not report. On September 22, 1983, still another USICA building--this time in Taegu--was set afire, which resulted in the death of one student and injuries to five others.[24]

As anti-Americanism surged in South Korea--fed in part by the conviction that in the last analysis what was propping Chun's regime was America[25]--Korean intellectuals showed renewed interest in the American President Theodore Roosevelt's endorsement as early as during the Russo-Japanese War (1904-1905) of Japan's eventual annexation of Korea.[26] The revived interest in this historical episode among the intellectuals were portentous in view of the very close and trusting relations that had been maintained between South Korea and the United States.

282

As he tackled the resurging domestic opposition in a new political milieu touched off by the over anti-Americanism, President Chun came under the same kind of peace offensive from the North that had put the late President Park constantly on the defensive. Indeed, as early as January 12, 1980, P'yongyang put the government in Seoul on the spot by calling for a meeting of the Prime Ministers of the two sides along with the opening of a "comprehensive political consultative conference" to resume the talks on unifying the country, the talks which had been suspended since the summer of 1973.[27] The shaky Ch'oe Kyu Ha government rejected the idea of the "comprehensive political consultative conference," because the proposed conference would be attended by hundreds or even thousands of governmental as well as nongovernmental representatives from each side and would minimize the role of the governments and might create social unrest in South Korea. Seoul, however, responded affirmatively to the meeting of the two Prime Ministers.[28]

As preliminary talks got under way from February 6, 1980 at P'anmunjom on the planned conference of the Prime Ministers, Seoul authorities took great pains not to raise the public's hopes for the convening of such a meeting. During the talks themselves, Seoul favored modest issues such as the reuniting of the separated families and related matters as the agenda of future Prime Ministers' meetings, while P'yongyang sought wide-ranging subjects including one on political reunification of the country.[29] Although the two delegations met several times to hammer out the differences, no progress was made. The negotiations finally foundered in April following P'yongyang's denunciation of Chun Doo Hwan as a "cancerous being," who was then consolidating his position.[30]

Meanwhile, on January 12, 1981 President Chun Doo Hwan proposed an exchange of visits between him and North Korea's Kim Il Sung to pave "the way to peaceful unification through unconditional resumption of the suspended dialogue." While stating that reunification was "the paramount national task" and "our nation's long-cherished goal," Chun emphasized that the goal could be reached when the North and South began "reaching agreements on the most amenable matters in the least sensitive areas and progress towards more difficult ones" and "a sense of trust" was restored.[31] Thus Chun was following Seoul's long-standing approach to unification, set forth during the aborted 1972-1973 reunification talks between the two Koreas. The North rejected Chun's proposal denouncing it as "a foolish burlesque designed to whitewash his dirty nation-splitting nature and gain public favor" in the forthcoming February 1981 presidential election.[32]

Undaunted, during his presidential inaugural address on March 3, Chun reiterated his invitation to the North Korean leader to visit Seoul, but in vain.[33] On January 22, 1982 Chun renewed his proposal of a year before for a direct meeting between him and Kim. The proposed summit parley would negotiate a provisional agreement governing the basic relations between the two Koreas until the time when the two halves were reunited. Notably, the suggested interim pact was to acknowledge the principles of equality of the two Koreas and of non-interference in each other's domestic affairs.[34]

In short, President Chun, like Presidents Park and Ch'oe, presented a scheme for a gradual political accommodation, leaving the status quo on the peninsula untouched for the time being. This proposal represented "the maximum position" of Chun's government on the reunification, in the word of a high-ranking Seoul official. To no one's surprise, P'yongyang wasted no time in rejecting Chun's overture, while calling him "a traitor" who was inciting confrontation between the two Koreas in order to keep the peninsula permanently divided.[35] On February 10, however, North Korea unsuccessfully called for a conference which would be attended by 100 delegates from each of the two Koreas to tackle directly the problems of reunification.[36]

In conjunction with P'yongyang's insistence on holding the comprehensive political consultative conference or the meeting of 100 political figures from each side, it should be remembered that already on June 23, 1973 Kim Il Sung had called for the opening of an All Nation Congress immediately following Park Chung Hee's proposal for simultaneous admission of the two Koreas into the United Nations as separate entities. Kim denounced Park's proposal as an attempt to perpetuate the division of the country, and demanded the convening of an All Nation Congress to establish a Confederal Republic of Koryo and that the North and South join the U.N. as a united body under that name.

It was obvious that in the latest exchanges of proposals and counterproposals between Seoul and P'yongyang, the latter was sticking to Kim's confederal scheme, while the former was adhering to the late Park's formula. Thus even though the Seoul authorities met with their northern counterparts from time to time in order to discuss the question of reunification, they hardly could afford to be enthusiastic about such meetings. Indeed, Seoul representatives approached the negotiations with the North always with caution and suspicion because of the potentially serious effects on South Korean domestic politics, which could emanate from the popular euphoria such contacts could generate. Thus as Park was doggedly plagued by northern peace overtures for the reunification of the divided peninsula, Chun was defensive and equivocal on the issue and failed to make a "credible effort" to achieve the goal.[37]

The Economy and the New Regime's Credibility Gap

As Chun was challenged externally and internally, the country's economy, which had shown signs of troubles even before Park's assassination, continued to ail. The problem was candidly conceded in December 1979 by a presidential spokesman, who stated that "our current economic situation is more serious than people generally think." When the Chun regime was launched in the fall of 1980, it reportedly realized that the revitalization of the sluggish economy was the most critical issue facing it.[38]

In 1979, the year oil prices doubled, South Korea's real exports fell by 2.3 percent. The trade deficit of the year was $4.29 billion, s sharp increase from $1.78 billion in 1978 and which was the largest trade imbalance thitherto. As a result, the total foreign debts reached some $22 billion, almost a 40 percent increase over the amount of the year before.[39] Among the reasons given by analysts for such a dismal outcome were the slowdown in the world economy, the increases in the costs of imported raw materials (especially oil), Seoul's weakening competitive position in the international market vis-a-vis other developing countries, and the country's political uncertainty following Park's murder.[40]

Because exports had been the "main engine" of South Korea's economic growth,[41] their decline spelled both slump and unemployment. The real GNP growth rate in 1979 was 7.1 percent--a sharp decline from 11.6 percent of the year before; and there were four times as many enterprises as the previous year that could not meet their payrolls. Inflation also remained high throughout the year 1979, with the retail prices running 20-25 percent higher than in 1978.[42]

As the country plunged into a fresh political turmoil in 1980, the economy performed even more dismally; the year's GNP in real terms declined by 5.7 percent, which was the first negative growth in 16 years. It was partly due to the year's disastrous grain harvest brought about by bad weather.[43] The minus growth was also caused by a continuing decline of exports, which occurred despite the devaluation in January 1980 of the won vis-a-vis U.S. dollar by 19.8 percent.[44] Incidentally, the 1980 exports increased over the year 1979 by about 17 percent nominally. However, this was far short of the year's inflation rate which climbed to 40-44 percent. Meanwhile, the year's trade deficit hit another high, $4.2 billion.[45]

As the economy dipped sharply in 1980, the inventories of the manufactured goods rose; and towards the year's end the country's plants were operating at no higher than 70 percent capacity, small and medium size plants operating only at half their capacity. As a result, the official unemployment rate rose from 3.8 percent in 1979 to 6.0 percent, the highest in 13 years. As the economy was gripped in a stagflation, the real incomes of the working people declined by 5.3 percent.[46] In all, the 1980 recession was the worst in more than two decades. Thereafter, the economy showed signs of recovery.

For example, the GNP growth rates were approximately 6.8 percent in 1981 and 5.3 percent in 1982 despite the continuing global recession. Inflation dropped from the high 40-44 in 1980 to 12.6 percent in 1981; and it further went down to 4.6-5.0 percent in 1982, which was one of the lowest in South Korea.[47] The figures cited above showed that the severe stagflation of 1980 was over; however, they were not strong enough to indicate the sluggishness of the economy itself had ended.

In order to remain "financially solvent" during 1982-1986 and to "minimize" unemployment in the face of some half a million people who annually joined the labor force (as of 1979-1980)--the South Korean economy needed a "real" or inflation-adjusted growth of seven to eight percent yearly.[48] Considered against these requisites and when adjusted against inflation, the economic figures of the years 1981-1982 revealed that "basically the economic situation in Korea isn't growing."[49] Meanwhile, the country's foreign debt, which was about $22 billion in 1979, increased precipitately; and by 1982 had reached nearly $40 billion, making South Korea one of the most indebted nations in the world.[50]

As the economy floundered in stagnation, many analysts wondered if the "economic miracle" of South Korea, Park's pride and foundation of his nation-building efforts, had finally evaporated with the advent of the Chun regime. And they asked that if Chun's regime could not acquire legitimacy in the eyes of the public on the basis of economic performance, from where could it draw public support for it, given the "unorthodox" way it had come to power. Thus the same observers perceived in the languidness of the exports, for long the mainstay of Seoul's "fabled" economy, a potential for the undercurrent of the domestic political opposition to swell, leading to a recurrence of the same kind of labor and political unrest that had preceded the demise of the Park regime.[51]

The ominous potential for such unrest was perceived by the analysts, especially because of the widening unevenness in the distribution of the nation's wealth. For example, South Korea's 10 top-notch business conglomerates, which accounted for 5.1 percent of the gross domestic product (GDP) in 1973, doubled the corresponding figure to a high 10.9 in 1978. Their annual growth rate of GDP during the 1973-1978 period was 28 percent, which was almost thrice the national rate of 9.9 percent for the same period. All these financial giants had diversified their holdings--deeply cutting into the manufacturing (23.4 percent as of 1978), construction (29.4 percent), banking and insurance (24.3 percent), and mass media and transportation (15.8 percent).[52]

Apparently, big businesses fared the 1980 economic crisis not as badly as lesser ones. Because as noted already, while South Korea's factories on the whole utilized 70 percent of their capacity, small and medium size factories operated at a much lower 50 percent of their capacity. This would mean that huge enterprises were not as much adversely affected by the economic slump as smaller ones, or possibly they did not suffer at all. Indeed, the GNP figures of various economic sectors for the first quarter of 1980 revealed that those spheres controlled by the financial giants enjoyed substantial growths. For example, the construction, banking and insurance, and transportation and communications--all under near monopoly by 46 affluent groups--grew at the rates of 12.1 percent, 10.1 percent, and 4.8 percent, respectively. The enterprises which suffered declines were generally small man's affairs such as those in agriculture and fishery and in the retail and restaurant businesses.[53]

Amidst the general economic hardship, the country's laborers began to stir, which led to disruption of the "uneasy calm" that had thithero prevailed on the labor scene under the Chun regime. The very first labor unrest to flare up since Chun's accession to presidency was the occupation on January 30, 1981 by 21 textile workers of an American labor institute in Seoul and the detention of its American director. This was done by the workers in an attempt to call international attention to the forcible closure by the government eight days before of the local Ch'ongge Garment Workers' Union.[54] After six hours of standoff, riot police moved in overpowering the intruders and freeing the American unharmed.[55]

Then on the night of June 2-3, 1982, a group of about 100 female workers held their two American executives hostage at the Seoul plant of the U.S.-owned Control Data Corporation. The two Americans were visiting Korea from their company headquarters in the United States to attend to complaints registered by the union at the Seoul plant that six of its leaders had been illegally dismissed in March over wage disputes. This union was composed of female assembly-line workers, and it and another at a textile company were said to be the only unions in South Korea whose officials had been freely elected.[56] On the opposite side of the union in the disputes were the company's non-union employees, among whom were about 30 male supervisors and engineers.

The irate women demanded that their American captives reinstate the fired union activists. Eventually, police were called in, who rescued the two Americans after more than nine hours of captivity. Coming on the heels of the firebombing of the U.S. cultural center in Pusan some three months before, the incident was regarded in Seoul as the most serious known labor clash since January of the previous year, when textile workers in Seoul took an American labor representative hostage.[57]

The South Korean economic scene, languid in productivity and marred by labor agitations, was rocked in May 1982 by a massive "curb loan scandal."[58] The scandal

involved manipulation of nearly one billion dollars worth
of promissory notes and defrauding of numerous investors
by more than two dozen high society persons. The key
figures among the defrauders were an ex-KCIA deputy chief
and his wife, who was a socialite curb market dealer.[59]
From the spring of 1981 the couple in question had made
high-interest cash loans to six major industrial firms,
demanding many times the value of the cash loaned in
promissory notes but pledging that the I.O.U.s would be
held only as collateral. However, trading on their political connections from the moment they made the first
cash loan of three million dollars, the couple resold the
promissory notes mostly on the curb market to discount
houses, banks, and individuals. With the cash thus generated, the man and wife obtained more notes from cor-
porate borrowers and resold them for additional cash in
spiralling deals.[60]

The devious practice continued until April 1982, when
a firm, whose promissory notes had been resold by the
couple despite the agreement to the contrary, complained
to the authorities; and the scam surfaced early in May,
as its two masterminds were arrested. Within a few days,
a score of additional arrests were made including two
former bank presidents. By then, the country's curb market transactions had come to a virtual standstill and
there was a run on the stock market. The government was
compelled to release billions of won from emergency funds
to shore up confidence in the nation's financial system.[61]

When the smoke had cleared, the average man in the
street learned that the knavish couple over a 14-month
period had handled a staggering sum of U.S. $988 million
in notes--about 17 percent of South Korea's entire money
supply which was estimated at $5.6 billion. In the
process, the couple had netted a huge sum of $250-300
million.[62] On the other hand, banks and other financial
institutions and curb market lenders--all found themselves holding "dishonored" promissory notes of one kind
or another bought from the guilty couple. The six corporations prominently involved in the scandal had either
bankrupted or teetered on the edge of bankruptcy.[63]

This multi-million dollar swindle was "the biggest"
financial scam in South Korea, according to the prosecution. In all, 29 culprits were involved in the scam
including an uncle of the First Lady. The uncle of
President Chun's wife, a retired general and a former

army provost marshall, had received $140,000 in cash and a house valued at $414,000 from the guilty couple in exchange for his promise to peddle his influence to further the couple's business interests.[64]

The eruption of the financial scandal was preceded by a bizarre incident on April 26, in which a provincial policeman went berserk for seven hours fatally shooting 56 villagers and wounding 37 others before taking his own life. The slaughter, which went on for so many hours without being halted by the authorities, profoundly shocked the public. The incident raised "serious doubts" about local defense capability in the country where authorities were "supposed to be constantly on the alert for infiltrators from the North."[65] Now the money scam--coming so close on the heels of such a politically embarrassing incident--touched off another public outcry; and it seriously undermined public confidence in Chun's two-year old rule, the official hallmark of which had been anti-corruption.[66]

The latest public controversy centered on: (1) how the masterminds of the scam had obtained the bulk, if not all, of the cash with which the scheme was initially launched, in view of the near impossibility of securing bank loans without political influence; (2) how the couple could have held sway over the country's financial establishment for more than a year, if they did not have political clout; and (3) where had the profits gone, which the scheming couple had acquired by trading in the $988 billion worth of the promissory notes.[67]

In an attempt to clear the public's suspicion and assuage their wrath, the authorities carried out wholesale arrests of those involved in the scam, including the uncle of the First Lady, while repeatedly stating that no money had gone to politicians or had been used as political slush funds. However, no amount of assurance by public leaders was able to persuade the public, who had grown "pathologically distrustful" of their officials, to accept the government's claim that its hands were clean. Instead, the man on the streets continued to suspect that the profits, made by juggling of the promissory notes, had been used for political purposes and that the major beneficiaries remained unpunished and in positions of power.[68]

Concerning the recent untoward incidents, the Tong-A Ilbo on May 21, 1982 commented as follows:

The people have understood that the principal
task of the DJP is to correct the fundamental
desolation of our society brought about by the
DRP's development policy [under Park] that was
materialistically oriented.

However, a series of incidents have been breaking
out in succession, which strike heavy frontal
blows at the 'just society' [to be realized]
through 'reformation of the way of thinking' [a
political slogan of the DJP]. A policeman,
regardless of his professional duty, shot all
night long the residents whom he had to protect.
As if this were not enough, leading members of
our society and their families...have committed
unjust acts, which have thrown our economy into
a great confusion.

What does all this tell about the state of our
society? It conjures up the saying: 'The DJP for
only themselves, the bureaucracy for only themselves, and the people for only themselves.'

The DJP's image continued to be tarnished as Chun's
anti-corruption campaign was further undermined by persistent financial scandals involving public figures.
Among the sensational of the new scandals were the
Myongsong and Yongdong cases in 1983 and corruption
charges against the ruling DJP Chairman Chong Nae Hyok
in 1984.

The Myongsong Corporation, a real estate developer,
amassed a fortune of $200 million in three years by
fraudulent means. Its leaders were indicted along with
more than a dozen officials, among whom was former air
force chief of staff Yun Ja Jung who served as the Minister of Construction in the first Chun cabinet.[69] In
the case of the Yongdong Development Corporation, five
employees of the corporation were indicted along with 19
Chohung Bank officials who had illegally extended a bank
payment in order to guarantee $230 million worth of com-
mercial papers floated by the corporation.[70] On the
other hand, the DJP Chairman Chong, faced with corruption
charges, gave up his national assembly seat and resigned
from the party chairmanship, while donating half of his
estimated property ($6 million) to the state.[71]

Indeed, the various signs--emanating from here and
there during the first few years of its existence--did

not bode well for the stability of the newly established Fifth Republic. Rather, they suggested that the future of the new republic would be stormy and precarious.

Notes

1. Economist, May 31, 1980, p. 12.
2. New York Times, January 4, 1981; and Sekai, No. 424, (March 1981), p. 225. KCIA directors' careers generally ended dismally. Kim Jae Kyu was hanged after he had killed Park; Kim Jong P'il, the agency's first head, and Lee Hu Rak, the sixth director, were held on charges of corruption and removed from political scene. Kim Hyong Wook, the third chief, disappeared in Paris in the fall of 1979, presumably a victim of the KCIA's own foul play. Kim Ke Won, the fourth director, was disgraced in connection with Park's assassination.
3. Washington Post, June 12, 1980.
4. Hanyang, No. 165, (March-April 1982), p. 68; and Patterson, "South Korea's Time of Testing," p. 216.
5. Tong-A Ilbo, July 30, 1980, June 12, 1981; and Shaplen, "Letters From South Korea," pp. 205-206.
6. Nakagawa Nobuo, "Kankoku Minshuka Tosono Chokumensuru Kadai" (The Problems Confronting the Struggle for Democratization in South Korea), Gekkan Shakaito (Tokyo), August 1981, pp. 175-176.
7. Ibid.
8. New York Times, March 1, 1981; and Sekai, No. 425, (April 1981), pp. 187-188.
9. Stokes, "Korea's Church Militants," p. 106; Patterson, "South Korea's Time of Testing," pp. 217-219; and Sekai, No. 425, (April 1981), p. 193.
10. Incidentally, no one had been able to define late Park's "Korean-style democracy."
11. Tong-A Ilbo, May 21, 1982.
12. Tong-A Ilbo, October 19, 1987; and Tong-A Daily News, San Francisco Section, November 27, 1987.
13. Maeda, Seoul karano Hokoku, p. 223; and Sekai, No. 432, (November 1981), p. 165.
14. New York Times, September 2, 1980; and Washington Post, March 4, 1981.

15. Sekai, No. 432, (November 1981), pp. 167-170. For example, Gen. Park Se Jik, Commander of the Capitol Garrison Command, was dishonorably retired from the service in August 1981 for alleged influence-peddling. Park, then 49, was a graduate of the 12th KMA class (one year junior to Chun's class) and also a native of Kyongsang Province, and he had "all the right credentials to climb up the ladder of power." Thus his dismissal fueled rumors that he was cashiered for "reasons other than the alleged corruption." Far Eastern Economic Review, August 14, 1981, pp. 12-13.

16. Stokes, "Korea's Church Militants," p. 104; and Sekai, No. 429, (August 1981), pp. 210-221.

17. Stokes, "Korea's Church Militants," p. 104.

18. Hanyang, No. 164, (January-February 1982), pp. 69, 70; and Sekai, ed., Gunsei to Junan, pp. 198-199.

19. Hanyang, No. 164, (January-February 1982), pp. 68, 69, 70; and New York Times, June 7, 1982.

20. Hanyang, No. 165, (March-April 1982), pp. 82-83; New York Times, September 2, November 10, 1980; and Christian Science Monitor, March 27, 1981. On September 1, 1980, the government reopened the nation's colleges and universities, which had been closed since May.

21. Since early 1970's, there had occasionally appeared anti-U.S. mottoes during campus rallies. But up until now, such mottoes had been used by a very small number of students.

22. Hanyang, No. 165, (March-April 1982), p. 82; and Sekai, No. 432, (November 1981), pp. 182-183, No. 433, (December 1981), pp. 171-174.

23. Asian Wall Street Journal, March 23, October 13, 1982.

24. Sekai, No. 424, (March 1981), p. 223; and New York Times, April 11, 1982.

25. Kim, "Panmi nun Odiso onunga," pp. 410-411.

26. For details of President Theodore Roosevelt's approval of Japan's takeover of Korea, see Andrew C. Nahm, "The Impact of the Taft-Katsura Memorandum on Korea-A Reassessment," Korea Journal, (Seoul), October 1985, pp. 4-17; and Howard K. Beale, Theodore Roosevelt and the Rise of America to World Power, (Baltimore: John Hopkins University Press, 1956), pp. 157-158, 314-325.

27. New York Times, January 13, 1980. The proposal was made by the North Korean Premier Lee Chong Ok in a letter dated January 12 and addressed to his South Korean counterpart Shin Hyon Hwack.

28. New York Times, January 19, 20, 25, February 3, 1980.

29. Washington Post, February 7, 20, March 28, 1980; Boston Globe, February 7, 20, March 24, 1980; and Christian Science Monitor, March 5, 1980. The Seoul delegation initially proposed that the two Prime Ministers meet at Geneva in Switzerland, while the northern counterpart favored Seoul and P'yongyang as the sites of the suggested meetings.

30. Nodong Shinmun, April 14, 1980; New York Times, January 22, 1982; and Far Eastern Economic Review, January 29, 1982, p. 9. In all, six contacts were made between February 6 and April 18, 1980 at P'anmunjom to arrange Prime Ministers' meetings.

31. Tong-A Ilbo, January 12, 1981.

32. New York Times, January 20, 1981; and Washington Post, January 20, 1981. The North formally rejected Chun's proposal on January 19 in the name of Vice President Kim Il.

33. Tong-A Ilbo, March 3, 1981.

34. Tong-A Ilbo, January 22, 1982. Chun made the offer while delivering his New Year's policy statement before the National Assembly.

35. The North rejected on January 26, again in the name of its Vice President Kim Il. Washington Post, January 25, 1982; and New York Times, February 11, 1982.

36. New York Times, February 11, 1982.

37. Asian Wall Street Journal, February 22, 1982; and Weinstein and Kamiya, Security of Korea, pp. 1, 74.

38. Koreatown, December 31, 1979, p. 9; and New York Times, September 2, 1981.

39. Tong-A Ilbo, January 2, 3, 15, February 16, 1980.

40. Tong-A Ilbo, November 29, 1979, January 1, 1980; and Kim, "American Technology and Korea's Technological Development," in Moskowitz, ed., From Patron to Partner, p. 78. Seoul's exports to Japan in 1978 increased by 22.6 percent over the previous year, Taiwan's by 35.8 percent, China's by 31.2 percent, Hongkong's by 42.6 percent, and Singapore's by 26.4 percent. In the first quarter of 1979 Seoul's exports to Japan grew by 48.4 percent over the same period of the previous year, Taiwan's by 66.4 percent, and Hongkong's by 60.4 percent. Seoul's competitive position in the international market weakened because of "rising labor costs that were outstripping gains in production."

41. Tong-A Ilbo, November 29, 1979; and Monthly Review of Korean Affairs, II, No. 1, (January 1980), p. 2. In 1981, exports accounted for 40 percent of south Korea's gross domestic products (GDP). Asian Wall street Journal, October 12, 1982.

42. _Tong-A Ilbo_, January 2, 3, 15, February 16, 1980; and Lee, "South Korea in 1979," p. 72.

43. The 1980 harvest fell some 30 percent below normal yearly yield, contributing at least two and possibly three percent to the record decline in the year's GNP. _Tong-A Ilbo_, January 2, May 8, 1980; _Christian Science Monitor_, March 17, 1981; and _Asian Wall Street Journal_, April 21, 1983.

44. _Tong-A Ilbo_, January 15, 1980.

45. _New York Times_, January 27, 1981; and _Christian Science Monitor_, March 17, 1981.

46. _Christian Science Monitor_, March 17, 1981; _New York Times_, June 8, 1980; and _Asian Wall Street Journal_, August 31, 1982. As of mid-1980, some 830,000 people were officially listed as unemployed.

47. _Asian Wall Street Journal_, August 31, 1982, April 21, June 29, 1983.

48. _Tong-A Ilbo_, December 31, 1979, July 10, 1982; and _Far Eastern Economic Review_, February 22, 1980, p. 18.

49. _Asian Wall Street Journal_, August 31, November 26, 1982.

50. The figure $40 billion was quoted in Suh Dae sook's "South Korea in 1982: A Centennial," _Asian Survey_, XX, No. 1, (January 1983), p. 100. The _New York Times_ on October 9, 1985 reported that South Korea's external debt stood at $45 billion, placing her in the top four debtor nations along with Brazil, Mexico, and Argentina. On the other hand, Kim Yong Sam, during his speech at the University of California at Berkeley in the fall of 1985, stated that Seoul's foreign debt had reached a whopping total of $50 billion in sharp contrast to the $18 billion accumulated during Park's 18-year rule. Kim further said that during Park's days many factories had been built with borrowed money but that he did not know what Chun had done with the enormous foreign debt incurred within a few years of his coming to power.

51. _Sekai_, No. 423, (February 1981), pp. 145-148; and _Asian Wall Street Journal_, August 31, 1982.

52. _Tong-A Ilbo_, April 7, 9, 1980.

53. _Tong-A Ilbo_, May 8, 1980.

54. With the passage of the new labor legislation, the famous Ch'ongge Garment Workers' Union, which had represented some 20,000 workers at the P'yonghwa Market in Seoul, was disbanded effective January 22, 1981 by the order of the mayor of Seoul. _Sekai_, No. 425, (April 1981), pp. 187-189.

55. The incident occurred at the office in downtown Seoul of the Asian-American Free Labor Institute. _New York Times_, March 1, 1981.

56. New York Times, June 7, 1982; and Asian Wall Street Journal, June 8, 1982.

57. New York Times, June 7, 1982; and Asian Wall Street Journal, June 8, July 21, 1982. The government-controlled South Korean news media did not report the incident at the Seoul plant of the Control Data Corporation. Incidentally, in July the plant, which had been in operation since 1967 manufacturing computer parts and had employed some 360 workers, announced that it would close the facility.

58. Because of the tight governmental control of banks, it was next to impossible to secure significant loans from banks without political connections. Thus frequently, the companies in need of cash turned to the unofficial curb market, and the transactions on the curb market were not illegal. The funds circulating in the curb market accounted for a quarter of the entire money supply of the country as of early 1982. Tong-A Ilbo, May 28, 29, 31, 1982.

59. The ex-KCIA deputy chief was Lee Ch'ol Hee, who was also a former National Assemblyman.

60. Asian Wall Street Journal, May 31, 1982; and New York Times, June 3, 1982.

61. Christian Science Monitor, May 19, 1982; and New York Times, August 10, 1982.

62. Tong-A Ilbo, June 2, 1982; and Christian Science Monitor, May 21, 1982.

63. Tong-A Ilbo, June 2, 1982.

64. Far Eastern Economic Review, June 11, 1982, p. 13. The First Lady's uncle in question was Lee Kyu Kwang.

65. New York Times, April 28, 1982; and Far Eastern Economic Review, May 7, 1982, p. 12. The incident took place in South Kyongsang Province.

66. New York Times, May 21, 1982; and Christian Science Monitor, May 21, 1982.

67. Far Eastern Economic Review, May 21, 1982, pp. 52-53, June 11, 1982, p. 13.

68. New York Times, June 3, 1982; and Far Eastern Economic Review, May 21, 1982, p. 53.

69. Tong-A Ilbo, June 27, 1985.

70. Yonhap Yongam 1984, pp. 138-139.

71. Yonghap Yongam 1985, p. 134. Chong, a retired general, had earlier served as minister of national defense.

CHAPTER 14

SOUTH KOREA UNDER A NEW REGIME (2)

It was under the political climate of anti-Americanism as well as public distrust of their leaders that the 12th national assembly election was held on February 12, 1985. The stage was set on November 30 of the previous year, when President Chun had lifted the ban on political activities for 84 persons who had been on his blacklist first drawn up in 1980 containing 567 names. This was the third time in four years that Chun removed former politicians from the blacklist, and it liberated all the names on the list except fourteen, among whom were "political heavyweights" such as the "three Kims."[1]

The Opposition New Korea Democratic Party

Among the individuals whose names had just been removed from Chun's blacklist, former opposition politicians formed in January 1985 the New Korea Democratic Party (NKDP) (Shinhan Minjudang) in preparation for the forthcoming election. Despite their different intra-party factional affiliations, the NKDP members were united in their commitment to democracy and in their opposition to Chun's rule. The new party was closely allied with the two best-known opposition politicians Kim Yong Sam and Kim Dae Jung, the latter returning to Seoul only four days before the election after more than two years of exile in the United States. As a matter of fact, the two Kims, though still banned from political life, were the de-facto leaders of the NKDP, and the party claimed that it--and not the more established main opposition group the Democratic Korea Party--was the leading anti-government force.[2]

The campaigning for the National Assembly officially lasted for 20 days ending on February 11. Focusing their campaigns on issues pushed by the two Kims, the NKDP candidates vowed to restore civilian supremacy in government along with the direct and popular election of the president. Simultaneously, they strongly denounced Mr. Chun's four-year rule, while not infrequently flouting laws banning "inflammatory" slogans. For instance, the NKDP president Lee Min Woo called the Chun government a "military dictatorship" and suggested that it relinquish its power in favor of a government that "follows the will of the people."[3] Such a campaign style of the NKDP was in sharp contrast to that of the DKP, whose candidates avoided a direct confrontation with Mr. Chun and preferred a gradual restoration of democracy.

Notwithstanding the brisk campaign atmosphere engendered by the hard-hitting tactics of the NKDP, the election results were anticipated not to have a significant impact on President Chun's grip on power and the general thrust of the national policies under him.[4] After all, the election had nothing to do with the country's presidency, the real base of power. Furthermore, the all-powerful president was elected indirectly by a presidential electoral college and Mr. Chun's term was not to expire until 1988. In addition, the National Assembly--as had been generally the case since the birth of the Republic of Korea in 1948--had not guided decisions made at the Blue House, which was the presidential office and also residence. Indeed, the National Assembly had not been an effective legislative body but a forum for airing grievances. Still more, given both the electoral rule, which heavily favored the government party, and the awesome resources at its disposal, it was difficult--some even claimed almost impossible--for the ruling DJP not to win a majority as it had done in 1981.

However, the election results could help the fundamentally weak legislature become a more vigorous political forum than it had been. More significantly, the forthcoming Assembly election--the second since Chun's seizure of power and the only kind planned before his retirement in 1988--was the first and the last meaningful opportunity for Chun to demonstrate that he had the popular support which his officials had claimed for him. Thus the DJP candidates asserted in their speeches that the previous four years had been marked by economic growth (which was 8.0 percent in 1984) and a steady rise in South Korea' international stature.[5]

The result of the 1985 Assembly election was a disappointment for Mr. Chun's DJP, while showing an impressive voter support for the NKDP. As expected of the ruling party, which invariably had the full backing of the police and local officials (who were all appointed by the central government), the DJP polled the largest number of votes, which, helped by the controversial electoral law, enabled the party to retain the majority status in the National Assembly. However, the DJP's share of the popular vote declined from 35.6 percent in 1981 to 35.3 percent, and it lost three seats it had won in 1981, winning a total of 87 district seats. With the additional 61 seats from the "proportional representation" slate, the party controlled 148 of the 176 Assembly seats--a majority, but three fewer than in 1981.[6]

Also, whereas in the 1981 election 85.9 percent of the successful 90 DJP candidates were top vote-getters in their respective districts, each of which elected two assemblymen, in 1985 only 66.3 percent of the party's 87 elected finished first in regular constituencies.[7] The election returns were a setback for President Chun and his government, and it could perhaps have been predicted.

What did surprise the observers, however, was the emergence of the NKDP, organized by the old foes of late President Park, as the major opposition party by eclipsing the more established number one opposition group, the Democratic Korea Party. Despite the fact that it was formed on the eve of the election and had just 20 days of restricted campaigning, the party garnered 29.2 percent of the popular vote, winning 50 contested seats. The NKDP's performance exceeded everyone's expectation including its own. With the addition from the "proportional representation" seats, the NKDP won a total of 67 seats.[8] The "tame" opposition DKP got 19.5 percent of the popular vote and picked up a total of 35 seats--a sharp decline from the 81 seats it had won in 1981; another mild opposition group, the Korea National Party captured 20 seats with 9.2 percent of the popular vote. Smaller groups and Independents divided the remaining six seats.[9]

In all, in the 1985 national assembly election, 64.7 percent of those who voted rejected the ruling DJP, and the two "genuine" opposition parties, the NKDP and DKP, together polled 48.7 percent of the total vote in contrast to the 35.3 percent garnered by the DJP. Thus the election outcome--especially the impressive showing of the "hardline" opposition NKDP--demonstrated a strong desire for democracy on the part of the voters, while indicating their alienation from the government.

Flushed with the election result, the NKDP assemblymen pressed their DJP counterparts for revision of the constitution, which was the NKDP's campaign pledge. Because the existing basic law provided for indirect election of the president, holding the possibility of the electoral votes being manipulated, it was almost a foregone conclusion that a person closely associated with Chun would succeed him in 1988 when he was scheduled to step down. The motions of the NKDP legislators to take up the issue inside the assembly, however, were met by the categorical rejection of the DJP.[10]

Having been frustrated, the NKDP launched a campaign to collect 10 million signatures nationwide (almost half of the electorate and a quarter of the population) in six months demanding constitutional revision. The campaign was started on February 12, 1986, the first anniversary of the previous year's assembly election. Once under way, the signature drive caught the authorities by surprise due to its "size and ferocity." From February 13 on, the police carried out a six-day crackdown nationwide on the signature drive. They raided the NKDP headquarters as well as dissident groups' offices and more than 100 universities in search of materials related to the signature campaign, while arresting campaign activists.[11]

However, the NKDP continued to press for constitutional revision, perhaps encouraged by the political development in the Philippines which led to the downfall of Marco's regime, while casting a shadow over South Korea.[12] Now President Chun began to back down step by step. On February 24, 1986 the Chun Administration expressed its willingness to consider "constitutional revision in 1989," after Chun's successor was chosen under the existing basic law. As the dissidents rejected such a gesture, the DJP Chairman Ro T'ae Woo on March 24 indicated that he might be inclined to reform the constitution before 1988, as demanded by the dissidents, provided a "compromise formula" could be worked out.[13] As it was gradually forced into a compromise posture with the opposition forces, Chun's DJP agreed to create in the National Assembly a Special Constitution Revision Committee, which was organized on June 14.[14]

However, it became immediately apparent that there were basic differences between the two opposing forces over the form of the government to be adopted. The DJP pushed for a parliamentary-cabinet system of government, while the NKDP held out for a presidential form of government

302

along with direct elections of the president. Given the long-standing records of anti-government and anti-authoritarian struggles by its likely presidential candidates (the two Kims), the NKDP was convinced that its prospective presidential standard-bearers had mass followings and good chances of getting popularly elected. Also for the NKDP, a cabinet system of government was only a mechanism to allow the ruling DJP and its military backers to cling to the reigns of power.[15] Neither side budging from its views, the newly established Special Committee was unable to produce a draft constitution.

Frustrated with the constitutional impasse, the NKDP planned a well publicized mass rally to be held in Seoul on November 29, 1986. But on the day the gathering was scheduled, the government dispatched a huge number of policemen (possibly as many as 70,000, or three times the entire New York city police force) to the streets of Seoul in order to block would-be demonstrators from reaching their rally-point. Faced with such a "massive show of force," the rally--a "democratic mobilization" intended to be a "dramatic show of the depth and breadth of opposition"--never made it to the streets.[16]

The government's attempts to "tame" the opposition NKDP in connection with the struggle over the constitutional reform had already been dramatically highlighted on October 16, when the NKDP Assemblyman Yu Sung Hwan was arrested for telling the National Assembly that the nation's policy priority should center on reunification and that "the nation and unification should be put above capitalism and communism."[17] The authorities arrested Mr. Yu, even though assemblymen were constitutionally immune from prosecution for remarks made on the assembly floor, and also despite the fact that both South and North Korea had been in agreement that their reunification must be achieved by transcending their ideological and other peculiarities. Yu was charged with making an antistate and pro-communist statement because his remark indicated that "the policy of anticommunism...can be dropped in favor of national unification...and that communism can be tolerated in the country."[18]

The NKDP--so assailed from outside by the government-- also suffered from internal dissensions and fractures in its ranks. Earlier, on April 3-4, 1985, out of the 35 newly elected assemblymen belonging to the moderate Democratic Korea Party, 29 switched their allegiance to the NKDP. With additional defections from still another minority party, the Korea National Party formed by supporters of the late President Park, the NKDP had increased its representation in the 276-member National Assembly to 102 seats.[19]

The NKDP's numerical strength, which was over one-third of the total assembly seats, secured for the party the right to call the assembly into session or to initiate a motion to dismiss a cabinet member. It also acquired the power to prevent the passage of any constitutional revision, which the ruling party might submit but would not be favored by the opposition. As it grew in its numerical strength, however, the "moderates" in the NKDP became critical of the "hardline" tactics of the party, which was controlled by the followers of the two Kims, who, barred from membership in the party, led it from behind the scenes.[20]

On December 31, 1985, 12 NKDP assemblymen quit the party in protest against what they termed its "befuddled" and "misguided leadership."[21] The defection of these 12--all of whom had come over to the NKDP from the DKP nine months before--brought the NKDP's strength to just two seats shy of one-third of the national assembly seats. Coming on the heels of well-publicized intra-party strife preceding the defections,[22] the latest splintering was particularly damaging to the public's perception of the NKDP, "a linch-pin in the whole struggle for democratic reform."[23]

The Rise of Extremism

With the constitutional dialogue among politicians having reached an impasse, and the NKDP, the biggest constitutional opposition group challenging the Chun regime, appearing as a strife-ridden motley group with varying degrees of commitment to democracy among its ranks, student demonstrations, now daily occurrences in South Korea, began to be marked by growing radicalization because of the increasing role played by extreme "leftist-leaning" students.

The extremism in the student movement emerged with a "vengeance" at the port city of Inch'on in May 1986, when an opposition rally calling for constitutional reform turned into a large-scale urban riot. During the tumult--planned by radical students, laborers, and religious "extremists"--the rioters simultaneously attacked

304

the ruling as well as the opposition parties by setting on fire the offices of both parties. As they showed their impatience with the wranglings among the "stationary party elite" by spreading violence and destruction, the rioters de-manded a "people's constitution," while shouting anti-American and anti-capitalist slogans.[24]

Then late in October, demonstrations, held at the Konguk University in Seoul by student activists from several universities, turned into "the worst outbreak of campus fighting" in many years, when some 8,000 policemen stormed the main library of the college, which was occupied by the demonstrators. After four days of siege, 1,525 students had been rounded up--most of them after battling policemen across roofs and through the blazing staircases of the library.[25]

In still another outbreak of anti-government violence--this time on November 13 in Seoul--some 500 students and laborers suddenly burst onto the streets of the Yongdungp'o District, and set several police vehicles on fire and firebombed a police-box. During the rampage, the mob displayed placards reading "Down With the Military Dictatorship," "Let Us Expel the U.S.-Japanese Imperialism that Blocks the Revolution of the Masses" and "Let Us Call A Constituent Assembly." When the violence was over after an hour or so, some 38 rioters had been taken into custody.[26]

The incident, along with the one at Inch'on in May, both of which were provoked jointly by students and workers, were symptomatic of a burgeoning alliance between college campus and labor. This had already become apparent in the violent resolution of a six-day labor strike at the Daewoo Apparel Company plant near Seoul in the summer of 1985. As the workers went on strike protesting arrests of their union leaders in conjunction with previous labor disputes, students demonstrated outside the plant's gates clashing with police.[27] The labor-student linkage was established by the students who had been banned from schools and taken up jobs in factories. And it was a big concern for the government because, taken to its limits, it could conceivably "throw a spanner in the engine" of the country's economy.[28]

As the extremism was on the rise among students and laborers, the relatively prudent traditional opposition leaders (like Kim Yong Sam and Kim Dae Jung) found themselves losing ground to the anti-American radicals. On the other hand, the government frightened the South Koreans by announcing on October 30, 1986 that North Korea was building at Mt. Kumgang a huge dam that could cause a catastrophe in Seoul and the Han River region if its water were maliciously released.[29] However, the announcement--especially given its timing--was construed by observers as "little more than an exercise to justify tougher actions" against the dissidents at the time when things were "not leaning the government's way."[30]

More extraordinary news followed on November 15-16, when the Defense Ministry in Seoul, quoting alleged broadcasts from North Korean loudspeakers placed along the demarcation line, announced the sudden death of North Korean President Kim Il Sung. However, a few days later on November 19 President Kim turned up at the airport in P'yongyang to greet the visiting Mongolian head of state Jambyn Batmonh. The whole incident, which attracted international attention, only served as an added blow to the credibility of President Chun's government.[31]

All this while, the anti-Americanism continued to manifest itself, largely in conjunction with the unceasing anti-government activities of students. As had been the case since the fire-bombings of the USICA offices in Kwangju in 1980 and Pusan in 1982 and Taegu in 1983, the intensity of the anti-American feeling was demonstrated in the form of violent physical assaults against American governmental as well as business and cultural interests. In May 1985, about 70 students (of whom 20 were coeds) occupied the USICA library in downtown Seoul for three days, protesting the U.S. role in the Kwangju massacre and demanding withdrawal of U.S. support of the Chun regime. Then on November 5, some 14 students briefly seized the Seoul office of the American Chamber of Commerce, while holding three people as hostages.[32]

The following month, students armed with gasoline bombs took over the office of U.S. cultural center in Kwangju and held it for nearly half a day. The anti-American violence showed no signs of abating. In May 1986, student protestors in Pusan occupied the U.S. cultural center and also carried out a bomb attack against the branch of the Korean-American Bank.[33] In addition to these instances of anti-Americanism, the hostility toward the United States was also finding expression in physical threats directed against American residents in Seoul, according to the June 15, 1986 issue of the <u>New York Times</u>. This kind of student-endorsed virulent hostility against the United States--a crucial external source of support for the troubled Fifth Republic--was finding sympathy in other segments of the population.[34]

The June 29th Democratization Package

On April 13, 1987, President Chun on national television told the nation that the ongoing debate on constitutional change, the country's dominant political topic following the February 1985 National Assembly elections, would be terminated immediately. The person who would succeed him after he steps down in the following February was to be selected under the then existing constitution, which provided for an indirect election by the electoral college. President Chun defended his decision by stating that, due to the intransigence of "superannuated politicians from a bygone era" in the opposition camp, there was little likelihood among political parties to reconcile their rival plans for choosing a new national leader, and that if he allowed the impasse to continue "there will be nothing but public divisiveness and social confusion."[35]

Mr. Chun's announcement was immediately followed by the government's "campaign of harassment"--in the form of seemingly legal actions--against the opposition's hard-line National Assemblymen. By mid-May at least a dozen anti-government legislators had found themselves either under investigation or indictment, or had been sentenced to prison terms for alleged criminal activities, some of which were suddenly revived after lying dormant for as long as 19 months.[36] Amidst the government's legal crackdown on its opponents, which was "largely political in nature" and could "whittle away at...wobbly-kneed legislators," the ruling DJP at its convention on June 10 formally chose Ro T'ae Woo, Chun's longtime military associate and the party chairman since March 1985, as the party's candidate for president in a national election set for later in the year.[37] As the DJP's presidential candidate, Ro appeared certain of victory under the electoral college voting system then in use.

President Chun's decision to terminate the constitutional debate was met with instantaneous and near universal disapproval of the South Koreans, who either lamented that Chun's action created "sorrow" for the country or denounced it as a "pretext" to prolong his rule. Following the DJP's nomination of Ro as its presidential candidate, the growing anti-government sentiment exploded into massive protest demonstrations across the country. As usual, the protests were led by the students, who had provided "the motor reflex of the opposition movement" in the country.[38]

Already since early March of the year, when the new school term began, students had been sporadically demonstrating, demanding "campus democratization" and a "democratic constitution."[39] Mr. Chun's decision to end the constitutional debate intensified the students' opposition to him, embroiling more and more campuses in anti-government disturbances.[40] At this juncture, the students were provided with additional impetuses: a business scandal involving South Korea's largest shipping company and the torture-death of a student activist at the hands of police.

The shipping firm, the Pan Ocean Shipping Company (Pomyang Sangsa), had been in serious financial trouble since the early 1980's. In April 1987, the firm was found unable to cope with its debt (U.S. $1.44 billion). According to government investigators, since 1979 the topmost two executives of the company had diverted U.S. $16.44 million abroad, in addition to embezzling won 5.1 billion in local currency. All this while, the company's massive debts had been met with government-subsidized financing, which prompted the public to wonder about the government "policies that for so long backed such a corrupt firm."[41]

A Seoul National University student, Park Chong Ch'ol, died in January during police questioning about his political connections. The authorities admitted that the death occurred during police interrogation, but covered it up as an accident. By May, however, the circumstances surrounding Park's death had been fully disclosed in Seoul publications. The revelation stirred a public outrage and further spurred students into anti-government demonstrations.[42] These demonstrations reached a crescendo following Mr. Ro's nomination as the DJP's presidential candidate on June 10.

Only hours after the selection of Ro as the DJP's standard-bearer, Seoul and more than 30 other cities across South Korea were hit by the outbreak of violent anti-government protests. For nearly three weeks, dem-

308

onstrators fought on and off the streets with teargas grenades-lobbing police, thus turning the country once again into "a battle ground."[43] The latest wave of demonstrations turned out to be "the most sustained and widespread street disorders" since Mr. Chun had come to power some seven years before. "In terms of the intensity of the protests," said one DJP lawmaker, "it is something we just did not expect."[44]

Particularly disturbing for the government was the presence among the protestors (largely students) of many middle-class Koreans, the country's "silent majority," suggesting that the dissatisfaction with the government was not confined to students, opposition politicians, and other traditional dissidents.[45] Indeed, South Korea, in the word of then Prime Minister Lee Han Gi, reached another "critical and crucial moment" in her political history that had been punctuated with a bitter cycle of violence.[46]

The raging civil disturbances racking the country recalled the fate of President Syngman Rhee, who was ousted by student demonstrations in 1960, and that of President Park Chung Hee, who was assassinated amidst social turmoil in 1979. Even if demonstrations had been quelled (probably only by the intervention of the military) and Ro T'ae Woo had won the presidential race, his ascension under the existing political arrangement would "still condemn him to carrying the same albatross of legitimacy that has plagued Chun."[47] However, given the fact that the unrest was spreading into the wider reaches of society, a military crackdown could risk an even larger-scale wave of violence of uncertain duration. A long siege of unrest could destroy the chance for successfully staging the 1988 Summer Olympic Games in Seoul, thus damaging the international image of South Korea for years to come.

As the political crisis in South Korea dragged on, the United States nudged President Chun to resume negotiations with the opposition on constitutional reform. At the same time, Washington urged the Seoul authorities to exercise restraint in dealing with the protestors, while making known its opposition to martial law or other forms of military intervention. To underscore U.S. concern with South Korean officials, Assistant Secretary of State Gaston Sigur visited Seoul for two days beginning June 23.[48]

The governing DJP had to act and act quickly to defuse the crisis. Yet the choices were few. On June 29, the party chairman Ro, whose presidential nomination had triggered the explosion of unrest, announced an eight-point democratization plan that embodied a wholesale acceptance of the opposition demands. The proposal, endorsed by President Chun two days later, pledged "the speedy amendment" of the constitution to allow for direct presidential election, the principal demand of the anti-government protestors.[49] The proposal also called for freedom of the press as well as amnesty for and restoration of civil rights to Kim Dae Jung, who had been banned from active political life since receiving a suspended 20-year prison term in connection with the 1980 Kwangju uprising. With this announcement, the violence that had racked South Korea for nearly three weeks, showed signs of abating.[50]

No sooner had the student-led demonstrations subsided than a wave of wildcat labor strikes jolted the country. According to the Ministry of Labor, some 2,000 job disputes had occurred during the two months since June 29; that is to say, labor disputes had broken out at the rate of some 33 a day, which was at least threefold as many as the rate during the turbulent month of April 1980. By early September, the strikes reached some 3,200--almost twice the total number in the previous 10 years.[51] There had never been such a flurry of labor disruptions in South Korea, which hit a wide range of industries. Some disputes were settled amicably but others deteriorated into violence such as the taking of company executives as hostages or physical clashes with police.[52]

The striking workers demanded free trade unions, higher wages, better working conditions, and payment of delinquent wages--the call for "democratic unions" topping the list. Indeed, many workers had for long regarded the country's umbrella labor organization, the Federation of Korean Trade Unions (which endorsed Mr. Chun's April 13th termination of constitutional debate), as a representative of government interests; and they had been trying to topple its leadership.[53]

While the labor strikes were unsettling the economy, the government--a traditional strikebreaker and management ally--expressed sympathy for striking workers and used riot police only sparingly. Throughout the labor unrest the government, on the whole, assumed a "neutral role" by urging both management and labor to reach "au-

tonomous solution."[54] This change of its role--perhaps
a reversal of its role--on the part of the government was
construed by observers as having stemmed from the consideration of the forthcoming presidential election,
which would be a direct election and would be held later
in the year.[55]

However, the government changed its attitude to the
current labor unrest after some dissident groups attempted to link the labor strikes with their own political movement following the death of a striking worker on
August 22 by a police teargas canister.[56] The authorities now began to pursue "a double tracked policy" by
arresting "militants" but continuously expressing general
support for the striking workers. By early September,
the police had detained a few hundred strikers, which led
to the arrests of students, lawyers, and other dissidents. By then, most of the labor disputes had been
settled, generally by management accedence to the demands
of the strikers.[57]

The December 1987 Presidential Election

While the labor strikes were going on, a National
Assembly bi-partisan committee, composed of members of
the ruling DJP and the main opposition Reunification
Democratic Party,[58] began to revise the constitution on
July 30.[59] On September 18, the committee submitted its
constitutional amendment bill to the National Assembly.
The bill was overwhelmingly approved (by a vote of 254
to 4) by the legislature on October 13.[60] The legislative passage of the amended bill surprised no one. The
action, nonetheless, marked an important milestone for
South Korea as it had come to terms with sweeping
democratic changes forced upon the government by the
widespread protests during the summer.

The latest amendment was the ninth of the kind since
the South Korean constitution was first proclaimed in
August 1948. Yet it was "the first undertaken with the
consensus of both the ruling and opposition parties and,
for that matter, of the people as a whole."[61] Under the
revised draft constitution, the country's next president
would serve a single five-year term after succeeding
President Chun on February 25, 1988. Compared with Mr.
Chun, who had exercised sweeping powers during his seven-
year term, the next president would be somewhat weaker.
The bill abolished the president's right to dissolve the

national assembly and gave lawmakers the right to investigate government affairs.[62]

The amended constitution was duly approved by the general public in a referendum on October 27 by 93.1 percent
of the voters, just 20 million or 78.2 percent of the
electorate. The new basic law was officially proclaimed
on October 29, clearing the way for a direct and popular
election of the president in December of the year--the
first such one in 16 years.[63]

On October 10, 1987, Kim Yong Sam, the head of the
Reunification Democratic Party (RDP) declared that he
would run in the forthcoming presidential election. On
November 9, the RDP formally nominated Kim as its standard-bearer in the presidential race, making it certain
that Kim would compete for the nation's highest political
office against one of his arch-political foes, the DJP's
candidate Ro.[64] The RDP was formed on May 1, 1987 by Kim
Yong Sam and Kim Dae Jung and others, who on April 8 had
broken away from the then main opposition NKDP because
of their differences with the rest of the party members
over the issue of the constitutional reform.[65]

As negotiations with the ruling DJP over the constitutional change were going nowhere, the two Kims and the
NKDP's other "hardliners," who had been unwavering in
their insistence on direct presidential elections, and
who constituted the mainstream faction of the party,
suspected that "opportunist elements" in the party were
willing to compromise with the DJP's formula of parliamentary cabinet system of government. The hardliners
especially suspected the party's nominal leader, Lee Min
Woo, who for a few months after the turn of the year
indicated to the ruling DJP that he would consider the
DJP's formula in exchange for DJP's guarantee of seven
basic democratic reforms, including the release of
political prisoners and freedom of the press.[66]

The NKDP's intra-party bickering came to a boil on
April 8--five days before President Chun's termination
of constitutional debate--when Kim Yong Sam and Kim Dae
Jung bolted the party, taking with them 66 of the 90 NKDP
lawmakers and leaving a minor party behind for Lee Min
Woo to preside over. The two Kims split from the NKDP,
which they had helped to create some 27 months before,
in order to form a "purged and purified" opposition
party, the RDP. With Kim Yong Sam as its president and
Kim Dae Jung selected as its standing adviser, the new

party had the largest opposition bloc in the National Assembly.[67]

No sooner had the June 29th democratization package been announced than a friction developed between the two most powerful leaders of the main opposition RDP--Kim Yong Sam and Kim Dae Jung--over who should be the party's standard-bearer in the forthcoming presidential race. During most of President Chun's seven-year rule, the two Kims had presented a united anti-government front, "resisting determined government efforts to undermine their alliance and morale."[68] The two men, however, were also longtime political rivals, their rivalry having already sharply surfaced in 1980, when the two men ran separate presidential races until stopped by Mr. Chun's seizure of power.

As the Chun government yielded in June to the demand for direct presidential election, and as amnesty was granted and civil rights were restored to Kim Dae Jung early in July, questions arose about how long the union of the two Kims would last if both men decided to run for the presidency.[69] The questions arose and persisted even though Kim Dae Jung the previous November had pledged that he would not seek the presidency even if Mr. Chun revised the Constitution to permit direct presidential election, which Chun agreed to do on July 1, 1987.[70]

The speculations about Kim Dae Jung running in the presidential race were fueled by Kim's own remark made on July 9 during his press conference. While remaining noncommittal on his candidacy, Kim stated that he had received "a strong protest from many people" because of his previous year's declaration not to run.[71] Eight days later, a coterie of Kim's political advisers at a gathering, where Kim himself was present, withdrew Kim's pledge not to run, merely explaining that "the situation was changed" by President Chun's action of April 13. The same advisers on August 27 announced that they would endeavor to promote Kim's presidential candidacy.[72]

Since the RDP head Kim Yong Sam had made few bones about his determination to run in the presidential election[73] and now that Kim Dae Jung appeared to be moving toward becoming another candidate, the possibility arose that the two Kims, as in 1980, would run separate races to chase the grand prize of the presidency. Under the circumstances, the alliance of the two Kims, widely characterized as "a political marriage of convenience," began to fall apart. This worried the broad anti-government forces, which had been exhilarated over the June 29th democratization package and had been pressing the two Kims to unite behind a single candidate against the ruling DJP candidate Ro.[74]

Within the RDP itself, Kim Yong Sam had the support of the majority of the party machinery, including the backing of as many as 40 of the party's 69 National Assemblymen. And he appeared to be almost guaranteed the party's nomination as its presidential candidate--the nomination Kim was to receive at the party convention on November 9. Kim Dae Jung, on the other hand, ruled out a vote showdown on the convention floor, while emphatically pointing out the political support he had been receiving from "the masses."[75]

Finally, on October 28--18 days after Kim Yong Sam's declaration of presidential candidacy--Kim Dae Jung, who for weeks had been hinting that he would run, formally announced that he would enter the approaching presidential race.[76] The following day, Kim Dae Jung and 23 National Assemblymen seceded from the RDP, which they had helped to form only six months before. On October 30, they, together with other followers of Kim Dae Jung, held a preparatory convention to form a new party, the Party for Peace and Democracy (PPD). The gathering selected Kim as the head of the new party.[77]

The collapse of the alliance between the two Kims, as symbolized by the breakaway of Kim Dae Jung and his followers from the RDP, dismayed many dissidents, who feared that the inability of the two Kims to join forces might enable the ruling DJP candidate Ro to glide into victory in the presidential race.[78] Also the split of the RDP and the emergence of the PPD once again confirmed the notion that South Korean politics had traditionally been based on factions dominated by strong leaders and that political parties had been created as vehicles to help these leaders to come to power.

Meanwhile, early in October, a third Kim, Kim Jong P'il, indicated that he too would seek the presidency as the nominee of a party which would be formed shortly by him and other pro-government politicians of the Park era. Kim, a chief architect of the 1961 coup and also former premier, said that he was running in order to "take the judgement of the electorate" on the Park years. The new party was to uphold the ideology of the defunct Democratic Republican Party.[79] On October 30, the new party, aptly named as the New Democratic Republican Party (NDRP), was inaugurated with Kim Jong P'il as its head and also as its presidential candidate.[80] The chances of the third Kim, a conservative, for winning the presidential race appeared remote, but his candidacy was expected to draw voters away from the ruling DJP's candidate Ro.[81]

Incidentally, it should be remembered that this was not the first time that this trio of ambitious Kims was facing off in the political arena. The three vied for the presidency in 1980 during the flowering of political freedom, that followed Park's assassination but which was quashed by Chun's seizure of power.

As the campaigning started in the fall for the presidential election (the 13th) set for December 16, 1987,[82] it became apparent that it was basically a three-way race among Ro T'ae Woo, Kim Yong Sam and Kim Dae Jung.[83] With three major contenders in the field, a simple plurality of votes was needed to win the race. At the heart of the campaign was the involvement in politics of the military, which had twice seized power since the birth of the republic and ushered in prolonged rule by military-dominated governments, while generating deep-seated resentment against military rule among the general public. The problem was highlighted by the enduring and undisguised hostility of army leaders to Kim Dae Jung's presidential candidacy and by their veiled threat that the army might intervene should Kim win the race.[84] The posture of army leaders created a stir and touched off strong public criticism.

Under the circumstances, the two rival opposition candidates, Kim Yong Sam and Kim Dae Jung, called on voters to choose them as the way to end military rule, while arguing that election of Ro, Chun's longtime army associate, would amount to granting President Chun's government a five-year extension.[85] Kim Yong Sam played his anti-military theme to the hilt by recruiting former four-star general and martial law administrator Chong Sung Hwa as the RDP's standing adviser and introducing him as such at the party's November 9 presidential candidate nomination convention.[86]

Emerging from a seven-year political exile, which he had to endure in connection with President Park's assassination, General Chong stated that the coup on December 12, 1979 was staged by General Chun Doo Hwan in collaboration with General Ro T'ae Woo and a few other army officers, and that it was a "mutiny" carried out by "politically motivated generals."[87] The public revelation of the army mutiny of eight years before was a serious setback for the candidacy of Mr. Ro, who tried to present himself as a nonmilitary "common man," while pointedly promising that the days of military rule in South Korea were over.

Indeed, all this while, Mr. Ro had been stressing that he initiated the June democratization package, leaving out the fact that the package was forced upon him by a mixture of street protests, U.S. pressure, and concern about the long-range consequences for the country's future. Mr. Ro also insisted that the "Kim-Kim feud" in the opposition camp showed that they were incapable of running a government, while presenting himself as "a stabilizing force" which would protect democracy and insure national security.[88] Meanwhile, Kim Dae Jung, who viewed himself as the voice of the politically disfranchised and aggrieved, projected himself as an "ardent" reformist. Kim Yong Sam, on the other hand, struck out a "centrist" position, that would put an end to the rule of the DJP but still would not "rock the boat too much."[89]

While the presidential hopefuls were hitting the campaign trails, the age-old regional rivalry and animosity--a "bane" of Korean politics--was rekindled. The regional antagonism--often expressed in physical assault against candidates from rival provinces in contrast to tumultuous welcome accorded to candidates of native provinces--was most conspicuously manifested between Kyongsang Province and Cholla Province.

Thus Kim Yong Sam, who had drawn a huge and enthusiastic crowd to his rally at his home base of Pusan on October 17, was forced to cut short his public appearance on November 14 in Kwangju, Kim Dae Jung's political turf, by a volley of rocks and eggs.[90] On the other hand, Kim Dae Jung, who enjoyed a rock-solid support in South Cholla Province, ran into trouble of his own on November 1, when he ventured into Pusan.[91] This regional rivalry, heightened by the evolving split of the two Kims and gripping the presidential campaigns, indicated that it would affect the voting pattern in the forthcoming election.

The ruling DJP candidate Ro, who was from Taegu in North Kyongsang Province, was dogged by a series of violent attacks during his appearances in Cholla Province.[92] Nonetheless, Ro's campaign was helped by government control of television, which was utilized to full advantage by Ro's campaign strategists, and by "the big money" at the disposal of the ruling DJP.[93]

On December 16, 1987, some 89.2 percent of the nearly 26 million South Korean registered voters cast their ballots to choose a new president. The returns showed that the ruling DJP candidate Ro won the race by receiving 35.9 percent of the popular vote. The RDP leader Kim Yong Sam finished second with 27.5 percent, trailed by the PPD head Kim Dae Jung, who garnered 26.5 percent. It should be noted that the two Kims together received 54 percent of the vote. The third Kim, the NDRP head Kim Jong P'il, lagged far behind, with 7.9 percent.[94] As anticipated, the level of voting support for each of the candidates closely coincided with his regional background, with Kim Jong P'il receiving the lion's share (43.8 percent) of the vote of his native South Ch'ungch'ong Province.

The two main opposition leaders, embittered over their defeat, declared the election results void because of what they called widespread vote fraud, and urged their followers into the streets to overturn the results.[95] Even as early as on December 17, when ballot counting was still going on giving the DJP candidate a lead over his opponents, dissidents took to the streets, protesting that the counting was fraudulent. For the next few days, the demonstrations continued in at least 12 cities at one time.[96]

However, in sharp contrast with what happened in June, the outcry of the protestors was largely ignored by the public, who believed that the rivalrous two Kims brought defeat on themselves by failing to field a single opposition candidate.[97] Indeed, Korean as well as Western observers--and even some opposition lawmakers--were of the opinion that the primary reason for the defeat of the opposition camp was the almost even split of the 54 percent of the vote garnered by the two Kims.[98]

The defeat of the opposition was a great disappointment for the majority of the South Korean electorate, who, apprehensive that the Ro presidency would be an extension of President Chun's military-dominated rule, voted for the two Kims. Cardinal Kim Su Hwan, who played an important role in pushing the government in June to compromise and allow free presidential elections, aptly expressed the sentiment of the disappointed public:

> Although we have a winner in this election, it
> is a shame that not everyone can share the joy
> of victory. The night is still long and the dawn
> of celebration still seems far away.[99]

Be that as it may, on February 25, 1988 Mr. Ro was sworn in as the new president, succeeding Mr. Chun and bringing an end to the Fifth Republic.[100]

Ro's election victory, however, was an "ambiguous" one,[101] as evidenced by the fact that only 35.9 percent of the voters supported him and the overwhelming majority cast their ballots against him or for other candidates. As such, President Ro needed to quickly follow through on his democratic reform blue-print laid down on June 29. Otherwise, the new President would inherit the same legitimacy problems that had dogged his predecessor Chun through his seven-year rule. Such an eventuality would continue the political instability which has been so characteristic of South Korea.

Notes

1. Korea Times, December 1, 1984.
2. New York Times, February 11, 12, 1985.
3. New York Times, February 12, 1985; and Far Eastern Economic Review, February 14, 1985, pp. 26-28, February 28, 1985, pp. 43-44.
4. New York Times, February 13, 1985; and Washington Post, February 5, 1985.
5. Tong-A Ilbo, January 30, 31, February 1, 1985; and Washington Post, February 5, 1985.
6. Tong-A Ilbo, February 13, 1985.
7. Tong-A Ilbo, February 13, 1985; and Washington Post, February 14, 1985.
8. New York Times, February 13, 1985; and Tong-A Ilbo, February 13, 1985.
9. Tong-A Ilbo, February 13, 1985.
10. Far Eastern Economic Review, August 22, 1985, p. 13, January 30, 1986, p. 15.
11. Tong-A Ilbo, March 7, 1986; Far Eastern Economic Review, January 30, 1986, pp. 15-16, February 27, 1986, p. 26; and Washington Post, February 15, 16, 18, 1986.
12. Ferdinand Marco fled the Philippines on February 25, 1986, ending 20 years of his rule. New York Times, February 26, 1986.
13. Tong-A Ilbo, March 7, 1986; and Far Eastern Economic Review, April 10, 1986, p. 21.
14. Korea Herald, June 25, 1986.
15. Far Eastern Economic Review, November 13, 1986, p. 15, December 11, 1986, p. 47, February 5, 1987, pp. 15-16.
16. New York Times, December 4, 1986; and San Francisco Chronicle, December 3, 1986.
17. Korea Herald, October 17, 1986.
18. Ibid. The government's assertion suggested that Chun regime implicitly equated unification with overthrow of North Korean communist system, which was unlikely to happen in the foreseeable future. By the way, the

government's request for the assembly's consent to take Mr. Yu into custody was approved by the DJP assemblymen alone, who had earlier slipped out of the assembly's main chamber and gathered in a conference room. This was the first time in 25 years that the national assembly--or one part of it--had given consent to the detention of a sitting assemblyman.

19. Tong-A Ilbo, April 6, 1985; and Far Eastern Economic Review, April 18, 1985, p. 46.

20. Far Eastern Economic Review, August 1, 1985, p. 32, August 15, 1985, p. 34; and Tong-A Ilbo, June 22, July 31, 1985.

21. Korea Times, December 31, 1985; and Far Eastern Economic Review, January 16, 1986, p. 22.

22. Tong-A Ilbo, June 22, July 31, 1985.

23. Far Eastern Economic Review, January 16, 1986, p. 23, January 30, 1986, pp. 15-16.

24. Yun Chae Kol, "Hanguk e Kupchin Seryok kwa Pan-Ch'eje Tanch'e" (The Radical Forces and the Anti-Establishment Groups in South Korea," Shin-Tong-A, No. 321, (June 1986), pp. 462-493.

25. Shin-Tong-A, No. 327, (December 1986), pp. 335-340.

26. Tong-A Ilbo, November 14, 1986.

27. The strike ended when company's non-union employees attacked the protestors with sticks and steel pipes; in December, a Seoul court sentenced three demonstrators to two years in prison. Far Eastern Economic Review, July 11, 1985, p. 12; and New York Times, December 15, 1985.

28. Far Eastern Economic Review, November 13, 1986, p. 14.

29. Asahi Shinbun, October 31, 1986.

30. Far Eastern Economic Review, November 20, 1986, p. 29, December 11, 1986, p. 31.

31. New York Times, November 19, 1986; and Korea Herald, November 19, 1986.

32. Washington Post, May 25, 26, November 5, 1985; and New York Times, May 24, November 5, 1985.

33. New York Times, December 3, 1985, June 15, 1986.

34. Monthly Review of Korean Affairs, VI, No. 1, (January/February 1984), p. 4.

35. Tong-A Ilbo, April 13, 1987.

36. Tong-A Ilbo, April 16, 17, 27, May 12, 13, 1987; New York Times, April 19, May 15, 1987; and Far Eastern Economic Review, May 7, 1987, p. 27.

37. Tong-A Ilbo, June 10, 1987; New York Times, April 21, 1987; and Far Eastern Economic Review, May 7, 1987, p. 27.

38. New York Times, April 14, 15, June 24, 1987.

39. Hanguk Ilbo, April 16, 17, 18, 1987; and Time, March 16, 1987, pp. 50-51.

40. Hanguk Ilbo, May 8, 12, 15, 16, 1987; New York Times, April 21, 1987; and Time, May 21, 1987, p. 46.

41. Hanguk Ilbo, April 28, May 17, 1987; and Far Eastern Economic Review, May 7, 1987, pp. 104-105.

42. Shin Tong-A, July 1987, pp. 256-173; and Hanguk Ilbo, May 22, 1987.

43. Tong-A Ilbo, June 27, 1987; Time, June 29, 1987, p. 23; Far Eastern Economic Review, June 25, 1987, p. 12; and New York Times, June 27, 1987.

44. New York Times, June 25, 1987; and Far Eastern Economic Review, July 2, 1987 p. 10.

45. Asian Wall Street Journal, November 30, 1987; New York Times, June 27, 1987; and Time, June 29, 1987, p. 24.

46. Tong-A Ilbo, June 20, 1987.

47. Time, June 29, 1987, pp. 22, 26; and U.S. News and World Report, July 6, 1987, pp. 31-32; New York Times, April 21, 1987; and Far Eastern Economic Review, June 4, 1987, p. 18, June 25, 1987, p. 18.

48. New York Times, June 20, 24, 25, 1987; and Time, July 6, 1987, p. 15.

49. Tong-A Ilbo, June 29, 1987; and New York Times, July 1, 1987.

50. New York Times, June 30, July 1, 1987.

51. Asian Wall Street Journal, August 31, 1987; Hanguk Ilbol, August 8, September 8, 1987; Los Angeles Times, August 28, 1987; and Han Sung joo, "South Korea in 1987: The Politics of Democratization," Asian Survey, XXVIII, No. 1, (January 1988), p. 58.

52. Hanguk Ilbo, July 31, August 7, 11, 14, 18, 19, 22, 27, 1987; New York Times, September 2, 3, 1987; Asian Wall Street Journal, August 31, 1987; and Far Eastern Economic Review, October 1, 1987, p. 20.

53. Hanguk Ilbo, May 12, August 23, 1987; Asian Wall Street Journal, December 7, 1987; New York Times, September 4, 1987; and Los Angeles Times, August 27, 1987.

54. Hanguk Ilbo, July 17, 31, August 11, 1987.

55. New York Times, August 19, 1987.

56. Hanguk Ilbo, August 23, 1987; New York Times, September 2, 4, 5, 7, 1987; and Far Eastern Economic Review, January 28, 1988, p. 60.

57. Hanguk Ilbo, September 8, 1987; New York Times, September 2, 4, 5, 7, 1987; and Far Eastern Economic Review, January 28, 1988, p. 60.

58. The origin of the Reunification Democratic Party, which was headed by Kim Yong Sam, will be explained.

59. Tong-A Ilbo, July 30, 1987.

60. Los Angeles Times, September 19, 1987; and New York Times, October 13, 1987.

61. Korea Times, October 13, 1987.

62. A full text of the bill, which subsequently became the new constitution, is in Hanguk Ilbo, October 30, 1987.

63. Hanguk Ilbo, October 29, 30, 1987.

64. Hanguk Ilbo, October 11, November 10, 1987; and Los Angeles Times, November 10, 1987.

65. Hanguk Ilbo, April 9, 30, May 1, 1987.

66. Han, "South Korea in 1987," p. 53; Far Eastern Economic Review, March 26, 1987, pp. 36-37, April 16, 1987, p. 24; and New York Times, June 24, 1987.

67. Hanguk Ilbo, April 30, May 1, July 10, 1987; and Asian Wall Street Journal, November 2, 1987. It was only after the lifting of the ban on his political activities in early July of the year that Kim Dae Jung formally assumed the role of the RDP's standing adviser.

68. Far Eastern Economic Review, October 1, 1987, p. 17.

69. Hanguk Ilbo, July 9, 1987; New York Times, June 24, 30, 1987; and Far Eastern Economic Review, July 9, 1987, p. 9.

70. New York Times, June 30, July 27, 1987; Time, July 13, 1987, pp. 36-37; and Far Eastern Economic Review, July 30, 1987, p. 27.

71. Hanguk Ilbo, July 10, 1987.

72. Hanguk Ilbo, July 18, August 28, 1987.

73. Time, July 13, 1987, p. 37.

74. Tong-A Ilbo, September 30, 1987; San Francisco Chronicle, October 10, 1987; and New York Times, June 24, October 11, 15, 1987.

75. For example, during his three-day tour early in September through his native South Cholla Province, Kim Dae Jung received tumultuous receptions. Hanguk Ilbo, July 18, August 28, September 10, 1987; San Francisco Chronicle, September 11, 1987; and New York Times, October 11, 28, 1987.

76. Hanguk Ilbo, October 29, 1987; and New York Times, October 28, 1987.

77. Hanguk Ilbo, October 30, 31, 1987; and Asian Wall Street Journal, November 2, 1987.

78. Asian Wall Street Journal, November 2, 1987.

79. Hanguk Ilbo, October 6, 1987; and Time, October 12, 1987, p. 36.

80. Hanguk Ilbo, October 30, 1987.

81. Asian Wall Street Journal, November 2, 1987; and Far Eastern Economic Review, October 15, 1987, p. 49.

82. It was on November 16 that President Chun formally opened one-month long presidential campaign, while setting the voting date for December 16. However, the campaigning had begun long before. Hanguk Ilbo, November 17, 1987; and Tong-A Ilbo, November 17, 1987.

83. In all, there were eight presidential hopefuls, including a woman. New York Times, November 17, 26, 1987.

84. Hanguk Ilbo, August 11, 1987; and New York Times, July 15, 27, 1987. On July 19, the Army Chief of Staff, General Park Hee To, during an off-the-record session with Korean reporters, stated that "something unhappy might happen if Kim Dae Jung ran for the president." Similar remarks were also made by two other high-ranking officers, including the head of the Defense Security Command. Incidentally, government officials denied Park ever had made the remark attributed to him.

85. Far Eastern Economic Review, November 19, 1987, p. 40; and New York Times, November 19, 28, 1987.

86. Hanguk Ilbo, November 10, 1987.

87. Chong served only three months of the seven-year prison term he had received for allegedly failing to take an appropriate action against Park's assassin Kim Jae Kyu. Far Eastern Economic Review, November 26, 1987, p. 4.

88. Time, October 12, 1987, p. 36; New York Times, November 19, 28, 1987; and Asian Wall Street Journal, November 16, 1987.

89. Newsweek, December 7, 1987, p. 57; Asian Wall Street Journal, December 28, 1987; and Far Eastern Economic Review, October 29, 1987, p. 23. Incidentally, the socio-economic views of the three major presidential candidates, which appeared in the November 2, 1987 issue of the Asian Wall Street Journal, hardly differed on basic issues. All three espoused a free economy, including Kim Dae Jung, who emphatically rejected socialism. On August 15, Kim Dae Jung proposed a confederation of North and South Korea as a formula to bring about an eventual reunification of the peninsula. The proposal, however, was met by a strong criticism from the ruling DJP, which attacked it as a "reckless idea" and forced Kim virtually to shelve it. Far Eastern Economic Review, September 3, 1987, p. 13.

90. Hanguk Ilbo, November 15, 1987; and Asian Wall Street Journal, November 16, 1987.

91. Hanguk Ilbo, November 3, 1987; and New York Times, November 2, 1987.

92. Tong-A Ilbo, October 23, 1987; New York Times, October 25, November 2, 30, 1987; and Hanguk Ilbo, December 11, 1987.

93. Asian Wall Street Journal, November 16, 1987; and Far Eastern Economic Review, December 3, 1987, p. 26. It was during the height of the presidential campaigns that a South Korean jetliner exploded over Thai-Burmese border, killing all those aboard. The tragedy, which occurred on November 29 and immediately attributed by South Korean authorities to North Korean sabotage, also could have helped Ro, who had stressed national security during his campaign appearances with voters, who were generally "security conscious." Hanguk Ilbo, December 1, 1987; and Asian Wall Street Journal, December 7, 1987.

94. The voting results are in Tong-A Ilbo, December 17, 18, 1987.

95. New York Times, December 18, 22, 1987; and Far Eastern Economic Review, January 7, 1988, p. 16. Most allegations of vote fraud focused on vote buying, voter intimidation, and tampering with absentee votes. Charges also surfaced that the voter registration rolls were padded in favor of Ro and that the computer used during ballot counting was rigged.

96. San Francisco Chronicle, December 18, 1987; New York Times, December 19, 22, 1987; and Asian Wall Street Journal, December 28, 1987. Probably, the worst single post-election protest occurred in the ward office compound in a working-class district, called Kuro, in the southern Seoul suburbs. There, on December 18, thousands of policemen stormed the ward office to end a three-day siege by protestors, who held hostage four disputed ballot boxes and a dozen election officials.

97. Asian Wall Street Journal, December 28, 1987; and Far Eastern Economic Review, December 31, 1987, p. 8, January 7, 1988, p. 16.

98. Han, "South Korea in 1987," p. 57; Time, December 28, 1987, p. 28; and U.S. News and World Report, December 28, 1987, p. 42. It was generally agreed that there were some irregularities in the ballot counting; as a whole, however, the election was considered fairly clean, and the opposition did not find evidence to back up its claims of massive fraud.

99. New York Times, December 22, 1987.

100. New York Times, February 26, 1988.

101. Asian Wall Street Journal, December 28, 1987.

324

CONCLUSION

The democratization of South Korea--long fought for by the opponents of the late President Park Chung Hee's authoritarian rule--appeared to have been provided with an opportunity for its realization following his assassination in the fall of 1979. Park's death put the end to his prolonged repressive rule and led to some easing of repression and granting of political freedom. Also until the spring of 1980, it appeared as if South Korea might finally move away from the oppressively tight Yushin rule and achieve a democracy under a genuinely civilian leadership. Thus Park's sudden demise presented South Korea with a chance to resolve its long drawn out political instability through democratization, aimed at establishing a new political center capable of developing a new consensus and of executing far-reaching reforms. At the same time, the public at large was full of expectation for a major change in the political structure of their country.

However, some of the army leaders, led by late Park "loyalist" Chun Doo Hwan, perceived a threat to their military careerism in the rising tides of public expectations for democratization, for which the Park's "nemesis" Kim Dae Jung was a prominent proponent. Irrespective of the popular mood and instead of learning a lesson from Park's tragic death, Chun and his coterie of relatively young officers moved to crush the democratization movement then under way and grasp the nation's highest political posts for themselves. The very first major step in this direction was their bloody but successful intra-army putsch within six weeks of Park's murder. This opened the way for Chun and his cohorts to climb to pivotal positions in the army and to control President Ch'oe Kyu Ha's interim civilian government from behind the scenes.

As social unrest grew among the proponents of democratization because of the uncertainty of political reform, Chun and his cohorts came to the forefront as an instrument of law and order, while muzzling the mounting clamors for liberalization. Furthermore, they took yet another decisive step in May 1980 by ordering troops into the city of Kwangju to suppress anti-government uprisings there. By September Mr. Chun had officially become the supreme ruler of the country by assuming the nation's presidency. Thus within one year after Park's death, the country had gone through successive stages of democratic aspiration, violence, repression, and finally settled back into authoritarianism.

Of deep concern in the cycles of change was that with the imposition of authoritarian rule under Chun, South Korea returned to a political deadlock similar to the one during Park's last days: a repressive rule by gun over an alienated population without the means of tapping their genuine support. Indeed, the Fifth Republic under Chun was a "successor regime" to Park's Yushin rule despite Chun's disavowal of his regime's identification with the Yushin rule. Chun's regime, like the late Park's, was an authoritarian one dominated and supported by the military--the nature of its authoritarianism probably being the merging of Yi dynasty Confucianism, Japanese colonialism, and 20th century authoritarian practices. Also in her external relations South Korea's posture under Chun remained basically the same as under Park.

Just as Park had his 1972 Yushin constitution approved in a referendum under martial law, Mr. Chun rammed through his political changes when the country was under military rule. Furthermore, Chun's slogans such as the "new society" and the "democratic welfare society" were the echoes of Park's "Korean-style democracy," which was a dictatorial rule in practice. Moreover, as Park substituted economic development and an impending Communist invasion for ideology, Chun heavily relied on the imperative of national security as a rallying point for the country, and crushed opposition in its name. However, the cry of "the Country in Danger," used consciously as the cement for holding together the social fabric, led to the politicization of the national security, producing cynicism, the very opposite of the result intended. All this is not surprising, because Mr. Chun was among the late Park's proteges and advisors, who had played a fateful role in leading the country into the extraordinary political crisis on the eve of Park's murder.

Despite the similarities, however, Chun was bound to have a much harder time consolidating his position than Park had experienced after the 1961 coup. On the eve of the 1961 military coup, the population--weary of the

disorder and confusion under the Chang Myon government--
was by no means unreceptive to a strong military rule.
Indeed, the South Korean society under the leadership of
Premier Chang was not unlike that of the French Fourth
Republic, which after years of "chaos and confusion" had
come to an end in the summer of 1958 paving the way for
the return to power of the authoritarian General Charles
de Gaulle. Thus it might even be said that Park had come
to power on the wave of popular discontent with the political backbiting and instability of the Chang regime.
Furthermore, the coup itself turned out to be bloodless.
In contrast, Chun rose to power against the general mood
of the population, and its path was gory.

Thus from the outset, Chun alienated a large segment
of the population permanently, while raising questions
about the legitimacy of his regime. The presidential and
national assembly elections that Chun and his associates
had undergone on the eve of their formal assumption of
power appeared in the eyes of many people merely as cha-
rades designed to present a democratic facade for a
regime that had come into being by naked force. The
doubt in the mind of the public about the validity of
Chun's authority was reflected in the incessant political
turmoil that had racked the Fifth Republic virtually ever
since its birth.

The problem was compounded by a series of financial
malfeasances involving high governmental officials and
even Chun's own relatives, that flew in the face of
Chun's own oft-raised motto of social "purification."
With the financial scandals involving public figures
erupting unceasingly, many people wondered if their government was willing or able to eradicate economic and
social wrongdoings. They even suspected that there might
have been a systematic collusion between the culprits and
those who were in power. As such, the public at large
became cynical about the slogans of "justice," "democracy," and "welfare society," raised by the ruling Democratic Justice Party.

When combined with the uncertainty of the future of
their political community revealed in the constant turmoil, the people's distrust of their political leaders--
prevalent from the latter years of the late Park's rule--
led many South Koreans to be driven by the impulse of
"every man for himself," making them work only for self-
aggradizement and for their own families. Thus, corruption on the part of the political elite debilitated the

national effort to rise up from poverty experienced until so recently by Koreans, as it eroded the cement that held the social fabric together and undermined the existing frameworks of the socio-political system.

With the Chun regime remaining in power despite the lingering doubt about its legitimacy, a growing number of South Koreans came to believe that ultimately it was the United States that was responsible for the continuation of such a regime. The American role was illustrated by such events as the release by U.S.-South Korea Combined Forces Commander Gen. John A. Wickham in May 1980 of Korean troops in order to retake rebel-held Kwangju, and Gen. Wickham's rather ill-timed interview of August 1980 in Seoul with a visiting American correspondent, the contents of which were selectively utilized by Chun to rally support for his last-minute efforts to become president.

The frustrations and anger of the foes of the Chun regime had given rise to anti-Americanism, which was manifested in the physical destruction of U.S. cultural centers or the holdings of Americans as hostages in conjunction with dissident activities of many young people. These were the first manifestation of overt anti-American sentiments since the Korean War, and they brought about a "new politics" in South Korea. Also closely related to the anti-U.S. sentiments was the problem of the unification of the peninsula. As noted, the Chun government indicated repeatedly that it was willing to relegate unification to the status of an aspiration to be fulfilled at some time in a distant future. The United States endorsed the position of Seoul because Washington, like Seoul, was more interested in maintaining "stability" in Korea than achieving unification.[1]

For South Korea, the appearance of the Fifth Republic under Chun's military backed regime was, in the last analysis, an "unnecessary coup." It did not alter the repressive internal political system that had led to the violent ending of the Park regime amidst widespread anti-government disturbances. On the contrary, by dragging the country into another round of repression--with the overwhelming majority of people opposed to it and with the armed forces split internally--Chun's regime laid the grounds for a deeper conflict for the country that had already suffered a series of upheavals and instabilities.

Indeed, South Korea was two mutually suspicious and antagonistic societies divided between conservatives led by the military and supported primarily by other state apparatus as well as big businesses, on the one hand, and reformists and radicals who were composed of students, Christian intellectuals, and a growing number of urbanites both from working and middle-class groups, on the other. The former camp stressed tight state control of citizen's political activities for the sake of economic growth and national security, while upholding the close U.S.-South Korea ties and taking a wary attitude toward any move that might lead to easing of tensions with P'yongyang. On the other hand, the latter camp favored participatory democracy and decreased military hegemony in politics, while in general advocating loosening or severance of the links with the United States and accommodation with North Korea.

Because the political aspirations of these two societies were sharply delineated and because the conservatives in control of the state apparatus responded to demands for political development with repression or viewed them with suspicion, there was a strong undercurrent of political alienation sweeping through South Korea. Thus for a great number of South Koreans, the formal governmental structures--developed generally to aggregate demands of various groups and process them in an orderly way--were essentially alien, extractive, and exploitative.

Aside from the conflicting political inclinations among the population at large, there emerged a cleavage of different nature in the army, revealed in a series of rumors of more army coups circulating since the mid-term of Chun's presidency. The primary cause of this rift was personal rather than ideological, including uneasiness of certain officers with the general drift of the country under Mr. Chun. This lack of internal cohesion in the army was largely a consequence of the conscious shifting of the army's role from an instrument of national politics to its arbiters by officers who had claimed themselves national leaders.

Mr. Chun repeatedly pledged that he would step down following the expiration in 1988 of his single presidential term, as constitutionally stipulated. That was a worthy goal, especially given the violent endings of all the previous governments in Seoul. But the problem for Chun was how he could pass on power without having to answer for his deeds to the outraged people. Chun's personal safety--in the volatile and often acrimonious political tradition of the country--would be the "safest" only if his party continued to be in power after his retirement. As such, while promising to give up power peacefully, Chun all along contrived to control the choice of his successor, either by keeping the indirect mode of selecting the president or by other self-serving ground rules backed by his party, that kept the majority status in the National Assembly. Mr. Chun's resolve not to open up the political process may have been reinforced by the inability of his military-backed regime to transcend its parochial power base and build a broad, public support around itself.

In the absence of voluntary allegiance of citizenry to it, the Chun regime's attempts to stay in power rested upon external control mechanisms such as the police, intelligence agencies, and the military. Various governmental institutions, instead of effectively aggregating and processing demands of various groups in an orderly way, rested uneasily upon the society, largely made up of a population oscillating between apathy and withdrawal of interests from the governmental institutions, on the one hand, and intensive outbursts of frustrations against and demands on these institutions for change, on the other. Under the circumstances, the Chun government became a captive of the chaos, moving from one crisis to another without any clear sense of where it was going, seemingly measuring its own success simply as a matter of staying in office.

As it was preoccupied with weathering through crises that swarmed around it, the Chun government resorted not only to force and the time-honored cry of "Country in Danger" but also to the traditional behavior patterns from the Yi dynasty--such as family-centrism, factionalism, and regionalism. The reliance upon such behavior patterns--all roundly condemned by contemporary Koreans as harmful for the general well-being of their society--was fostered and perpetuated by the continuous lack of political stability. Yet, families and other private groups remained the only element that provided security to the individual in South Korean society, which was going through a most wrenching period of continually recurring crises.

As the people became wary and introspective amidst uncertainty in their society, the government remained

unable to articulate a constructive vision to marshall
the energy of the whole society; meanwhile, the continuing conflict between the government and its foes raised
the level of violence and bitterness on the political
scene, while widening and deepening mutual distrust.
The clashes between the two opposing forces were so
enervating for the country that they took on the aspect
of fratricide, carried on in the eyes of the world, and
were crushing to the national pride of South Koreans.

The time was long overdue for South Korea to overcome
the cycle of political violence and instability by building political institutions based on a popularly accepted
political order. When the political order is erected on
a broad ideological consensus among various social strata, the political center will be capable of directing and
changing the society in an orderly and sustained fashion,
as is sorely needed for South Korea. Such a political
center will be forthcoming when it is created by the will
of the people--that is, by a democratic political pro-
cess--in a society where the proceeds of economic moder-
nity are generally and equitably shared. Yearning for
democracy, with its ennobling ideas of fundamental human
rights and civil liberties, has been clear and enduring
among South Koreans. When a government is popularly
elected and legitimized by the public, the country's
military institutions and economic accomplishments will
become meaningful parts of the national strength, because
a nation is as strong as the degree to which it has found
its own identity and has achieved social and political
cohesion.

Notes

1. Kim, "Panmi nun Odiso onunga," p. 413.

POSTCRIPT

On April 8, 1988, the government announced that the election for the 13th National Assembly, which had been expected for some time, would be held on April 26.[1] The new legislature was to have a total of 229 seats--a 23 seat expansion from the previous two legislatures. Of the 299 lawmakers, 224 were to be elected from single-member electoral districts, a departure from the recent practice of electing two legislators from each of 92 constituencies. The remaining 75 seats were to be nationally distributed among rival parties on a "proportional" basis, which was a reduction by 17 seats of "proportional" representation from the 92 seats divided among major parties following the previous two elections.[2]

There was an average of five candidates competing for each of the 224 district seats. The opposition was split between three major parties--the RDP, the PPD, and the NDRP--and 10 minor parties, plus independent candidates. The main division of the opposition, as in the previous December, was between the RDP and the PPD.[3]

The campaign themes for the elections were generally a rerun of the previous December. The opposition portrayed the ruling DJP as nothing but an embodiment of the rule of the unpopular former president Chun, and tried to link the DJP by association to the corruption scandal swirling around the previous government because of the implication in the scandal of Mr. Chun's younger brother.[4] The younger brother in question, Chun Kyong Hwan, a retired lieutenant colonel, was arrested on March 31 on suspicion of embezzlement and influence-peddling perpetrated during his seven-year tenure as the head of the Saemaul Undong, the post he held during the presidency of his elder brother.[5] The ruling DJP candidates, on the other hand, capitalized on the split of the main opposition camp between the RDP and PPD. While holding up a spectre of legislative turmoil and paralysis in the case of the opposition victory, the DJP candidates asserted that there would be no political stability unless their party won.[6]

The returns of the April 26 National Assembly elections showed that most South Koreans continued to hold anti-government views, while preferring the opposition as a whole. Indeed, the voters stripped the government party of its parliamentary majority, the first time since the early 1950's, while reviving the opposition dispirited by its failure in the previous December.[7] With 33.2 percent of the popular vote (less than the 35.9 percent Ro received in December), the DJP won 87 of the 224 district seats. Kim Yong Sam's RDP followed with 23.7 percent of the vote and captured 47 contested seats. Kim Dae Jung's PPD received only 19.2 percent of the vote, far below the 26.5 percent he himself had received four months before. However, the PPD, whose leader Kim Dae Jung had pressed hardest to change the electoral system to the present single-member system,[8] performed strongly in the seat total by winning 55 and emerging as the number one opposition party.[9] Kim Jong P'il's NDRP captured 27 district seats with 15.3 percent of the vote. Independent candidates won eight district seats.[10]

As the party which won the largest number of the contested seats, the DJP was awarded half (not two-thirds) of the 75 "proportional representation" seats. This gave President Ro's party a total of 125 seats in the 299-member National Assembly, 25 seats shy of a simple majority. The remaining 37 "proportional representation" seats were distributed proportionately among the PPD, the RDP, and the NDRP. As a result, the PPD held a total of 71 seats in the National Assembly, the RDP 60 seats, and the NDRP 35 seats. Thus the three opposition parties together held 166 seats.[11]

In addition to the stunning setback for the DJP and the emergence of the PPD as the main legislative opposition group, the parliamentary election returns showed a clear-cut regional breakdown of the electorate, which, though expected, increasingly worried those who were concerned.[12] For instance, Kim Dae Jung's PPD captured all but one of the 32 district seats in his native Cholla region. At Taegu, Ro's hometown, his DJP swept all eight contested seats. Also, in Pusan, Kim Yong Sam's home base, his RDP won 14 of the 15 seats. The DJP and RDP together wrapped up 40 of the 43 seats in the surrounding North and South Kyongsang Provinces. The NDRP, whose leader Kim Jong P'il is from South Ch'ungch'ong Province, took 13 of the province's 18 seats.[13]

On May 30, 1988, the 13th National Assembly inaugurated its four-year term. It was also the occasion for the leaders of the three opposition parties to return to the National Assembly after a prolonged involuntary absence. Kim Dae Jung regained his parliamentary seat for the first time in 17 years.[14] Kim Yong Sam resumed his seat nine years after being ousted from the Assembly by the then majority DRP of President Park. Kim Jong P'il returned after being forced into exile when Chun Doo Hwan seized power eight years before.[15] Indeed, the political careers of the three Kims suffered when Mr. Chun, aided by Ro and others, seized power in 1980.

Notes

1. Tong-A Ilbo, April 8, 1988; and Hanguk Ilbo, April 1988.

2. Tong-A Ilbo, March 9, 1988; New York Times, April 9, 1988; and Far Eastern Economic Review, March 24, 1988, pp. 32-33. The single-member constituency system had been practiced up to the time of the establishment of the Yushin System in 1972.

3. Korea Times, April 26, 1988; Christian Science Monitor, April 22, 1988; and New York Times, April 26, 1988. In preparation for the National Assembly elections, the leaderships of the RDP and the PPD had made a series of attempts to reunify their parties, but in vain. Tong-A Ilbo, February 15, March 3, 11, 12, 1988.

4. Tong-A Ilbo, March 11, 12, April 9, 1988; Hanguk Ilbo, April 6, 9, 1988; Christian Science Monitor, April 22, 1988; and New York Times, April 14, 1988.

5. Hanguk Ilbo, April 7, 1988; Korea Times, April 14, 1988; Asian Wall Street Journal, March 28, 1988; and Far Eastern Economic Review, July 7, 1988, p. 27.

6. New York Times, April 26, 1988.

7. Korea Times, April 28, 1988; and Tong-A Ilbo, May 30, 1988.

8. Tong-A Ilbo, February 10, 1988; and Far Eastern Economic Review, March 24, 1988, pp. 32-33.

9. Kim Yong Sam and Kim Dae Jung, both of whom had been severely criticized for failing to come up with a single challenger to the DJP candidate in the previous December, gave up their party presidencies, the former on February 8 and the latter on March 17. Both men, however, remained the guiding forces of their parties, and both resumed their party presidencies following the April 26 Assembly elections, Dae Jung on May 7 and Yong Sam on May 13. Tong-A Ilbo, February 9, March 18, 1988; and Hanguk Ilbo, May 8, 13, 1988.

10. Tong-A Ilbo, May 30, 1988; and Korea Times, April 28, 1988.

11. _Tong-A Ilbo_, May 30, 1988; and _Korea Times_, April 28, 1988.

12. _Tong-A Ilbo_, March 9, 1988; and _Hanguk Ilbo_, April 7, 1988.

13. _Korea Times_, April 28, 1988.

14. Unlike Kim Yong Sam and Kim Jong P'il, Kim Dae Jung did not run for a district seat. Instead, he was placed on his party's list of candidates for "proportional" seats. _Korea Times_, May 31, 1988.

15. _Tong-A Ilbo_, May 30, 1988; _New York Times_, May 31, 1988; and _Korea Times_, May 31, 1988.

BIBLIOGRAPHY

(In English)

A. Books and Documents

Almond, Gabriel A. and Verba, Sidney. The Civic Culture: Political Attitudes and Democracy in Five Nations. Princeton, N.J.: Princeton University Press, 1963.

Bards, William J., ed. The Two Koreas in East Asian Affairs. New York: New York University Press, 1976.

Bartz, Patricia M. South Korea. London: Oxford University Press, 1972.

Beale, Howard K. Theodore Roosevelt and the Rise of America to World Power. Baltimore: John Hopkins University Press, 1956.

Boettcher, Robert, and Freedman, Gordon L. Gifts of Deceit: Sun Myung Moon, Tongsun Park and the Korean Scandal. New York: Harper and Row, 1980.

Bunge, Frederica M., ed. South Korea, A Country Study. Washington, D.C.: American University Press, 1982.

Bunge, Frederica M., and Shin Rin-sup, eds. China: A Country Study. Washington, D.C.: American University Press, 1981.

Buss, Claude A. The United States and the Republic of Korea. Stanford, CA: Hoover Institute Press, 1982.

Choy Bong-youn. A History of the Korean Reunification Movement: Its Issues and Prospects. Peoria, Illinois: Bradley University Press, 1984.

Clough, Ralph N. Deterrence and Defense in Korea: The Role of U.S. Forces. Washington, D.C.: Brookings Institution, 1976.

Cole, David, and Lyman, Princeton N. Korean Development: The Interplay of Politics and Economics. Cambridge, MA: Harvard University Press, 1971.

Cumings, Bruce. The Origins of the Korean War: Liberation the Emergence of Separate Regimes, 1945-1947. Princeton University Press, 1981.

Curtis, Gerald L., and Han Sung-joo, eds. The U.S.-South Korea Alliance: Evolving Patterns in Security Relations. Lexington, MA: D.C. Heath and Company, 1983.

The Economic and Social Modernization of the Republic of Korea. Cambridge, MA: Harvard University Press, 1980.

Eisenstadt, Samuel Noah. Modernization: Protest and Change. Englewood Cliffs, NJ: Prentice-Hall, Inc., 1966.

Frank, Charles R., et. al. Foreign Trade Regimes and Economic Development: South Korea. New York: National Bureau of Economic Research, 1975.

Fukuda Tsunehari. Future of Japan and the Korean Peninsula (trans. from Japanese by K. Jahng). Seoul: Hollym International Corp., 1978.

Grahm, Robert. Iran: The Illusion of Power. New York: St. Martin's Press, 1980.

Hahm Pyong-choon. The Korean Political Tradition and Law. Seoul: Hollym International Corporation, Publishers, 1967.

Han Sungjoo. The Failure of Democracy in South Korea. Berkeley: University of California Press, 1974.

Harrison, Selig S. The Widening Gulf: Asian Nationalism and American Policy. New York: The Free Press, 1978.

Hasan, Parvez. Korea: Problems and Issues in A Rapidly Growing Economy. Baltimore: John Hopkins University Press, 1976.

Henderson, Gregory. Korea: The Politics of Vortex. Cambridge, MA: Harvard University Press, 1968.

Hinton, Harold C. Korea Under New Leadership: The Fifth Republic. New York: Praeger Publishers, 1983.

340

Hong Wontack, and Kreuger, Anne O., eds. Trade and Development in Korea. Seoul: Korea Development Institute, 1975.

Hwang In K. The Neutralized Unification of Korea in Perspective. Cambridge, MA: Shenkman Publishing Company, Inc., 1980.

Janowitz, Morris. The Military in the Political Development of New Nations. Chicago: University of Chicago Press, 1964.

_____. The Professional Soldier: A Social and Political Portrait. New York: The Free Press, 1971.

Jones, Leroy P., and Sakong Il. Government, Business, and Entrepreneurship in Economic Development: The Korean Case. Cambridge, MA: Harvard University Press, 1979.

Keon, Michael. Korean Phoenix: A Nation from the Ashes. Englewood Cliff, NJ: Prentice-Hall, 1977.

Kihl Young Whan. Politics and Policies in Divided Korea: Regimes in Contest. Boulder, Colorado: Westview Press, 1984.

Kim Chong Lim. Political Participation in Korea: Democracy, Mobilization and Mobility. Santa Barbara, CA: ABC-CLIO Press, 1980.

Kim Dae Jung. Prison Writings (trans. by Choi Sung-il and David R. McCann). Berkeley: University of California Press, 1987.

Kim Joungwon Alexander. Divided Korea: The Politics of Development 1945-1972. Cambridge, MA: Harvard University Press, 1975.

Kim Kwan Bong. The Korea-Japan Treaty Crisis and the Instability of the Korean Political System. New York: Praeger Publishers, 1971.

Kim Kyong-Dong. Man and Society in Korea's Economic Growth: Sociological Studies. Seoul: Seoul National University Press, 1985.

Kim Se-Jin. The Politics of Military Revolution in Korea. Chapel Hill: University of North Carolina Press, 1971.

Kim Se-Jin, and Cho Chang H., eds. Government and Politics of Korea. Silver Spring, Maryland: Research Institute of Korean Affairs, 1972.

Kim Young C., and Halpern, Abraham., eds., The Future of the Korean Peninsula. New York: Praeger Publishers, 1977.

Korea Annual 1964. Seoul: Haptong News Agency, 1964.

Korea Annual 1981 and 1982. Seoul: Yonhap News Agency, 1981, 1982.

Kuznets, Paul W. Economic Growth and Structure in the Republic of Korea. New Haven, Conn.: Yale University Press, 1977.

Lee Changsoo, and De Vos, George. Koreans in Japan. Berkeley, CA: University of California Press, 1981.

Lee Hahn-Been. Korea: Time, Change, and Administration. Honolulu: East-West Center, 1968.

McCormack, Gavan, and Selden, Marck, eds. Korea, North and South: The Deepening Crisis. New York: Monthly Review Press, 1978.

Military Revolution in Korea. Seoul: The Secretariat, Supreme Council for National Reconstruction, 1961.

Moskowitz, Karl, ed. From Patron to Partner: The Development of U.S.-Korean Business and Trade Relations. Lexington, MA: D.C. Heath and Company, 1984.

Oh John K.C. Korea: Democracy on Trial. Ithaca: Cornell University Press, 1968.

Oliver, Robert T. Syngman Rhee, The Man Behind the Myth. New York: Dodd Mead Company, 1955.

Pak Chi-Young. Political Opposition in Korea, 1945-1960. Seoul: Seoul National University Press, 1985.

Palais, James B. Politics and Policy in Traditional Korea. Cambridge, MA: Harvard University Press, 1975.

Palmer, Spencer J. Korea and Christianity: The Problems of Identification with Tradition. Seoul: Hollym Corporation, Publishers, 1967.

Park Chung Hee. Major Speeches by Korea's Park Chung Hee. Seoul: Hollym Corporation, Publishers, 1970.

_____. Our Nation's Path: Ideology and Social Reconstruction. Seoul: Tong-A Publishing Company, LTD, 1964.

_____. To Build A Nation. Washington, D.C.: Acropolis Books, 1971.

Pihl, Marshall R., ed. Listening to Korea: A Korea Anthology. New York: Praeger Publishers, 1973.

Shaplen, Robert. A Turning Wheel: The Decades of the Asian Revolution as Witnessed by a Correspondent for the New Yorker. New York: Random House, 1979.

Starr, John Bryan, ed. The Future of U.S.-China Relations. New York: New York University Press, 1981.

Suh Dae-sook and Lee Chae-Jin, eds. Political Leadership in Korea. Seattle: University of Washington Press, 1975.

Sullivan, John and Foss, Roberta. Two Koreas--One Future? Lanham, MD: University Press of America, Inc., 1987.

Sunoo Harold Hakwon. American Dilemma in Asia: The Case of South Korea. Chicago: Nelson-Hall, 1979.

Vreeland, Nena, et. al. Area Handbook for South Korea. Washington, D.C.: American University Press, 1975.

Weinstein, Franklin B., and Kamiya Fuji, eds. The Security of Korea: U.S.-Japanese Perspectives on the 1980's. Boulder, Colorado: Westview Press, 1980.

White, Nathan N. U.S. Policy Toward Korea: Analysis, Alternatives, and Recommendations. Boulder, Colorado: Westview Press, 1979.

Wright, Edward Reynolds, ed. Korean Politics in Transition. Seattle: University of Washington Press, 1975.

343

Yang Sung Chul. <u>Korea and Two Regimes:</u> A Study of Kim Il Sung and Park Chung Hee. Cambridge, MA: Schenkman Publishing Company, Inc., 1981.

B. Articles

Ahn Byung-joon. "South Korea and the Communist Countries," <u>Asian Survey</u>, XX, No. 11 (November 1980), pp. 1098-1107.

Baker, Edward J. "Politics in South Korea," <u>Current History</u>, April 1982, pp. 173-174, 177-178.

Benjamin, Roger. "The Political Economy of Korea," <u>Asian Survey</u>, XII, No. 11 (November 1982), pp. 1105-1116.

Choi Chang-yoon. "Korea: Security and Strategic Issues," <u>Asian Survey</u>, XX, No. 11 (November 1980), pp. 1123-1139.

George, Douglas E. "The Transformation of a 'Hermit': North Korean Foreign Policy Before and After the Vietnam War," unpublished term paper submitted on June 15, 1987 to National Security Affairs Department, Naval Postgraduate School, Monterey, CA (59 pages).

Hahn Bae-ho. "Korea-Japan Relations in the 1970's," <u>Asian Survey</u>, XX, No. 11 (November 1980), pp. 1087-1097.

Han Sungjoo. "South Korea and the United States: The Alliance Survives," <u>Asian Survey</u>, XX, No. 11 (November 1980), pp. 1075-1086.

_____. "South Korea 1978: The Growing Security Dilemma," <u>Asian Survey</u>, XIX, No. 1 (January 1979), pp. 41-50.

_____. "South Korea 1978: The Politics of Democratization," <u>Asian Survey</u>, XXVIII, No. 1 (January 1988), pp. 52-61.

Ho Lee Young. "Military Balance and Peace in the Korean Peninsula," <u>Asian Survey</u>, XXI, No. 8 (August 1981), pp. 852-864.

Ho Samuel P. S.   "Rural-Urban Imbalance in South Korea
   in the 1970's," Asian Survey, XIX, No. 7 (July 1979),
   pp. 645-659.

_____. "South Korea and Taiwan: Development
   Prospects and Problems in the 1980's," Asian Survey,
   XXI, No. 21 (December 1981), pp. 1175-1196.

Imazu Hiroshi.   "A New Era in Japan-South Korea Relations," Japan Quarterly, XXXI, No. 4 (October-December
   1984), pp. 358-364.

Jo Yung-Hwan.   "Japanese-Korean Relations and Asian
   Diplomacy," Orbis, XI, No. 2 (Summer 1967), pp. 582-
   593.

Kamiya Fuji.   "The Korean Peninsula After Park Chung
   Hee," Asian Survey, XX, No. 7 (July 1980, pp. 744-753.

Kauh Kwang-man.   "Problems concerning Student Participation in Korean Society," Korea Journal (Seoul), VIII,
   No. 7 (July 1968), pp. 29-34.

Kim C. I. Eugene.   "South Korea in 1985: An Eventful Year
   Amidst Uncertainty," Asian Survey, XXVI, No. 1 (January
   1986), pp. 66-77.

_____. "South Korea in 1986: Preparing For a Power
   Transition," Asian Survey, XXVII, No. 1 (January 1987),
   pp. 64-74.

_____. "Significance of Korea's 10th National
   Assembly Elections," Asian Survey, XIX, No. 5 (May
   1979), pp. 523-532.

_____. "Significance of the 1963 Korean Elections,"
   Asian Survey, IV, No. 3 (March 1964), pp. 765-773.

Kim Son-ung, and Donaldson, Peter J.   "Dealing with
   Seoul's Population Growth: Government Plans and Their
   Implementation," Asian Survey, XIX, No. 7 (July 1979),
   pp. 660-673.

Koh B. C.   "The 1985 Parliamentary Elections in South
   Korea," Asian Survey, XXV, No. 9 (September 1985), PP.
   883-897.

_____. "Inter-Korean Relations: Seoul's Perspective," _Asian Survey_, XX, No. 11 (November 1980), pp. 1108-1122.

Koo Youngnok. "Future Perspective of South Korea's Foreign Relations," _Asian Survey_, XX, No. 11 (November 1980), pp. 1152-1163.

Lee Chae-Jin. "South Korea in 1984: Seeking Peace and Prosperity," _Asian Survey_, XXV, No. 1 (January 1985), pp. 80-89.

_____. "South Korea in 1983: Crisis Management and Political Legitimacy," _Asian Survey_, XXIV, No. 1 (January 1984), pp. 112-121.

Lee Chong-Sik. "South Korea in 1980: The Emergence of A New Authoritarian Order," _Asian Survey_, XXI, No. 1 (January 1981), pp. 125-143.

_____. "South Korea in 1979: Confrontation, Assassination and Transition," _Asian Survey_, XX, No. 1 (January 1980), pp. 63-79.

Nahm Andrew C. "The Impact of the Taft-Katsura Memorandum on Korea--A Reassessment," _Korea Journal_ (Seoul), October 1985, pp. 4-17.

Nam Koon Woo. "North-South Korean Relations: From Dialogue To Confrontation," _Pacific Affairs_, Winter 1975-1976, pp. 477-499.

Niksch, Larry A. "U.S. Troop Withdrawal From South Korea: Past Shortcomings and Future Prospects," _Asian Survey_, XXI, No. 3 (March 1981), pp. 325-341.

Olsen, Edward A. "Korean Politics and U.S. Policy: Higher Pressure and Lower Profile," _Asian Survey_, XXVII, No. 8 (August 1987), pp. 839-861.

Park Moon Kyu. "Interest Representation in South Korea: The Limits of Corporatist Control," _Asian Survey_, XXVII, No. 8 (August 1987), pp. 903-917.

Park Tong Whan. "The Korean Arms Race: Implications in the International Politics of Northeast Asia," _Asian Survey_, XX, No. 6 (June 1980), pp. 646-660.

Patterson, Benjamin. "South Korea's Time of Testing,"
 America, October 17, 1981, pp. 214-219.

Reischauer, Edwin O., and Baker, Edward J. "A Time Bomb
 Is Ticking in South Korea," _The New York Times Sunday
 Magazine_, November 16, 1986, pp. 51, 80, 82-84, 86, 88.

Rhee Kang Suk. "North Korea's Pragmatism: A Turning
 Point?," _Asian Survey_, XXVII, No. 8 (August 1987), pp.
 885-902.

Shaplen, Robert. "Letters From South Korea," _The New
 Yorker_, November 17, 1980, pp. 174-207.

Stokes, Henry Scott. "Korea's Church Militants," _The New
 York Times Sunday Magazine_, November 28, 1982, pp. 67-
 69, 104-111.

Suh Dae-sook. "South Korea in 1981: The First Year of
 the Fifth Republic," _Asian Survey_, XXII, No. 1 (January
 1982), pp. 107-115.

_____. "South Korea in 1982: A Centennial," _Asian
 Survey_, XXIII, No. 1 (January 1983), pp. 94-101.

Suh Sang-chul. "South Korea's International Economic
 Relations," _Asian Survey_, XX, No. 11 (November 1980),
 pp. 1140-1151.

Tanaka Akira. "Japanese-South Korean Relations in the
 1980's: An Uneasy Partnership," _Japan Quarterly_, XXX,
 No. 2 (April-June 1983), pp. 126-129.

C. Newspapers and Periodicals

Asian Wall Street Journal (Hong Kong)

Boston Globe

Boston Herald American

Christian Science Monitor

Economist (London)

Far Eastern Economic Review (Hong Kong)

Japan Quarterly (Tokyo)

Korea Herald (Seoul)

Korea Times (Seoul)

Korean Newsletter (Washington, D.C.)

Koreatown (Los Angeles)

Los Angeles Times

Monthly Review of Korean Affairs (Arlington, Virginia)

New York Times

Newsweek

San Francisco Chronicle

San Francisco Examiner

Time

U.S. News and World Report

Washington Post

(In Korean or Japanese)

A.   Books and Documents

Chong Chin Sok. Hanguk Ollon Kwange Munhon Saegin (An
    Index to Communication Studies in Korea: A Guide to
    Bibliography on Communication). Seoul: National
    Assembly Library, 1978.

Hanguk Inmyong Sajon (A Korean Biographical Dictionary).
    Seoul: Haptong T'ongshinsa, 1977.

Hanguk Inmyong Sajon (A Korean Biographical Dictionary).
    Seoul: Haptong T'ongshinsa, 1980.

Hapton Yongam 1975, 1976, 1977, 1980 (Haptong Yearbook
    1975, 1976, 1977, 1980). Seoul: Haptong T'ongshinsa,
    1975, 1976, 1977, 1980.

Hong Sung Myon, et. al., eds. Haebang Isipnyon (The Twenty years of Liberation). Seoul: Semunsa, 1965.

Kim Hyong Wook. Kenryoku to Inbo (Power and Intrigue). Tokyo: Kodo Shuppansha, 1980.

Kim Chae Chun. Pomyong'gi (Diary of an Ordinary Man), Vol. II. Toronto, Canada: Ch'ilsong Kwang'gosa, 1982.

Maeda Yasuhiro. Seoul karano Hokokuk: Dokyumento Kankoku 1976-1980 (Report From Seoul: A Document on Korea 1976-1980). Tokyo: Diamond Kaisha, 1981.

Nakagawa Nobuyuki. Chosen Mondai eno Kihonteki Shikaku (Korean Problems Viewed from Fundamental Angles. Tokyo: Tobata Shotten, 1976.

Sasaki Harutaka. Hangukchon Pisa (Hidden History of the Korean War, trans. from Japanese by Kang Ch'ang Koo), Vol. I, II, III. Seoul: Pyonghaksa, 1977.

Sekai, ed. Kankoku karano Tsushin (Letters from South Korea). Tokyo: Iwanami Shotten, 1974.

_____. Zoku Kankoku karano Tsushin (The Second Series of Letters from South Korea). Tokyo: Iwanami Shotten, 1975.

_____. Daisan Kankoku karano Tsushin (The Third Series of Letters from South Korea). Tokyo: Iwanami Shotten, 1977.

_____. Gunsei to Junan: Daishi Kankoku karano Tsushin (Military Rule and Tribulation: The Fourth Series of Letters from South Korea). Tokyo: Iwanami Shotten, 1980.

Tong-A Yongam 1975 (Tong-A Yearbook 1975). Seoul: Tong-A Ilbosa, 1975.

Yonhap Yongam 1981, 1982, 1983, 1984, 1985 (Yonhap Yearbook 1981, 1982, 1983, 1984, 1985). Seoul: Yonhap T'ongshinsa, 1981, 1982, 1983, 1984, 1985.

B. Articles

Bae Tong Ho. "'Hanmi Kongdong Songmyong' un Pundan
Kojonghwa Ch'aektong" (The 'South-Korea-U.S. Joint
Communique' is a Scheme to Freeze the Division),
Hanyang (Tokyo), No. 149 (July-August 1979), pp. 60-
67.

Chang Byong Jo. "Hanguk Chongdang'i koro'on Kil" (the
Path Treaded by Korean Political Parties), Shin-Tong-
A (Seoul), No. 190 (June 1980), pp. 121-129.

Ch'oe Il Nam. "Nongch'on un so'oe tang'hako itta" (Farm
Villages Are Being Alienated), Shin-Tong-A, No. 322
(July 1986), pp. 304-329.

Fuji Haruo. "Shin Nikkan Yuchaku no Shoten, II: Nikkan
Gunji Taisei no Jitsuzo" (The Focal Point of the New
Union of Japan and South Korea, II: The Reality of
Japanese-South Korean Military System), Sekai (Tokyo),
No. 432 (November 1981), pp. 115-121.

Im Ch'un Ung. "Chaeya Seryok iran Nukuinga" (Who Are the
Forces in the Field?), Shin-Tong-A (Seoul), No. 190
(June 1980), pp. 150-160.

Kamada Mitsunori. "Boku Daitoryo Ansatsu no Hamon" (The
Impact of the Assassination of President Park), Supplement to Special New Year Edition of Chuo Koron (Tokyo)
1982, pp. 121-132.

Kang Song Chae. "80 Nyon Pom Kuk'hoe Kae'hon Tuk'i e
Chwajol" (The Collapse of the 1980 Spring National
Assembly Special Committee on Constitutional Revision),
Shin-Tong-A, No. 322 (July 1986), pp. 262-285.

_____. "Park Chung Hee wa Minjong Iyang Chonya"
(Park Chung Hee and the Eve of the Transfer of Power
to Civil Government), Shin-Tong-A, No. 325 (October
1986), pp. 256-272.

_____. "Park Chung Hee e 'Poni' wa Kwollyok Naebu
e Amt'u" (Park Chung Hee's 'Reversal of Will' and the
Secret Feud Within the Ruling Group), Shin-Tong-A, No.
327 (December 1986), pp. 279-301.

_____. "Park Chung Hee ege Onsong Nop'in Mitaesa
'Berger'" (American Ambassador Samuel Berger Who Raised
Voice to Park Chung Hee), Shin-Tong-A, No. 328 (January
1987), pp. 324-345.

Kim Sang Chun. "Panmi nun Odiso onunga" (Where From Is the Anti-Americanism Coming?), Shin-tong-A, No. 322 (July 1986), pp. 408-415.

Kim Yong Sam. "Minjung Chudo e Sae-sidae rul yonda" (A New Era of Leadership by the Masses Opens), Hanyang, No. 149 (July-August 1979), pp. 54-59

Lee Kyong Chae and Park Ki Chong. "'Sam Kimssi' rul Umjikinun Saramdul" (The People Who Move the 'Three Kims'), Shin-Tong-A, No. 190 (June 1980), pp. 138-149.

Lee Sang Woo. "Hanguk kwa Miguk: ku Kaltung e Choryu" (Korea and the United States: The Undercurrent of Conflict), Shin-Tong-A, No. 322 (July 1986), pp. 442-467.

_____. "Park Chongkwonha e Ollon T'anap" (The Suppression of the Press Under the Park Regime," Shin-Tong-A, No. 325 (October 1986), pp. 290-318.

_____. "Park Chongkwon ha Kwollyokhyong Pup'ae e Chongch'e" (The True Character of Power-Associated Corruption Under the Park Regime), Shin-Tong-A, No. 328 (January 1987), pp. 279-295.

_____. "Yushin Ch'iha Chonggyoge'e Panch'eje Undong" (The Anti-Establishment Movement of Religious Circles Under the Yushin Rule," Shin-Tong-A, No. 320 (May 1986), pp. 414-439.

Maeda Yasuhiro. "Zen Tokan Seiken no Jinmyaku" (the Human Connections of the Chun Doo Hwan Regime," Sekai, No. 432 (November 1981), pp. 156-170.

Nakagawa Nobuo. "Kankoku Minshuka Tosono Chokumensuru Kadai" (The Problems confronting the Struggle for Democratization in South Korea), Gekkan Shakaito (Tokyo), August 1981, pp. 173-181.

"O'il Ch'iril Ihu e Hanguk Hakksaeng Undong" (the Korean Students' Movement After the May 17th), Hanyang, No. 165 (March-April 1982), pp. 59-86.

Park Sil. "Hanguk Ollon Sunansa" (A History of the Sufferings of Freedom of Speech and Writing in South Korea), Shin-Tong-A, No. 295 (April 1984), pp. 258-284.

Utsunomiya Tokuma. "Naniga Chosen Josei o Kincho sasete iruka" (What Is Causing Tension in Korea?), Sekai, No. 433 (December 1981), pp. 71-76.

Yun Chae Kol. "Hanguk e Kupchin Seryok kwa Pan-Ch'eje Tanch'e" (The Radical Forces and the Anti-Establishment Groups in South Korea), Shin-Tong-A, No. 321 (June 1986), pp. 462-493.

C. Newspapers and Periodicals

Asahi Shimbun (Tokyo)

Hanguk Ilbo (Seoul)

Hanyang (Tokyo)

Nihon Keizai Shimbun (Tokyo)

Nodong Shinmun (P'yongyang)

Sekai (Tokyo)

Shin-Tong-A (Seoul)

Tong-A Ilbo (Seoul)

Yomiuri Shimbun (Tokyo)

Constitutional Amendment Deliberation Committee, 207, 211
Control Data Corporation, labor strike at, 288, 297
corruption (of officials), 236, 237, 249, 289-290
curb loan scandal, 289-290, 297

Daewoo Apparel Company, labor dispute at, 305, 320
December 12th intra-army coup, 185-190, 205, 280
Declaration for Democracy and National Salvation, 98-99
Defense Security Command, 186, 190, 240, 241
Defense Tax Law, 86, 120
Demilitarized Zone, 104, 146
Democratic Justice Party, 244, 268, 269, 301, 302, 334;June 10, 1987 convention, 307
Democratic Korea Party, 244, 269, 276, 301, 304
Democratic Nationalist Party, 5, 17
Democratic Party:origin of, 6, 7, 10, 17;factionalism of, 11, 13;conservatism of, 12, 14
Democratic Republican Party: origin of, 29;schism in, 30-31, 47-48;as governing party, 52-53, 58, 97;since Park's death, 191, 193-194
Democratic Socialist Party, 244
Democratic Unification Party, 59, 67, 144, 181, 185
"democratic welfare state," 240, 250, 279, 326
dissidents, 74-74, 76, 81, 92, 184;the core members, 75;catchword of, 75, 80; concern over split of op-

[dissidents]
position camp (presidential rivalry of two Kims), 314

economic development plans: First Five-Year Plan (1962-1966), 27, 39, 45, 50, 119; Fourth Five-Year Plan (1977-1981), 119, 121;Second Five-Year Plan (1967-1971), 50; Third Five-Year Plan (1972-1976), 50, 119, 121
Economic Planning Board, 123, 206
economy:recession, 132-133, 285-288;for foreign debt, see trade;foreign investments, 65;gross national products, 18;growth rate, 18, 39, 48-49, 285, 286; inflation, 44, 49;manufactured goods, 120; technology, 126, 127, 137; employment, 44, 140;development strategy, 49, 50, 126-127, 134
education, 78, 86, 87.See also students and professors.
Education Law (1975), 86, 87
Ehwa Women's University, 212, 219
eight-point democratization plan (of June 29, 1987), 310
Election Management Committee, 102-103, 269, 276
elections:presidential, 6, 7, 31-32, 40, 51-52, 268, 311-318;of national assembly, 3, 4, 5, 10, 32, 40, 52-53, 58-59, 111, 118, 144-145, 152, 268-269, 299-302, 333-335
emergency decrees (presidential), 76, 83;number nine, 85-86, 100, 108, 118, 147,

355

leftists, xiii, 304-305; under American Military Government, 3, 21, 70; agitation during the Second Republic, 26-27
Legislative Council for National Security, 242-246, 269, 278
Liberal Party, 5, 6, 17, 243;disintegration of, 10

Magruder, Carter B., General, 25
martial law, 27, 38, 57, 168, 179, 181, 198, 220
Masan, 9, 168-169, 172;Free Export Zone in, 128
McGovern, George, 115
military (South Korea).See armed forces.
Mindan.See the Korean Residents' Association in Japan.
miners, strikes of, 126
Minju Chonson, x, 160
Minju Kungmin Yonhap.See National Association for Democracy.
Mokp'o, rebellion in, 222, 228
Moon Ik Hwan, 100
Moon Pu Shik, 160, 161
Moon Sun Myung, 105
Moon Tong Whan, 181
Muskie, Edmund M., 259, 262
Myondong Incident, 98-101, 114
Myongsong Corporation, financial scandal of, 291

Nam Duck Woo, 240
National Assembly:violence in, 38, 48, 82, 165-166;of Second Republic, 10;elections for, 3, 4, 5, 10, 32, 40, 52-53, 58-59, 111, 144-145, 152, 299, 302; special committee on constitutional revision, 181,

[National Assembly] 207-208, 302-303, 311
National Association For Democracy, 143
National Coalition For Democracy and Unification, 146, 183-184, 240
National Conference For Unification, 58, 141, 142, 198
National Council For the Restoration of Democracy, 80, 99;disbanded, 89
National Council of Christian Churches, 99, 109
National Defense Corps, scandal, 4
National Federation of Democratic Youth-Students, 76, 77
National Security Law, 7, 8, 181, 255
National Students' Defense Corps, 87, 212
National Traitors' Law, 243, 251
New Democratic Party, 13, 40, 52, 53, 58;factionalism in, 101-103, 110-111, 149-150, 163, 196;in line with government policy, 88, 110-111;on the offensive, 77, 149-151, 160; since Park's assassination in 1979, 191, 193
New Democratic Republican Party, 315
New Faction (of Democratic Party), 13, 18, 31
New Korea Democratic Party: origin of, 40, 299, 300; dissension in, 303-304, 312
New Village Movement, 121, 131
news media:under government attack, 27, 28, 37, 69, 78, 79, 82, 85, 92, 118, 235-236, 248;intimidated

Urban Industrial Mission, 125, 136, 149, 162, 278
urbanization, 6, 66
U.S. reconnaissance plane EC 121, shoot down of, 48
U.S.S. Pueblo, its seizure by North Koreans, 48
U.S.-South Korea Combined Forces Command, 187, 201, 224, 281, 328

Vance, Cyrus R., 174
Vietnam:dispatch of Korean troops to, 39;revenues from, 46, 51, 136;withdrawal of Korean troops from, 51, 65;impact of its fall in Korea, 84-86, 95-96

wages.See labor.
Wickham, John A., 224, 238-239, 249, 281
workers.See labor.
World Bank, report from, 122, 152

Y.H. Industrial Company, labor dispute at, 161-162, 166, 181
Yi Dynasty:education during, 71;factional strife, xv, xvi, 159-160
Yi Ki Bung, 6, 8, 9
Yi Shi Yong, 5
Yi Wan Yong, 54, 66
Yongdong Development Corporation, 291
Yongnam University, 167
Yonhap News, 245
Yonsei University, 77, 109, 219
Yosu-Sunch'on Incident (military rebellion), 3, 21
Yu Byong Hyon, 232
Yu Ch'i Song, 244, 276
Yu Chin San, 77, 91
Yu Hak Song, 238
Yu Kil Chun, 89

Yu Sung Hwan, 303, 320
Yujonghoe (Political Fraternity for Yushin), 59, 145, 209, 210
Yulsan, an industrial group, 133, 140
Yun Ch'i Ho, 89
Yun Ja Jung, 291
Yun Po Son;his presidency, 12, 25, 28;resigns presidency, 44;political activities of, 32, 40;as dissident, 76, 80, 99, 100, 108, 143, 146
Yushin Constitution, 57-59;its impacts on unification talks, 59;criticisms of, 75-80, 96-97, 180-181, 183, 184, 185
"Yushin generals," 190